The Great Prairie Fact

and Literary Imagination

The Great Prairie Fact
and Literary Imagination

Robert Thacker

University of New Mexico Press
Albuquerque

Library of Congress Cataloging-in-Publication Data

Thacker, Robert, 1951–
   The great prairie fact and literary imagination / Robert Thacker.
— 1st ed.
    p. cm.
   Bibliography: p.
   Includes index.
   ISBN 0–8263–1150–4
   1. American literature—History and criticism. 2. Prairies in
literature. 3. Great Plains in literature. 4. West (U.S.) in literature.
5. Landscape in literature. 6. Frontier and pioneer life in literature.
7. Canadian literature—History and criticism. 8. Prairies in art.
I. Title.
PS169.P7T4 1989
813'.009'32145—dc20   89-4816
                                                               CIP

Contents

For Debbie

(who understands me but not my enthusiasms),

Alison, and Melissa

The health of the eye seems to demand a horizon. We are never tired, so long as we can see far enough.

Ralph Waldo Emerson
Nature

The train clonks on and on. Through the prairies. She looks out at the flat lands, which from the train window could not ever tell you anything about what they are. The grain elevators, like stark strange towers. The small bluffs of scrub oak and poplar. . . . The crocuses used to grow out of the snow. You would find them in pastures, the black-pitted dying snow still there, and the crocuses already growing, their greengrey featherstems, and the petals a pale greymauve. People who'd never lived hereabouts always imagined it was dull, bleak, hundreds of miles of nothing. They didn't know. They didn't know the renewal that came out of the dead cold.

Margaret Laurence
The Diviners

Once in his life a man ought to concentrate his mind upon the remembered earth, I believe. He ought to give himself up to a particular landscape in his experience, to look at it from as many angles as he can, to wonder about it, to dwell upon it. He ought to imagine that he touches it with his hands at every season and listens to the sounds that are made upon it. He ought to imagine the creatures there and all the faintest motions of the wind. He ought to recollect the glare of noon and all the colors of the dawn and dusk.

N. Scott Momaday
The Way to Rainy Mountain

Preface

This book had its beginnings in a desire to cross borders. Having been born in southern Ohio (a descendant of Iowa homesteaders some of whose offspring turned about and moved east to live on the edge of the prairie), I decided some years ago to develop an expertise in Canadian literature. In the process, I began pursuing a long-standing interest in the frontier by focusing upon the literary wests of both Canada and the United States. During doctoral work at the University of Manitoba, I became convinced that while important scholarship was being produced on western literature on each side of the forty-ninth parallel, virtually no one was conversant with both sides of the border. And while at Manitoba, I had the enormous good fortune to serve as managing editor of the *Canadian Review of American Studies,* giving me a vantage point from which to observe and participate in the interdisciplinary activities of scholars working in several disciplines. This convinced me in turn that the Canadian-American border was not the only boundary in need of crossing, that the work and insights of geographer, historian, and art historian were not only relevant to North American literature, they were, and are, an essential part of it. The correspondences between the disciplines and across the forty-ninth parallel are so numerous and significant that an inclusive interdisciplinary approach seems not merely sensible—it seemed, and still seems, mandatory.

By analyzing epistemological and esthetic responses to the prairie revealed by some of the texts left by people of European descent, this book is both broadly inclusive and, at the same time, almost as broadly exclusive. Texts and figures very frequently the concern of historians are treated here for their literary value while, at the same time, literary texts are placed in particular historical relation to prairie exploration and settlement. And while every attempt has been made to base this argument on as broad a survey of prairie writing as possible, much material—from both sides of the prairie border-land—goes undiscussed in favor of more detailed treatment of established figures, full Canadian and American coverage, and a complete chronology. At the same time, this book involves a broad range of frontier-related studies; it uses perceptual geography and generalizes about a landscape that is not always as homogeneous as it might be seen to be, whatever general impression it sometimes seems to offer; it recognizes the gender implications of various aspects of the discussion without claiming to have dealt with them completely; and it offers additional consideration of some figures very thoroughly analyzed already as well as looking at some texts very few have read, let alone analyzed. Cutting so wide a swath, my discussion may disappoint anyone who comes to it seeking a strictly disciplinary, thematic, or otherwise narrow point of view. The aim here has been to offer a synthesis, to combine in a single discussion the disparate observers and equally disparate literary figures who converged on the prairie between the mid-sixteenth century and the present; together, they offer a reasonably complete, if not yet completed, picture of European adaptation to prairie landscape as it is evident in the written record.

As is usual in a project of this size, I have many people to thank. The commonplacedness of such expressions of gratitude in no way diminishes their sincerity, nor does saying thanks repay the numerous debts. Scholarly insight freely and generously offered is a wonder to behold, an ongoing delight; I have benefited from too many individuals' generosities to note. Among such people, first and foremost is Professor Evelyn J. Hinz (University of Manitoba), who supervised the beginnings of this as a doctoral thesis and provided me with the encouragement, the zest, (and occasionally) the zeal necessary to pursue an interdisciplinary project; throughout, she displayed a mind ever curious, equally sensitive to nuance as well as major connections. For similar help, though at a bit greater remove, thanks are due to Professor John J. Teunissen (University of Manitoba).

More recently, Professor Susan J. Rosowski (University of Nebraska—Lincoln) has offered freely of her exhaustive knowledge of Willa Cather's work by reading earlier versions of chapter 4 and suggesting important revisions; more than that, she has encouraged me in countless ways over the past decade—Sue is my ideal of the generous scholar-teacher (and a good friend besides). Professor Michael A. Peterman (Trent University) read portions of this in earlier form and made many valuable comments, as did my St. Lawrence colleague, Professor Bruce I. Weiner. And I want to thank Elizabeth Hadas, Director of the University of New Mexico Press, for her invaluable

Introduction:

The Great Fact Was the Land Itself

The North American prairie, Wallace Stegner has written, is a land "notable primarily for its weather, which is violent and prolonged; its emptiness, which is almost frighteningly total; and its wind, which blows all the time in a way to stiffen your hair and rattle the eyes in your head." Though written during the mid-twentieth century, this description is a fitting point of departure for a book examining literary adaptations to the prairie, because it encapsulates the essence of European man's imaginative response to the landscape. Ever since Spaniards wandered onto the prairies during the sixteenth century, Europeans and their descendants have been vexed by the imaginative impact of prairie space. Pedro de Castañeda, who left a narrative of Coronado's visit, wrote that the prairie "seemed as round as if a man should imagine himself in a three-pint measure,"[1] and, eerily, Stegner seems to echo his response to the roundness of prairie sky almost four centuries later, writing that the landscape "is a long way from characterless; 'overpowering' would be a better word. For over the segmented circle of earth is domed the biggest sky anywhere, which . . . sheds down on range and wheat and summer fallow a light to set a painter wild, a light pure, glareless, and transparent" (7).

Stegner wrote these descriptions in *Wolf Willow: A History, A Story, and a Memory of the Last Plains Frontier* (1962), a volume that speaks directly to the purpose of this book. *Wolf Willow* is an odd book, something of a generic anomaly that offers, as its subtitle suggests, a mixture of authorial impulses—the same impulses that lie behind the texts examined here. In it, Stegner describes a pilgrimage he made to his boyhood town—Whitemud, Saskatchewan, where his family homesteaded during the 1910s—to see what was still there. Throughout, the landscape exerts a pull on his imagination, as

1

land, through memory, and through its history. But to Stegner, the prairie is emphatically a personal landscape, one that seems to elude his struggle to express it. Thus, however oddly, Stegner's book blends memory, history, and fiction to offer one man's evaluation of his place, a personal landscape at a particular time, a series of associations seemingly as coincident as the aroma of the local shrub, wolf willow. Indeed, its scent is a kind of personal talisman for Stegner, for it encapsulates his feelings about his boyhood home; as he says: "if I am native to anything, I am native to this" (20).

It is fitting that such an anomalous text as *Wolf Willow* should emerge from the prairie, given its unique topography; from Coronado's time on, the prairie has offered vistas ever at odds with the western European notion of "landscape." It was, and is, unlike any landscape conventionally thought pleasing. Rather than the variety and contrast of the picturesque, or the majesty of the sublime, the prairie presents instead, as Sir William Francis Butler described it during the second half of the nineteenth century, "a view so vast that endless space seems for once to find embodiment, and at a single glance the eye is satiated with immensity." Thus Stegner's apparent difficulties in finding suitable form for his feelings about southern Saskatchewan point to the essential problem examined here: the relationship between prairie landscape, esthetic conventions, and individual experience within literary texts. Willa Cather, the most subtle artist yet to record the landscape, wrote that on the prairie "the great fact was the land itself."[2] It still is, and this book attempts first to define and then to trace the processes—recorded in literary texts—by which Europeans and their descendants came to understand the imaginative demands of prairie space and to incorporate them into esthetic conventions.

These reactions, moreover, point up the difficulties involved in the transformation of the prairie from "virgin land" to "home place." Historically ill-equipped to view and to understand the prairie landscape, Europeans did not foresee and often misunderstood the practical and epistemological problems posed by prairie topography, which had to be reckoned with as the region was explored, traveled through, and ultimately settled between the sixteenth and nineteenth centuries. Coronado, for example, found no gold in present-day Kansas, just grass and buffalo—the prairie in its natural state. The area was like nowhere else he had ever been, and Coronado was frustrated to find that the only way he could keep his party together was by collecting piles of buffalo dung and sun-bleached bones and using them to mark the way. By adapting in this fashion, Coronado and his party began a process that was to continue for centuries: the creation of landmarks in a region that seemed—at least to Europeans—to be without them. In turn, the records left by these Spaniards constitute the beginning of a series of documents that reveal the imaginative adaptation—the placing of mental landmarks—required of those who attempted to understand the prairie, whether for purposes of exploration, travel, settlement, or fiction.

Scholars have dealt with the North American West and the frontier, including the prairie, extensively. They take for granted an affective, even determinative, relationship between New World landscapes and New World cultural assumptions and character. Canadian commentators have been much more inclined to analyze the relationship of prairie landscape with literary texts than scholars of American literature have; some of their assumptions undergird the following chapters. Thus Henry Kreisel, in "The Prairie: A State of Mind," offers an axiomatic generalization: "All discussion of the literature produced in the Canadian West must of necessity begin with the impact of the landscape on the mind." Robert Kroetsch, the Canadian novelist, poet, and critic, carries Kreisel's point further when he asks in "On Being an Alberta Writer," "How do you write in a new country?" and then goes on to say: "Our inherited literature, the literature of our European past and of eastern North America, is emphatically the literature of a people who have *not* lived on prairies. We had, and still have, difficulty finding names for the elements and characteristics of this landscape."[3] Here as elsewhere—both in criticism and his own fiction—Kroetsch wonders about the processes of esthetic adaptation brought about by the collision between inculcated esthetics and literary convention, on the one hand, and prairie landscape, on the other. This book seeks to define and analyze that collision.

But if Canadian critics have focused most precisely on the prairie landscape, critics of American literature have offered the most sophisticated analyses of the imaginative processes involved in claiming the west as literary landscape. Their work on these processes, unlike the more recent work of Canadian scholars, has not been limited to the prairie region but rather treats the whole history of North American exploration and settlement. In his revered *Virgin Land* (1950), Henry Nash Smith argues that "The character of the American empire was defined . . . by a relation between man and nature—or rather, even more narrowly, between American man and the American West." Continuing in the same vein, Richard Slotkin discusses the literary dimension of contact between Europeans and North American space and defines the process of adaptation in *Regeneration Through Violence* (1973), noting that "The one constant in the American environment has been the wilderness in its varying forms of forest, plain, mountain, and desert." Slotkin continues to delineate the ways that the metaphors used in New World descriptions were "constantly adjusted to suit American conditions," and, as a result, they "began to metamorphose, to take on some of the shape and coloration of the colonists' experience of America and her landscape." Along the same lines, Stephen

Fender has recently done a detailed study of the rhetoric involved in this process of metamorphosis along the California Trail, *Plotting the Golden West* (1981), seeing in the writing of overlander and literary figure alike that "the more plotless the landscape"—that is, culturally empty—"the more plotted the writing."[4] Focused on prairie writing, this book charts the same process of metamorphosis Slotkin defined, and confirms Fender's analyses of the relationship between landscape and text as well.

At the same time, Fender's generalization implicitly points to another important concern: the various ways—based on age, gender, background, intention, and other individual characteristics—by which authors were able to first see, then respond to, and ultimately describe for others the landscapes they experienced, prairie as well as other types. Perceptual geographers such as David Lowenthal and Yi-Fu Tuan have used literature to reconstruct past attitudes toward the environment. Lowenthal, for example, argues that "Landscapes are formed by landscape tastes"—people see in a landscape what they expect to see. According to J. Wreford Watson, who has considered the "role of illusion" in this process, "This is especially true of new environments; it is not what people actually see there so much as what they want to see, or think they see, which affects their reaction." And Tuan, whose work concentrates on individual attachment to particular landscapes, holds that intention directs response to a given landscape. The very process of evaluating a landscape, he maintains, requires a conscious separation of the self from surrounding space.[5] Applied to the prairie landscape described and used within a literary text, such analyses suggest the need to carefully evaluate the role played by landscape in each separate work while, at the same time, analyzing each writer's background and purpose equally carefully. The following chapters are meant to analyze the literary implications of the prairie landscape within the fiction, rather than what they might suggest about the dynamics of perception alone.

The particular concern historians and literary critics have shown for the role of gender in western studies over the past several years should also be highlighted, since the implication of their work is crucial to this study. Revisionist historians of the nineteenth-century overland trails and settlement have taken up women's attitudes—as seen in the letters, diaries, and autobiographies such people left—and contrasted them with the attitudes of their husbands, fathers, and brothers—who have long been the primary focus of frontier studies. Thus Glenda Riley recently has argued the existence of a "female frontier" in her *The Female Frontier: A Comparative View of Women on the Prairie and the Plains* (1988) where "frontierswomen's responsibilities, life-styles and sensibilities were shaped more by gender considerations than by region." This work has both highlighted women's activities in the westward movement and, at the same time, debunked such stereotyped images of western women as "prairie madonnas" or, as Sandra L. Myres calls them in her *Westering Women and the Frontier Experience, 1800–1915* (1982), "sunbonnet saints." Such stereotypes derive, of course, from some of the fictional works considered here as well as the larger popular culture itself, but the salient point in the discussion is that, until very recently, as Myres argues, "our perceptions of westering women have been shaped by male writers who did not read what women themselves wrote about the West."[6] Historians such as Myres and Riley have redressed this neglect admirably, persuasively arguing a gender-based process of adaptation on the frontier in which women's values are clearly differentiated from those of men as pioneering gave way to settlement.

Reaction to the landscape itself, however, is more complex since gender is but one factor in any individual's estimation of her new surroundings. Martha Mitten Allen has noted that over fifty years ago Walter Prescott Webb argued that "Men were more apt to experience elation, freedom, and exultation" on the prairies "while women tended to sense the loneliness" of the landscape. Recent scholarship on women's perceptions of the prairie landscape has shown Webb's generalization to be a vast oversimplification. Yet despite the considerable attention given to the issue, the degree to which women actually differed from men in their esthetic estimation of the prairie landscape remains arguable. Indeed, the most ambitious analysis of the question has come from a literary scholar, Annette Kolodny; eschewing the narrow focus of many historians as well as the male myths of westering seen in R. W. B. Lewis's *The American Adam* (1955), she analyzes the West as women's symbolic landscape—one borne of its informing myths—arguing in *The Land Before Her: Fantasy and Experience of the American Frontiers, 1630–1860* (1984) that "men sought sexual gratifications from the land, while women sought there the gratifications of home and family relations." The prairie landscape, particularly, "spoke to women's fantasies. And there, with an assurance she had not previously commanded, the newly self-conscious American Eve proclaimed a paradise in which garden and home were one."[7]

By incorporating the approaches and arguments of these diverse groups of scholars as they converge, so to speak, on the prairie, this study seeks to use their insights to further define and, ultimately, to understand the relationship between prairie landscape and prairie fiction. That this undertaking requires the crossing of disciplinary, ideological, and national boundaries is without question, certainly, since the process of literary adaptation on the prairie—like the larger process of settling the continent—has required adjustments, seemingly, to all aspects of human culture. Imaginative writing is a conscious synthesis of human experience, a projection of both our deepest desires and fears (what Kolodny calls "fantasy"); as such, fiction combines the geography, history, sociology, and, ultimately, epistemology of prairie adaptation within its compass—it is, finally, where the story of prairie exploration, settlement, and being is told most urgently.

The prairie, a phenomenon unique to North America, is defined as that area of generally level unforested farmland—formerly grassland—between the Ohio River and the plateaus of the West that extends north into Canada to include portions of the provinces of Manitoba, Saskatchewan, and Alberta, and south to include the area extending to the gulf coast of Texas. Its significance in the history and development of North American literature stems mainly from its singularity: no Old World topography equals the prairie's stark expanses (barring, of course, the Russian Steppes, with which few North American settlers were familiar). To Europeans glimpsing it for the first time, the prairie was the most unfamiliar of landscapes. The hardwood forests of the Atlantic seaboard, though dense and foreboding, presented much the same topography as European forests, as did the Appalachian Mountains. The North American prairie, however, was another matter altogether.[8]

This definition is based on Walter Prescott Webb's; in *The Great Plains* (1931), he defines it as follows:

> A plains environment is characterized by a plane, or level, surface, is treeless, and is sub-humid. The High Plains have all three characteristics. Eastward of the High Plains the limits of the Plains environment are marked by the timber line, including a humid, but treeless, level surface called the Prairie Plains. West of the High Plains the surface is broken, no longer plane; but two other characteristics remain,—the absence of trees and semiaridity,—and these two characteristics are generally found in conjunction all the way to the Pacific slope. Thus we find the High Plains flanked on either hand by land belts exhibiting two of the three essential elements of a plains environment. The High Plains in the center, the Prairie Plains on the east, and the arid mountainous section on the west constitute the Great Plains environment in the United States.

The environmental determinism Webb argues has been controversial among historians since his book was published, certainly, but his definition of the region—with its northern extension into Canada that Webb ignores—is quite suitable here. In Canada, the environment of which Webb speaks extends, in a roughly triangular shape into Alberta, Saskatchewan, and Manitoba—the prairie provinces. The plains environment is bordered on the north by parklands, which are characterized by gentle hills and valleys, fertile soil, and lakes; these, in turn, are bordered to the north by forests that stretch to the treeline and the arctic. For literary purposes, ultimately, level, plane, surfaces—providing a largely uninterrupted view to the horizon line—and treelessness are the salient features of the prairie.[9]

As the first attempts to write about the prairie, to fit and frame its vastness within the confines of the written page, commentaries such as Castañeda's constitute the necessary point of departure for the study of esthetic adaptation to the landscape. During the period of exploration and expansion into the region, stretching from 1534 through the late nineteenth century, numerous explorers left written records of what they saw, heard about, and surmised while on the prairie. These records take the form of journals, narratives, and letters; some are elegantly written while others are mere factual descriptions in terse language. Chapter 1 isolates and details European reaction to the landscape as it was first seen and assessed through descriptive writing. Stretching as they do from the mid-sixteenth through the late nineteenth centuries, such first-person accounts—written by travelers, traders, missionaries, and tourists, as well as explorers—establish the ways in which the prairie landscape, both practically and imaginatively, affected those who traveled through it. Largely without any avowed literary intentions, these writers record directly the interaction of the European mind with the prairie landscape—at first impression, at initial comprehension, and at eventual understanding.

Although the nonliterary accounts provide the basis for this transformation, they do not delimit its accomplishment—that phase lies within the realm of art. But because the prairie was no more a conventional subject for art than it was a familiar landscape to the European, its use in both painting and literature produced conflicts between conventional esthetic assumptions and the actual nature of the land. Just as early commentators were hesitant to pronounce a prairie vista sublime, so early pictorial artists and literate travelers were reluctant to focus directly upon the vastness of the land, preferring more conventional subjects and methods. Only gradually did they adapt their techniques to its imaginative demands. Chapter 2 considers well-known figures who offer "first views": George Catlin, Paul Kane, Karl Bodmer, and Alfred Jacob Miller. The selection of writers, similarly, has been dictated by notoriety and timing; Washington Irving and Francis Parkman left literary travel narratives rather than overt fictions; their published texts, moreover, may be compared to their (also) published trip journals, so immediate reactions may be seen as counterpoint to later "worked up" literary forms.

Turning then to the first writers who used the prairie in fiction—whether as setting or as source of metaphor and allusion—chapter 3 traces the role the prairie played in nineteenth-century literature. Beginning with one of the best-known prairie novels, James Fenimore Cooper's *The Prairie* (1827), this chapter extends through the writing of the early twentieth century, concluding with discussions of Hamlin Garland and Arthur Stringer. It defines the transformation of the prairie into a literary landscape, and suggests the relationship between nonliterary first-person accounts—very often source texts for nineteenth-century authors such as Cooper and Melville—as depiction of the prairie in fiction moved from a landscape of the imagination to that of a pioneered land. Concurrently, this transformation sees a movement from the mode of romance to that of realism.

From the late nineteenth century on, the sheer number of prairie novels and stories makes a complete survey impossible here. Thus the writers and texts treated in the final two chapters—which take up prairie fiction at its fullest— are intended to be representative rather than exhaustive. Texts have been selected on the basis of the reputation and stature of the novelists and their works, as well as the extent to which landscape figures in the writing. At the same time, the survey undertaken for purposes of text selection has been sufficiently broad to ensure that the works treated here are representative.[10]

Accordingly, chapter 4 takes up relatively few texts, but they are the important ones that define what is perhaps the central tale of prairie fiction: pioneering. It is preferable to treat prairie pioneering in terms of the imaginative effects and authorial techniques related to the land, to consider major figures in some depth rather than cursorily examining numerous thematic examples culled from scores of novels. Thus the four authors discussed— Cather, Rölvaag, Grove, and Stegner—encapsulate prairie pioneering as depicted in fiction; the preeminence of the first three in discussions such as this is unquestionable. Stegner, however, might seem an odd choice. His *On a Darkling Plain* (1939) offers an unusual motivation for pioneering—his protagonist, Edwin Vickers, takes up a homestead in Saskatchewan in order to flee the First World War—and, since he wants to write, *On a Darkling Plain* offers direct consideration of the difficulties involved in writing from the prairie landscape. Without question, numerous other texts, both American and Canadian, might have been used to do the same thing. But when taken together, the four figures offer a composite picture of prairie pioneering representing that found in prairie fiction as a whole.

Lastly, chapter 5 considers those who depict the postpioneering prairie as well as those writers who have been born and raised on the prairie, ending with a consideration of contemporary writing. Again, the criterion of selection has been significance, although this chapter tries to treat Canadian and American writers equally. Thus, after consideration of two representative postpioneering novels, the writers of the dust bowl thirties—John Steinbeck, Sinclair Ross, and W. O. Mitchell—are evaluated as they depict, respectively, exodus from the dust bowl and the prairie small town. Following this, Wright Morris, the American writer who has concentrated most emphatically on his Nebraska beginnings, is examined prior to considering the enormous literary activity on the Canadian prairie today. Canadian writers, particularly Robert Kroetsch, are among the most articulate in defining their relation to their prairie beginnings. Throughout, the intention has been to analyze the degree to which twentieth-century prairie writers continue the imaginative struggle begun by Coronado during the sixteenth century.

Such diversity in writing and writers over five centuries includes a multiplicity of purposes, allegiances, and interests on the part of those who used the prairie—and these variables affected their texts. Whether explorer's journal, travel narrative, or novel, each one poses critical problems of assumption, intent, audience, and scope that convey its author's treatment of the landscape. Owing to these various other interests, accurate (or even inaccurate), depiction of the prairie landscape was often the farthest thing from an author's mind. Thus the intention here has been to isolate and define the ways that writers have employed the prairie landscape, remaining always attuned to the dictates of each separate text.

Without question, the individual's gradual understanding of the strange new environment parallels the prairie landscape's incorporation within the larger literary tradition. Like Coronado, who had to devise means of finding his way through a land that was (to his mind) without landmarks, authors have had to devise techniques designed to articulate the vast essence of the prairie landscape; they have had to develop ways of communicating the feelings evoked by prairie space. In doing so, their inherited European and eastern assumptions and metaphors metamorphosed; they were adapted to prairie conditions. Thus as this book seeks to demonstrate, prairie landscape conventions and techniques of symbolic depiction have been derived from the essential elements of the land itself, the same elements described by Stegner in the first paragraph of *Wolf Willow*. Prairie writing reveals that whether a person is traveling through, settling on, or living on the prairie, "the great fact" has always been and is still "the land itself."

Part

Visitors

1

Beyond the Borders of Culture:

Explorers, Traders and Travelers

First Views: 1534–1807

The first Europeans to glimpse the prairie were motivated by a variety of impulses, the least of which was to appreciate the esthetic character of this new world. Alvar Nuñez Cabeza de Vaca, the first European to have seen it, about 1534, came because he was lost.[1] He was followed in 1540 by Coronado, who was seeking gold in an area the Spaniards had been told was called Quivira, present-day Kansas. Traveling there, Coronado sent patrols off in various directions and Pedro de Castañeda, who wrote the most extensive narrative of the expedition, states that one such group returned "and told the general that in the twenty leagues they had been over they had seen nothing but cows and the sky."[2] The trackless quality of the land—the absence of European landmarks—draws considerable attention from Castañeda because of the numerous practical problems it offered: "It was impossible to find tracks in this country, because the grass straightened up again as soon as it was trodden down" (331). He reports that one man who went off to hunt was entirely lost because of the tracklessness of the prairie, and many others were nearly lost:

> Many fellows were lost at this time who went out hunting and did not get back to the army for two or three days, wandering about the country as if they were crazy, in one direction or another, not knowing how to get back where they started from. . . . Every night they took account of who was missing, fired guns and blew trumpets and beat drums and built great fires, but yet some of them went off so far and wandered about so much that all this did not give them any help, although it helped others. . . . It is worth noting that the country there is so level that at midday, after one has wan-

dered about in one direction and another in pursuit of game, the only thing to do is to stay near the game quietly until sunset, so as to see where it goes down, and even then they have to be men who are practised to do it. (336)

That Coronado shared Castañeda's frustration is indicated by a letter he wrote to his king on October 20, 1541, while still on the expedition:

> After nine days' march I reached some plains, so vast that I did not find their limit anywhere that I went, although I travelled over them for more than 300 leagues. . . .
>
> . . . .
>
> I travelled five more days as the guides wished to lead me, until I reached some plains, with no more landmarks than as if we had been swallowed up in the sea, where they [the guides] strayed about, because there was not a stone, nor a bit of rising ground, nor a tree, nor a scrub, nor anything to go by. There is much very fine pasture land, with good grass. And while we were lost in these plains. . . .[3]

Antedating as it does Castañeda's *Narrative,* Coronado's letter provides an immediate, on-the-spot reaction to the prairie environment by one of the first Europeans to experience it; at the same time, his attempt to present the prairie in terms that the king and his ministers at court can understand is consistent with Richard Slotkin's view of the metamorphosis of metaphor as Europeans assimilated New World conditions (18–19). Ever mindful of his audience— far removed in Spain—Coronado likens the prairie to the ocean, and his litany of absent landmarks is made up of things a European expects to use as landmarks; that is, objects not found on the prairie. The landscape is singular for what it does *not* have, and for what it is *like,* not for what it *is.* In the same letter Coronado describes the number and extent of the buffalo herds, and this leads to his comment on the suitability of the prairie as pasture lands. Yet this appreciative comment is far outweighed by the general's knowledge that he has found no gold and cannot, moreover, keep his bearings in this strange land. He knows he has been lost much of the time.

Whereas Cabeza de Vaca had passed through only the southern fringe of the prairie, Coronado and his men marched directly into its center. Seeking stone dwellings with rooms full of gold in Quivira, Coronado found only grass huts inhabited by Wichita Indians. Upon hearing the actual conditions in Quivira, Coronado expressed his disappointment: "This news troubled me greatly, to find myself on these limitless plains, where I was in great need of water, and often had to drink it so poor that it was more mud than water. Here the guides confessed to me that they had not told the truth in regard to the size of the houses, because these were of grass. . . ."[4] Realizing he was not going to find any gold, Coronado was understandably despondent, since gold was the unit of measure of his expedition's success and he had every reason to consider himself a failure; indeed, upon his return to Spain he was treated as such. But as this letter suggests, Coronado's disappointment was also aggravated by the prairie environment's singular strangeness, with its infinity of sky countered only by endless, flat, land; the landscape defied comprehension.

Another member of the expedition comments that Coronado and his men were forced "to mark the road by which they went with cow dung, so as to return, since there were no stones or anything else."[5] Castañeda, when he notes the same action, does so in a chapter near the end of his account, which is thus curiously out of place within the chronological pattern of his *Narrative,* and greatly inflates the size of Coronado's party:

> My silence was not without mystery and dissimulation when, in Chapter 7 of the second part of this book [the proper place of the prairie in the chronology], I spoke of the plains and the things of which I will give a detailed account in this chapter, where all these things may be found together; for these things were remarkable and something not seen in other parts. I dare to write of them because I am writing at a time when many men are still living [c. 1565] who saw them and who will vouch for my account. Who could believe that 1,000 horses and 500 of our cows and more than 5,000 rams and ewes and more than 1,500 friendly Indians and servants, in travelling over those plains, would leave no more trace where they had passed than if nothing had been there—nothing—so that it was necessary to make piles of bones and cow-dung now and then, so that the rear guard could follow the army. The grass never failed to become erect after it had been trodden down and, although it was short, it was fresh and straight as before. (381–82)

Herbert E. Bolton, in *Coronado: Knight of Pueblos and Plains,* accounts for this anomaly, noting that Castañeda observes that "men are still living who saw" the strange sights of the plains and suggests that the annalist avoided going into much detail about the plains in the earlier chapter because he feared being discredited "for telling such whoppers." Later, however, Castañeda reconsidered his previous decision and elected to write a special chapter on the plains; such indecision might also account for his amazed tone and approach to the prairie landscape: "Who could believe. . . ."[6] Moreover, the style of the passage suggests that a major factor was Castañeda's awe in the presence of the landscape and his concurrent feeling of insignificance. Hence the mystery, the special treatment of the subject, the exaggerated numbers, the rhetorical question and, of course, his emphatic repetition of "nothing."

Later in the same chapter, Castañeda returns to his discussion of the extent and habits of the buffalo. Again he is at pains to communicate his response in arithmetical terms: "Another thing worth noticing is that the bulls travelled without cows in such large numbers that nobody could have counted them, and so far away from the cows that it was more than forty leagues from where we began to see the bulls to the place where we began to see the cows" (383). Castañeda's previous descriptions of the prairie landscape, in the earlier sections of his *Narrative,* were literal and factual; as he continues his description of the buffalo here, however, he seems compelled to resort to symbolism and metaphor:

> The country they travelled over was so level and smooth that if one looked at them the sky could be seen between their legs, so that if some of them were at a distance they looked like smooth-trunked pines whose tops joined, and if there was only one bull it looked as if there were four pines. When one was near them, it was impossible to see the ground on the other side of them. The reason for all this was that the country seemed as round as if a man should imagine himself in a three-pint measure, and could see the sky at the edge of it, about a crossbow shot from him, and even if a man only lay down on his back he lost sight of the ground. (383–84)[7]

His own amazement over the vastness of prairie space (and of the attendant difficulties in comprehending it), like Coronado's letter to the king, appeals to his assumed audience in Spain, the people he lived among as he wrote. Each writer assumes that he will be disbelieved, so he strives in his writing to stress the land's strangeness while, at the same time, incorporating familiar metaphors and allusions (ocean, three-pint measure) in order to, in effect, translate his experiences for his reader. Castañeda anticipates incredulity and seeks, in his descriptions, to combat it, as seen particularly in his rhetorical question: "Who could believe . . ."

Since approximately twenty-five years elapsed between the expedition and his composition of the *Narrative,* Castañeda's account attests in another way to the impact the prairie landscape had on its author: even after almost a quarter of a century, his impressions of the prairie remained vivid. And the effects of the prairie on the Spaniards—disorientation, difficulties, and disbelief—are mentioned by many who left accounts of their experiences during this expedition,[8] so that its documents offer a crucial first assessment of European man's initial prairie experiences. Indeed, the Coronado expedition illustrates what Bernard DeVoto describes as "the paradox of minds which were as logical as any today and, further, were here working not with myth but with the most concrete realities but were betrayed by sheer strangeness." As DeVoto also explains, the problem of practical adaptability compounded the problem of imaginative adjustment for the early Spanish explorers: "The principal reason why Coronado went no further than he did but turned back was that his supplies of corn were short and his men and horses might starve. For the horses there was only buffalo grass, the most nutritious grass in the New World, and for the army only buffalo meat, the most complete single food that mankind has ever known."[9] Hence Coronado turned back, fearing starvation, when all he needed was staring him, quite literally, in the face.

Yet DeVoto's phrase, "sheer strangeness," points up the underlying imaginative problem posed by the prairie to the European mind, demonstrated for the first time by Coronado and his men through the documents they left. In the detail and depth of their reaction to the landscape, Castañeda's *Narrative* and Coronado's on-the-spot explanations reveal deep and heartfelt reactions to what Slotkin calls "the psychological terrors of the wilderness" (18). They express, emphatically, their authors' sense of exile from society as they know it, embodied in their European metaphors of half-pint measure and ocean, and are given urgency by their implicit need to explain and justify their actions, certainly, but more importantly, their perceptions. Hence the Coronado texts are a point of departure here, but also a paradigm of European response to the "sheer strangeness" of the landscape to the occidental mind. They reveal that—at first incursion—Europeans sought refuge in their audience, back home, sharing this incomprehensible place of only sky and land, proclaiming their inability to be at ease there. In so saying, Coronado and his men reveal a "need to confront and comprehend the insistent prairie spaces, to 'learn the landscape's language.'"[10]

Coronado and his men were using land routes, however, and to judge by the journals and letters of French exploration of the Mississippi basin during the latter half of the seventeenth century, this was a crucial factor. When the prairie is mentioned in these writings, it is usually seen through gaps in the trees along a riverbank, and often buffalo herds receive more detailed consideration than the landscape.[11] Thus the "beautiful prairies" seen by the seventeenth-century French explorers constitute a very different landscape from that seen by their Spanish precursors. It appears, then, on the basis of these two groups of explorers, that their different impressions of the prairie varied according to their purpose, direction, and expectations; the French documents convey positive reactions to the landscape because the land meets their expectations.

In striking contrast to Castañeda's account, therefore, is the following passage from the *Jesuit Relations:*

> We proceeded, continuing always to coast along the great prairies, which extend farther than the eye can reach. Trees are met with from time to time, but they are so placed that they seem to have been planted with design, in order to make avenues more pleasing to the eye than those of orchards. The base of these trees is often watered by little streamlets, at which are seen large herds of stags and hinds refreshing themselves, and peacefully feeding upon the short grass. We followed these vast plains for 20 leagues and repeated many times, "Benedicite opera Domini Domino."[12]

The speaker here is Fr. Allouez, a Jesuit missionary, and the scene he describes is the field of his mission. Allouez is able to describe the scene in this manner, seeing the prairie as a garden, because he is traversing it at one of its most well-watered points and because he knows where he is going, having only to watch the scenery drift by. Moreover, prairie seen from the water is vastly different than prairie seen from horseback in mid-July. Not surprisingly— since prairie means "meadow" in French—this passage typifies these accounts; the prairie in Allouez's description has the features of a work of art, its sublime proportions neatly arranged to reflect its creator.

While the Spaniards were exasperated by the prairie and the French were awed by it, the first recorded Englishman to travel through the area was, by comparison, laconically factual. In 1690, at the behest of his employer, the Hudson's Bay Company, twenty-year-old Henry Kelsey traveled southwest up the Hayes River–Nelson River complex from York factory on Hudson Bay. He accompanied a group of Indians and for two years traveled with them as the only European. His exact route cannot be traced, but his journals reveal that he reached the Canadian prairie, was the first Englishman to see a buffalo hunt, and traveled in the area of both the South Saskatchewan and Assiniboine rivers. His first reference to the prairie echoes the words of Coronado's returning scouts a century and a half earlier: "This plain affords nothing but Beast & grass/ And over it in three days time we past/ getting unto ye woods on the other side/ It being about forty six miles wide." Though in keeping with his fur-trading purpose Kelsey goes on to note, "there is beavour in abundance but no Otter/ with plains & ridges in the Country throughout,"[13] he is first impressed by "Beast & grass," just as Coronado's scouts reported they had seen nothing for twenty leagues but "cows and the sky." Thus though Kelsey's descriptions are laconic, to say the least, we readily discern his strong reaction to the basic elements of prairie landscape—"Beast & grass."

Anthony Henday, another employee of the Hudson's Bay Company sent inland to drum up business, followed Kelsey's presumed route to the prairie and is recognized as the first European to see the Rocky Mountains. Like Kelsey, too, he traveled as the sole white man among Indians. His journal, however, while actually quite terse and laconic, seems almost copious when compared to Kelsey's. Leaving the French trading post at the location of The Pas, Manitoba, in late July 1754, Henday followed the Saskatchewan River for a short while before heading southwest into the prairie along the present Manitoba-Saskatchewan border, traveling overland. The daily entries in his journal are notable when taken as a whole, rather than individually. In the entry dated August 11, Henday notes: "Travelled 11 Miles S. W. b. W. Level lands, short grass; no woods; and no water but what is salt." Two days later, the entry reads: "Tuesday. Travelled 7 Miles W. S. W. Level land, short Grass, Dry-woods, and several salt water lakes. We are now entered Muscuty plains, and shall soon see plenty of Buffalo, and the Archithinue [Blackfoot] Indians hunting them on Horse-back." [14] Entries for the next two months are similar, and include observations concerning the "Level land," the amount and type of wooded areas about, the incidence of buffalo, and comments on the Indians and their habits.

Like Kelsey, Henday is struck by the scale of prairie space, which he characterizes as "Level Barren land, not one stick of wood to be seen, & no water to drink" (330). But whereas a reader must infer Kelsey's exasperation at traveling across the vast flatness of the prairie, there is no mistaking Henday's; he keeps noting "Level land" and, more importantly, keeps repeating "we are yet in the Muscuty plains" (331 [two entries], 335). On October 5 he exclaims: "We are still in the Muscuty Country" (336) and on the twenty-ninth he is finally able to note "Left Muscuty plains, which I have been in since 13th of August. . . ." (341). Thus, though Henday's journal lacks any literary flair, his numerous repetitions reflect the apparent sense of strangeness and discomfort he felt as he traveled across the prairie. The land vexed him by its inescapable breadth, its enormity, frustrating his efforts to get out of the "Muscuty plains."

The next significant figure to venture into the prairie stands quite alone. David Thompson, for twenty years employed by both the major fur-trading companies—first the Hudson's Bay Company, then the North West Company—was an explorer, geographer, and cartographer. His travels between 1784 and 1812 gave him an unequalled understanding of the country from the upper Great Lakes to Hudson Bay and west to the mouth of the Columbia River. Thompson's *Narrative,* which he began when he was over seventy and which was not published until 1916, is a synthesis of a lifetime of travel, work, and knowledge; it is unequalled in breadth by any other work of the fur trade and exploration period of North American history. While other works, like Mackenzie's *Voyages* or the Biddle Lewis and Clark, present a particular expedition, Thompson's *Narrative* is the product of twenty years of experience in the west.

Thompson's book, moreover, reveals a literary artist at work; his prose may not be as polished as some, but he clearly structured his *Narrative* with his audience, and with the desire to produce particular effects upon that audience, in mind. As T. D. MacLulich explains, Thompson sought "to convey an understanding of the large regions into which the American Northwest was divided, and to evoke the life of the distinctive tribes which inhabit each region," a fact that he accomplished by concentrating on two themes: "The land and its peoples. . . ." But Thompson deliberately tries, by the manner in which he presents his materials, to create particular effects. Thus the *Narrative* is characterized by "a *unity of vision*" whereby Thompson allows himself the freedom to shift his authorial point of view as long as it accords with his understanding of the land and its peoples; Thompson "does not view space as the narrow ribbon of landscape he passes through on his journeys; he does not view distance merely as so many miles of obstacles to overcome. Instead he tries to present the pattern which the land's features form in space. . . ."[15]

Thompson defines his perspective: "I shall not at present attempt to describe the great plains, having had opportunities for the space of twenty years after this to traverse them in many directions. . . ."[16] In chapter 11 of the *Narrative* he provides a short analysis of the size, extent, and other factual matters relating to the plains—which he calls them throughout—and two chapters later he describes his journey to the Mandan villages along the Missouri River in late 1797. After describing the circumstances surrounding the trip, Thompson states: "As my journey to the Missisourie is over part of the Great Plains, I shall give it in the form of a journal, this form, however dull, is the only method in my opinion, that can give the reader a clear idea of them" (161). Since Thompson was writing at least forty years after the trip, and was working from his journals, it is evident that, like Castañeda, the effect upon his imagination of the prairie landscape, and of travel across such a landscape, was still clear in his mind. Additionally, he was bent on recreating that dullness for his reader by his organic technique, the only extended use of the journal form in the entire *Narrative*.

As a result of the journal form, the reader never forgets that the party is traveling across the prairie in the dead of winter. They depart for the Mandan villages on November 28, 1797; they do not reach their destination until December 30. So the reader traverses some thirty daily entries, each designed to remind him of the temperature, the exposed quality of the party, and the strength and direction of the wind. On November 30, for example, they set off when the temperature was −32°F.

One entry, describing a time after his party has become lost, particularly illustrates the way that Thompson is able to evoke the frustration and anxiety of those who crossed the prairie overland:

> we now came on a rising ground at 1 PM. but the Turtle Hill was not in sight; and all before and around us a boundless plain; and Monsr Jussomme [their guide] could not say where we were; the weather appeared threatening and preparing for a Storm; our situation was alarming: and anxiety [was] in the face of every man, for we did not know to which hand to turn ourselves for shelter: I mounted My Horse and went to the highest ground near us, and with my telescope viewed the horizon all around, but not the least vestige of woods appeared; but at due North West from us, where there appeared the tops of a few Trees like Oaks. They anxiously enquired if I saw Woods. I told them what I had seen, and that with my old Soldier I should guide myself by the Compass, and directly proceed as the Woods were far off; McCrachen and a Canadian joined us; the other six conferred among themselves what to do, they had no faith in the Compass on land, and thought best to march in some direction until they could see woods with their own eyes; but had not proceeded half a mile before all followed us, thinking there would be better safety by being all together. The Gale of Wind came on, and kept increasing. (162)

At seven P.M. Thompson and his party managed to reach the woods, marching six hours to cover the distance his telescope covered in an instant. Here then is Thompson's presentation of travel across a "boundless plain," complete with its dangers, not the least of which is disorientation. The Canadians who accompany the explorer ironically do not trust "the Compass on land" (apparently they have faith in it while afloat); the irony lies, of course, in their inability to see the similarity between a snow-swept prairie and a body of water. Thompson's entry also illustrates another reason for the European preference for wooded areas, already seen in the observations of Kelsey and Henday: not only do such "islands" provide fuel, they also provide shelter.

Once Thompson realized that they were lost, his first reaction was to seek out the nearest roll in the surface of the prairie and, upon attaining its height, scan the horizon to locate a clump of trees. Natural enough in itself, this becomes the European's characteristic action on the prairie: whenever a European explorer or traveler wanted to understand the prairie scene before him, to encompass it visually, and to describe it in specific detail, he sought out the local height of land to get above the prairie.

Another fur trade employee, Alexander Henry the Younger, carried his desire to get above the prairie to some extreme. The nephew of another fur-trading Alexander Henry known as "the Elder," Henry established a North West Company trading post in 1800 at the confluence of the Park River and the Red River of the North, just south of the present-day U.S.–Canadian border in North Dakota. After a year there, he removed his post down the Red to its junction with the Pembina River, where he remained until 1808 when he was sent to a Saskatchewan River post.

Henry kept one of the most voluminous journals of the fur trade and his references to the surrounding prairie are both frequent and detailed. Among the tasks Henry assigned, upon arriving on the Park River, was the trimming of a large oak tree:

> *Sept. 11th.* I climbed up a tall oak, which I had trimmed for that purpose, at the entrance of the plain, from the top of which I had an extensive view of the country. Buffalo and red deer were everywhere in sight, passing to and fro. The weather being perfectly serene, I could distinguish the Hair hills on the W., though they were scarcely perceptible—nothing more than a blue stripe, running N. and S. The interval is a level meadow, with nothing to attract the eye but the winding course of Park river, whose wood is lost to the sight long before it reaches the hills. The distance may be between 12 and 15 leagues. [17]

As in the case of Thompson, Henry seeks an elevation in order to gain perspective, but his description of what he sees is also structured in terms of pictorial "perspective." First he alludes to the foreground scenery, which is made up of buffalo and deer. Their numbers are such that they may be just in the foreground, immediately around the post, or they may well stretch off into the distance; "everywhere in sight" seems to imply the latter. Then Henry moves to the distance with his description of the Hair hills and, after that, he fills in the middle distance before moving away again into the far distance by describing the woods along the Park River.

Yet, unlike Thompson, Henry does not really have any artistic intentions—his journals were a part of his responsibilities as head of the trading post; they do not reveal a man given to imaginative flights. His descriptions offer factuality with a minimum of subjectivity, written by a practical man doing his job; a comprehension of the landscape—with its strange features and infinite breadth—was necessary for the trading post's very survival, as well as its success. Thus in the passage above, he follows the pictorial presentation of the scene with an attempt to estimate the distance in practical terms. A week after the previous entry was written, for example, Henry remarks over the almost unfathomable number of buffalo surrounding the post, and this subsequently becomes a favorite theme of his: "*Sept. 18th.* I took my usual morning view from the top of my oak and saw more buffaloes than ever. They formed one body, commencing about half a mile from camp, whence the plain was covered on the W. side of the river as far as the eye could reach. They were moving southward slowly, and the meadow seemed as if in motion" (1: 99). Four months later, he writes:

> *Jan. 14th.* [1801] At daybreak I was awakened by the bellowing of buf-
> faloes. I got up, and was astonished when I climbed into the S. W. bastion.
> On my right the plains were black, and appeared as if in motion, S. to N.
> Opposite the fort the ice was covered; and on my left, to the utmost extent
> of the reach below us, the river was covered with buffalo moving northward.
> Our dogs were confined within the fort, which allowed the buffalo to pass
> within a few paces. I dressed and climbed my oak for a better view. I had
> seen almost incredible numbers of buffalo in the fall, but nothing in com-
> parison to what I now beheld. The ground was covered at every point of the
> compass, as far as the eye could reach, and every animal was in motion. (1:
> 167)[18]

As these examples suggest, if Henry's tree climbing was prompted by practical motives, the result was a heightening of the impact of the prairie and awe at its vastness, and the difficulty in understanding it.[19]

The significance of Alexander Henry's journals lies in the first-person impressions of a man who, once he entered the prairie, lived for an extended period of time in one locale. Unlike Thompson and those who came before him, both in the northern part of the region and in the southern, Henry was not just passing through. Though he frequently resorted to stock phrases ("as far as the eye could reach"), "his sharp eye [also] caught the detail necessary to bring out varieties in the flat land,"[20] so that his journals reveal a European becoming gradually accustomed to life on the prairie. Henry's changed attitude is revealed by his progressively less frequent tree-climbing as his familiarity with the prairie increased. Near the end of the journals such activities disappear altogether; such adaptation supports Slotkin's view that the formation of American myths rests upon the metamorphosis of metaphor, whereby hitherto European parallels waned and gradually came to reflect the mores and circumstances of the New World.

No single expedition into western North America received more attention, praise, and comment than Lewis and Clark's trip overland to the Pacific during the years 1804–06. Essentially the result of President Jefferson's charge to keep a specific daily journal of precise accounts of the land, distances traveled, and other observations, the *Original Journals of the Lewis and Clark Expedition, 1804–1806* (1904–05) runs to eight volumes. Having been published in the form in which they were written, they have little stylized polish. The *Original Journals* thus provide an unadulterated record of early responses to the prairie with minimal editorial interjection.

Like the French who traveled the Mississippi by canoe during the seventeenth and eighteenth centuries, Lewis and Clark traveled by boat on the Missouri and their view of the prairie reflects this perspective—the high bluffs on the lower river often precluded a direct view of the surrounding land. Captain Clark, however, often traveled on foot along the bank of the river and frequently ascended the bluffs to walk through the surrounding prairies. In his first significant reference to the Missouri prairie on June 10, 1804, he states: "I walked out three miles, found the prarie composed of good Land and plenty of water roleing & interspursed with points of timber land." He goes on to compare these lands with the "barrens" of the east: "[These] Praries are not like those, or a number of those E. of the Mississippi void of every thing except grass, they abound with Hasel Grapes & a wild plumb. . . ."[21] With respect to the fertility of the land, Lewis and Clark apparently agreed with their sponsor, Thomas Jefferson. The president, who was also their mentor regarding what they should expect on their travels, argued that the reason the trans-Mississippi west was treeless was because the soil was too fertile for the growth of forests. In addition, Lewis and Clark did not travel through the more arid areas of the west and, consequently, they saw the west largely as a garden.[22]

As the expedition moves farther up the Missouri, references to both prairie and plains become more numerous; they do not, however, become more extensive nor more detailed when the commentator, usually Clark, is speaking of the view from the river. Clark's descriptions of the prairie vary only when, as was the case on June 13, he is able to get above the surrounding landscape.[23] On July 12, he ascends a tributary stream and walks out onto the prairie, where he finds several artificial mounds:

> from the top of the highest of those Mounds I had an extensive view of the Serounding Plains, which afforded one of the most pleasing prospect I ever beheld, under me a Butifull River of Clear Water of about 80 yards wide Meandering thro: a leavel and extensive meadow, as far as I could See, the prospect much enlivened by the fiew Trees & Srubs which is bordering the

bank of the river, and the Creeks & runs falling into it, The bottom land is covered with Grass of about 4½ feet high, and appears as leavel as a smoth surfice. . . . (1: 75)

Thus like Alexander Henry's, Clark's imaginative grasp of the surrounding prairie landscape is greatly enhanced by the simple expedient of getting above it.

Apparently, neither explorer considered the prairie landscape worthy of sustained esthetic contemplation. The only time in the first two volumes of the *Journals* that Clark uses a "literary" term to define a scene is in connection with his view of the river valley as they are approaching the Great Falls of the Missouri: "This countrey has a romantick appearance river inclosed between high and steep hills cut to pices by revines but little timber and that confined to the Rivers & creek, the Missouri has but a fiew scattering trees on its borders . . ." (2: 187). In Clark's mind, apparently, "romantick" is a term to be reserved for scenes of vertical impressiveness and for scenes that are "inclosed"—in short, European or eastern North American vistas.[24]

Similarly, the sight of the Great Falls occasions Lewis to employ the phrase "sublimely grand" (2: 154), using it in the sense of "great height, lofty, and towering." Looking back over his attempt to describe the Falls, furthermore, Lewis expresses his dissatisfaction in ways that at once suggest that he was certainly capable of extended imaginative response and that his inability to appreciate the sublimity of the prairie must be traced to popular esthetic assumptions of his time.

> after wrighting this imperfect discription I again viewed the falls and was so much disgusted with the imperfect idea which it conveyed of the scene that I determined to draw my pen across it and begin agin, but then reflected that I could not perhaps succeed better than pening the first impressions of the mind; I wished for the pencil of Salvator Rosa [*a Titian*] or the pen of Thompson, that I might be enabled to give to the enlightened world some just idea of this truly magnifficent and sublimely grand object, which has from the commencement of time been concealed from the view of civilized man; but this was fruitless and vain. I most sincerely regreted that I had not brought a crimee [camera] obscura with me by the assistance of which even I could have hoped to have done better but alas this was also out of my reach; I therefore with the assistance of my pen only indeavoured to trace some of the stronger features of this seen by the assistance of which my recollection aided by some able pencil I hope still to give the world some faint idea of an object which at this moment fills me with such pleasure and astonishment;

and which of its kind I will venture to ascert is second but to one in the known world. (2: 149–50; Thwaites' interpolation)

Such a passage—which shows Lewis reacting strongly, if conventionally—confirms that esthetic assumptions colored what perceivers found beautiful; Lewis ignores the uniqueness of the prairie in favor of the conventional "sublime" of a waterfall, depicting it as a sight that is "second but to one in the known world," given the esthetic norms he employs.

The sole instance in which either explorer does focus esthetically upon a scene containing plains country occurs when they reach the Three Forks of the Missouri. There Lewis notes that "at the junction of the S. E. fork of the Missouri . . . the country opens suddonly to extensive and bea[u]tifull plains and meadows which appear to be surrounded in every direction with distant and lofty mountains. . . ." (Thwaites' interpolation). Lewis halted the party for breakfast and ascended a nearby limestone cliff, from which he "commanded a most perfect view of the neighbouring country." He notes an "extensive green meadow" and, beyond it, "a high wide and extensive plain," and describes all the while the disappearing courses of the three rivers which converge to form the Missouri; the whole scene is ringed round by the distant mountains (2: 275–77). Here the beauty Lewis perceives arises from the relation of the plains and the meadows to his obtained height and, as well, to the mountains beyond the plains and converging streams before him.

Of the entries recording the outward journey of the expedition, the only extended description of the plains involves an appreciation of them in contrast to other, more perpendicular landscapes, and is subordinated by other concerns. Beyond the comments recorded during the first few months of the expedition, the *Journals* of Lewis and Clark do not include any prolonged or explicit analyses of or reactions to the flat expanse of prairie-plains through which the expedition passed. Viewing a scene on the upper Missouri, which he notes "the country back [from the river] on either side as far as the eye can reach entirely desittute of trees or brush," Lewis comments: "nothing remarkable in the appearance of the country" (2: 227), and this blasé attitude is typical of the reaction for the latter part of the trip to Missouri.

Lewis and Clark's expedition marks the end of the period of occasional incursions into the prairie-plains. By the end of the first decade of the nineteenth century, easterners were continually pushing into the prairie. And because of general interest in western North America, as well as the contemporary predilection for travel literature, those who went on such trips often published some account of their travels and exploits. One of these accounts was by Zebulon Montgomery Pike, a young army officer who made a trip up the Mississippi from St. Louis while Lewis and Clark were still on their expedition (1805–06) and who later embarked on a trip to the Rocky Mountains as they were returning (1806–07). It was on this second trip that Pike lent his name to a mountain, although there is some question as to whether or not he even saw it; he certainly never climbed it. His *An Account of expeditions to the sources of the Mississippi . . .* was published in 1810. It presents several key reactions to the prairie-plains region, and the historical significance of his account is unquestionable: for by way of it Pike becomes one of the first to advance the idea of a Great American Desert, though he did not use that descriptive phrase himself.[25]

Pike makes his most telling observation about man's position on the prairie, not when he is traveling across such a plain but rather when he is crossing a frozen lake in what is now Minnesota during January 1806. Looking for houses on the other shore after night had set in, Pike comments: "I was fearful of loosing ourselves on the Lake (the consequence of which, can only be imagined by those who have been exposed on a Lake, or naked plain— a dreary night of January, in the Latitude of 47°N.—where the Mercury of *Reamour* stood at 27 below 0.)."[26] Whether written immediately after the incident in question, or after he had traveled across the plains to the Rocky Mountains and then down to Mexico and back, Pike's analogy between a frozen lake and a frozen prairie recalls Coronado's prairie/sea analogy in his letter to his king. And like Thompson in his record of his overland journey to the Mandan villages in the winter of 1797, Pike articulates the fear of exposure on the plains in winter.

Pike provides detailed descriptions of the animals living on the plains, especially buffalo, wild horses, and the black-tailed prairie dog,[27] but he also offers an esthetic reaction to the prairie consistent with Lewis and Clark's. In his first description from the perspective of a mountainside, looking down on a prairie scene from above, Pike compares the mountains with the plain below. After spending a night on the side of the mountain with no shelter, he explains that the party "Arose hungry, dry, and extremely sore, from the inequality of the rocks. . . ." But, he says, they were "amply compensated for toil by the sublimity of the prospects below. The unbounded prairie was overhung with clouds, which appeared like the ocean in a storm; wave piled on wave and foaming, whilst the sky was perfectly clear where we were" (1: 350).

At the same time, a discernible esthetic ambivalence characterizes Pike's views, such as one from "a high hill":

we had a view of all the prairie and rivers to the north of of us; it was at the same time one of the most sublime and beautiful inland prospects ever presented to the eyes of man. The prairie lying nearly north and south, was probably 60 miles by 45.

The main river bursting out of the western mountains, and meeting from the north-east, a large branch, which divides the chain of mountains, proceeds down the prairie, making many large and beautiful islands, one of which I judge contains 100,000 acres of land, all meadow ground, covered with innumerable herds of deer; about six miles from the mountains which cross the prairie, at the south end, a branch of 12 steps wide, pays its tribute to the main stream from the west course. . . . In short, this view combined the sublime and the beautiful; the great and lofty mountains covered with eternal snows, seemed to surround the luxuriant vale, crowned with perennial flowers, like a terrestrial paradise, shut out from the view of man. (1: 375–76)

Although Pike appreciates the vastness of the prairie in this scene, he nonetheless feels compelled to frame it by reference to the surrounding mountains and to domesticate it by referring to the serpentine rivers and streams running through it; the latter, apparently, constitute in his mind those elements of the vista necessary for esthetic appreciation. Recalling Pike's earlier application of "sublime" to the prairie landscape when he and his party were traveling overland, it is significant that, when juxtaposed against the mountains, the prairie is merely "beautiful"; "sublime" is reserved for the peaks. Of the two, "beautiful" is clearly inferior to "sublime," for like Lewis in his awe of the Great Falls of the Missouri and of the three forks that form the river, Pike reserves his unqualified admiration for the more familiar and "vertical" formations of the west.[28] He and Lewis reflect the dominant popular esthetic mode and, accordingly, suggest how prairie landscapes were valued esthetically: they were appreciated only when adjacent to other, more lofty features. As a landscape, the prairie offered the epistomological challenge demonstrated by Coronado and his men; it conflicted with the dominant European esthetic— popular as well as aesthete—and so from the first Europeans were forced to adapt esthetically, practically, and imaginatively to the prairie landscape.

Later Views: 1811–84

A few years after Pike's second expedition a new sort of traveler ventured into the prairie and later published accounts of their experiences: the tourist.

Distinguishing their writings from previous reports, first of all, is their literary cast: some were men of letters, others had them as editors. Second, they look at the prairie with a spectator's eye only: unconcerned with the responsibilities of exploration or fur trading, they responded mainly to the esthetic qualities in the landscape—along with its sights and sounds. After the wide distribution of Pike's *Account* and of the *History* of the Lewis and Clark expedition, of course, as well as the greater frequency of visits to the Upper Missouri and Saskatchewan country, such visitors had a better idea—though initially it was still hazy—of what they would find on the prairie than did their predecessors, just as they also had their eyes on the almost insatiable literary market for travel narratives. These men were the first of scores of tourists who ventured into the prairie West during the first half of the nineteenth century and most, so it seems, rushed back east to write up their impressions for the ready market.

Thus, by the 1840s writers were less concerned with detailing the prairie as a strange landscape since, by then, it was not really an unknown land. After official explorers and travelers published their accounts during the first third of the century, the land's salient qualities became known. Additionally, as subsequent chapters show, James Fenimore Cooper, William Cullen Bryant, and Washington Irving—literary visitors—popularized the prairie West through their writings during the 1820s and 1830s. And, through the activities of artists such as Samuel Seymour (who accompanied the Long expedition, 1819–20) and George Catlin, Karl Bodmer, and Alfred Jacob Miller (each of whom visited the prairie during the 1830s), illustrations and paintings of prairie scenes began to appear with regularity. Given this, the descriptive writers of the period were far more concerned with defining the feeling of prairie landscape, of prairie space, than they were in simply discovering its features, although, to be sure, reliable maps did not become available for some time.

Concurrently, newspaper editors in the second decade of the century began to debate the possibilities of traversing the plains to reach the West Coast. Their debates ultimately chronicled the overland exodus of Americans—spurred on by land hunger—from the East through the plains to Oregon and California, an exodus that reached its greatest proportions in the 1840s and 1850s. Though migrants did not really begin to settle the prairie beyond the Mississippi, except for eastern Kansas and Nebraska, until after the Civil War, by the 1830s and 1840s what had been the unknown prairie had become widely known, if not experienced. It was no longer a place of exotic delights. By 1860, the prairie along the Overland trail had been experienced by some 300,000 overlanders.[29] Tourists, traders, trekkers, and trappers (the latter of whom had been traveling the plains all along)—as well as additional exploration parties first commissioned to observe settlement possibilities, then to chart railroad routes—combined to create a public perception of the prairie west. Their writings, though better informed as to the conditions to be found there, still reveal perceptual difficulties with prairie space as the writers strove to comprehend its demands despite, at times, extensive prairie experience.

Characteristic of the tourists, and one of the earliest, is Henry Marie Brackenridge, son of the novelist and later a distinguished jurist and author in his own right. He accepted the invitation of Manuel Lisa, the Missouri fur trader, to accompany him on a trip up the Missouri, embarking in the spring of 1811. As he begins his journey, Brackenridge's observations are very general, noting that "There is an immense extent of prairie on both sides of the river." Later, having grown accustomed to such scenes, he writes, "an immense level plain stretches out, bounded only by the horizon. The hunter informs me that it extends nearly a hundred miles with little variation."[30] When he is able to alight from the boat, and walk out onto the prairie by himself, however, his descriptions become at once more detailed and poetic:

> Passed through a most delightful prairie, the grass short and close, of a deep blue, and intermixed with a great variety of beautiful flowers. With what delight could I roam over these lovely meads, if not under restraint from the fear of meeting some party of Indians, who may be lurking about. The plain was strewed with the ordure of the buffaloe, which gave it the appearance of an immense pasture field. (91)

Brackenridge is like some English squire here—off to taste nature's delights, roaming at will, and this passage clearly reflects the conventions of eighteenth-century landscape appreciation. Equally indicative of an *a priori* frame of mind, however, is his fear that there "may" be Indians "lurking about," a fear derived from the eastern American colonial experience.

Like Fr. Allouez on the Mississippi and Alexander Henry on the Red River of the North, Brackenridge also describes the prairie in pictorial or compositional terms:

> The scenery this evening is beautiful beyond any thing I ever beheld. . . . The sky as clear as that represented in Chinese painting. The face of the country enchanting. The flowery mead, the swelling ground, the romantic hill, the bold river, the winding rivulet, the groves, the shrubberies, all disposed and arranged in the most exquisite manner. (91–92)

Such a "classical" description, however, soon gives way to a "romantic" response and a very ambivalent comparison of the old world with the new:

> No idea can be conveyed to the mind, but by recurring to one which would be as sad as this is pleasing. Suppose for a moment, the most beautiful parts of France or Italy should at once be divested of their population, and with it their dwellings and every vestige of human existence—that nothing but the silent plains and a few solitary groves and thickets should remain, there would be some resemblance to the scenery of the Missouri; though the contemplation would produce grief instead of pleasure. Yet even here, I could not feel as if there existed a painful void—something wanting—"a melancholy stillness reigns over the interminable waste"—no animated beings—
>
> ————scarce an insect moves
> Its filmy wing—and o'er the plain, naught breathes
> But scouling blasts, or th' eternal silence
> Breaks—save when the paling thunder roars.
>
> In fact, I saw no living thing in the course of my evening ramble, except a few buzzing insects.

Significantly, this ambivalence totally disappears as Brackenridge then goes on to imagine the future of the prairie:

> But there is a pleasure in giving wing to fancy, which anticipates the cheerful day when virgin soil will give birth to millions of my countrymen. Too happy, if my after fame might but survive on the plains of the Missouri. If the vast expanse of ocean is considered as a sublime spectacle, this is even more so; for the eye has still greater scope, and, instead of its monotony, now reposes upon the velvet green, or feeds on the endless variety of hill and dale. Instead of being closed up in a moving prison, deprived of the use of our limbs, here we may wander at our will. The mind naturally expands, or contracts, to suit the sphere in which it exists—in the immeasurable immensity of the scene, the intellectual faculties are endured with an energy, a vigor, a spring, not to be described. (92)

Having shifted from a classical eighteenth-century stance to a European romantic one, Brackenridge now becomes romantic in what was to be in the American epic vein, with his use of the ubiquitous prairie/ocean analogy, anticipating Melville's metaphors. His comments on the effect of the prairie on the mind also anticipating Emerson's theories of correspondence and self-reliance. Similarly, although he continues to see the present uninhabited landscape as a problem, his task now is essentially one of trying to describe such a situation:

> Herds of buffaloe could be seen at such a distance as to appear like black spots or dots. How different are the feelings in the midst of this romantic scenery, from those experienced in the close forests of the Ohio? At four o'clock hoisted sail with a fair wind. From the moment of our departure, we were hardly ever out of sight of herds of buffaloes, feeding on the hills and in the plains, and in the course of the day saw elk and antelopes in abundance. These objects enliven the scenery, but there is something strange in thus passing day after day without meeting any human beings. A vast country inhabited only by buffaloes, deer, and wolves, has more resemblance to the fictions of the "Arabian Nights Entertainments" than to reality. (109–10)

As this passage indicates, not only did the prairie challenge Brackenridge's esthetic sense; as in the case of the first explorers and traders, it also forced him to reassess his concept of "reality."

This situation, in turn, may explain the interesting combination of esthetic appreciation and scientific reasoning in Brackenridge's attempts to come to terms with prairie phenomena. After comparing the deep blue of the prairie sky to that seen in a "Chinese painting," for example, he takes up the possible causes for the sky's hue at some length:

> I could not help remarking the clearness of the air, and the enchanting blue of the sky. Whether it is to be attributed to the Alpine height, to which we have attained, or to the openness of the country, which permits every breeze to have its full scope, and thus chase away the vapors, I am not able to say.

He continues by estimating his elevation above sea level and then states:

> It is said, that on the high plains of Switzerland, between the mountains, the sky is observed to possess a deeper azure; the same cause may produce the like effect on these plains. Here, we are elevated above the fogs and mists of lakes and rivers, and the sun does not transmit his rays through the white medium of clouds. (135–36)

Using this general knowledge, he then attempts to account for the particular case in question: "The light dress of vegetation, with which these plains are clothed, may likewise be considered. Where the vegetation is luxuriant, dense vapours arise during the night; and noxious gases are produced, which floating into the atmosphere, lessen its brightness as well as its purity" (136). Ultimately, however, he turns from consideration of cause back to a statement of effect: "But, whatever may be the cause of the superior beauty of the azure in the heavenly vault, I experienced a particular pleasure in contemplating it" (136).

Similar to this tendency to introduce scientific explanations in the midst of esthetic appreciation are Brackenridge's frequent reader-conscious asides. As the party was approaching a particular island in the river, for example,

> our ears were assailed by a murmuring noise. As we drew near it grew to a tremendous roaring, such as to deafen us. On landing we discovered the grove crowded with buffaloe, the greater part engaged in furious combat— the air filled with their dreadful bellowing. A more frightful sight cannot easily be imagined. Conceive several thousand of these furious animals, roaring and rushing upon each other, producing a scene of horror, confusion, and fierceness, like the fight of armies: the earth trembled beneath their feet, the air was deafened, and the grove was shaken with the shock of their tremendous battle. I am conscious that with many, I run the risk of being thought to indulge in romance, in consequence of this account: but with those who are informed of the astonishing number of the buffaloe, it will not be considered incredible. We soon discovered that a herd of males had broken in amongst a number of females and that these were the cause of a conflict, which raged with unparalleled fury. (149–50)

Brackenridge's vivid description, indicative of his wonder over the scene itself (and by extension, with wonder at a land which contains such sights), might well be criticized as romantic hyperbole by those who had never been to such a place. As numerous other first-person accounts attest, however, during buffalo mating season such sights were common.[31] Brackenridge continues:

> We fired amongst them but without producing much effect; we then embarked and proceeded on our voyage. On the hills in every direction [buffalo] appeared by the thousands. Late in the evening we saw an immense herd in motion on the sides of the hill, at full speed: their appearance had something in it, which, without incurring ridicule, I might call sublime—the sounds

of their footsteps, even at the distance of two miles, resembled the rumbling of distant thunder. (150)

Again, Brackenridge's defensive syntax indicates his uneasiness over whether his audience will share his opinion that such a scene might legitimately be called "sublime." Among the cultured of the eastern United States and of England, for whom Brackenridge was writing, the image of thousands of hairy, wild cattle stomping down a hillside might not be thought deserving of such an adjective. To some of them, indeed, Lewis's description of the Great Falls of the Missouri probably seemed closer to sublimity.

But Brackenridge's defensive syntax suggests that he is readjusting his assumptions to fit the imaginative demands of the new world into which he had ventured. His tone is one of amazement, but instead of the "brave new world" of *The Tempest,* he finds the "strange new world" of the North American prairie. His combination of esthetic reaction and scientific description—reveals an individual "beyond the borders of his culture," in Stephen Fender's words, attempting to understand by precise description and inculcated esthetics and shared comparisons—the only tools he has. Thus Brackenridge finds himself in the midst of a cultural void, assuaged only partly by his tentative useage of terms such as *sublime.* Indeed, he doubts the efficacy of such terminology on the prairie, though there is no doubt as to the esthetic challenge the prairie poses to his imagination.[32]

Before turning to travelers with extended experience of the prairie, Edmund Flagg should be considered briefly. Although he traveled to the prairie twenty years after Brackenridge, his *The Far West* (1838) demonstrates that an alternative to elaborate factuality in the face of a strange landscape is romantic hyperbole. Having just graduated from Bowdoin College prior to his western tour, Flagg also suggests that the prairie was being assimilated into the eastern consciousness, however impressionistically and vaguely. Thus Flagg includes a quotation from William Cullen Bryant's poem, "The Prairies" (1833) to close an extended landscape description:

> I was struck, as is every traveller at first view of these vast plains, with the grandeur, the novelty, and loveliness of the scene before me. For some moments I remained stationary, looking out upon the boundless landscape before me. The tall grasstops waving in the billowing beauty in the breeze; the narrow pathway winding off like a serpent over the rolling surface, disappearing and reappearing till lost in the luxurient herbage; the shadowy, cloud-like aspect of the far-off trees, looming up, here and there, in isolated masses along the horizon, like the pyramidal canvass of ships at sea; the

deep-green groves besprinkled among the vegetation, like islets in the waters; the crimson-died prairie-flower flashing in the sun—these features of inanimate nature seemed strangely beautiful to one born and bred amid the bold mountain scenery of the North, and who now gazed upon them "for the first."[33]

Flagg's approach and reaction to the prairie landscape is romantisized and convention-laden—this passage is followed immediately by more direct quotation from Bryant's "The Prairies,"—but, even so, he keeps in sight the landscape before him. His flowery outpourings take the forms of interpretive analogies; the prairie is yet again likened to the sea.

Flagg's effusions are more significant, however, when he considers the esthetic potential of the prairie landscape; not surprisingly, this is found within a description of a prairie sunset, at once conventional and, on the prairie, singular:

The blue heavens of Italy have tasked the inspiration of an hundred bards, and the warm brush of her own Lorraine has swept the canvass with their gorgeous transcript! But what pencil has wandered over the grander scenes of the North American prairie? What bard has struck his lyre to the wild melody of loveliness of the prairie sunset?

In turn, with a nationalist flair, Flagg inverts the typical expression of unfamiliarity: "I cannot tell of the beauties of climes I have never seen; but I have gazed upon all the varied loveliness of my own fair, native land from the rising sun to its setting, and in vain have tasked my fancy to image a fairer" (26: 251). Earlier, of course, Flagg contrasts the prairie with the northern landscapes of his native New England—each landscape seen as proof of the American nation's splendor—and, in like manner, while describing the prairie in moonlight, Flagg begins by employing the typical ocean analogy but then goes on to mention the literary genre most frequently associated with such scenes: "There was a dash of fascinating romance about the scene" (26: 332). And finally he concludes by claiming for America an exotic setting comparable to those most fabled elsewhere; while northern Asia may boast of her "boundless *pastures* and *steppes*" and Africa "her Bedoin *sands*" and "India her *jungles*," the "vast regions of the 'Far West' " may boast of their "broad-rolling *prairies*" (26: 343).

At one point Flagg is caught in a thunderstorm; his description, which begins chronicling the dusty, rainless forty days which preceded the storm, leads up to it by way of foreshadowing. The description of the storm itself is replete with literary allusions and, after recounting his impression of it, Flagg concludes:

> I have witnessed thunder-storms on the deep, and many a one among the cliffs of my native hills; but a midnight thunder-gust upon the broad prairie-plains of the West is more terrible than they. A more sublimely magnificent spectacle have I never beheld that that, when one of these broad-sheeted masses of purple light would blaze along the black bosom of the cloud, quiver for an instant over the prairie miles in extent, flinging around the scene a garment of flame, and then go out in darkness. (26: 217–18)

Unlike Brackenridge, Flagg does not hesitate to assign the term *sublime* to a prairie scene; he even tries to amplify its meaning by yoking it to the adjective *magnificent*. Brackenridge, however, was describing a herd of buffalo; he thought the view sublime, but he hesitated to pronounce it so since it was so very unlike any other spectacle usually so called. In Flagg's case, his scene is not outside of conventional assumptions of the sublime—indeed the awesome power of nature is all the more visible to Flagg on the prairie.

John Palliser, who led the most famous exploratory expedition into the Canadian prairie in the late 1850s, represents another type of tourist—the hunter, for which purpose he undertook a trip into the American prairie during 1847 and 1848. His book, *Solitary Rambles and Adventures of a Hunter on the Prairies* (1853) is largely a guidebook for hunters and his perspective is slightly different from those examined thus far. Because hunting is a sport that requires a keen attention to the terrain as habitat for the animals sought, Palliser pays closer attention to the terrain than did some of his predecessors. Like some of them, Palliser notes the prairie's optical effects; seeing distant objects is "almost like looking through a telescope." Like many of them, too, he remarks upon the difficulty of a land without landmarks: "The eye ranges over a sea of short waving grass without a single intervening object to afford it the accustomed means of estimating relative size and distance."[34]

Palliser's most telling comments, however, relate to how the prairie makes him feel. Though he begins with a discussion of the local vegetation, he concludes by revealing his personal reaction to the prairie itself:

> The vegetation in this part of the prairie was very rank, and in some places gigantic, the grass growing over thousands of acres from five to eight feet high. For two days we travelled through this without intermission, occa-sionally meeting with willows and small spots of timber. Everything around—the huge coarse grass—weeds that I never saw before, rank and

tangled in their unchecked growth—and the eternal illimitable sweep of the undulating prairie, impressed on me a sense of vastness quite overwhelming." (87)

Similarly, while later struggling still through this landscape, Palliser remarks:

> I know not when I have felt so forcibly conscious of my own insignificance, as when struggling through this immense waste, and feeling as though I were suddenly carried backward into some remote and long past age, and as though I were encroaching on the territories of the Mammoth and the Mastodon. (88)

The prairie, according to Palliser, is a primordial landscape—it makes him feel small and insignificant. Unlike the earliest commentators, therefore, Palliser does not describe the prairie mainly in terms of comparison with known things—his strange feelings of insignificance seem to require the unknown, so he alters his allusions accordingly. Similarly, so overpowering is the impact of the prairie that it overrides any conventional landscape notions Palliser may have had before he ventured into it. Instead he searches for the appropriate words.[35]

These three travelers form a representative group. None appears wholly comfortable with his descriptions of prairie sights—all suggest both uncertainly and tentativeness about their subjects. At the same time, their writings demonstrate the role played by personal background in landscape perception since, in contrast to his fellows, Palliser offers virtually no esthetic allusions in his landscape descriptions. Taken together, narratives such as Brackenridge's *Account,* Flagg's *The Far West,* and Palliser's *Solitary Rambles* demonstrate the esthetic and epistemological vacuum offered by the prairie landscape during the prewar period. Just as their precursors Lewis and Clark and Zubulon Pike reserved esthetic terminology for Rocky Mountain scenery that only happened to include the prairie, so too were men of letters hard pressed (even though they understood contemporary esthetics more precisely) to understand the prairie, to feel comfortable in it. Brackenridge, on the one hand, strives mightily to describe precisely the land and its sights, tentatively suggesting that terms such as *sublime* might be applicable to the prairie. Flagg, on the other hand, charges forward with only conventional romantic gush and etherial vagaries—ultimately, he says nothing precise nor new about the prairie; his view is wholly conventional, and he never gets beyond it. Palliser describes his feelings of insignificance directly, though he too invokes science through his primordial allusions. In Stephen Fender's terms, each tries to plot an unplotted wilderness through the language of science or, conversely, the language of inherited romantic literary convention. They do not succeed, for the prairie which emerges from these narratives is only marginally better understood than that which emerges from Castañeda's *Narrative*. The rhetorical directness of the Spaniard's "Who could believe . . ." is missing, but the tone, the feeling, and something of the description, of having seen a strange land and of having not really understood it remains.[36]

While tourists began finding their way into the prairie, official exploratory expeditions kept heading west throughout the nineteenth century. Of the reports they left, Edwin James's *Account of an Expedition from Pittsburgh to the Rocky Mountains, performed in the Years 1819, 1820 . . . under the Command of Maj. S. H. Long* (1823),[37] is probably the most significant. James, who was botanist and geologist to the expedition, which was itself essentially scientific in character, wrote the account in consultation with Major Long and other members of the party. Perhaps because the expedition struck out overland from the Missouri toward the Rocky Mountains, James repeatedly complains of the monotony of the view as they cross "the same uninteresting and dreary country as before," although he is "constantly amused at observing the motions of the countless thousands of bisons" which usually surrounded the party (15: 255). At other points in his description James agrees with Pike as to the desert character of much of the region (17: 147–48) and was, in fact, the person who coined the usual nineteenth-century descriptive designation for the area, "The Great American Desert."

But James's *Account* is most revealing in its comments on the interaction between his culture and the prairie. Thus after explaining that their "path lay through extensive and fertile meadows, stretching away to the distant horizon, and bounded sometimes by the margin of a forest" he goes on to observe:

> The elk, the deer, and the bison, the indigenous inhabitants of these delightful meadows, had been long since driven away by the incursions of the white settlers, scattered at remote intervals on the borders of the forests. The dense and uniform growth of grass had risen untrodden and uncropped, and was now waving with ceaseless undulations, as the wind swept lightly over the surface of the plain. (15: 171)

Conversely, he records how the same day the expedition was overtaken by a thunderstorm that included, for a time, hail:

> The wind soon rose to a tempest; and hailstones of uncommon magnitude began to fall, accompanied by thunder and lightning. Our first thought was

to dismount from our horses, and shelter ourselves from the hail on the leeward side of their bodies. We were in the middle of an extensive prairie, where no other protection could be looked for. (15: 172)

As the prairie is rendered barren by man's incursions, in short, so it also exposes him to the forces of the elements—engendering feelings of vulnerability.[38]

James, owing to his background and the scientific character of the expedition, articulately and precisely defines natural phenomena; the vast line of sight afforded by the prairie landscape, while noted by James's predecessors, is accurately described by him for the first time:

Nothing is more difficult than to estimate, by the eye, the distance of objects seen in these plains. A small animal, as a wolf or a turkey, sometimes appears of the magnitude of a horse, on account of an erroneous impression of distance. Three elk, which were the first we had seen, crossed our path at some distance before us. The effect of the *mirage,* together with our indefinite idea of the distance, magnified these animals to a most prodigious size. For a moment we thought we saw the mastodon of America, moving in those vast plains, which seem to have been created for his dwelling place. An animal seen for the first time, or any object with which the eye is unacquainted, usually appears much enlarged, and inaccurate ideas are formed of the magnitude and distance of all surrounding objects; but if some well-known animal, as a deer or a wolf, comes into the field of vision so near as to be recognized, the illusions vanish, and all things return to their proper dimensions. (15: 184)

James is the first commentator to analyze the manner by which unfamiliar animals or objects are apprehended on the prairie: through the commingling of previous experience (both personal experience and acculturated experience embodied in conventions) with new experiences; such is the process of man's adaptation. As he states, "illusions vanish" upon recognition; that is, they vanish upon the establishment of a correspondence in the mind between what one is seeing and what one has seen previously. But until that correspondence is established in a new landscape like the prairie, the uninitiated are forced to suffer the discomfort of their "illusions."

This same situation is reflected, but in a more threatening aspect, when James later notes an alarm caused when some of the party reported that they had seen Indians on horseback, traveling at a distance:

but of this there could be no certainty, the imagination often representing a herd of antelopes, or other animals, seen at a distance, and perhaps distorted by the looming of the prairie, as so many mounted Indians. We had often found ourselves more grossly abused by our eye-sight, than is supposed in this instance, having mistaken turkeys for bisons, wolves for horses, &c. (15: 259)

Like Brackenridge's reference to "lurking" Indians, James here reflects the way in which the illusions that vexed travelers often took the form of imported and projected fears. Human eyesight is "abused" by the prairie because there accurate visual perspective is difficult to obtain, even impossible to obtain in the case of an uninitiated prairie traveler; the imagination, allowed a free rein, often filled in the gaps left vacant—hence James's Indians on horseback and, before them, his vision of the "mastodon of America" off in the distances.

Like most other observers, James also provides his most extensive description of the buffalo when he views them from above. After climbing a local height, an "undulation," in one instance he describes them as "obscuring . . . the verdant plain" and covering the entire field of vision. He notices small clouds of dust here and there, raised by both playful and earnest scuffles between individual bulls, and finally concludes: "On the distant bluffs, individuals were constantly disappearing, whilst others were presenting themselves to our view, until, as the dusk of the evening increased, their massive forms, thus elevated above the line of other objects, were but dimly defined on the skies" (15: 239). Both Castañeda and Henry record similar sights but, unlike them, James registers his impressions largely in terms of visual perspective rather than numerical estimates of the herd's size. Although he mentions numbers, saying "at least ten thousand here burst on our sight in the instant," James emphasizes a panoramic view of the herd. And because he describes individual buffalo at the horizon line, moving in and out of sight, his description dramatizes the spectacle of buffalo "as far as the eye could reach." The party, moreover, was moved by the view afforded them by their vantage point and the prairie landscape: "We retired to our evening fare, highly gratified with the novel spectacle we had witnessed, and with the most sanguine expectations" for the next morning's hunt. But when morning came, when they "again sought the living picture," James and his fellows were shocked to find that "not one remained" (15: 239)—his dismay over such a radical change being registered through his vivid diction.

A last American exploration report, though written during the 1850s, underscores James's reaction to the prairies, and echoes Palliser's comments by asserting that his text is essentially mute regarding the vastness of the region.

John Lambert, topographer to the American railway exploratory party led by I. I. Stevens in 1853–54, traveled west from the Red River of the North as far as present-day Idaho; having done so, he writes:

> The eye grows weary travelling over the naked outlines of the successive plateaux. . . . It is difficult to convey an adequate idea of these dreary solitudes. Let it be remembered that a few minutes' reading embraces sections which require tedious weeks to traverse; and that even travelling over and observing them with the patient labor of months, leaves but a *feeling* of their vastness, which baffles the effort to express it. The impressive silence of succeeding days is broken at rare intervals by the crack of some stray hunter's rifle, or perchance by the yell of painted warriors on a foray; but when the twilight wanes over the peaceful camp, when the evening meal is over, and the incidents of the march are recounted, then the "drowsy ear of night" is roused to listen to the prolonged and melancholy cry of prowling wolves.[39]

Even Lambert, after months of travel, has but a *"feeling"* of the prairie's vastness, "which baffles the effort to express it." He knows that, since description summarizes, any description reduces the impression of the prairie left with the reader to one that is, because of its attendant reduction, essentially inaccurate. Lambert's details, like Palliser's, present images that reinforce his feeling of vastness—solitary rifles and howling wolves—and also give a romantic cast to the scene. Ironically, it is as if Lambert feels that the only hope of describing the prairie accurately is by pointing up the difficulty in doing so: details can be pointed to and feelings described, but the prairie landscape eludes definition. That someone traveling over the prairie in the mid-nineteenth century would hold such an opinion is not surprising, but that a topographer would focus upon his imaginative impression, rather than discussing the fine differences in the land that his trained eye could isolate, reflects the strong, perhaps overwhelming impact of the land; in this passage, at least, his imaginative response took priority over his scientific objectivity.

Lambert was objective, however, in offering his opinion regarding the aridity of the upper Great Plains. Writing while the idea of the Great American Desert still had currency, Lambert is careful not to use the term "desert." The possibility of barrenness, he wrote,

> must be greatly qualified, if not removed, by the fact that all these regions are the pasture-grounds of frequent herds of various kinds of deer, particularly of the graceful antelope, with quantities of inferior game and spe-

cies of vermin, and, last and greatest, the unfailing millions of the uncouth and ponderous buffalo. (152)

Because during the pre–Civil War period, Americans "were used to judging the fertility of new land by the kind of trees growing on it," as Henry Nash Smith has observed, Lambert carefully couches his observation so as to combat this prejudice by suggesting another litmus test for fertility: the animals supported by the land.[40]

James's *Account* is significant largely because it provides one of the best single objective narratives of a march directly across the prairies. Since he was a scientist, and it was a collaborative official scientific report, James's narrative offers crucial evidence of the epistomological challenge offered by the prairie that corroborates that found in the earlier first-person accounts. James's responses, though couched in terms of scientific objectivity, nonetheless echo those of his predecessors, and speak for the entire party's reactions. The Long expedition was among the last of the initial exploration parties, those undertaken by men who were not especially sure of what to expect, such was the information available. Given this, the almost eerie consistency of their reactions suggests that prior reading did not amount to very much. This analysis is confirmed by the reactions of tourists and, thirty years later, those of Lambert. A person had to experience the prairie's infinities himself, he had to try to comprehend its seemingly incomprehensible spaces on his own terms, whether he traveled alone or with a group, for business or for pleasure.

Before turning to yet another sort of prairie text—those written after considerable experience—something needs to be said about the audience for western travel accounts. Numerous commentators have detailed the popularity of the west as a topic during the nineteenth century, most notably Henry Nash Smith in *Virgin Land;* Americans and Europeans alike bought books about the American west in vast numbers for the period and, as indicated above, travel narratives were no exception. The James *Account* of the Long expedition was the first western exploration report to be lavishly printed and was widely distributed, though Pike's *Account* had been popular—as was, to a lesser extent, the Biddle *History* of the Lewis and Clark expedition. The 1820s through the 1840s saw the popularity of Cooper's Leatherstocking series, Irving's western works, and George Catlin's *Letters and Notes on the Manners, Customs, and Conditions of the North American Indians* (1841). These decades also saw the popularization of the American west by John C. Frémont, who was called "the Great Pathfinder" but ought to have been called "the Great Path Publicizer," according to one historian, so important were his reports and so crucial were they in establishing the popular images of the American west.[41]

Josiah Gregg's *Commerce of the Prairies* (1844), the final American prairie narrative to be considered in this chapter, was among the most popular western accounts of the 1840s. Between first publication and 1856 Gregg's book went through eleven printings, including British editions and four German translations. Apart from its popularity, *Commerce* differs from those works treated above by the perspective Gregg offers. Like Thompson, his writing reflects extensive prairie experience, not just a single trip; at the same time, it differs from Alexander Henry's journals in that it digests nine years of experience. Gregg was a Sante Fe trader from 1831–40, traveling across the prairie from the U.S. into Mexican territory and back again. He originally went west seeking relief from an illness, and according to his own testimony, found it. On the prairie,

> Most chronic diseases . . . are often radically cured; owing, no doubt, to the peculiarities of diet, and the regular exercise incident to prairie life, as well as to the purity of the atmosphere of those elevated unembarrassed regions. An invalid myself, I can answer for the efficacy of the remedy, at least in my own case.

The effect of the atmosphere on Gregg's health undoubtedly accounts for his "passion for Prairie life."[42]

Gregg made eight round trips through the prairie, and throughout the *Commerce* he speaks as one who is intimately acquainted with it:

> Our route had already led us up the course of the Arkansas river for over a hundred miles, yet the earlier caravans often passed from fifty to a hundred [miles] further up before crossing the river; therefore nothing like a regular ford had ever been established. Nor was there a road, not even a trail, anywhere across the famous plain, extending between the Arkansas and Cimmarron rivers, a distance of over fifty miles, which now lay before us—the scene of such frequent sufferings in former times for want of water. It having been determined upon, however, to strike across the dreaded desert the following morning, the whole party was busy in preparing for the "water scrape," as these droughty drives are very appropriately called by prairie travellers. (19: 218–19)

What deserves notice in this description is the way that Gregg combines his previous knowledge and experience with the action taking place immediately before him. The area Gregg describes is along the Arkansas river—where Coronado bemoaned the lack of water and complained of the quality of that which was available—and his perception of the land itself is the same as the Spaniard's:

> This tract of country may truly be styled the grand "prairie ocean"; for not a single landmark is to be seen for more than forty miles—scarcely a visible eminence by which to direct one's course. All is level as the sea, and the compass was our surest, as well as principle guide. (19: 219)

The analogy with the ocean, which Coronado first used had, however, become a literary commonplace by the time Gregg was writing, and his dependence on his compass recalls in inverted fashion the Canadians who accompanied Thompson to the Mandan villages in 1797. They, of course, did not trust a compass "on land."

Like other travelers, too, Gregg uses the scaling of an eminence for his most prolonged and detailed analysis of the prairie and its effects upon those who travel through it. Both as a landmark and as a perch, a hill Gregg calls "the 'Round Mound'" serves as his vantage point for analysis of the surrounding landscape:

> We were yet at least three miles from this mound, when a party sent out on foot to ascend it, in order to get a view of the surrounding country. They felt confident it was but half a mile off—at most, three-quarters; but finding the distance so much greater than they had anticipated, many began to lag behind and soon rejoined the wagons. The optical illusions occasioned by the rarified and transparent atmosphere of these elevated plains, are often truly remarkable, affording another exemplification of its purity. One would almost fancy himself looking through a spy-glass, for objects frequently appear at scarce one-fourth of their real distance—frequently much magnified, and more especially elevated. (19: 241)

Gregg continues to attest, like James, that objects and animals seen from a distance on the prairie are taken for much larger things or beings. A herd of buffalo, for example, "upon a distant plain often appear so increased in bulk that they would be mistaken by the inexperienced for a grove of trees" (19: 242). Like Castañeda and James, Gregg observes that this illusion has the greatest effect on those who are inxperienced, and that it vanishes when one recognizes familiar objects and is less likely to recur as one gains prairie experience.

Gregg then speaks of "a continual waving and looming" on the prairies "which often so writhe and distort distant objects," reflecting his knowledge of the optical effects of heat rising; the phenomenon "seems to be occasioned by gaseous vapors rising from the ground while the beaming rays of the sun are darting upon it" (19: 242). As he also notes, however, the increased density of the air along the surface of the earth creates another optical illusion: "false ponds," or the desert mirage. "Even the experienced traveller," Gregg maintains,

> is often deceived by these upon the arid plains, where a disappointment is most severely felt. The thirsty wayfarer, after jogging for hours under a burning sky, at length espies a pond—yes, it must be water—it looks too natural for it to be mistaken. He quickens his pace, enjoying in anticipation the pleasure of a refreshing draught: but lo! as he approaches, it recedes or entirely disappears; and when upon its apparent site, he is ready to doubt his own vision—he finds but a parched plain under his feet. (19: 242)

After his lengthy digression about optical illusions, Gregg allows some of his party to experience the view from the summit of the Round Mound—"a full and advantageous view of the surrounding country, in some directions to a distance of a hundred miles or more" (19: 243). After so doing, Gregg launches into a description of the plains themselves:

> These immense bordering plains, and even the hills with which they are interspersed, are wholly destitute of timber, except a chance scattering tree upon the margins of the bluffs and ravines, which but scantily serves to variegate the landscape. Not even a buffalo was now to be seen to relieve the dull monotony of the scene; although at some seasons (and particularly in the fall) these prairies are literally strewed with herds of this animal. Then "thousands and tens of thousands" might at times be seen from this eminence. (19: 243–44)

Like others before (and after) him, Gregg uses the view from the summit to unify and encompass the whole of the prairie landscape spread before him, but because of his experience he also provides a larger context for each individual scene. To the same effect, after concluding his comments on the buffalo, Gregg continues to take advantage of the view from atop the mound, and describes his caravan as it heads farther west, moving in four parallel columns (19: 246–47).

Thus Gregg's dramatic, synthetic narrative techniques reflect his extended experience of the prairie; by collapsing eight round trips into one and so taking his reader on a "typical" trip from the American frontier during the 1830s to Santa Fe, Mexico, he presents the land in the *Commerce of the Prairies* as an understood, familar entity and not just the incidental topography seen in narratives based on a single trip. His descriptions are in no way impressionistic—they reflect a keen understanding of the prairie and its imaginative and practical effects. That Gregg's descriptions, and those written by others of equal prairie experience, are consistent with those of travelers and one-time explorers suggests that the prairie's imaginative challenges are continual; while one may come to understand their workings over time, the feelings of strangeness the landscape engenders initially do not seem totally to abate. Man may begin to comprehend—and so become more at ease with, prairie spaces—but, even so, its infinities and thus its inscrutability, remain. [43]

During the 1820s through the 1840s, women also began to enter the prairie in numbers as overlanders, settlers, and tourists; so like the explorers and traders who had preceded them, they were faced with the new imaginative demands of prairie space. To be sure, native women had been present throughout the exploration period and had played crucial roles, but not until the first decades of the century, which saw the settlement of Illinois and other areas in the upper Mississippi region, were white women a significant presence. [44] Accordingly, it was only in the nineteenth century that women began leaving written records of their perceptions of the West in any number. And, as noted in the Introduction, until recently pioneering the prairie West was seen by— mostly male—scholars as a masculine enterprise. Thus the recent historical scholarship of Julie Roy Jeffrey, John Mack Faragher, Sandra L. Myres, Glenda Riley, Martha Mitten Allen and others has been an important corrective. It has illuminated women's actual roles and attitudes during this period and contrasted women's writings with those by men within the social context of the time, thus shattering many of the myths surrounding women's roles in pioneering. Jeffrey warns against "viewing women solely as reluctant pioneers" since, despite the widespread acceptance of that stereotype, one created in part by fictions written by men, the record suggests that many women took to the overland trail enthusiastically. And as she concludes in *Frontier Women,* "women knew" that during the frontier period "they had been at their best":

> Had they known what lay in store, some admitted, they would not have set out so lightheartedly so many years before. Although they remembered the pioneer period with distaste, these women also described themselves as courageous and brave. They had not been weak but strong; they had not been passive but active. They had triumphed over frontier conditions heroically. [45]

The gender-based differences which are significant in understanding the relationship between men's and women's writings in response to the prairie landscape derive from their separate social spheres and the different sets of values that define their roles. The men saw "overland emigration," according to Faragher, as "an archetypal nineteenth-century event, for it was conceived in the spirit of progress, publicly designated to fulfill economic goals, yet infused and overlaid with male projections and identifications." The women, on the other hand, "only reluctantly participated in these male fantasies." "They went," Faragher concludes, "because of the terms of obedience which marriage had imposed and which they had accepted." In her important corrective, Annette Kolodny makes the point more positively, writing in *The Land Before Her* that: "What women were apparently less willing to accept was the single-minded transformation of nature into wealth without any regard for the inherent beauty of the place."[46]

Such objections speak directly to the role of women in early nineteenth-century America, which Myres has summarized:

> Banned from the marketplace and displaced from their earlier economic roles
> within the family, women sought a new meaning for their lives, and this was
> provided by the idealization of women as the moral guardians of home and
> family life. Women were assigned a new role confined within the carefully
> defined sphere of woman's place. Women were expected to remain domestic
> and demure, withhold themselves from competition with men, and shield
> home and family from the rapidly changing and often frightening values of
> an increasingly materialistic society. By the nineteenth century, this portrait
> of women's place was enshrined within the cult of true womanhood.[47]

Frontier conditions, particularly the six months spent traveling the overland trail, flew in the face of such concerns; women were thrust into continual contact with men other than their husbands or relatives, and simply maintaining the family in the face of such hardship was often a major challenge.

How these gender-based differences affected assessments of the prairie landscape is another matter. Faragher notes that, on the basis of his content analysis, three major themes emerge from the 169 narratives he studied: "the practical aspects of the trip, the health and safety of traveling kith and kin, and the natural beauty of the landscape." "In terms of sheer preponderance," he continues, "men and women emigrants mentioned the beauty of the setting more than any other single subject." Ultimately, Faragher concludes that "these mid-nineteenth-century men and women were part of a common culture, that they were, indeed, more alike than different." Myres, on the other hand, notes that "women's journals contained some of the most detailed accounts of the trip and vivid descriptions of the countryside." As to the prairies themselves, the guidebooks which the overlanders consulted offered conflicting reports as to nature of the terrain—whether desert or garden.[48]

Most women, however, "were not attracted to the open prairies in the new country," according to Myres, assuming that trees were an indication of fertility and, traveling the plains farther west, "the overwhelming sentiment expressed by most travelers was boredom." Yet just as among men, both poles of response to the prairies are represented in women's writings. Describing the Illinois prairie, Eliza W. Farnham writes in *Life in Prairie Land* (1846):

> The great, silent plain, with its still streams, its tender verdure, its lovely flowers, its timid birds and quadrupeds, shrinking away from our sight; its soft winds, its majestic storms—was a sublime spectacle! Occasionally a herd of deer bounded across our path, or a solitary pair of grouse, startled from their parental cares, rose and cleft the air like arrows of their old pursuers; but save these we were alone, the silence broken only by our own voices.[49]

Passages such as this echo romantic responses to the landscape that are first articulated by visitors such as Brackenridge and Flagg, and these responses continued to appear—in progressively more popular books, as here or in Irving's *A Tour on the Prairies*—throughout the century. At the same, however, women reacted negatively to the prairies, perhaps most graphically in a passage by Mrs. A. M. Green, an "unwilling emigrant to the colony at Greeley, Colorado" noted by Allen, who wrote of "those dreadful, hateful, woeful, fearful, doleful, desolate, distressed, disagreeable, dusty, detestable, homely and lonely plains." Ultimately, though, the initial esthetic response of women to the prairie landscape was fundamentally the same as men, in keeping with their shared culture; Sandra L. Myres summarizes the view of nineteenth-century women:

> Women's writings also reveal both realistic and romantic attitudes toward wilderness. Women, like men, evaluated the productivity and potential of the landscape, but, also like men, they were influenced by the nineteenth-century ideas of sublimity in nature and the romantic wilderness cult. The better read made frequent allusions to classical and romantic literature and painting in their descriptions of the wilderness, but even poorly educated women made use of romantic terms and phrases in recounting their experiences. In regard to the physical wonders of nature, men and women experienced similar reactions. Women were no more repelled by wilderness than

were men. They saw beauty in even the most unexpected places—in the rocks, the barren spaces, the solitude of the open prairies. Women found wilderness both attractive and repelling, inviting and desolate, both Arcadia and desert.[50]

Owing to climate and different immigration and emigration patterns, the Canadian prairie west was explored and settled later than its American counterpart. While settlers crossing the prairie on their way to Oregon and California were frequent from the mid-1830s on, such movement into the Canadian prairie did not come until the late 1880s. So when Lambert was weighing the possibilities of the Dakotas during the 1850s, British North Americans were virtually ignorant of the prairie region of the British possessions. Fur traders had operated in the area for well over a century, but since settlement was extremely limited, the Canadian North West was virtually unknown. The first official forays into the area were not undertaken until the late 1850s—although Paul Kane, the artist, traveled through the area during the mid-1840s—when two separate expeditions under Palliser and Henry Youle Hind, respectively, were accomplished. With the transfer of the Hudson's Bay territories to Canada in 1869 and the first Riel (Manitoba) uprising that resulted from the transfer, however, attention became focused on the northern prairie—and official and autobiographical accounts began to appear in increasing numbers. Perhaps not surprisingly, these accounts offer much the same responses to the prairie landscape as those by individuals who encountered it south of the border.[51]

Of the two initial expeditions, only Hind's report reflects an imaginative reaction. Describing White Horse Plain (just west of present-day Winnipeg)—"a vast, slightly undulating prairie, bounded by the horizon in every direction but the south, where the distant woods of the Assinniboine [River] afford some relief to the eye"—Hind expresses the monotony felt by James and Flagg, among others, in the United States. At the same time, however, he registers his esthetic appreciation of the novelty of the scene:

> The vast ocean of level prairie which lies to the west of Red River must be seen in its extraordinary aspects, before it can be rightly valued and understood in reference to its future occupation by an energetic and civilised race, able to improve its vast capabilities and appreciate its marvellous beauties. It must be seen at sunrise, when the boundless plain suddenly flashes with rose-coloured light, as the first rays of the sun sparkle in the dew on the long rich grass, gently stirred by the unfailing morning breeze. It must be seen at noon-day, when refraction swells into the forms of distant hill ranges the an-

cient beaches and ridges of Lake Winnipeg, which mark its former extension; when each willow bush is magnified into a grove, each distant clump of aspens, not seen before, into wide forests, and the outline of wooded river banks, far beyond unassisted vision, rise to view. It must be seen at sunset, when, just as the huge ball of fire is dipping below the horizon, he throws a flood of red light, indescribably magnificent, upon the illimitable waving green, the colours blending and separating with the gentle roll of the long grass in the evening breeze, and seemingly magnified towards the horizon into the distant heaving swell of a parti-coloured sea. It must be seen, too, by moonlight, when the summits of the low green grass waves are tipped with silver, and the stars in the west disappear suddenly as they touch the earth. Finally, it must be seen at night, when the distant prairies are in a blaze, thirty, fifty, or seventy miles away; when the fire reaches clumps of aspen, and the forked tips of the flames, magnified by refraction, flash and quiver in the horizon, and the reflected lights from rolling clouds of smoke above tell of the havoc which is raging below.

Hind's description neatly encompasses the various sights of the prairie other commentators have noticed: the wind, the sunset, and moonlight noticed by Flagg; the effect upon eyesight caused by the prairie as seen in James, Gregg, and Palliser; and finally the unconstrained line of sight touched upon by virtually every commentator. At the same time, his synthesis offers what I. S. MacLaren has called "the epitome of the sublime in landscape description," one that will "impart to a prospective settler a great desire to emigrate," and one that stands in marked contrast with Palliser's comments on the prairie grasslands of the North West. Palliser, MacLaren holds, "practised an aesthetic of elision" when viewing a prairie scene, omitting those elements in the scene which render it distasteful, so his descriptions are more like Pike's or James's.[52]

Another view of the prairie was offered by Sandford Fleming, Chief Engineer for the Canadian Pacific Railway, who published several documents dealing with the topography of the prairie. Most of these are by way of progress reports and deal, mainly, with engineering problems offered by the terrain and with the potential adaptability of the region to farming. In 1884, however, he published a personal narrative of his travels, entitled *England and Canada,* and in doing so he introduces a new perspective from which to view the prairie: from the window of a speeding railway car.

We continue through a genuine prairie without tree or shrub. Our point of vision is really and truly the centre of one vast, grassy plain, the circumference of which lies defined in the horizon. As we look from the rear, the two rails gradually come closer till they are lost, seemingly, in one line; the row of telegraph poles recedes with the distance to a point. I should estimate the horizon to be removed from us from six to eight miles. The sky, without a cloud, forms a blue vault above us; nothing around is visible but the prairie on all sides gently swelling and undulating, with the railway forming a defined diameter across the circle. Looking along the track in the distance there is a small cloud of vapour discernable, indicating that an engine is following us. The train itself is not visible. There is certainly no little monotony in a railway journey over the prairie. The landscape is unvaried: a solitude, in which the only sign of life is the motion of the train.[53]

Despite the novelty of his vantage point, there is in Fleming's description that same quality of frustration seen in Henday's "We are still in the Muscuty plains," James's "weary march," and Lambert's reference to "tedious weeks": although the traveler is moving, the vastness of the prairie makes it seem as if he is making little progress—his vision stretches ever-outward to the vanishing point where rails and sky meet. Nor, as Fleming's observation suggests, does mechanized transport do anything to mitigate the sense of endlessness— on the contrary, it serves to accentuate it.[54]

The single best-known volume on the Canadian North West during this period, however, is Sir William Francis Butler's *The Great Lone Land* (1872). Having traveled through the United States in order to rendezvous with the Wolseley expedition at Red River, Butler first confronted the prairie as he was traveling northwest from St. Cloud, Minnesota. He describes approaching a log hut "which stood out upon the level sea of grass and was visible miles and miles before one reached it," and later, describes the appearance of the Red River seen from a distance: "the windings of the river are marked by a dark line of woods fringing the whole length of the stream—each tributary has also its line of forest—a line visible many miles away over the great sea of grass."[55] Despite his use of the prairie/sea analogy, Butler's descriptions here are mainly factual; he soon turns, however, from such factual descriptions to matters of perspective on the prairie: "As one travels on, there first rise above the prairie the summits of the trees; these gradually grow larger, until finally, after many hours, the river is reached. Nothing else breaks the uniform level" (94). Hence Butler presents to his reader the effect of approaching a river from the prairie: its trees are continually in sight, but the river takes "many hours" to reach.

Not only does Butler reiterate the comments of other travelers with regard to the appearance of rivers from a distance, however; his next comment encapsulates the basic European impulse in the face of the prairie landscape:

"Standing upon the ground the eye ranges over many miles of grass, standing on a waggon, one doubles the area of vision, and to look over the plains from an elevation of twelve feet above the earth is to survey at a glance a space so vast that distance alone seems to bound its limits" (94–95). After spending some time in Red River, Butler was commissioned by Lieutenant-Governor Archibald of Manitoba and the North West Territories to travel to the Rockies and report on the Indians and the conditions he encountered. His journey, accomplished during the harshest conditions of the prairie winter, took 199 days and covered nearly three thousand miles. At one point in the account of his trip, Butler devotes a lengthy paragraph to an evaluation of the tendency among early geographers to represent the interior of the North American continent as a vast inland sea:

> an ocean there is, and an ocean through which men seek the treasures of Ca-thay, even in our own times. But the ocean is one of grass, and the shores are the crests of mountain ranges, and the dark pine-forests of the sub-Arctic regions. The great ocean itself does not present more infinite variety than does this prairie-ocean of which we speak. In winter, a dazzling surface of purest snow; in early summer, a vast expanse of grass and pale pink roses; in autumn too often a wild sea of raging fire. No ocean of water in the world can vie with its gorgeous sunsets; no solitude can equal the loneliness of night-shadowed prairie; one feels the stillness, and hears the silence, the wail of the prowling wolf makes the voice of the solitude audible, the stars look down through infinite silence upon a silence almost as intense. This ocean has no past—time has been nought to it; and men have come and gone, leaving behind them no track, no vestige, of their presence. (199–200)

Thus Butler brings the prairie/sea analogy full circle, arguing that the legend of the inland sea was literally wrong but imaginatively correct.

Butler's response to the vast featurelessness of the prairie is similarly revisionist and paradoxical. Focusing in *The Wild North Land* (1873) upon "around four hundred miles of horizon," for example, he describes

> a view so vast that endless space seems for once to find embodiment, and at a single glance the eye is satiated with immensity. There is no mountain range to come up across the sky-line, no river to lay its glistening folds along the middle distance, no dark forest to give shade to foreground or to fringe perspective, no speck of life, no track of man, nothing but the wilderness.

Whereas this was the very situation that made it difficult for Lewis to respond esthetically to the prairie, Butler continues "Reduced thus to its own nakedness, space stands forth with almost terrible grandeur." In one of his letters Fr. De Smet—a Belgian missionary with considerable American prairie experience—observes that "when one travels over the plains, he feels more inclined to prayer, meditation, [and] confidence in God. . . ." Butler's reaction in *The Great Lone Land* to "the vague dark immensity around" him is similarly religious, although it leads him to focus on "that strange mystery called death" (206). And in *The Wild North Land* Butler concludes his response to the "terrible grandeur" of the prairie in Melvillian fashion: "One is suddenly brought face to face with that enigma which we try to comprehend by giving to it the names of endless, interminable, measureless; that dark inanity which broods upon a waste of moorland at dusk, and in which fancy sees the spectral and the shadowy."[56]

If the significance of the first phase of prairie commentary lies in the unprecedented nature of the encounter, the significance of the second phase lies in the extent to which such accounts identify the problems that confronted those who attempted to depict the prairie in art. By defining a person's sense of being on the prairie, in particular, these second-phase accounts reflect the clash between conventional notions of landscape—cultural as well as esthetic—and the almost incomprehensible infinities the prairie offered, the way the landscape makes a person feel. In so doing, these texts suggest the ways that the landscape impinged upon, even directed, the narrative techniques used to describe it.

But however viewed, the writings of prairie exploration, trade, and travel attest to the landscape's effect on the human imagination. From Castañeda to Butler, the prairie exerted a tangible influence on its descriptive writers as they strove to explain, describe, encompass and, at times, justify the sights they had seen and the feelings they had felt. That they were largely without literary intention or pretension, and that their reactions are virtually indistinguishable regardless of extent of experience, purpose, or nationality are crucial considerations as this chapter concludes. These writings define a body of shared reactions untouched by overt literary intention, reactions dependent upon imaginative responses to the land itself. These texts define the features of a new land which subsequent fiction writers have, haltingly, mythologized as fictional setting. The process was halting, these writers show, because the infinities of prairie landscape are imaginatively strange, difficult; "the great fact was the land itself" on the prairie, so new metaphors had to be found, metaphors based on the land itself, before the prairie could become a literary landscape. The nascent beginnings of this transformation are to be seen in descriptive writing from Castañeda through Butler, as the great fact of the land held its sway.

Romantic Sensibility and the
Prairie Landscape:
Artistic Visitors, 1819–49

Artists were among those who traveled west during the first half of the
nineteenth century, but the first were painters and illustrators, not literary
figures. Samuel Seymour, a British-born painter and engraver, was one of the
Long expedition; he made some 150 landscape views and Indian scenes, of
which six were published in the atlas that accompanied James's *Account*. Many
others followed him, some officially employed by expeditions or travelers,
others working on their own. The paintings, sketches, and engravings record
a confrontation between their inculcated European esthetic and the prairie, a
landscape offering them what William H. Goetzmann calls "new experience
in nature."[1] This confrontation, born of a tension between what an artist was
taught to see and value in a landscape and what he actually saw on the prairie,
is analogous to that experienced by literary figures who sought to use the
prairie in their art. Both derive from the imaginative effects occasioned by the
landscape itself, the effects already seen in the nonliterary exploration and
travel narratives. By offering an analogue to literature that is, so to speak,
more visible, the artists who depicted the prairie landscape during the 1830s
and 1840s illustrate the esthetic transformation effected by the prairie landscape and recorded most extensively in prairie fiction.

The challenge to early nineteenth-century esthetics found in prairie pictures and prose is a part, of course, of the tension during the period between
romanticism and realism. Each view offered its own approach to the artist's
role, whether to interpret or merely reflect, to serve as "lamp," or "mirror."[2]
Esthetic theories aside, for the moment, the 1830–50 prairie should be seen
as a flashpoint for such concerns, since its infinite spaces seemed to defy
imaginative control, thereby rendering imported esthetic assumptions neu-

tral, almost moot. Thus, as preliminary to a discussion of prairie setting in fiction, this chapter takes up the first confrontation between the prairie landscape and figures with avowedly artistic purposes and backgrounds as a way of gauging the relationship between the landscape and the artist's inculcated esthetic assumptions.

Painters

The first major illustrator of the West, George Catlin, also wrote *Letters and Notes on the Manners, Customs, and Conditions of the North American Indians* (1841). *Letters and Notes* is prominent within the travel literature of the period because it was the first copiously illustrated book dealing with the West.[3] Unable to interest a publisher in the well-illustrated book he envisioned, Catlin had it privately printed and used as illustrations line drawings he made from his own paintings. It ran through numerous reprintings and editions; like Gregg's *Commerce of the Prairies,* Catlin's *Letters and Notes* was one of the most widely known books dealing with the American West during the prewar period. Lilian Schlissel cites a passage from the overland trail diary of Harriet Sherril Ward, for example, who made the trip to California from Wisconsin in 1853 and wrote that she " 'at once recognized one of George Catlin's beautiful views upon the Mississippi.' " "The journey, to her educated tastes," Schlissel notes, "was a procession of scenic views. In describing Independence Rock, she wrote: 'Cold chills come over me and tears would flow in spite of my efforts to repress them.' "[4]

Catlin was embarked on a romantic quest. Having studied or associated with Thomas Sully, John Meagle and several of the natural scientists who were prominent in Philadelphia during the 1830s, he established himself there as a portrait painter of some reputation. Catlin's romantic resolve stemmed, in part, from his experience with the Indians of the eastern United States; observing their fatal adaptation to white ways, he realized that the Indians of the far West were equally doomed, and he found his fears articulated in Cooper's Leatherstocking series, especially *The Prairie.* Acting on this realization, he ignored the protests of his family and, in 1830, headed west to St. Louis to begin painting western Indians. Recalling the purpose of his art, Catlin emphasizes the need to portray the Indian life-style while, paradoxically, he praises the absence of an art tradition as the primary attraction of the native for the painter:

Man, in the simplicity and loftiness of his nature, unrestrained and unfet-
tered by the disguises of art, is surely the most beautiful model for the
painter—and the country from which he hails is unquestionably the best
study or school of the arts in the world: such I am sure, from the models I
have seen, is the wilderness of North America. And the history and customs
of such people, preserved by pictorial illustrations, are themes worthy of the
life-time of one man, and nothing short of the loss of my life, shall prevent
me from visiting their country, and of becoming their historian.[5]

In his paintings Catlin best serves as historian of the prairie environment,
documenting the land and its people, seeing them as existing in a kind of
symbiotic relationship. Thus, his pictorial work—despite certain limitations—could be described as realistic. His prose, on the other hand, is
characterized by romantic excesses, very often reminiscent of Edmund Flagg.
This discrepancy may be explained by perspective; most of Catlin's paintings
were done on the spot, in great haste and under extremely difficult conditions,
but he wrote much of his book while he was living in London during 1839–
40, where he displayed his "Indian Collection" (made up of his paintings,
drawings, sketches, assorted memorabilia and, later, Indians acting out pan-
tomimes of scalping, skulking, and other colorful activities). Thus a double
kind of nostalgia may have been operating as he wrote of Indians in their
natural environment, far away on the prairie.[6] Indeed, this same tendency
may be seen in prairie scenes Catlin painted years later, such as *Elk and Buffalo
Making Acquaintance, Texas* (1846–48) (fig. 1), where his treatment of landscape is far more mannered and conventional than his on-the-spot renderings
of 1832–33.

Although experiences of this "historian" of the prairie Indian were in
keeping with his previously held esthetic assumptions, the landscape and its
peoples forced him to push those assumptions to their farthest limit, their
apotheosis. In this case he was not alone. The imaginative adjustment Catlin
makes in the most florid terms in *Letters and Notes*—seeing the prairie as the
most romantic landscape, the Indian as the most romantic being, the buffalo
as the most impressive beast—is characteristic of esthetically inclined travelers. The new land was in their minds excessively romantic and radically
different from its European counterpart: the air was too clear, the sun too
bright, the sights too exotic, the landscape too vast. Imaginatively and
practically, the artist had to adjust his conventions. Thus the tension defined
by Catlin's separate visions—realistic pictures versus romantic prose—makes
him a paradigm of the nineteenth-century artist on the prairie during this
period, whether painter or writer. His romantic prose, by contrasting strik-

ingly with his painted images, points up the same tension in the work of the more subtle figures who followed him.

After spending two years in and around St. Louis painting Indians who visited the city and traveling up the South Platte, Catlin embarked for the upper Missouri in March 1832 on board the American Fur Company's steamboat, *Yellow Stone,* itself a ubiquitous presence in the travel literature of the 1830s and 1840s. Recounting his voyage, Catlin describes the shoreline with a painterly eye; after remarking over some cottonwood trees growing along the banks, he comments that

> The greater part of the shores of this river, however, are without timber, where the eye is delightfully relieved by wandering over the beautiful prairies; most of the way gracefully sloping down to the water's edge, carpeted with the deepest green, and, in distance, softening into velvet of the richest hues, entirely beyond the reach of the artist's pencil. (1: 18)

Without question, Catlin's sheer joy over having embarked finally upon his quest colors this passage; but his artistic predilections and vocabulary are apparent as well.[7] Whereas Lewis and Clark, seeing such scenes from their boats, simply mentioned a "beautiful" prairie or plain, Catlin dissects the nature of that beauty and employs the synecdoche of the observer becoming his eyes only. So while other travelers, notably Brackenridge, responded imaginatively and esthetically to the prairie, Catlin is the first to describe it in terms that suggest a relation between the landscape and the artist. And while commentators like Lambert had expressed the inadequacy of words to describe the prairie, Catlin notes the limitations of the visual artist's medium. Catlin is conscious as well of being one of the first to have come west for artistic purposes, and it is from this vantage point that he criticizes the accounts of his predecessors:

> It has been, heretofore, very erroneously represented to the world, that the scenery on this river was monotonous, and wanting in picturesque beauty. This intelligence is surely incorrect, and that because it has been brought perhaps, by men who are not the best judges in the world, of Nature's beautiful works; and if they were, they always pass them by, in pain or desperate distress, in toil and trembling fear for the safety of their furs and peltries, or for their lives, which are at the mercy of the yelling savages who inhabit this delightful country. (1: 18)

Though Catlin here seems to take into account the extent to which practical considerations conditioned early responses to the prairie, his last curious observation also seems to suggest that the artist sees dangers differently than does an ordinary man.

But Catlin's description of a caravan may be positively contrasted with Gregg's more factual report:

> From this elevated spot, the horizon was bounded all around us by mountain streaks of blue, softening into azure as they vanished, and the pictured vales that intermediate lay, were deepening into green as the eye was returning from its roamings. Beneath us, and winding through the waving landscape was seen with peculiar effect, the "bold dragoons," marching in beautiful order forming a train of a mile in length. Baggage waggons and Indians (*engagés*) helped to lengthen the procession. From the point where we stood, the line was seen in miniature; and the undulating hills over which it was bending its way, gave it the appearance of a huge black snake gracefully gliding over a rich carpet of green. (2: 45–46)

Catlin's painter's eye is upon the visual here (colors changing, movement from background to middle distance, line, and symmetry) and his esthetic background informs the whole description. As in the case of "the yelling savages who inhabit this delightful country," there is also in Catlin's final analogy the curious appreciation of what would normally be thought sinister, although at the same time his likening of the caravan to a "huge snake" may be an unconscious registering of his negative feelings about western expansion and the "fall" of the Indian which he sensed would be the result.

Catlin's enthusiasm for the West was not enough to keep him perpetually excited over the prairie landscape, however. Traveling overland from the mouth of the Teton River on the upper Missouri, he admits to the depressing effects of a particularly level stretch of land; significantly he does so, however, not only in terms of the by now almost clichéd analogy but with a certain self-conscious awareness of its conventionality:

> For two or three of the first days, the scenery was monotonous, and became exceedingly painful from the fact, that we were (to use a phrase of the country) "out of sight of land," *i.e.* out of sight of anything rising above the horizon, which was a perfect straight line around us, like that of the blue and boundless ocean. The pedestrian over such a discouraging sea of green, without a landmark before or behind him; without a beacon to lead him on, or define his progress, feels weak and overcome when night falls; and he stretches his exhausted limbs, apparently on the same spot where he has [*sic*] slept the night before, with the same prospect before and behind him; the

same canopy over his head, and the same cheerless sea of green to start upon in the morning. (1: 218)

Before Catlin had criticized those who allowed practical issues to interfere with esthetic response, but here he seems to admit their interrelationships: "It is difficult to describe the simple beauty and serenity of these scenes of solitude, or the feelings of feeble man, whose limbs are toiling to carry him through them—without a hill or tree to mark his progress, and convince him that he is not, like a squirrel in his cage, after all his toil, standing still" (1: 218). Whereas other commentators had expressed the difficulty of describing the prairie, Catlin also observed the difficulty of describing the physical effort of prairie travel and the moral frustration it engenders.

As frustrating as the lack of landmarks, according to Catlin are the spectral images the traveler's mind conjures up in their stead:

One commences on peregrinations like these, with a light heart, and a nimble foot, and spirits as buoyant as the very air that floats along by the side of him; but his spirit soon tires, and he lags on the way that is rendered more tedious and intolerable by the tantalizing *mirage* that opens before him beautiful lakes, and lawns, and copses; or by the *looming* of the prairie ahead of him, that seems to rise in a parapet, and decked with its varied flowers, phantom-like, flies and moves along before him. (1: 218)

To a painter like Catlin, mirages are especially disconcerting since they serve to remind him that his eyesight is not always to be trusted.

Judged alone, without reference to the images he left, Catlin's reactions to and descriptions of the prairie landscape in *Letters and Notes* offer observations virtually identical to those left by his nonartistic fellows, Flagg, for example, or Lambert. But it is what Catlin did with his observations in his paintings that best encapsulates his evocation of the prairie and its Indian peoples, and shows most directly the collision between a need to document ("mirror") and a need to illuminate ("lamp"), a collision caused by the new land itself.

Art historians have debated Catlin's talent and ability for some time; without venturing into that debate, one might observe that what sets Catlin apart from Kane, Bodmer, and Miller is the extreme haste in which he worked. During 1832 while in the upper Missouri country, for example, Catlin made at least 140 paintings. Indicating his fervor, this pace also had a decided effect on the quality of his work. Indeed, much of the debate deals in possibilities, suggesting that had Catlin taken as much care with his western works as with his earlier portraits in Philadelphia, his technical achievements would have been greater.[8]

Yet even conceding his haste and the subordination of landscape to portraiture, Catlin's landscapes showing scenes of Indian life—literal as they are—make apparent the challenge offered by the prairie landscape. In his depiction of buffalo, and the hunting thereof, Catlin was forced to present them in their native habitat. In those scenes where he uses a prairie uninterrupted by a hill or some other obstruction, though, his pictures have no real depth; in fact, in one, *Band of Sioux Moving Camp* (fig. 2) his Indians look like figures moving across the top of a slightly curved table; in another, *Prairie Meadows Burning* (fig. 3), the scene is only roughly sketched, offering strong feelings of terror, but little detail. In the latter picture Catlin blocks the view to the horizon by the swirling flames and smoke in the middle distance, and this technique is especially apparent in his depiction of hunting scenes, such as *Buffalo Chase in Winter, Indians on Snowshoes* (fig. 4), where two hills or bluffs, one in the left foreground and the other in the right middle distance, sandwich a line of buffalo traveling Indian file into the distance.

In numerous other hunting scenes Catlin employs the same device, blocking the horizon with hills or undulations, so the viewer's eye cannot extend farther than the middle distance. This strategy is especially apparent in *Buffalo Chase with Bows and Lances* (fig. 5), for the scene is definitely that of a prairie landscape; but Catlin has depicted his Indians hunters from an angle that is only slightly raised above the landscape itself. As a result, the undulations in the prairie are given a greater prominence than they would have had if he had shown the scene from a sharper angle; indeed, his lower angle of vision accentuates the undulations so that they loom in the middle distance, enclosing the foreground scene. In a similar manner, when he attempts landscape as landscape—for example, *Big Bend on the Upper Missouri, 1900 Miles Above St. Louis* (fig. 6)—Catlin adopts a conventional raised, bird's-eye perspective, but it is one seemingly demanded by the prairie, as Alexander Henry and others learned.

Whether such techniques indicate that Catlin was in a hurry or compensating for a weakness with perspective or, and perhaps less knowingly, reacting to the vast space of the prairie by curbing it in this manner is difficult to say.[9] Yet the recurrent "diagramatical" use of hills, bluffs, and a raised perspective—particularly in view of the relatively few flat prairie scenes—suggest a need in Catlin to control western space, to adapt his art to its demands. Without question, Catlin did so in use of color: "To duplicate" the Indians' appearance, Catlin "forged a palette that would have shocked most of his colleagues in New York, but which was, in fact, the most effective ingredient in his vivid portrayal of the Indian."[10] In view of such an adaptation, one begins to appreciate more fully the significance of those sights that Catlin described as depressing: "The pedestrian over such a discouraging sea of green, without landmark before or behind him, without a beacon to lead him on, or define his progress, feels weak and overcome when night falls . . ." (1: 218). What he could readily admit in words, apparently, Catlin could not accommodate as readily into his paintings. Despite the roughness of his work, the evident struggle in them between his need to document and his need to interpret— the one goal at least compatible with haste, the other emphatically not— Catlin attests to the imaginative, esthetic challenge the prairie offered to its first artist. Both a romantic and documentary artist, the one in prose, the other in pictures, George Catlin was esthetically ever at cross purposes.

Paul Kane is a Canadian counterpart to George Catlin; like the American, he recorded the land and its peoples before large-scale settlement. His book, *Wanderings of an Artist among the Indians of North America* (1858), was inspired, at least in part, by the success of Catlin's *Letters and Notes;* he probably met Catlin in London just prior to his return to Canada in 1842. At the time of his arrival in Toronto, Kane was resolved to undertake his trip west, but his plan was not effected until 1845.[11] As Kane expressed his mission himself, his intention was to "represent the scenery of an almost unknown country" and to "sketch pictures of the principal chiefs" (51). He departed from Toronto in early summer 1845 but did not reach the prairie until a year later; in the meantime he had lived among and painted the Indians living in the Great Lakes region and also had the enormous good fortune to be befriended by Governor Simpson of the Hudson's Bay Company, who authorized him free transportation on all company boats and "hospitalities" at all posts. In effect, this gave Kane carte blanche to travel at will throughout the west.

Initially, Kane was not much taken with the prairie landscape; describing the country around present-day Winnipeg, he writes: "The country here is not very beautiful; a dead level plain with very little timber, the landscape wearing more the appearance of the cultivated farms of the old country with scarcely a stick or stump upon it" (68). After he had become accustomed to the prairie, however, Kane is more positive; recording his travels along the banks of the North Saskatchewan River, heading toward present-day Edmonton, he writes:

> It was the commencement of Indian summer; the evening was very fine, and threw that peculiar soft, warm haziness over the landscape, which is supposed to proceed from the burning of the immense prairies. The sleepy buffaloes grazing upon the undulating hills, here and there relieved by clumps

of small trees, the unbroken stillness, and the approaching evening, rendered it altogether a scene of most enchanting repose. (80)

Kane proceeds here in the same painterly manner as Catlin, presenting the scene as if he were describing a picture. First, he is concerned with the visual nature of the scene, then he turns to its component parts—buffalo, hills, and trees—and only then does he evaluate it subjectively.

Kane's talents were more adaptable to the prairie landscape than Catlin's. Yet Kane also used certain pictorial conventions, especially those of composition, to play down the effect of the prairie's vastness. In *The Man that Always Rides* (fig. 7), for example, Kane composed his canvas almost exactly as Catlin had in his portrait of *BA-DA-AH-CHON-DU (He Who Jumps Over Everyone) . . on Horseback* (fig. 8), depicting his Indian also on horseback, looking out over the outstretching prairie. But Kane benefited from his European study, and he was in less of a hurry, so his means of emphasizing his central figure at the expense of the prairie context is more sophisticated than Catlin's. The latter set his Indian against a vague cloudbank, while Kane pictures his just after dusk, and accentuates his figure by means of a light source shining down on the Indian and his horse from above like a spotlight. Thus the prairie's vastness is apparent in the painting, but it is deemphasized, darkened by the painter's use of chiaroscuro. Similarly, a portion of the prairie is closed off by a foreground obstruction which rises immediately behind the horse; it also blocks the view to Kane's dusky horizon, his distant light source.[12] In another of his paintings, *Winter Travelling in Dog Sleds (A Wedding Party Leaving Fort Edmonton)* (fig. 9), Kane minimizes the vastness of the prairie by arranging his foreground hills and trees in the same manner as Catlin did in his various hunting scenes.[13]

While Kane's treatment of the prairie is direct and accurate in the watercolor sketches like *Camping on the Prairies* (fig. 11), two of his paintings in particular, *Assiniboine Hunting Buffalo* (fig. 12) and *Brigade of Boats* (fig. 13), reflect his retreat into conventions. The horses depicted in the former painting are known to have been modeled upon those in an Italian engraving, and the trading boats in the latter, which are supposedly plying the Saskatchewan River, "have the dignity of Roman galleys" according to J. Russell Harper. The skies in these paintings, as in most of Kane's prairie oils, glow above the expansive landscape amid billowing clouds, reflecting a rainbow of colors, and shine upon the scenes below—buffalo hunts, Indian rituals, and portraits. They do so in a manner quite conventionally European and, also, quite unnatural.[14] Even when he takes up a subject that forces him to confront prairie space directly, as in *A Prairie on Fire* (fig. 14), Kane treats it in a way that emphasizes its putative profundity. In a studio version in oils of a scene he rendered in watercolors near Edmonton, Kane changed the scene from day to night and produced an eerie, if conventionally mannered, effect. Its serenity is in marked contrast to Catlin's almost frenzied version of a similar occurrence (fig. 3).

Paul Kane is in many respects a mirror image of George Catlin. While Catlin's romanticism is more apparent in his prose—often purple prose—than in his painting, Kane's painting is far more romantic than his writings. *Wanderings of an Artist* displays the same descriptive, matter-of-fact perspective that characterizes Kane's on-the-spot sketches. Only when he was away from his subject in his studio did Kane, like Catlin, depart from his documentary perspective and imbue his canvases with the European conventions demanded by his audience and training. And with Kane the initial impression is readily separable from the subsequent artifice; though he had seen the West as it was, he tried after the fact to make the landscape and its people fit a conventional, preconceived, idea of what constitutes "profound" art.

Unlike Catlin and Kane, who were emotionally attracted to the West and who went out of a personal desire to record the native way of life, other painters came because it was their job, attached to an exploratory expedition or hunting trip. Two such figures were Karl Bodmer and Alfred Jacob Miller, the first formally trained painters to depict the West, both of whom traveled west during the 1830s immediately after Catlin. Bodmer, a Swiss, was hired by German naturalist Maximilian, Prince of Wied-Neuwied, to illustrate his trip up the Missouri in 1833, which also was taken aboard the *Yellow Stone,* a year after Catlin's journey. The prince was a scientist and demanded scientific precision from his illustrator who, though practiced in landscape engraving in the manner of Claude Lorrain, was as self-taught in portraiture as Catlin. Though scholars have suggested that Maximilian oversaw Bodmer closely, so as to curb his natural romantic fancy, it is more likely that his lack of experience with the human form "compelled him to exercise special care in composing his Indian portraits."[15] Without question, Bodmer's Indian portraits offer a degree of precise detail which totally eluded Catlin; Bernard DeVoto sees in Bodmer's Mandan Indian portraits "the force and selectivity of medical art . . . a clarity, emphasis, and separation of parts beyond the capacity of the camera lens." Such achieved effects suggest Bodmer's scrupulous technique and precise draftsmanship—his art is as laborious and careful as Catlin's was frenzied and expedient.

Yet Bodmer's landscapes, while far more finished and technically accomplished compositions than Catlin's, or even Kane's studio oils, confront the prairie even less directly than theirs. Relatively few in number and virtually all river scenes, they reveal an accommodation of the land to the esthetic conventions Bodmer assumed; they certainly offer sophisticated, finished images of the upper Missouri country in 1833–34, and perhaps capture what William H. Goetzmann calls "misty exoticism and mystery of the Indian villages" which had eluded Catlin, but they do not confront the new landscape offered by the prairie. In *View of the Mandan Village Mih-Tutta-Hang-Kusch* (fig. 15), of which Goetzmann says "nobody ever painted the far western landscapes quite as Bodmer did in this unforgetable picture," the prairie landscape is only hinted at by the middle distance horizon line above Fort Clark on the opposite shore. Goetzmann's assertion is literally true: no one had painted western landscapes prior to Bodmer, but that is because no artist—Bodmer included—was esthetically prepared to really see the far western landscape, the prairie.

Nor, according to Thomas Flexner, was this accidental: Bodmer's "sophisticated eye," he says, "bothered by the weird hues of the plains and the badlands, fled from such unacceptable reality into formulas, often keyed to the salmon-pink skies beloved of the European romantics." Flexner's observation complements DeVoto's assertion that when artists reached the far West "they had to deal with vaster spaces and greater intensity of light than American painters had been accustomed to work with before." Indeed, Goetzmann notes that Bodmer's imagination was so taken by the "romantic sinuosities of the tangled undergrowth" along river banks "that for the rest of his life he painted countless similar scenes in the forests of Barbizon."[16]

While Bodmer left only a few western landscapes, Alfred Jacob Miller left scores and, very often, several different versions of the same composition. Formally trained in Paris after some rudimentary schooling in his native Baltimore, Miller was hired to illustrate one of Captain (later Sir) William Drummond Stewart's hunting trips up the Platte River to the Rockies in 1837. Miller had neither Catlin and Kane's sense of mission nor Bodmer's commission to be scientifically accurate; as one critic has noted, his task "was to record, for future transcription into large oils, a miraculous holiday."[17]

Upon his return Miller dutifully traveled to Scotland and transcribed his western work into large oils to adorn his patron's castle. He later established himself as a portrait painter in Baltimore and did a brisk business in producing copies of his western works. For one such commission Miller wrote a series of notes to accompany his pictures and to serve as authorial commentary on the scenes of western life they depict.

Unlike Bodmer, whose treatment of the prairie is circumspect, Miller—who traveled overland—depicted the prairie landscape in numerous paintings. In keeping with his conventional esthetics, however, he did not often present the prairie as his central subject: instead, it is most often a portion of the picture (usually the background) and serves to provide perspective to the foreground scene. A representative example of this approach is to be found in a painting entitled *Noon-day Rest* (fig. 16). Here Miller's fellow travelers are reclining on a knoll on the prairie and, in addition to the trees which serve as a backdrop for their figures, they fill the immediate foreground and the left diagonal portion of the canvas; that is, the foot of the knoll, and hence the foreground scene, begins its incline in the lower-right corner of the picture and its bushes and trees continue to the upper-left corner. The prairie, stretching off to the horizon, and speckled in the middle-distance with other reclining figures, followed by the far-distant figures of wagons and grazing horses, makes up but a small portion of the remaining right triangle of the picture. The bulk of this area is a blue-orange sky. Thus, though Miller's composition, when considered as a whole, is a pleasing one, it is also one that effectively nullifies the vast spaces of the prairie.

Noon-day Rest is representative of Miller's usual treatment of the prairie landscape. His formalized arrangement of figures against the prairie, with a prominent foreground stretching through the middle distance to the background, is, of course, entirely to be expected, given his training and background. Given Catlin's haste, it is questionable whether his repeated use of knolls and other obstructions to obscure the background distance was the result of his attempt to hide his failure to depict perspective adequately or whether it was the result of a personal preference. With Miller, however, we have a painter sufficiently skilled to depict a prairie landscape directly and who did so on a few occasions, but one who by and large chose to play down its vastness by devoting only a portion of his space to the prairie, filling the rest of the frame with his foreground scenes. Like Catlin, too, he often enclosed his scene by showing mountains and hills in the far background; on other occasions, he combined the foreground eminence and background mountain conventions in order to frame the intermediate prairie. Finally, in such paintings as *Indians on the War Path* (fig. 17) Miller shows his figures on the open prairie and obscures the background distance through the use of a certain vague shape behind his figures. In this particular work, the obscuring shape may be intended as a dust cloud raised by the Indians' horses; whatever these vague shapes are taken to be, however, they block the view of the distant horizon.

Taken together, Miller's various techniques suggest that, like Bodmer, he also tended to flee the "unacceptable reality" of a prairie landscape, adapting the landscape to the conventions of his art rather than attempting the reverse. That is, these various techniques use the prairie not as vast space, but rather as space, properly viewed—so as to produce a particularly balanced effect. In turn, the conventions that these artists are using belong to what William

Gilpin would call the tradition of the "beautiful" rather than the sublime. [18] This is not surprising, of course, for Miller's purpose in painting was quite different from the missions undertaken by Catlin and Kane, and different too from the exact requirements expected of Bodmer. Captain Stewart, his employer, was a romantic who had fought at Waterloo and he saw his western trips as exotic adventures, full of Indian maidens, buffalo hunts, and feats of horsemanship. He was not interested in a literal view of the West, preferring to see the Indian as a mysterious figure, wild and unpredictable, yet noble in his natural freedom, and he expected this romantic view of Miller's canvases. This requirement suited Miller well. In a letter to Brantz Mayer written before departing from St. Louis, the artist explained his own attitude: "It's best never to be too explicit (I have found in a painting that whenever I left anything for the imagination to fill up, that invariably did me more justice.)" Stewart concurred, for he admired an early work of Miller's in which the sun was "throwing a mysterious haze over every object." Miller recognized the basis for the praise, recording in his journal that "this mistiness was pleasing to the observer [Stewart] because it leaves his imagination at full play." [19]

The adherence of these artists to the tradition of the "beautiful," moreover, is evidenced by their tendency to depict the prairie in relation to other, more impressive, landscape elements. Both Catlin and Bodmer painted Missouri River scenes, viewed from above, and Miller's *Snake Indians* (fig. 18) is a representative example of this particular mode of treatment. Miller pictures a plain in the middle distance, sandwiched between a background mountain and a foreground promontory, on which the Indians stand. Thus ringed round and framed by background and foreground, Miller's viewpoint is exactly the sort which prompted Lewis to call a plain "beatifull": when "surrounded in every direction with distant and lofty mountains" (2: 275).

Miller treats the prairie landscape directly, giving it central importance within his composition, only when such a depiction is dictated by his choice of subject. In *Buffalo Turning on his Pursuers* (fig. 19), Miller shows three hunters, two of them dismounted to finish off two wounded buffalo nearby; against the far horizon is the herd from which they have been separated. Because the great distance between foreground and background is characteristic of the buffalo hunt, Miller has to detail the setting. In the notes accompanying two other works, *The Lost Greenhorn* (fig. 20) and *Prairie Scene: Mirage* (fig. 21), Miller himself suggests how this rationale operated. He recounts an incident in which the party's cook, an Englishman named John, boasted of his great skill as a buffalo hunter; Captain Stewart, upon hearing these boasts, allowed him a chance to go off and make good his claims. The man thereupon got lost for three days, was unable to kill any buffalo he found, and subsisted on berries until he was found by the party's hunters. Inspired by this story,

Miller's *Greenhorn* shows a man on a horse standing upon a rise, looking off into the distance, surrounded only by the outspreading prairie and the sky.[20] In the second painting, Miller depicts a caravan setting out on the prairie and, in the distance, he shows a prairie mirage. In his note he explains:

> The caravan is proceeding at its usual steady pace, both men and horses suffering for want of water,—the day is hot and oppressive. Suddenly in the distance, an extensive Lake looms up,—delightful to the eye, the surface reflecting islands, and trees on its borders;—but what is the matter with the horses?—they neither raise their ears, quicken their motion, or snort, as is their wont on such occasions.
>
> Poor brutes!—well do they know there is no water for them. It is the mirage, an optical delusion;—the deception is so perfect that you can scarcely credit your senses.[21]

Because a prairie mirage requires an uninterrupted line of sight, Miller was forced by his subject to open the whole of his canvas to the landscape. In any case, it is significant that when Miller pictures four other scenes peculiar to the prairie—a buffalo "jump," a prairie fire, a buffalo "surround" and the prairie itself—his landscape treatment is similarly direct.

At the same time, however, these prairie subjects also seem to have had the effect of engendering in Miller an appreciation of the prairie in its own right, enforcing its own imaginative adaptation. Thus in his note describing the surround he seems to be suggesting that these subjects owe their impressiveness to the landscape: "the dexterity and grace of the Indians and the thousands upon thousands of Buffalo moving in every direction over the illimitable prairie form a scene altogether, that in the whole world beside, cannot be matched" (Note facing Plate 200). Just as the first travelers on the prairie often required the impetus of the sight of a vast buffalo herd at mating season or of the shock of a prairie mirage to startle them into an imaginative reaction to the prairie landscape, Alfred Jacob Miller apparently required the same sights to shock him out of his conventional concept of landscape. But while the travelers' recognition can be gauged only by the tone and nature of their descriptions, Miller's recognition may be gauged by the altered technique evident in his art.[22]

If Catlin and Kane mirror one another, they are brought into sharper focus by Karl Bodmer and Alfred Jacob Miller. Bodmer and Miller's role in this group of prairie artists is pivotal; their training and experience before heading west schooled them in European artistic conventions, but unlike Catlin and Kane, they had no personal axes to grind. Bodmer readily met the scientific expectations of Prince Maximilian in depicting the Indians and their land, but his severely limited use of what Goetzmann has called "a wholly new land of awesome space, immense distances" and "infinite horizons," in light of his obvious preferences for the "romantic sinousities of the tangled undergrowth" along riverbanks, suggests a need to flee the "unacceptable reality" of the prairie.[23] Likewise, because Miller cared little for recording accurately and romantisized according to the dictates of his esthetic and the expectations of his patron, leaving room "for the imagination to fill up," he too serves as a gloss on Catlin and Kane. His works, academic and romantic as they are, nevertheless reveal the same need to adjust the requirements of artistic convention to the depiction of a new land and its peoples. That Catlin and Kane—as self-appointed artistic pathfinders—reveal a tension between reality and convention, between the mirror and the lamp, is not surprising. Though they tried, they could not record and interpret at once, so they had to choose one or the other. Thus, when Alfred Jacob Miller and Karl Bodmer were unable to maintain their European artistic conventions in facing the prairie landscape their adaptation is revealing. Despite disinterested motivations, they too adapted their works to prairie space by controlling it or ignoring it; by doing so through their more subtle art, they confirm and underscore the common tension produced in the attempt to represent this new land in art.[24]

Writers

In 1832 America's most celebrated contemporary author, Washington Irving, returned to his native country after seventeen years in Europe. Eager to see something of the changes that had taken place during his absence, Irving traveled into the West and, quite by accident, met Henry L. Ellsworth, who had just been appointed an Indian commissioner and was about to embark on a trip to investigate problems among the tribes of the Oklahoma territory; he invited Irving to accompany him and the author readily agreed. As Irving later wrote to his brother Peter,

> The offer was too tempting to be resisted: I should have an opportunity of
> seeing the remnants of those great Indian tribes, which are now about to dis-
> appear as independent nations, or to be amalgamated under some new form
> of government. I should see those fine countries of the "far west," while still

in a state of pristine wildness, and behold herds of buffaloes scouring their native prairies, before they are driven beyond the reach of a civilized tour- ist.[25]

"Civilized tourist" is an apt description of Irving on the prairie because, like tourists before him, such as Brackenridge and Flagg, he had no urgent business to transact—he wanted only to experience the "pristine wildness" of his country's West. Ellsworth, Irving, and the author's two traveling compan- ions accompanied a party of mounted rangers on the tour, leaving Fort Gibson for a month on October 8, 1832. The direct result of the trip was Irving's *A Tour on the Prairies,* which was published in 1835 as the first volume of *The Crayon Miscellany.* It had been long awaited by the American public, even from the time Irving started west, and its reviews were glowing.[26]

In many respects, Irving represents a literary equivalent of Alfred Jacob Miller, for he too was well-schooled in European romantic conventions, and his trip west was, like the painter's, something of a lark. He had only to travel about, see things and, given his clamoring audience, "work up" his experi- ences into a suitable literary form. Irving visited the prairie but, because of his background, his inherently romantic temperament, and his addiction to literary convention, he adamantly refused to see it. Given this background, his spontaneous decision to make the trip, and the public's demand for his account, Irving could hardly have been expected to produce a book radically different from *A Tour,* but as the first sustained literary work by an author who had traveled the prairie, Irving's description of that landscape is vague, unimpressive, and ultimately disappointing.[27]

Literary conventions colored everything Irving saw on the prairie. Writing to his sister while in Independence, Missouri on the outward trip, he explains:

> Many parts of these Praries of the Missouri are extremely beautiful, resem-
> bling cultivated countries, embellished with parks and groves, rather than
> the savage rudeness of the wilderness Yesterday I was out on a deer hunt in
> the vicinity of this place, which led me through some Scenery that only
> wanted a castle, or gentlemans seat here and there interspersed, to have
> equalled some of the most elaborate park Scenery of England. (725)

Thus even before Irving embarked on his tour he had already adapted the prairie to his preconceptions.

In his journal of the trip, as well as in *A Tour* itself, Irving sees the landscape solely in terms of his previous experience. He writes on one occasion, for example: "scale a hill—limestone rock & stones full of shells & miniature basalt like giant causeway—boundless view of silent Praries—distant hill like Paté de Strasburg."[28] Later, he writes: "Left encampt this morning and rode through mist which gradually cleared up & shewed wide prarie—with distant line of green woody hills that looked like cultivated country. It seemed as if we could distinguish fields of grain—groves [—] pasturages—glades &c" (96; editor's interpolation). Similarly, when he celebrates camp life on the prairie, Irving's emphasis is not on the land itself, but on various elements in the scene and how they make him feel:

> The weather is in its perfection Golden sunshine, not oppressive but ani-
> mating—Skies without a cloud—&[?] if there be clouds, of feathery texture
> and lovely tints—air pure, bland, exhilarating—an atmosphere of perfect
> transparency—and the whole country having the mellow tint of autumn.
> How exciting to think that we are breaking thro a country hitherto untrod/-
> den by whiteman, except perchance the solitary trapper. A glorious world
> spread around us without an inhabitant (127; editor's interpolation)

Thus while Irving is keen to pick up on the effects of the prairie landscape— the vivid way in which nature's elements are available here—he does not consider the landscape itself as the causal agent of such effects. Indeed, Irving's emphasis here and throughout *A Tour* is upon human feeling and human society, an emphasis that is reflected in his romantic conception of himself as a pathfinder—a role derived from his relation to eastern society.

In understanding *A Tour* and especially Irving's presentation of the prairie landscape in that work, however, the *Journals* play a key role. In the case of Paul Kane, the painter's on-the-spot sketches of the prairie landscape are preferable because they are without the conventional clichés of his later, and larger, oils. But Irving's *Journals* reveal that he had already become ac-customed to thinking in literary clichés when he arrived on the prairie; his *Journals* are more direct than *A Tour*, certainly, but they suggest that he was constitutionally almost incapable of seeing the prairie without reference to conventional verities.

Irving begins *A Tour* by whisking his reader off to a remote land:

> In the often vaunted regions of the Far West, several hundred miles beyond
> the Mississippi, extends a vast tract of uninhabited country, where there is
> neither to be seen the log house of the white man, nor the wigwam of the
> Indian. It consists of great grassy plains, interspersed with forests and groves
> and clumps of trees, and watered by the Arkansas, the grand Canadian, the
> Red River, and all their tributary streams.[29]

Thus in keeping with his "civilized" background, Irving emphasizes the lack of human habitation, while in keeping with his romantic proclivities he later muses over the freedom of the animals, especially the wild horses, they encounter on the prairie: "Over these fertile and verdant wastes still roam the Elk, the Buffalo, and the wild horse in all their native freedom" (9). Irving characterizes the land as a "waste," a desert which is ironically "verdant" and "fertile."[30] But Irving does not attempt to come to terms with the landscape he presents: instead, he summarizes it through a few phrases ("vast tract," "great grassy plains" and "fertile and verdant wastes") and moves on to his far more detailed presentation of various western Indian tribes.

Indeed, Irving is not moved to comment on the landscape again until his sixth chapter; and then his focus is not on the prairie itself but rather on a vista in which the prairie is but one element. As with other contemporary observers, Irving's delight in this scene stems from its diversity—its accordance with the eighteenth-century concept of the beautiful. When he is more detailed in his observations, furthermore, it is as means to an end that has little to do with prairie per se, as his description of his impressions as he travels through a forest suggests:

> We were overshadowed by lofty trees, with straight smooth trunks, like stately columns, and as the glancing rays of the sun shone through the transparent leaves, tinted with the many coloured hues of autumn, I was reminded of the effect of sunshine among the stained windows and clustering columns of a Gothic cathedral. Indeed there is a grandeur and solemnity in some of our spacious forests of the West that awaken in me the same feeling I have experienced in those vast and venerable piles, and the sound of the wind sweeping through them, supplies occasionally the deep breathings of the organ. (25)

Thus, he here seems more interested in the opportunity that the prairie provides for analogy and in the elaboration of the analogy than in its appropriateness.

Irving's concern with the elemental forces of the prairie also appears to be in evidence only when he has some other, and usually more literary, purpose in mind. His experience of being caught in a thunderstorm on the prairie, for example, is presented in the following manner:

> The rain came rattling upon us in torrents and spattered up like steam along the ground; the whole landscape was suddenly wrapped in gloom that gave a vivid effect to the intense sheets of lightning, while the thunder seemed to

burst over our very heads, and was reverberated by the groves and forests that checquered and skirted the prairie. (58)

This passage recreates the imaginative effect of a storm in a manner superior to James's rendering of one, but unlike James, Irving does not dwell upon it. He moves on to its logistical effect and in turn to a related analogy: "Man and beast were so pelted, drenched and confounded that the line was thrown in complete confusion . . . [the] scattered cavalcade looked like a tempest tost fleet . . ." (58). He then continues to narrate the events of the day. When he later returns to this thunderstorm, and to its imaginative impact, he does so merely by way of prefacing his presentation of Indian beliefs and legends concerning such phenomena: "A thunder storm on a prairie as upon the ocean, derives grandeur and sublimity from the wild and boundless waste over which it rages and bellows" (59). Irving then moves from the wildness of the land to the wildness of its people.

Irving's evocation of the prairie thunderstorm is a part of a larger dramatic context that is clearly more important to him than landscape description. Before noting the effect of the storm and summarizing the tales of the natives, he had described his group sitting around the campfire:

> The grove thus fitfully lighted up by the ruddy glare of the fires resembled a vast leafy dome, walled in by opaque darkness; but every now and then two or three quivering flashes of lightning in quick succession would suddenly reveal a vast champaign country where fields and forests and running streams, would start as it were into existence for a few brief seconds, and, before the eye could ascertain them, vanish again into gloom. (58–59)

Thus the prairie, Irving's "champaign country," is given scant attention, just as the impact of the storm is subordinate to the romantic effect he is trying to create. And after summarizing his Indian beliefs and tales, he goes on to observe:

> These are simple and artless tales, but they had a wild and romantic inter- est heard from the lips of half savage narrators, round a hunter's fire, in a stormy night with a forest on one side and a howling waste on the other: and, where peradventure savage foes might be lurking in the outer darkness. (59)

The "howling waste" becomes simply an element in Irving's dramatic render- ing of fear of the unknown; if the prairie is symbolic, it operates mainly to evoke the conventional emotion of fear. His symbolism is imposed from without, obscuring the actual qualities of a landscape which, while certainly capable of evoking fear, does so not in Irving's manner, but rather unconventionally.

Some of this imposition seems to have been the result of afterthought, as certain differences between his *Journal* and *A Tour* suggest. For example, whereas in the journal Irving simply refers to the lack of human habitation on the prairie, in *A Tour* he goes on to explain: "It was as if a ban hung over this fair but fated region. The very Indians dared not abide here but made it a mere scene of perilous enterprize, to hunt for a few days and then away" (48). Irving cannot accept the notion that the land is simply wild, uninhabited, and different from the east; he infers some presumably dire and mysterious reason for the land's lack of human inhabitants.

Irving's tendency to impose his values on the landscape is so pervasive throughout *A Tour,* however, that it must on the whole be described as a congential disposition rather than as the result of recollection. Thus in describing an instance in which he was greatly pleased to come upon a prairie—having emerged from a more difficult (and wooded) terrain—he writes:

> Here one of the characteristic scenes of the Far West broke upon us. An immense extent of grassy undulating, or as it is termed, rolling country with here and there a clump of trees, dimly seen in the distance like a ship at sea; the landscape deriving sublimity from its vastness and simplicity. To the south west on the summit of a hill was a singular crest of broken rocks resembling a ruined fortress. It reminded me of the ruin of some Moorish castle crowning a height in the midst of a lonely Spanish landscape. To this hill we gave the name of Cliff Castle. (61)

Irving begins his description by treating the prairie landscape directly but quickly passes over it to concentrate on the "crest of broken rocks" he sees in the distance. Without further reference to the landscape that made such a view possible, or its esthetic qualities, Irving retreats into his conventional, familiar European metaphors—Moorish castles amid Spanish landscapes. This is not to criticize Irving unduly for using familiar analogies, but to suggest that passages like this reveal that he did far more than simply interpret the prairie landscape in terms of his previous experience; he substituted his own values and conventions.

At the same time, it must be admitted that Irving's attitude toward the landscape and toward nature in general fluctuates throughout *A Tour* in accordance with the various situations in which he finds himself. At one point the party's route took them through a heavily wooded area, called "cross timbers," and one of Irving's companions says of him: "I never saw a man more impatient, to be out of them [the cross timbers], than Mr. Irving. . . ."[31] Thus frustrated, Irving is in a position to appreciate the prairie landscape. Looking across the cross timbers from the top of a hill, he writes:

> the eye stretched beyond this rugged wilderness of hills, and ravines and ragged forests, to a prairie about ten miles off, extending in a clear blue line along the horizon. It was like looking from among rocks and breakers upon a distant tract of tranquil ocean. Unluckily our route did not lie in that direction, we still had to traverse many a weary mile of the "cross timber." (86)

Irving's vexation is like that of Anthony Henday, who decried his continual weary march across the Muscuty plains. Henday, however, longed for wooded country; Irving longs for prairie:

> we emerged towards midday from the dreary belt of the Cross Timber, and to our infinite delight beheld "The Great Prairie" stretching to the right and left before us. . . . The landscape was vast and beautiful. There is always an expansion of feeling in looking upon these boundless and fertile wastes; but I was doubly conscious of it after emerging from our "close dungeon of innumerous boughs." (97)

Not only is delight apparent in his description, but Irving admits that his delight is caused by the prairie, and this constitutes his most effusive comment on that landscape in the whole of *A Tour*. Although he clothes his feelings in the hackneyed "boundless and fertile wastes," and gravitates at once to an allusion to Milton's *Comus,* and although his feelings may have been prompted by the contrast that the prairie provided to the scene of his discomfort, he responds here to the landscape itself.

On another occasion, similarly, Irving was forced to confront prairie vastness when he was separated from his companions while chasing buffalo; thus he experienced the prairie landscape most acutely when he was lost. He writes:

> I now found myself in the midst of a lonely waste in which the prospect was bounded by undulating swells of land, naked and uniform, where, from the deficiency of land marks and distinct features in inexperienced man may become bewildered and lose his way as readily as in the wastes of the ocean. The day too was overcast, so that I could not guide myself by the sun; my

only mode was to retrace the track my horse had made in coming, though this I would often lose sight of, where the ground was covered with parched herbage. (100)[32]

Irving's description is admirably direct, including only the "waste" of his prairie/sea metaphor as a literary word choice. In fact, this passage embodies the same sort of disorientation noted by Castañeda when he described members of Coronado's party who were forced to wait by their killed game in order to see the direction of the setting sun. And Irving's subsequent observation embodies the same feelings of exposure expressed by others:

> To one unaccustomed to it there is something inexpressibly lonely in the solitude of a prairie. The loneliness of a forest seems nothing to it. There the view is shut in by trees, and the imagination is left free to picture some livelier scene beyond. But here we have an immense extent of landscape without a sign of human existence. We have the consciousness of being far, far beyond the bounds of human habitation; we feel as if moving in the midst of a desert world. (100)

Bereft of human companionship for the first time on his trip, Irving is forced to experience the prairie landscape rather than simply look at it, and in the process, significantly, he admits that such direct apprehension prevents one from indulging in escapist flights of fancy.

Describing himself retracing his steps, Irving's diction also has a suitability not seen elsewhere in *A Tour:*

> As my horse lagged slowly back over the scenes of our late scamper, and the delirium of the chase had passed away, I was peculiarly sensible to these circumstances. The silence of the waste was now and then broken by the cry of a distant flock of pelicans stalking like spectres about a shallow pool. Sometimes by the sinister croaking of a raven in the air, while occasionally a scoundrel wolf would scour off from before me and having attained a safe distance, would sit down and howl and whine with tones that gave a dreariness to the surrounding solitude. (100)[33]

Because he is lost, Irving quite legitimately sees the landscape as bleak and threatening, and though his personifications of the menacing creatures are melodramatic, they derive from his genuine dismay over his disorientation. His description grows directly out of his subject here; his impressions have not been imposed on the landscape, but rather, it has at last imposed itself upon his imagination.

Irving's lapse, however, was only momentary. Immediately afterward he discovers another from his party and his sense of isolation vanishes. The two men decide to continue their hunt and, glimpsing a herd of buffalo two miles off, Irving reverts to a socially oriented perspective; the buffalo are "scattered apart and quietly grazing near a small strip of trees and bushes. It required but little stretch of fancy to picture them so many cattle grazing on the edge of a common and that the grove might shelter some lowly farmhouse" (100–01). When lost on the prairie, even for a short time, Irving could not deny the hegemony of nature—he was forced to confront the "inexpressibly lonely" quality "in the solitude of a prairie." But returned to society, he seems to forget this unpleasant experience and conjures up a "common," a conventional, domestic scene in which humans dominate nature. [34]

Margaret Fuller, the next literary visitor to the prairie, took a more accommodating view of the landscape than Irving, although when she first glimpsed it during her western trip in 1843, her immediate reaction was negative. As she recalls in *Summer on the Lakes* (1844):

> At first the prairie seemed to speak of the very desolation of dullness. After sweeping over the vast monotony of the lakes to come to this monotony of land, with all around a limitless horizon—to walk, and walk, and run, but never climb, oh! it was too dreary for any but a Hollander to bear. [35]

Fuller's reaction is, like Irving's, governed by her Eastern and European values; but upon inspection she is willing to reconsider:

> But after I had ridden out and seen the flowers, and observed the sunset with that calmness seen only in the prairies, and the cattle winding slowly to their homes in the "island grove"—most peaceful of sights—I began to love because I began to know the scene, and shrank no longer from "the encircling vastness." (26)

That she couches her newfound appreciation in language borrowed from Bryant's "The Prairies" confirms that she had a foreknowledge of the landscape, although she herself goes on to address the problem of expectation:

> It is always thus with the new form of life; we must learn to look at it by its own standard. At First, no doubt, my accustomed eye kept saying, if the mind did not, "What! no distant mountains? no valleys?" But after a while I

would ascend the roof of the house where we lived and pass many hours, needing no sight but the moon reigning in the heavens or starlight falling upon the lake, till all the lights were out in the island grove of men beneath my feet, and felt nearer heaven that there was nothing but this lovely, still reception on the earth; no towering mountains, no deep tree-shadows, nothing but the plain earth and water bathed in light. (26–27)

From the vantage point of her elevated perspective, here Fuller shows that, unlike Irving, who had to be forced into seeing the prairie landscape directly and ultimately recoiled from it, she learned "to look at it by its own standard."

Yet in so saying, a pause is necessary here to take up a gender-based distinction that is evident between Fuller and Irving, especially in light of Annette Kolodny's *The Land Before Her,* a book that offers a chapter on Fuller and *Summer on the Lakes.* As in this study, Kolodny uses the literary tourists of this period to move, as she entitles this section, "From Promotion to Literature." Both Irving and Fuller prefer what might be called domesticity in a prairie vista yet, as argued above, Irving's preference appears to be primarily a literary pose designed to meet the romantic expectations of his eastern audience. Because of Kolodny's argument and the context in which it is offered, the same cannot be said of Margaret Fuller.

If, as indicated above in the discussion of esthetic reactions to the prairie on the overland trail, men and women responded to the landscape in the same fashion, initially, clear evidence exists suggesting that such similarities on the trail gave way to differing imaginative relationships with the prairie once men and women were settled on it with the intention to remain. Fuller's *Summer on the Lakes* demonstrates the point for, while she may indeed have learned to look at the prairie "by its own standard" while there, her own gender's perspective created a relationship with the land different from that of most men. As historians have noted, women on the overland trails noticed the "wild prairies covered with luxuriant grasses and wild flowers" and, what is more, the imagery of their descriptions, like Fuller's, stressed domesticity by likening the prairies to gardens. Such images may be traced back to the French explorers of the seventeenth century, and are consistent with the commonly held view of the West as garden, but their preponderance in women's writings of the early nineteenth century is especially strong.[36]

Kolodny, for her part, differs from social historians such as Jeffrey and Myres although she is not strictly writing literary history either; what she offers in *The Land Before Her* is a discussion of "the sequence of fantasies through which generations of women came to know and act upon the westward-moving frontier." Put another way, her "purpose is to chart women's private responses to the successive American frontiers and to trace a tradition of women's public statements about the West." Kolodny deserves consideration in some depth because, as the second statement suggests, her work bridges the private and the public in order to define the ways in which "women's public writings about the West purposefully and self-consciously rejected (or refined) male fantasies, replacing them with figures from the female imagination." Those figures derive, of course, from women's private writings. Throughout her book, moreover, Kolodny views landscape "as a symbolic (as opposed to geographic) realm," and she carefully foregrounds her discussion of Fuller with a consideration of the prairie promotional tracts such as *Texas* (1833) by Mary Austin Holley and *Life in Prairie Land* (1846) by Eliza Farnham and follows it with a chapter on Caroline Kirkland.[37]

Fuller is thus seen within a tradition of women's writing, one in which the prairie landscape is especially important:

> The beauty of the view did not become a recurrent theme for women, however, until the early decades of the nineteenth century brought them out of the forests and onto the open prairies of Illinois, Wisconsin, and Texas.
> . . . .
> [When] Margaret Fuller declared the Rock River country of Illinois "the very Eden which earth might still afford." The American Eve had at last found her proper garden. With their parklike and flowered expanses alternating with stands of trees, the prairies seemed to offer nothing of the claustrophobic oppression of a wooded frontier. If anything, they resembled in large the treed lawns and flower beds with which women had always dreamed of surrounding home.
> More than that, the prairies invited metaphors of intimacy—as had the forests for men. (8)

Without rehearsing the whole of Kolodny's argument, she clearly establishes a connection between women's private responses to the prairie landscape—embodied in the imagery of domesticity—and what she calls women's "deepest dreams and aspirations" (8).

Thus Margaret Fuller, who wrote in *Summer on the Lakes* that "nature still wore her motherly smile" (43–44), encapsulates for Kolodny women's reaction to the prairie landscape; she sees the Illinois trip, moreover, as key to understanding Fuller, and her concerns for women expressed in *Women in the Nineteenth Century* (1855). On the prairies, Kolodny writes, Fuller found "the palpable incarnation of a little girl's garden retreat" (117), a larger version of her girlhood Cambridgeport garden that Fuller "irrevocably lost" when her father moved this family to Groton, Massachusetts. There Fuller (who had opposed the move) was immersed in "household drudgery" and ministering to the numerous illnesses in her family (117–19). By couching her discussion of Fuller in terms that demonstrate a response similar to that found in Holley's and Farnham's promotional tracts—far better known than Fuller's book, despite her preferred literary status today—moreover, Kolodny argues persuasively for a shared women's fantasy, one fulfilled by the prairie landscape. Thus Kolodny writes:

> What Holley and Farnham projected onto the Texas and Illinois prairies,
> therefore, represented more than their unique personal psyches. Their projec-
> tions encompassed the very imagery through which most women of their day
> either experienced or wished to experience their lives. (111)

In other words, like men, women projected their expectations onto the prairie landscape and, also like them, owing to their gender-induced roles and personal preferences, these projections defined women's own wishes and hopes for the future through the imagery of the domestic sphere. Rather than seeking to dominate the prairie—either physically by subduing it to the plow or, like Irving, imaginatively by enforcing inappropriate literary allusions upon it—women sought to see and respond to the land's garden-like qualities, to respond to its potential for domestication.

When brought back to the discussion of texts offered here, Kolodny's argument deepens the relationship between prairie landscape and texts by literary visitors, since Fuller's reaction is demonstrably different from Irving's—though the two literary figures do share, certainly, many esthetic and romantic assumptions. Even so, Irving and Fuller's separate responses to the landscape confirm that the same tensions—between conventions, expectation, and actuality—apparent in the exploration and travel narratives, and apparent in the painters and illustrators' pictures and prose, are evident as well in literary travel accounts. Indeed, in view of Francis Parkman's *The Oregon Trail* (1849), the responses of literary figures are arguably more urgent and persistent than those of their nonliterary counterparts.

When he headed onto the prairie in spring 1846, Francis Parkman was newly graduated from Harvard and had written none of the volumes on which his reputation now rests, although he had begun to plan the first of these, and came west in part to see Indians in their native environment. Parkman and his cousin Quincy Adams Shaw traveled west primarily for adventure and the joy of a summer spent "out of bounds," so a holiday air often permeates *The Oregon Trail*. Historians Mason Wade and Bernard DeVoto have lamented Parkman's inexperience in 1846 for, on the Oregon trail among its emigrants, he saw firsthand many of the important players in the westward movement at a crucial time; yet, because of his youth, they claim Parkman did not understand what he was looking at.[38] He was, however, most "experienced" in another way: prior to his trip he had read Gregg's *Commerce of the Prairies,* Maximilian's *Travels,* and Frémont's *Report,* among the first-person accounts; he had seen Catlin's paintings in London and read his book (through Maximilian's book, of course, he knew Bodmer's paintings), and he had read all of Irving's western works. Finally, he knew Cooper's Leatherstocking novels "almost by heart" and could quote Bryant's western poems from memory.[39]

Thus Francis Parkman, unlike Irving, was a literary visitor steeped in contemporary western description confronting the West for the first time. His expectations, as well as his notions of literary convention, accordingly, come into play as he describes the prairie landscape in *The Oregon Trail.* And, just as it is possible to compare Kane's on-the-spot sketches and watercolors with his large, after-the-fact oils, the availability of Parkman's Oregon Trail journal allows a comparison between his immediate reaction to the prairie landscape and the "worked-up" version which is *The Oregon Trail.*[40] As a well-educated person, moreover, Parkman had distinct ideas about the nature of literature; indeed, before turning wholly to his histories, he wrote not only *The Oregon Trail* but also a critical essay on Cooper, and *Vassall Morton* (1856), a novel.

Parkman and his party left Westport, Missouri, the traditional "jumping off" point for both the Oregon and Santa Fe Trails, in early May 1846 and traveled up the Platte to Fort Laramie; they then traveled south along the eastern side of the Rocky Mountains before turning east and following the Arkansas River back to the settlements, returning in late September to the area around Westport. Parkman's overall assessment of the prairie West is found in a letter written to his father immediately upon his return to the settlements: "There is no place on earth," he wrote, where a person "is thrown more completely on his own resources." He first saw the prairie just outside of Westport; his immediate impression was as follows:

> we had a sight of the great green ocean of the prairies; for the forest terminates at this place, where also is the boundary of the State of Missouri. A lofty forest, all fresh and verdant in the spring—then a tract of shrubbery and crab-trees full of fragrant blossoms—and then the great level expanse of prairie.[41]

In *The Oregon Trail,* Parkman's rendering of the same description places a greater emphasis on the visual: "Looking over an intervening belt of bushes, we saw the green, ocean-like expanse of prairie, stretching swell beyond swell to the horizon." This description also emphasizes the spreading vastness of the prairie but, after describing the blossoming trees, he interjects a new element: "I was half inclined to regret leaving behind the land of gardens, for the rude and stern scenes of the prairie and the mountains" (10). Implicitly, Parkman equates the settlements and forests of the East with "gardens"—the tamed and the known—while the prairie equals a strange new landscape—wild, un-tamed, and unknown. This was, in fact, its aspect for Parkman, but by interjecting this consideration—a longing to stay—he prepares his reader for what lies ahead on the trail.

Such is the usual technique to be found when passages in *The Oregon Trail* are compared to their precursors in Parkman's journals. He often took the germ of an idea in the journals and, through elaboration, explanation, and amplification, produced a passage that is far more detailed and articulate. These passages, too, often take on a larger structural significance within the whole of *The Oregon Trail*. Writing in the journals some two weeks after they had left Westport, Parkman notes that "the expanse of prairie stretched for mile after mile without tree or bush—we ascended swell after swell and could see nothing but the vast, green level. At last, turned aside from the road to a clump of trees in the distance" (*Journals*, 2: 424). This observation is quite similar to those made by others but, when writing (or rather dictating) *The Oregon Trail*, Parkman seized upon this descriptive passage as his occasion for the parallel consideration of the real prairie versus its literary reputation. Thus he writes in a protracted preliminary to the passage just quoted:

> Should any one of my readers ever be impelled to visit the prairies, and should he choose the route of the Platte (the best, perhaps, that can be adopted), I can assure him that he need not think to enter at once upon the paradise of his imagination. A dreary preliminary, a protracted crossing of the threshold, awaits him before he finds himself fairly upon the verge of the "great American desert,"—those barren wastes, the haunts of the buffalo and the Indian, where the very shadow of civilization lies a hundred leagues be-hind him. The intervening country, the wide and fertile belt that extends for several hundred miles beyond the extreme frontier, will probably answer tol-erably well to his preconceived ideas of the prairie; for this it is from which picturesque tourists, painters, poets, and novelists, who have seldom pene-trated farther, have derived their conceptions of the whole region. If he has a painter's eye, he may find his period of probation not wholly void of interest. The scenery, though tame, is graceful and pleasing. Here are level plains too wide for the eye to measure; green undulations, like motionless swells of the

ocean; abundance of streams, followed through all their windings by lines of woods and scattered groves. (34–35)

Because he is writing in retrospect, Parkman knows what lies ahead of this fertile tract of land—the High Plains; when he wrote the entry in his journal he did not. Thus this passage provides the reader with a distillation of Parkman's own experience; presumably, the "fertile-belt" he describes answered his own "preconceived ideas of the prairie" but in retrospect he is aware that those ideas—garnered, no doubt, from his readings and the paintings he had seen—are severely limited. While he understands the esthetic reaction to the fertile prairies ("If he has a painter's eye"), Parkman is conscious that the esthetic reaction is only a part of prairie experience; coupled with it are a variety of more pressing—and elemental—considerations:

But let him be as enthusiastic as he may, he will find enough to damp his ardor. His wagons will stick in the mud; his horses will break loose; harness will give way; and axle-trees prove unsound. His bed will be a soft one, consisting often of black mud of the richest consistency. As to food, he must content himself with biscuit and salt provisions; for strange as it may seem, this tract of country produces very little game. As he advances, indeed, he will see, mouldering in the grass by his path, the vast antlers of the elk, and farther on the whitened skulls of the buffalo, once swarming over this now deserted region. Perhaps, like us, he may journey for a fortnight, and see not so much as the hoof-print of a deer; in the spring, not even a prairie-hen is to be had.

Yet, to compensate him for this unlooked-for deficiency of game, he will find himself beset with "varmints" innumerable. The wolves will entertain him with a concert at night, and skulk around him by day just beyond rifle-shot; his horse will step into badger-holes; from every marsh and mud-puddle will arise the bellowing, croaking and trilling of legions of frogs, infinitely various in color, shape, and dimensions. A profusion of snakes will glide away from under his horse's feet, or quietly visit him in his tent at night; while the pertinacious humming of unnumbered mosquitoes will banish sleep from his eyelids. When, thirsty with a long ride in the scorching sun over some boundless reach of prairie, he comes at length to a pool of water and alights to drink, he discovers a troop of young tadpoles sporting in the bottom of his cup. Add to this that, all the morning, the sun beats upon him with a sultry, penetrating heat, and that, with provoking regularity, at about four o'clock in the afternoon a thunderstorm rises and drenches him to the skin. (35–36)

Clearly, some of Parkman's romantic expectations—he knew Cooper's Leatherstocking tales, after all, "almost by heart"—were exploded by the hard realities he found on the prairie. The two views of the landscape and its qualities he provided here—the preconceived and the actual—act as a corrective for his readers. Having read much of what was in print at the time concerning the prairie West himself, Parkman is visibly conscious that such descriptions provided at best a partial picture only, partial both in terms of the extent of the travels these works delineate and partial in the view that they take.

Like those travelers who preceded him onto the prairie and plains, Parkman comments on the strange sights he found; like them, he notes huge buffalo herds (82), optical illusions (310), the clarity of the air (369) and takes advantage of hilltop views. As we have seen, also, he used the ocean metaphor for the prairie. But the fact that he noticed these elements is not as important, for the purposes of this discussion, as his literary use of them in *The Oregon Trail*.

One such instance concerns some thunderstorms that he describes in his journal factually and chronologically (*Journals* 2: 425). In rewriting this incident for *The Oregon Trail*, Parkman passes quickly over the initial storm so that, by this shift of emphasis, his party is racing dramatically against the impending storm at the end of a long march:

> Not a breath of air stirred over the free and open prairie; the clouds were like light piles of cotton; and where the blue sky was visible, it wore a hazy and languid aspect. The sun beat down upon us with a sultry, penetrating heat almost insupportable, and as our party crept slowly along over the interminable level, the horses hung their heads as they waded fetlock deep through the mud, and the men slouched into the easiest position upon the saddle. At last, towards evening, the old familiar black heads of thunderclouds rose fast above the horizon, and the same deep muttering of distant thunder that had become the ordinary accompaniment of our afternoon's journey began to roll hoarsely over the prairie. Only a few minutes elapsed before the whole sky was densely shrouded, and the prairie and some clusters of woods in front assumed a purple hue beneath the inky shadows. Suddenly from the densest fold of the cloud the flash leaped out, quivering again and again down to the edge of the prairie; and at the same instant came the sharp burst and the long rolling peal of the thunder. (48)

As in the journal entry, the party rushes to the shelter of a clump of trees and hurriedly sets camp, and they sit through the storm in their tents, which

Parkman considers but ineffectual shelters. He then notes that "Towards sunset, however, the storm ceased as suddenly as it began. A bright streak of clear red sky appeared above the western verge of the prairie; the horizontal rays of the sinking sun streamed through it, and glittered in a thousand prismatic colors upon the dripping groves and the prostrate grass" (49). Parkman concludes his description in *The Oregon Trail* by emphasizing the point at which the journal entry began—the description of a thunderstorm at night on the prairie:

> Scarcely had night set in when the tumult broke forth anew. The thunder here is not like the tame thunder of the Atlantic coast. Bursting with a terrific crash directly above our heads, it roared over the boundless waste of prairie, seeming to roll around the whole circle of the firmament with a peculiar and awful reverberation. The lightning flashed all night, playing with its livid glare upon the neighboring trees, revealing the vast expanse of the plain, and then leaving us shut in as if by a palpable wall of darkness. (49–50)

By passing over the previous night's thunderstorm, Parkman makes the situation more dramatic by way of the race against the swirling cloudbanks. Likewise, by leading up to the description of the prairie landscape at night through the party's movements during the day, Parkman is able to accentuate a visibly striking aspect of the landscape: the darkened prairie suddenly, momentarily illuminated and then followed by "a palpable wall of darkness." When compared to a similar description in James's *Account* of the Long expedition (*EWT,* 15: 172), Parkman's is more vivid, more visual, and more direct.

To a certain extent, therefore, *The Oregon Trail* stands in a different relation to Parkman's journal than Kane's large oils to his on-the-spot sketches, or Irving's journals versus *A Tour.* Instead of merely applying literary conventions to his immediate observations, Parkman in *The Oregon Trail* questions their very validity in describing the West—thus his overview of the well-read traveler's expectations and the reality he finds (34–36). Certainly, the holiday air that infuses the book has all the trappings of romance (Parkman frequently refers to his guide as "another Leatherstocking"), but Parkman's writings most often amplify and embellish sentiments expressed in his journal, and hence improve their clarity.

This is especially so with regard to the prairie landscape. As with thunderstorms, when Parkman recalled his experiences on the prairie while dictating *The Oregon Trail* he developed his impressions (as seen in the journal); he made them clearer and more precise. For example, after traveling for several days overland prior to striking the Platte river, Parkman is understandably anxious to reach it; game had been scarce and the travel monotonous: "hour after hour over a perfect level" (*Journals*, 1: 430). After traveling a good part of the day with the buttes of the Platte in sight, Parkman writes: "and after a long and gradual ascent, saw the Platte from the summit—apparently one vast, level plain, fringed with a distant line of forest—the river ran invisible in sluices through the plain, with here and there a patch of woods like an island" (*Journals*, 2: 431). Parkman's rendering of the same scene in *The Oregon Trail* is both more detailed and concerned with his emotional and esthetic response:

> At length we gained the summit, and the long-expected valley of the Platte lay before us. We all drew rein, and sat joyfully looking down upon the prospect. It was right welcome,—strange, too, and strking to the imagination; and yet it had not one picturesque or beautiful feature; nor had it any of the features of grandeur, other than its vast extent, its solitude, and its wildness. For league after league, a plain as level as a lake was outspread beneath us; here and there the Platte, divided into a dozen thread-like sluices, was traversing it, and an occasional clump of wood, rising in the midst like a shadowy island, relieved the monotony of the waste. No living thing was moving throughout the vast landscape, except the lizards that darted over the sand and through the rank grass and prickly pears at our feet. (65)

While the journal entry provides the bare bones of the incident, Parkman here recalls his emotional response and analyzes it. He knows that his reaction is both strong and imaginative, but at the same time he is uneasy because he is aware that this particular vista includes none of the conventional "features of grandeur" associated with the beautiful, the picturesque, or the sublime. Finally, too, he is aware that his imagination has been struck by a landscape that contains no living things to animate the scene.

This is most clearly seen when, as Irving did earlier, Parkman becomes lost. Describing it in his journal, Parkman writes:

> Got separated from the others—rode for hours westwardly over the prairie— saw the hills dotted with thousands of buffalo. Antelopes—prairie-dogs— burrowing owls—wild geese—wolves, etc. Finding my course wrong, followed a buffalo-track northward, and about noon came out on the road. Awkward feeling, being lost on the prairie. (*Journals*, 2: 434–35)

Parkman's last sentence (with which his numerous predecessors would have agreed) becomes the basis for a lengthy passage of description and analysis in *The Oregon Trail:*

> I looked about for some indications to show me where I was, and what course I ought to pursue; I might as well have looked for landmarks in the midst of the ocean. How many miles I had run, or in what direction, I had no idea; and around me the prairie was rolling in steep swells and pitches, without a single distinctive feature to guide me. I had a little compass hung at my neck; and ignorant that the Platte at this point diverged considerably from its easterly course, I thought that by keeping to the northward I should certainly reach it. So I turned and rode about two hours in that direction. The prairie changed as I advanced, softening away into easier undulations, but nothing like the Platte appeared, nor any sight of a human being: the same wild, endless expanse lay around me still; and to all appearance I was as far from my object as ever. I began now to think myself in danger of being lost, and, reining in my horse, summoned the scanty share of woodcraft that I possessed (if that term be applicable on the prairie) to extricate me. It occurred to me that the buffalo might prove my best guides. I soon found one of the paths made by them in their passage to the river: it ran nearly at right angles to my course; but turning my horse's head in the direction it indicated, his freer gait and erected ears assured me that I was right. (81)

Here Parkman makes plain to his reader the nature of his "awkward" feeling: on the prairie, he realizes, none of the conventional means of orientation applies. One who is lost in a landscape without landmarks must rethink the applicability of the term "woodcraft" to such a landscape. Instead of, like Castañeda, looking for a "distinctive feature" in a landscape that is largely without such things, Parkman eventually realizes that he must work with those features that do exist on the prairie; instead of looking up for some upright thing in order to obtain orientation, Parkman realizes that on the prairie one is better served by looking down and following the way of a buffalo trail. Parkman's growing frustration over his disorientation is palpable too in this passage, along with his growing awareness that he must adapt imaginatively in order to find his way. Thus the passage in *The Oregon Trail* is explicit and dramatic while the journal entry, taken immediately after the incident, suggests only the nascent feeling: awkwardness. Just as earlier he was uncertain about why the prairie around the Platte struck him as beautiful, now he is forced to probe the nature of his "Awkward feeling" at being lost on the prairie.[42]

Finally, if Parkman's most succinct assessment of the prairie's effect upon an individual is found in the letter he wrote his father immediately upon his return to Westport, then his most telling evaluation of its effect on conventional esthetic assumptions is seen in a passage included in the 1849 edition, but subsequently deleted. Immediately after his description of their first sight of the Platte—in which he sees no features of beauty but is imaginatively struck nonetheless—Parkman wrote:

> And yet stern and wild associations gave a singular interest to the view; for here each man lives by the strength of his arm and the valor of his heart. Here society is reduced to its original elements, the whole fabric of art and conventionality is struck rudely to pieces, and men find themselves suddenly brought back to the wants and resources of their original natures.[43]

Parkman's metaphorical destruction of artistic conventions, embodied in an image, encapsulates the more acute problems of the first artists to visit the prairie. Unlike the first explorers and travelers, who had to learn only how to travel through and live for a time within the environment while, perhaps, describing it a bit, those of artistic intentions had to both do this and to communicate the experience. Accordingly, they had to adapt and accommodate inherited esthetic assumptions and conventions. That both painters and writers reveal a tension within their works as they strove to do so suggests the gulf between European esthetics and the salient qualities of prairie space in the nineteenth century—a gulf between the dominant romantic sensibility and the "new experience in nature." Of those surveyed here, only Parkman seems to have in any way bridged this gulf when he defined the prairie as "strange, too, and striking to the imagination," and then continued to acknowledge the metaphorical destruction of conventions by the landscape. Even so, his literary evocations of the land in *The Oregon Trail* are initial steps only, suggesting the time and distance needed for the prairie to become a literary setting.

Fig. 1. George Catlin, *Elk and Buffalo Making Acquaintance, Texas.* National Museum of American Art, Smithsonian Institution. Gift of Mrs. Joseph Harrison, Jr.

Fig. 2. George Catlin, *Band of Sioux Moving Camp.* National Museum of American Art, Smithsonian Institution. Gift of Mrs. Joseph Harrison, Jr.

89

Fig. 3. George Catlin, *Prairie Meadows Burning*. National Museum of American Art, Smithsonian Institution. Gift of Mrs. Joseph Harrison, Jr.

Fig. 4. George Catlin, *Buffalo Chase in Winter, Indians on Snowshoes*. National Museum of American Art, Smithsonian Institution. Gift of Mrs. Joseph Harrison, Jr.

Fig. 5. George Catlin, *Buffalo Chase with Bows and Lances.* National Museum of American Art, Smithsonian Institution. Gift of Mrs. Joseph Harrison, Jr.

Fig. 6. George Catlin, *Big Bend on the Upper Missouri, 1900 Miles Above St. Louis.* National Museum of American Art, Smithsonian Institution. Gift of Mrs. Joseph Harrison, Jr.

91

Fig. 7. Paul Kane, *The Man that Always Rides.* Courtesy of the Royal Ontario Museum, Toronto, Canada.

Fig. 8. George Catlin, *BA-DA-AH-CHON-DU (He Who Jumps Over Everyone) . . . on Horseback.* The Paul Mellon Collection, Virginia Museum of Fine Arts, Richmond.

Fig. 9. Paul Kane, *Winter Travelling in Dog Sleds (A Wedding Party Leaving Fort Edmonton)*. Courtesy of the Royal Ontario Museum, Toronto, Canada.

Fig. 10. John Mix Stanley, *Herd of Bison, Near Lake Jessie*. Taft Collection, Kansas State Historical Society.

Fig. 11. Paul Kane, *Camping on the Prairie.* Stark Museum of Art, Orange, Texas.

Fig. 12. Paul Kane, *Assiniboine Hunting Buffalo.* National Gallery of Canada, Ottawa. Transferred from Parliament, 1955.

94

Fig. 13. Paul Kane, *Brigade of Boats.* Courtesy of the Royal Ontario Museum, Toronto, Canada.

Fig. 14. Paul Kane, *A Prairie on Fire.* Courtesy of the Royal Ontario Museum, Toronto, Canada.

Fig. 15. Karl Bodmer, *View of the Mandan Village Mih-Tutta-Hang-Kusch.* Joslyn Art Museum, Omaha, Nebraska.

Fig. 16. Alfred Jacob Miller, *Noon-day Rest.* Walters Art Gallery, Baltimore.

Fig. 17. Alfred Jacob Miller, *Indians on the War Path*. Walters Art Gallery, Baltimore.

Fig. 18. Alfred Jacob Miller, *Snake Indians*. The Gund Collection of Western Art, Cleveland.

Fig. 19. Alfred Jacob Miller, *Buffalo Turning on his Pursuers.* Walters Art Gallery, Baltimore.

Fig. 20. Alfred Jacob Miller, *The Lost Greenhorn.* Walters Art Gallery, Baltimore.

Fig. 21. Alfred Jacob Miller, *Prairie Scene: Mirage.* Walters Art Gallery, Baltimore.

Part

Pioneers

3

Breathing Life and Fire into a Circle of Imagery:

Prairie as Nineteenth-Century Literary Landscape

Among the glowing reviews greeting Irving's *A Tour on the Prairies* was a long laudatory piece in the *North American Review*. Edward Everett lavished praise on Irving's presentation of "the whole unhackneyed freshness of the West," ultimately turning to his actual subject, Irving's grand stature within contemporary American letters:

> we glow with rapture as we see him coming back from the Prairies, laden
> with the poetical treasures of the primitive wilderness,—rich with spoil
> from the uninhabited desert. We thank him for turning these poor barbarous
> *steppes* into classical land;—and joining his inspiration to that of Cooper, in
> breathing life and fire into a circle of imagery, which was not known before
> to exist, for the purposes of the imagination.

Seeing Irving as using uniquely American materials, really, for the first time in his career, Everett proclaims with nationalist fervor that "a better day is dawning on American letters."[1]

Though Irving *was* employing truly American material—as opposed to recycling old-world tales as he had previously—his *A Tour* tells far more about Irving than it does the prairie. Yet by taking up the prairie West as subject, Irving acknowledged its status as an overriding concern of early nineteenth-century America, perhaps even its obsession. Certainly, *A Tour* did have the effect of "breathing life and fire" into a subject that had previously been treated—with the glaring exception of Cooper's *The Prairie*—only in explorers and travelers' first-person accounts; but because Irving imposed his literary assumptions on his material—in just the inaccurate manner remarked upon by Parkman in *The Oregon Trail*—it remained for others to transform the West into the literary landscape Everett envisions. Irving's prairies remain ever "barbarous *steppes.*" And like Irving's western book, Parkman's also received lavish attention from reviewers, among them the novelist Herman Melville, who had recently published *Mardi* and would later in 1849 bring out *Redburn.*[2] While he attacked Parkman's attitude toward the Indian, Melville otherwise praises *The Oregon Trail* highly, pausing occasionally to point up western images he finds particularly appealing. Most importantly, Melville's enthusiasm illustrates the literary appeal of the prairie West during the 1830s and 1840s while Everett's allusion to Cooper suggests the nascent beginnings of the prairie as a literary landscape.

During the nineteenth century the prairie was an evolving, if not always acknowledged, literary setting. James Fenimore Cooper began its transformation graphically and dramatically in 1827 in *The Prairie,* but it was not until 1913, in Willa Cather's *O Pioneers!,* that the landscape was again called upon to play so crucial a role in a major American novel. From Cooper's tale on, the prairie began its evolution from simply a source of unusual images and symbols and of allusions invoking the westward movement into a literary setting as westerners, particularly realists like Hamlin Garland, drew upon their newly settled land as setting for fiction. Throughout, the prairie's features exerted their primacy—as they had in the first-person accounts and painters' canvases—in shaping the landscape's role as a literary setting. It is a critical commonplace that nineteenth-century American literature reveals a tension between romance and realism, but in looking at prairie fictions between Cooper and Cather, it becomes clear that tension was exacerbated by the nature of the landscape itself, forcing the demands of prairie space into literary consciousness. Indeed, judging from the literature it has inspired, the prairie landscape might well be seen as a battleground between romance and realism, for the harshness of the land tested whatever idealized expectations its pioneers brought along with them. Just as overlanders jettisoned some of their possessions on the trail, so too did they cast off some of their cultural baggage as they adapted imaginatively to the land.

Cooper, Bryant, and the Writers of the American Renaissance

Margaret Fuller wrote that she came "to the West prepared for the distaste" she "must experience at its mushroom growth," and she hoped to "foresee the law by which a new order, a new poetry, is to be evoked from this chaos" of growth (22) in the West. Such fervor and interest also affected contemporary writers who remained comfortably in the East. As a result, many of the classical works of nineteenth-century American literature abound with western allusions.[3] To James Fenimore Cooper and his successors, the appeal of the prairie had mainly to do with its availability as a symbolic value. Two comments by Fuller's contemporaries, neither specifically about the prairie, help to explain this view. Speaking of landscape depiction, Thoreau observes:

> Not only has the foreground of a picture its glass of transparent crystal spread over it, but the picture itself is a glass or transparent medium to a remoter background. We demand only of all pictures that they be perspicuous, that the laws of perspective have been truly observed. It is not the fringed foreground of the desert nor the intermediate oases that detain the eye and the imagination, but the infinite, level, and roomy horizon, where the sky meets the sand, and heavens and earth, the ideal and the actual, are coincident, the background into which leads the path of the pilgrim.

Thoreau's notion of the far distance, on the horizon where the ideal and actual meet, neatly presents the approach to the prairie landscape used by the leading writers of the period. For them, the prairie was both ideal and actual; it was an actual landscape which could be used metaphorically to make vivid their concept of scope. All the more so because it was largely uninhabited—it was, for them, a place of experiment and definition. Similarly, in *Nature,* Emerson observes: "The health of the eye seems to demand a horizon. We are never tired, so long as we see far enough."[4] As with Thoreau, Emerson is not speaking of the prairie landscape, yet his stress on imaginative potential seems to demand that landscape, just as Alfred Jacob Miller preferred a landscape with room left "for the imagination to fill up."[5]

Critics have long noted the effect of prairie landscape on the whole of Cooper's *The Prairie,*[6] though such criticism does not go much beyond a comment by James Franklin Beard that the setting of the novel "is not simply a backdrop to the action, and hence incidental to the meaning: it is an integral part of the action *and* the meaning."[7] Whatever the landscape's role in the novel, the question is of course complicated by the fact that Cooper never saw the landscape he chose as his setting. He relied on published first-person exploration accounts for landscape detail, most heavily Edwin James's rendering of the Long expedition. Given this, Cooper's contemporaries were quick to point out that the West he depicts in *The Prairie* is inaccurate; his factual mistakes led those familiar with the region, such as Lewis Cass, Timothy Flint, and Daniel Drake, to dismiss his novel altogether, an attitude which still persists.[8] Yet because of the symbolic function of the landscape in the novel, the issue is not so much one of accuracy or inaccuracy; rather it is one of imaginative transformation, how one interprets—in relation to the novel's action and purpose—the role of the landscape as Cooper presents it.

By using the James *Account* of the Long expedition as the basis of his fictional setting, Cooper transformed the prairie landscape from an actual, experienced one, into a symbolic, mythic one. In *The Prairie,* meaning resides not only in the experience or perception of the characters who are on the prairie but also within their understanding of the meaning assigned to the landscape by Cooper. In previous accounts examined here, the authors revealed subjective reactions to prairie landscape; the landscape itself is passive, static. But in *The Prairie,* for the first time in such writing, Cooper's art charges the landscape with symbolic meaning, so that within the novel perceiver and object form a symbiosis. His technique in the Leatherstocking series, as recent criticism has convincingly argued, was aimed at "a comprehensive survey of the variety of American experience."[9] In accomplishing this, Cooper saw fit to transform the strange landscape he found in his sources into a pictorial projection that complemented his themes. He thus seized on the prairie's salient visual and psychological effects, the very effects that had accosted the European imagination since Coronado.

The role of his sources in this is ultimately secondary; Cooper's fiction vis-à-vis his sources is not a matter of right or wrong but rather one of his imaginative interpretations of his sources.[10] Speaking of *The Pioneers,* James D. Wallace has offered an assessment that applies equally to *The Prairie:*

> By merging the resources of the explorer's journal with those of the American novel he had invented in *The Spy,* Cooper advanced his claim to be Fielding's true historian, "a describer of society as it exists and men as they are," and by teaching us to read *The Pioneers,* he sought to teach us to be Americans.[11]

By boldly setting his novel, which he saw as the final volume of a trilogy, in a landscape alien to his readers, he gave himself the task of teaching his audience to "read" that landscape—thematically, pictorially, and symbolically. Certainly, no landscape could better serve Cooper's elegiac purposes in the novel than the western prairie, since to eastern sensibilities the prairie, as a part of the Great American Desert, was barren, a barrier to settlement.[12]

Cooper's use of the prairie as the organic setting for a moralistic tale is evident from the first page of the novel, where he describes the region as "a barrier of desert to the extension of our population in the west." Defining this theme more concretely, Natty Bumppo sees the "barren belt of Prairie, behind the States" as a warning, a bitter jest of God: "Look around you, men; what will the Yankee choppers say, when they have cut their path from the eastern to the western waters, and find that a hand, which can lay the 'arth bare at a blow, has been here, and swept the country, in very mockery of their wickedness."[13] So Cooper appropriates the concept of the Great American Desert for thematic purposes; as a result, he emphasizes the treeless quality of the prairie and downplays other features. For example, his single buffalo stampede notwithstanding, Cooper makes little of the vast herds that James described, perhaps thinking a land that supported such herds might not be as much a barrier as he sought. In any case, Cooper makes the treeless character of the plains the most striking element of the setting in the novel, not other elements discussed by explorers and travelers. That Cooper consciously did so, moreover, is apparent through the long discussion between Bumppo and Dr. Bat in chapter 22, in which Natty—underscoring his comments here—sees the prairie as a testament to human folly.

After providing his summary account of both the Louisiana Purchase and the Westward Movement at the very beginning of the novel, Cooper describes the Bush caravan as it heads west over the plains in the fall of 1805. Although the trapper and Ishmael Bush, a squatter, contrast in virtually every respect, both have been driven into the prairie as a result of differences with eastern law. The prairie landscape is pictured at the outset of the novel as a wasteland for Cooper's latter-day Ishmael and, as well, a place of exile for his hero, who in old age has sunk from hunter to subsistence trapper:

> The appearance of such a train, in that bleak and solitary place, was rendered all the more remarkable by the fact, that the surrounding country offered so little, that was tempting to the cupidity of speculation, and, if possible, still less that was flattering to the hopes of an ordinary settler of new lands.
>
> The meagre herbage of the Prairie promised nothing in favor of a hard and unyielding soil, over which the wheels of the vehicles rattled as lightly as if they travelled on a beaten road; neither wagons nor beasts making any deeper impression, than to mark that bruised and withered grass, which the cattle plucked, from time to time, and as often rejected as food too sour for even hunger to render palatable. (11)

Cooper's impression of the landscape is reflected throughout in his adjectives; and as the book proceeds the reader becomes so accustomed to certain phrases ("interminable tracts") that they have the quality of clichés by its end, but they are nonetheless definitive tags that Cooper uses to remind his readers of his earlier descriptions.

After describing Ishmael Bush and selected members of his party, Cooper turns his attention once more to the landscape, noting after the fashion of Lewis the "little valleys" between the divides that partially enclose the view: on the sides that remain open, the "meagre prospect" runs "off in long, narrow, barren perspectives, but slightly relieved by a pitiful show of coarse, though somewhat luxuriant vegetation." Then, like almost every explorer or traveler who ever walked the prairie, Cooper obtains his best vantage point from the height of an undulation; his resulting description echoes all of the basic elements observed by travelers and explorers:

> From the summits of the swells, the eye became fatigued with the sameness and chilling dreariness of the landscape. The earth was not unlike the ocean, when its restless waters are heaving heavily, after the agitation and fury of the tempest have begun to lessen. There was the same waving and regular surface, the same absence of foreign objects, and the same boundless extent to the view. Indeed so very striking was the resemblance between the water and the land, that, however much the geologist might sneer at so simple a theory, it would have been difficult for a poet not to have felt that the formation of the one had been produced by the subsiding dominion of the other. Here and there a tall tree rose out of the bottoms, stretching its naked branches abroad, like some solitary vessel; and, to strengthen the delusion, far in the distance appeared two or three rounded thickets, looming in the misty horizon like islands resting on the waters. (13)

Cooper consciously relied for his landscape data almost totally on the James *Account* of the Long expedition; his deliberation, furthermore, is suggested first by his comment that, though the geologist might sneer at the prairie/sea analogy, to the poet it is inescapable. And having adopted the analogy (his novel played some considerable part in making the comparison a cliché), Cooper uses it repeatedly. Even when direct landscape descriptions recede as the plot takes over, his repetitions remind the reader of the setting, particularly through prairie/sea parallels.[14] He was, of course, drawing on his own seafaring experience but, more than that, the prairie/sea metaphor was for him an apt means of making a strange landscape imaginatively available; economically vivid, it reflected the usual European reaction to a treeless landscape, and was thematically connected with his notion of the prairie as a barrier to settlement. As such, Cooper was teaching his audience to read the prairie landscape.

That this was a conscious technique is evident from close comparisons of Cooper's landscape passages and the James *Account.* James's imagination, of course, was affected by the prairie landscape. Striving to be accurate by consulting the most up-to-date, official information, Cooper, while reading the James *Account* was similarly, although vicariously, struck, and he adapted those elements in them that best served his artistic purposes. Overland has argued, for example, that the passage just quoted was lifted virtually whole from the *Account,* Cooper being content to add a detail or two—the appearance of tall trees and the prairie/sea "theory."[15] But in so saying, he oversimplifies the author's creative process and thereby underestimates Cooper's artistry. James speaks of "here and there an insular grove of trees," but Cooper retained this and added: "Here and there a tall tree rose out of the bottoms, stretching its naked branches abroad like some solitary vessel" (14). Overland is correct when he holds that Cooper added the simile, but he fails to notice that Cooper also contributed the "naked" solitary trees; Cooper needed these trees, certainly, to signify fuel and shelter to his readers, but also for the Bushes to cut down the evening of their first meeting with Natty. Abiram White, more symbolically, is sentenced at the end of the novel to carry out his own execution from a dead and solitary willow tree. Thus Cooper foreshadows one of his starkest images in his first extended description of the landscape that made that image available; in so doing he used an element of prairie landscape—uninterrupted line of sight—dramatically. Imagining the vista as James described it, Cooper saw how its various elements could be used dramatically, and he structured his tale accordingly.[16]

No single scene in *The Prairie* makes this more apparent than the occasion when, as the Bushes trudge westward across the "interminable tracts," they are confronted by Natty Bumppo. Backlighted by the setting sun, Cooper's hero seems to them "a spectacle as sudden as it was unexpected":

> The sun had fallen below the crest of the nearest wave of the Prairie, leaving the usual rich and glowing train on its track. In the centre of this flood of fiery light a human form appeared, drawn against the gilded background, as distinctly, and seemingly as palpable, as though it would come within the grasp of any extended hand. The figure was colossal; the attitude musing and melancholy, and the situation directly in the route of the travellers. But embedded, as it was, in its setting of garish light, it was impossible to distinguish its just proportions or true character. (14–15)

This is perhaps the single most memorable, and symbolic, scene in the whole of the Leatherstocking series; and like Cooper's initial description of the prairie, it was inspired by James's *Account*. James had noted that "Nothing is more difficult than to estimate, by the eye, the distance of objects seen in these plains" because of mirage effects (15: 184). Immediately after his first description of the landscape, Cooper prepares the reader for Natty's entrance by commenting "the sameness of surface, and the low stands of the spectators exaggerated the distances" (14), other details taken from the Long expedition *Account*. But he appears to have saved most of the details regarding the optical effects of the prairie for Natty's first appearance, where they could be used to best advantage.

James also wrote that he and his party "had often found ourselves more grossly abused by our eye-sight" (15: 259) while traveling the prairie. Cooper seized upon such optical effects in presenting Natty Bumppo at the outset of *The Prairie,* for the Bush caravan is brought to a grinding halt by the "spectacle" they find before them; like James's eyesight, theirs is being similarly, and dramatically, abused. The colossal figure of Natty, standing "directly in the route of the travelers," represents Cooper's adaptation of James's observations. For James, who was a botanist and geologist (and perhaps Cooper's model for Dr. Bat), the optical illusions of the prairie are notable phenomena, data for science. Adapted by Cooper, they are a basis for archetypal presentation of his crucial character—and his crucial ideas. As his author's masculine ideal, Natty is alone, huge, palpable, and bathed in a golden light, standing as a questioning presence, a consciousness, at a time when the nation was undertaking western settlement. Ultimately, too, it is the prairie landscape that allows Cooper to write "it was impossible to distinguish its just proportions or true character." This is, of course, just what *The Prairie* is about. Whether one is Ishmael Bush, casual reader, or literary critic, each must tackle Natty's "true character" in order to grasp Cooper's message. Thus a central fact of the prairie landscape, attested to by James, Pike, Gregg, and numerous other travelers, offered Cooper at the beginning of *The Prairie* with a strikingly visual means of presenting Natty symbolically, stripped of all but his essential meaning.

The Bushes, like the reader, are affected immediately by this vision; its result, Cooper writes, "was instantaneous and powerful. The man in front of the emigrants came to a stand, and remained gazing at the mysterious object, with a dull interest that soon quickened to superstitious awe" (15). As with Cooper's "naked" trees dotting the prairie, Cooper here foreshadows the direction his narrative will take since, like many of the characters and the readers as well, Ishmael Bush fluctuates between "interest" and "superstitious awe" as he attempts (and is sometimes forced) to understand Bumppo and his values.[17]

Cooper's use of the prairie sunset as a technical device therefore allows him to lend symbolic and thematic significance to Bumppo before he has actually been introduced to the reader. This accomplished, Cooper turns the sunset off, as it were, when "the proportions of the fanciful form became less exaggerated, and finally distinct" (16). Transforming a "fanciful form" to a figure that is distinct by turning down the light, Cooper lays bare his technique—he has employed the sunset illusion to create a particular dramatic effect. Once this has been done, he moves on to his plot, but always defining the trapper in terms of his first colossal, metaphorically larger-than-life, presentation. Thus, before answering Bush's polite request for "necessaries for the night," Bumppo insists that his own—and thematically more significant—query be answered first: " 'Is the land filled on the other side of the Big River!' demanded the old man, solemnly, and without appearing to hearken to the other's question; 'or why do I see a sight I had never thought to behold again?' " (16–17). This question answered to the best of Ishmael's ability, Natty undertakes the role he plays throughout: guide for and mediator between the various characters and, as well, guide for and mediator between the whites and the strange prairie landscape.

All of Cooper's characters, with the exception of the trapper and the Indians, are puny figures within the landscape and are affected by its vastness at every turn. Like the Bushes at the beginning of the novel, they need Bumppo's "prairie-craft," and all continue to need him throughout. Only he is able to realize the presence of Hard-Heart, to lead the captive Inez away from Bush's rock tower without being detected, and to know the difference between a brilliant sunrise and the glow of a prairie fire. His character is defined by his ability to be at one with the land, even as seemingly harsh, trackless, and vacant a land as Cooper's prairie. The starkness of the prairie landscape is exploited by Cooper to make the moral relations in the novel vivid. Natty Bumppo stands golden, colossal at the beginning (and he is bathed in the same glow when he dies) while Abiram White's quivering form stands upon its perch at the farthest extreme of the prairie horizon, symbolizing his reformed brother-in-law's apparent new knowledge. The setting prairie sun highlights both men, but to radically different moral conclusions.

Cooper's use of the prairie landscape to imagistically invoke and define the moral relations between his characters is seen particularly when the Bushes are forced to move to their rock tower due to the Sioux raid of the previous night. Here and throughout the novel Cooper's emphasis is on the pictorial qualities in his scenes. [18] The morning after the raid, Bush and several of his party walk "in profound and moody silence to the summit of the nearest swell, whence they could command an almost boundless view of the naked plains." Here they saw only "a solitary buffaloe," which Ishmael assumes is one of his animals left by the Sioux to mock him. Then follows a discussion between

Bush and Bumppo over the quality of the prairie land and the growth of the country; Leatherstocking tells the emigrant: "If you have come in search of land, you have journeyed hundreds of miles too far, or many leagues too little" (75). The prairie as a metaphor—treeless land, barren, a barrier to settlement, the final refuge of the Indian—makes Cooper's ideas on the exploitation of America more effective, especially to an audience that had never seen such a landscape. And, because of the ways in which he seized the salient features of the landscape from his sources, Cooper projects, for the first time in a work of fiction, the imaginative reactions of many explorers and travelers—Castañeda, Brackenridge, Flagg, Greeley, and others—who were forced to reconsider their notion of the word *landscape*. Thus, his imaginative invocation of the region as a literary setting is, in many points at least, an amplification and ordering of views held by actual prairie travelers.

Telling the emigrant that the open prairie "is but a naked spot, for a dozen men to make head in, ag'in five hundred," Natty prevails upon Bush to repair to another, more defensible, place three "long miles from this spot" (79, 80). When presenting Bush's decision to move elsewhere, however, Cooper is careful not to provide an immediate description of the party's destination. Instead he describes the landscape they must traverse in order to move from one encampment to the other:

> The heavens were clothed in driving clouds, piled in vast masses one above the other, which whirled violently, in the gusts, opening, occasionally, to admit the transient glimpses of the bright and glorious sight of the heavens, dwelling in a magnificence by far too grand and durable, to be disturbed by the fitful efforts of the lower world. Beneath, the wind swept across the wild and naked Prairies with a violence that is seldom witnessed, in any section of the continent less open. It would have been easy to have imagined, in the ages of Fable, that the god of the winds had permitted his subordinate agents to escape from their den, and that they not rioted, in wantonness, across wastes, where neither tree, nor work of man, nor mountain, nor obstacle of any sort opposed itself to their gambols. (85)

For mythic creatures, the prairie is a playground, where they may "gambol" at will; for man, however, the essence of the land is his exposure amid the vastness of nature. Sky and land only. Thus, Cooper concentrates on the swirling clouds above, while below upon the "wild and naked prairies," the wind sports about with unchecked violence. And his final sentence, cataloguing those elements that are not present to provide man's comfort, echoes the descriptions of a multitude of prairie travelers and explorers. Doubtlessly, the passage has its source in James's description of being caught in a hailstorm on the prairie (15: 172), yet as Cooper uses it—especially through his placement of it—this passage's meaning far exceeds James's immediate landscape description. Through it, the reader sees the essentially exposed quality of all the characters who have ventured into "the wild and naked prairies."

But because this passage is placed so that the reader has to traverse it in order to follow the Bushes from their first camp to their rock tower, Cooper emphasizes the symbolic weight of each place. Thus once the Bushes have left the camp, Bumppo tarries, musing over the abandoned site and the "deserted logs at his feet," which the day before had been standing trees:

> "Ay!" he muttered to himself, "I might have know'd it! I might have knowed it! Often I have seen the same before, and yet I brought them to the spot myself, and have now sent them to the only neighborhood of their kind, within many long leagues of the spot where I stand. This is man's wish, and pride, and waste, and sinfulness. He tames the beasts of the field, to feed his idle wants, and having robbed the brutes of their natural food, he teaches them to strip the 'arth of its trees, to quiet their hunger." (83)

Immediately afterwards, Paul Hover appears and makes comments that prompt the trapper's recollection of his early manhood in New York, so this scene and Natty's soliloquy link *The Prairie* to the earlier Leatherstocking Tales. But Bumppo's comments are fitting preliminary to Cooper's introduction of Bush's monument to hubris, his own Tower of Babel.

While he is in the midst of the prairie—an elemental landscape of wind, earth, and sky, only—Ishmael Bush needs Natty Bumppo. Once safely ensconced in his rock tower, which permits him to rise above the landscape and so "control" his knowledge of it, Bush scorns the trapper's help and proceeds on his own course. That course, however, is one that involves pacts with the Sioux, further involvement with Abiram White, and the latter's murder of Bush's eldest son. Only when he recants and recognizes Natty's true character is Bush able to cease his wandering and, as the final trial scene dramatizes, become a just man, if only nominally.

Cooper's placement of a "single, naked, and ragged rock," "at least, two hundred feet above the level of the plain" (84, 88) is based on such eminences, such as Castle Rock, mentioned in his source.[19] Allowing Bush to command a good part of the novel's action, its height can be seen from any vantage point in the area of the action and, at night, the fire at its summit serves as a beacon. Natty must guide his fellows carefully as they make their getaway from the tower after rescuing Inez, for he knows the danger of detection by anyone standing upon its summit. Likewise, as the Bushes return after discovering Asa's corpse, they strain to espy Ellen standing at its pinnacle. As Cooper describes their view from the prairie: "The hill had gradually risen, as they approached, like some tower, emerging from the bosom of the sea, and when within a mile, the minuter objects that crowned its height came, dimly into view" (144). The tower, according to Natty, is "the only neighborhood" of the Bushes' kind for miles, too (83), and Bush, ironically, is unaware that the threat to him is not from without, to be repelled from the tower, but within the bosom of his family: Abiram White.

Structurally and dramatically, the tower is the fixed point in Cooper's composition, and most of the action takes place within its radius. But its symbolic and technical use is made possible, and demanded, by the landscape itself. Cooper had to look no further than his primary source, the James *Account.* Moreover, and apart from its appearance in his source, his desire to insert a monumental upright tower into an essentially flat landscape must have been motivated—as actual prairie travelers were—by a need to encompass the landscape imaginatively. Throughout, Cooper stresses the "monotony of view" afforded by prairie landscape and, in the passage which defines and describes the "interminable" in oft-repeated "interminable wastes" he notes "neither tree, nor work of man, nor mountain, nor obstacle of any sort" to impede the force of prairie winds. As a first-time visitor to the prairie, albeit in imagination, Cooper was affected as many actual visitors were; Alexander Henry the Younger climbed a tree—James Fenimore Cooper created a tower. Teaching us to read the prairie, he sought techniques—like the tower—that would bring about our understanding of the new land he chose as setting.

Cooper's ability to take the basic elements of the prairie landscape and to charge those elements with relevant meaning reaches its apex in the death of Abiram White. Held as a prisoner for the murder of Asa Bush, White is taken east with the caravan when "the squatter turned his back towards the setting sun." Bush, who ostensibly has recanted and become a just man, is now described in contemplation as a figure analogous to Bumppo himself, in an image underscored by the repetition of elements of Cooper's first symbolic presentation of Natty: "his huge figure was seen standing on the summit of some distant swell, with his head bent towards the earth, as he leaned on his rifle . . ." (355). While not backlighted, Bush is larger than life, like Natty, and is also seen from the top of a swell.

Cooper draws upon the landscape once more when he introduces the means for White's eventual execution. First noting that the country had improved—through the incidence of hillocks and trees—as the party moved east, he then describes a dead "solitary willow" beside a large rock. Though still standing, it symbolically proclaims "the frailty of existence, and the fulfillment of time"

(356). After his discussion with his wife concerning White's execution, Bush intends to shoot him, just as White shot Asa; but in response to White's pleas for time Bush relents and, after noticing the configuration of willow and rock platform, leaves White to decide his own moment of death by hanging. Bush turns and departs across the plain without looking back until he reaches "the boundary of the visible horizon from the rock." Gazing to the west once again, he sees another figure against the setting sun, one without any of Natty's heroic proportions: "The sun was near dipping into the plains beyond, and its last rays lighted the naked branches of the willow. He saw the ragged outline of the whole drawn against the glowing heavens, and he even traced the still upright form he had left to his misery" (361–62). Thus, just as the prairie landscape allows Ishmael a symbolic glimpse of Natty's character at the tale's beginning, it also allows him a symbolic glimpse of what he has learned from the trapper at its end.

To underscore the bleak image of his ogre-against-the-sky, Cooper makes White's figure a part of the chillingly threatening landscape that has defeated, yet enhanced, Ishmael Bush:

> For the first time, in a life of so much wild adventure, Ishmael felt a keen sense of solitude. The naked Prairies began to assume the forms of illimitable and dreary wastes, and the rushing of the wind sounded like the whisperings of the dead. It was not long before he thought a shriek was borne past him on a blast. It did not sound like a call from earth, but swept frightfully through the upper air, mingled with the hoarse accompanyment of the wind. (362)

Just as Bumppo's prairie-craft is a symbolic counterpoint to his character, here the natural forces of the prairie symbolize what Ishmael has come to learn; he has recognized his own puniness in nature. To do so he had to move, symbolically, from his hubristic tower of rock to that fallen from by White. And, as the harsh prairie wind carries Bush's intimation of White's shriek to his ears, it emphasizes the squatter's—putative, at least—new knowledge of his social responsibility.

Thus, in *The Prairie* Cooper offers us the first sustained use of the prairie as setting and for the first time presents a prairie landscape explained through its own terms, rather than those imported from the East. Cooper is at great pains not to present the landscape as a "blank slate," as some critics have held, but rather as one that—in its harshness, vastness, and apparent barrenness—enforces adaptations of its own. Though many argue that Cooper's denouement is unconvincing, there is no doubt that he dramatizes the landscape in order to affect his characters and thereby his readers. The features of the landscape—monotony, mirage, and the rolling quality of the prairie—are, within Cooper's novel, the major elements in a symbolic landscape. Just as Francis Parkman amplified and embellished a single journal entry ("Awkward feeling, being lost on the prairie") into an extended page of description in *The Oregon Trail,* and Paul Kane worked up massive oils from on-the-spot sketches, so Cooper ordered, embellished, and dramatized the landscape materials that he took from the James *Account.* In doing so, he provides the reader with an image of the prairie not to be found again in any sustained manner until Cather's *O Pioneers!.*

Another author to use the prairie as setting—uncharacteristically, since the prairie has seemed to demand prose—was the poet, William Cullen Bryant, who traveled to Illinois in 1832. His immediate esthetic response to the prairie was unfavorable: "I believe this to be the most salubrious, and I am sure it is the most fertile, country I ever saw," he wrote to his wife, "at the same time I do not think it beautiful." Implicit in Bryant's denial of beauty in the prairie is his eastern bias and his esthetic associations with the painters of the Hudson River school. Significantly, though, Bryant does go on to qualify his negative responses: "Some of the views, however, from the highest parts of the prairies are what, I have no doubt, some would call beautiful in the highest degree, the green heights and hollows and plains blend so softly and gently with one another."[20] Insofar as he is able to admit to the possibility of beauty in a prairie vista Bryant, like other prairie travelers requires an elevated perspective.

What Bryant first required, apparently, was a different medium of expression. For Bryant, that form was poetry, and in "The Prairies" (1833) he evokes the vast spaces of the western landscape. The difference between his prose sketches (written on the spot in 1832) and the poem (written in 1833) suggests that distance in time and space may also have been an important factor. The most important requirement, however, was literary precedent, such as provided by Cooper's *The Prairie,* a book that Bryant reviewed shortly after its publication and praised as a work of genius.

In his review, Bryant observed that "This is not very promising matter . . .; the prairie is, to be sure, a new scene . . . it is the wilderness still," but "the store of images and situations it offers is soon exhausted."[21] In his own poem, ironically, Bryant calls up this same store of images: he speaks of the prairie as ocean, its "airy undulations," its constant movement, of the play of cloud and wind over its surface, and of "that advancing multitude / Which soon shall fill these deserts." The bee, moreover, is the harbinger of this "multitude" as it moves west, into the "verdant waste," pushing the "red man" and bison before it. Bryant also notes, echoing Natty Bumppo, that

"The hand that built the firmament hath heaved / And smoothed these verdant swells, and sown their slopes / With herbage, planted them with island groves. . . ."[22]

Since Bryant reviewed Cooper's novel in 1827 and did not go to Illinois until 1832, however, an explanation of why the influence of *The Prairie* did not manifest itself in his prose sketches as well is needed. Why were his responses there not of the positive kind found in his poem? Paradoxically, one explanation may be that Bryant was seeing the prairie through Cooper's eyes. Having read *The Prairie*, Bryant encountered the landscape with preconceived notions of the sort to which Francis Parkman drew attention at the outset of *The Oregon Trail*. Whatever the explanation, the fact remains that "The Prairies" echoes the *The Prairie* much more so than it does Bryant's sketches; the parallels are so numerous that they suggest Bryant's notions of literary treatment of the prairie were formed by Cooper's novel—a situation that suggests, in turn, that with "The Prairies" we have the beginnings of literary influence in prairie landscape depiction.

That such influences were felt is confirmed by the growing frenzy over the American West accompanying Manifest Destiny, with western allusions becoming frequent in contemporary works. A good index of this is Edgar Allan Poe, who published his (never finished) *Journal of Julius Rodman* in 1840. Considered by critics to be a hoax, it testifies to the currency of the West as subject, and to the popularity of the travel narrative in particular; in it, Poe blatantly "plagiarized" from the travel and exploration accounts of Lewis and Clark, Mackenzie, and Irving among others. Some critics have seen the *Journal* as a parody of western travel literature in the 1830s and such a reading is consistent with Poe's comic presentation of Rodman's reaction to the prairie landscape.[23] After a meditation on the enormity of the land through which he was passing, for example, Rodman exclaims:

> At that moment I seemed possessed of an energy more than human; and my animal spirts rose to so high a degree that I could with difficulty content my-self in the narrow limits of the boat. I longed to be with the Greelys [typical Kentuckians] on the bank, that I might give full vent to the feelings which inspired me, by leaping and running in the prairie.[24]

Through this bizarre image of a frenzied frolic, Poe satirized the conventional reaction to the prairie, just as a few pages later he satirizes the clichés of landscape description.

The attraction of the prairie as image and symbol for Herman Melville and the other major writers of the American Renaissance is not surprising. Hawthorne and Emerson offer chance allusions, and to suggest that virtually no Eastern writer, however reclusive, seems to have been unaware of the prairie landscape during this period so too did Emily Dickinson.[25] Besides these admittedly minor allusions, there are also more major examples to be found in the work of Thoreau. In *Walden,* (1854), one of the most quoted assertions Thoreau makes is "I have travelled a good deal in Concord." His travels often took him imaginatively onto the prairie, though he did not respond with Melville's enthusiasm.[26] Whitman's references to the prairie, not surprisingly given the inclusiveness of his subjects, are numerous—yet he too is much more concerned with the idea of the prairie West than he is with the landscape as setting. And, since he did not visit the prairies until 1879, relatively late in his life, his early references to it suggest great enthusiasm but little knowledge.[27]

Herman Melville, in *Moby-Dick,* was the only writer of this period who used the prairie with anything like the depth and power of Cooper. In his review of Parkman's *The Oregon Trail,* he points up western images he found particularly appealing and discusses them at some length; one of these was the prairie as ocean. That Melville was attracted to the prairie landscape before reading Parkman is certain, but the book reaffirmed his attraction and, more importantly, his enthusiasm illustrates the literary currency of the prairie West in mid-nineteenth-century America. Melville, who had used western references incidently in his earlier works, seems to have redoubled his efforts from *Redburn* on; in "Hawthorne and his Mosses" he tells his American reader "your own broad prairies are in [Hawthorne's] soul; and if you travel away inland into his deep and noble nature, you will hear the far roar of his Niagara." As here, the West in general and the prairie in particular constitute a major pattern of allusion in *Moby-Dick,* and *The Confidence Man* deals with a symbolic voyage down the Mississippi. Melville actually took only one trip into the far American West, in 1840, to Gelena, Illinois, when he was twenty-one years old. Yet judging by his writing (he was still drawing upon the prairie frontier in 1888 with a book of poems: *John Marr and Other Sailors*), Melville visited the prairie West repeatedly through his imagination.[28]

Edwin Fussell has said that in *Moby-Dick*

> there are more references to the American West than to Polynesia (or England; or the ancient world; or the Near East; or the history of philosophy; or anything else); and all these references appear to head in one direction, as if arranging themselves along the lines of force in a pre-existing magnetic field. There are almost more allusions to the West than to whaling; and the whales themselves, we quickly learn, are as often as not buffaloes.[29]

Melville's first direct reference to the prairie occurs in "Loomings," when Ishmael, while discussing the meditative effects of bodies of water, and having just described the role of a stream in the painting of a "romantic landscape," admonishes his reader to "Go visit the prairie in June, when for scores on scores of miles you wade knee-deep among Tiger-lilies . . ." (13).

Elsewhere, however, such uses are not just minor allusions, for they appear dramatically in key scenes. In "The Quarter-Deck," for example, just after Ahab gives his "pasteboard masks" speech to Starbuck, and after he nails the doubloon to the mast and whips up the crew's ardor in the search for Moby Dick, the captain conducts his communion service with the three harpooneers and his mates. Ahab, Melville writes, "stood for an instant searchingly eyeing every man of his crew. But those wild eyes met his, as the bloodshot eyes of the prairie wolves meet the eye of their leader, ere he rushes on at their head in the trail of the bison . . ." (145). Here Melville uses the prairie to help define Ahab's quest, character, and the means he employs to obtain the crew's vigilance in his search. He continues the analogy, moreover, to reveal the outcome of such loyalty: "but alas!" the prairie wolves follow "only to fall into the hidden snare of the Indian" (145). Much later in the novel Melville likens Ahab to a "lone, gigantic elm" on the plains that men flee upon the coming of a hurricane (418).

Another instance in which the prairie helps to define a particularly dramatic scene is to be found in "The First Lowering," in which Ishmael, for the first time, mans a boat in pursuit of a whale. The boat is swamped although the crew remain in it: "The wind increased to a howl; the waves dashed their bucklers together; the whole squall roared, forked, and crackled around us like a white fire upon the prairie, in which, unconsumed, we were burning; immortal in these jaws of death!" (194). Melville's allusion to a prairie fire provides him with another landscape that accentuates the vulnerability of man in the face of elemental forces. At the same time, the analogy operates to dramatize the Manichean nature of the universe: on the prairie—and in the case of a fire—water is the answer; on the ocean what is needed is the hot and dry, i.e., fire. Thus Melville goes on to cap off the analogy with a description of Queequeg holding a lantern aloft: "There, then, he sat, holding up that imbecile candle in the heart of that almighty forlornness. There, then, he sat, the sign and symbol of a man without faith, hopelessly holding up hope in the midst of despair" (195).

Additionally, Melville devotes two chapters to a specific consideration of prairie phenomena. "The Whiteness of the Whale," the chapter in which Ishmael probes those considerations of which "the Albino whale was the symbol," is a long meditation on the nature of whiteness, its quality of attracting as it repels. After citing numerous preeminent examples of white-ness, among them that of the albatross, Ishmael invokes "the White Steed of the Prairies" who "was the elected Xerxes of vast herds of wild horses, whose pastures in those days were only fenced by the Rocky Mountains and the Alleghanies." This horse is "A most imperial and archangelical apparition of that unfallen, western world, which to the eyes of the old trappers and hunters revived the glories of those primeval times when Adam walked majestic as a god, bluff-bowed and fearless as this mighty steed." Here the prairie is deemed a suitable setting for this white paragon, and in his invocation of the Eden archetype, Melville implies that the relationship between horse and prairie is symbiotic: "Whether marching amid his aides and marshals in the van of countless coherts that endlessly streamed" an apparition of the unfallen world "over the plains, like an Ohio; or whether with his circumambient subjects browsing all around at the horizon, the White Steed gallopingly reviewed them with warm nostrils reddening through his cool milkiness . . ." (165). The prairie only appears to be an Eden, however, so the White Steed also evokes in Ishmael "a certain nameless terror" (166), a terror sensed by the Vermont colt that recoils when he smells the musk of "the black bisons of distant Oregon" (169). Thus just as Melville uses prairie analogies to describe magnificent beauty so he uses prairie references to define the "demonism of the world."[30]

Besides using the animals of the prairie to invoke beauty and terror, Melville also uses the featurelessness of the prairie in winter to elaborate his response to whiteness. Thus Ishmael speaks of the mirages created by the continual whiteness of "the scenery of the Antarctic seas" and in turn of "the backwoodsman of the West, who with comparative indifference views an unbounded prairie sheeted with driven snow, no shadow of tree or twig to break the fixed trance of whiteness" (168). After this, Ishmael considers the young Vermont Colt and combines his various examples to explain his per-sonal reaction to whiteness:

> Though thousands of miles from Oregon, still when [the colt] smells that savage musk, the rending, goring bison herds are as present as to the de-serted wild foal of the prairies, which this instant they may be trampling into dust.
>
> Thus, then, the muffled rollings of a milky sea; the bleak rustlings of the festooned frosts of mountains; the desolate shiftings of the windrowed snows of prairies; all these, to Ishmael, are as the shaking of that buffalo robe to the frightened colt! (169)

Melville found in the snow-covered prairie that same quality that Ishmael and Ahab saw in Moby Dick: "a dumb blankness, full of meaning, in a wide landscape of snows" (169). The prairie, when covered with snow, furthermore, presents the same inscrutable visage as Moby Dick; though the backwoodsman might view such a scene with indifference, Ishmael does not: "It was the whiteness of the whale that above all things appalled me" (163).

Melville's greatest emphasis on the featurelessness of the prairie landscape is to be found in the chapter entitled "The Prairie," in which his earlier implicit comparison between the landscape and Moby Dick constitutes his method and concern throughout. The prairie is referred to only in the chapter title, so that Ishmael's discussion of the appearance of a Sperm whale's brow is an extended metaphor. It begins with Ishmael's explanation that he is "but ill qualified for a pioneer" (291), and he then goes on to explain the features of the whale's brow in the way in which travelers and explorers attempted to come to terms with the prairie. Just as they were struck by the lack of landmarks and required a promontory, so he notes the absence of a nose; just as they argued from the known and familiar, so he argues from human physiognomy; and just as they contrasted the featureless prairie with domesticated scenes, so he draws an analogy to landscape gardening, where "a spire, cupola, monument, or tower of some sort, is deemed almost indispensible to the completion of the scene; so no face can be physiognomically in keeping without the elevated open-work belfry of the nose." And finally, just as some of them were able to overcome their esthetic preconceptions and to respond imaginatively to the grandeur of the prairie, so Ishmael is able to pronounce the full frontal nose of a Sperm whale as not only "imposing" but also as "sublime" (291). As for the question of why Melville chose to keep his analogy of the prairie and Moby Dick implicit, perhaps the best answer is to be found in his sense of the similarities between these two majestic natural phenomena: in both equally he found "dumb blankness, full of meaning"—besides, both prairie and Sperm whale were unknown quantities that had no familiar counterparts. In any case, Melville's description of the whale, in conjunction with his discussion of whiteness and reference to the western landscape through *Moby-Dick*, make this sea novel one of the most artistic evocations of the prairie.

Writers from Cooper to Melville were attracted to the prairie landscape by its currency in the national consciousness and used it, ultimately, to stress its imaginative evocativeness, its romantic attraction. Their use of the prairie, like their use of the West generally, is neatly summarized by an observation made by a travel writer of the period, George William Curtis. In his *Lotus Eating* (1852), Curtis observed, "The *idea* of the great western rivers and of lakes as shoreless to the eye as the sea, or of magnificent monotony of grass or forest, is as impressive and much less wearisome than the actual sight of them."[31] Curtis's view is confirmed by Irving's on-the-spot rejection of prairie as a literary landscape and Parkman's tentative, qualified, acceptance. Unhampered by extended prairie experience, Cooper, Bryant, and Poe, as well as Melville and the other writers of the American Renaissance, each in his own way, began to transform the prairie into a literary landscape through their imaginative writings; in doing so, each confirmed Curtis's comment, since their work shows far more rapture over the state of mind the landscape evoked and could be used to symbolize than with the prairie as place.

Early Romances and the Beginnings of Realism

Evocative as Cooper and Melville's uses of the prairie are, they do not offer a setting based on authorial experience. If one turns now to early writers who were really familiar with the landscape, the rough passage of the prairie from a personally felt landscape to literary setting can be seen. Scrutinized closely, the process recapitulates the individual's experience of the prairie as it has been seen in the descriptive texts; like explorers and travelers who responded to the prairie with both romantic elation and realistic displeasure, writers during the latter half of the nineteenth century gravitated between the poles of romance and realism, offering their readers some combination of the two modes. Like Francis Parkman, they were not able to see the landscape as wholly one or the other.

Albert Pike, the first writer of western fiction who had actually been in the area and who had traveled through the prairie, offers the earliest example. After traveling through the prairie he chose as his setting the southwest around Santa Fe, explaining himself in *Prose Sketches and Poems* (1834). There, he registers three stages of response to the prairie. In the first of these his emphasis is upon the absence of life in such a setting:

> Imagine yourself, kind reader, standing in a plain to which your eye can see no bounds. Not a tree, not a bush, not a shrub, not a tall weed lifts its head above the barren grandeur of the desert; not a stone is to be seen on its hard beaten surface; no undulation, no abruptness, no break to relieve the monotony; nothing, save here and there a deep narrow track worn into the hard plain by the constant hoof of the buffalo.[32]

Pike then goes on to present the various animated forms his reader may imagine in such a scene: buffalo, wild horses, antelope, "white, snow-like wolves prowling about," prairie dogs, and "a band of Comanches, mounted on noble swift horses . . .," and concludes: "if you imagine" the Commanches "hovering about in the prairie, chasing the buffalo or attacking an enemy, you have an image of the prairie, such as no book ever described adequately to me" (10). In his final response, however, it is again the "dead quiet" of the landscape which strikes him as the forces of natural elements provide animation. The problem the prairie poses, therefore, is its unprecedented character and its elusive strangeness, one that withholds a concrete impression while imparting a more powerful overall feeling. Like Zebulon Pike, who compared being lost on a frozen and storm-blown lake to being lost on the snow-blown prairie, Albert Pike is forced to confront the play and power of nature amid the prairie landscape. And like Washington Irving, Pike finds his romantic illusions vanishing when he faces the landscape directly:

> Its sublimity arises from its unbounded extent, its barren monotony and desolation, its still, unmoved, calm, stern, almost self-confident grandeur, its strange power of deception, its want of echo, and, in fine, its power of throwing a man back upon himself and giving him a feeling of lone helplessness, strangely mingled at the same time with a feeling of liberty and freedom from restraint. (11)

Here, then, is a likely rationale for Pike's decision to avoid the prairie as setting for his conventionally romantic tales; it has none of the conventional mystery of the Spanish southwest and is, seemingly, inimical to romance, since it both demands and eludes exact description, creating a strong impression while withholding features to which this impression may be attributed. Pike, like Irving and his European allusions, is able to wax romantic over the prairie only by describing the prairie's inhabitants, but these as he realizes are not essential to the landscape. And even such animation as was available on the prairie did not satisfy the requirements of conventional romance, as a review of Irving's *A Tour* suggests: "the mind becomes wearied with the monotony of a journey through the solitudes of the Western Prairies, and after we have once formed a tolerably distinct idea of a buffalo hunt, and the lasoing of the wild horse, we become tired of the repetition of adventures, which possess so little variety."[33]

Pike's experience reflects, as well, on Cooper's *The Prairie,* since his decision not to use the prairie landscape as setting for his fiction further defines the relationship between the prairie landscape, on the one hand, and Cooper's method of landscape depiction versus Irving's on the other. Indeed, judging by the extended hiatus of first-rank prairie fiction between Cooper's novel and Willa Cather's *O Pioneers!* (1913), it might be argued that Cooper had an advantage in never having seen the landscape he used. Thus detached, but with suitable resource material in James's *Account* before him, Cooper imagined a land to suit his needs, unhampered by facts, and so rendered the prairie articulate and symbolic. No subsequent romancer, neither Washington Irving nor Albert Pike, was able to accomplish anything even remotely similar. Nor did they try. Certainly desire, talent, and interest may have kept each of the latter from attempting to use the prairie as fictional setting, but they were hampered, ironically handicapped, by their personal prairie experience. Both men discovered that their desire to see the prairie as a romantic landscape did not make it one, could not make it one; each was faced, in Pike's words, with "a feeling of lone helplessness" which forced romantic illusions to vanish. James Fenimore Cooper, aware of his personal ignorance of the prairie and undaunted by it, consciously strove to accommodate his art to its peculiarities; had he the personal experience of an Irving or a Pike, one wonders if he would have tried.

The first writers to use the prairie as a setting for fiction after Cooper were British tourists who, like Palliser, were sportsmen seeking game in the wilderness of North America. Their first-hand experiences are subordinated to the demands of the conventions of popular romantic fiction, with its hackneyed plots and devices, noble heroes and heroines, and dark villians. A representative example is Charles Augustus Murray's *The Prairie-Bird* (1844). Murray, a wealthy British sportsman, went hunting on the prairie in 1835 and, before trying his hand at fiction, wrote *Travels in North America* (1839). In *The Prairie-Bird* he simply took the ingredients of popular romance and gave them a prairie backdrop.[34] Unlike Murray's romance, George Frederick Ruxton's *Life in the Far West* (1848) does not slavishly follow the conventions of popular romance. During 1846–47, Ruxton hunted in the prairie, lived among mountain men, and spied for the British. Much of *Life* reads like a travel account, rather than a work of fiction; describing the prairie, Ruxton writes that his characters passed through "the beautiful undulating scenery of this park-like country": "The grass was everywhere luxuriously green, and gaudy flowers dotted the surface of the prairie." He then contrasts this area with that farther west, "the flat monotony of the Grand Plains."[35]

Despite the incompatibility of the prairie and the conventions of popular romance to which the work of Murray and Ruxton each in its own way attests, another conventional romancer, Emerson Bennett, sensed no such problem. In *The Prairie Flower* (1849), which is said to have sold over 100,000 copies, he is emphatic about the suitability of the prairie for romance purposes and shows, moreover, Bryant's influence in his landscape descriptions.[36] Yet Bennett's transparently romantic depiction of the prairie landscape attests to the existence in 1849 of conventional modes of presenting the western lands. Although the prairie landscape provided the initial impetus for these conventions, and sustained them briefly, as seen in the writings from Brackenridge to Butler, even the most romantic of temperaments could not render the prairie perpetually exhilarating. Despite the azure of blue sky, monotony eventually breaks in, and when it does, romance vanishes. As such, the empty hollowness of Bennett's unfelt platitudes is deafening; he neither understands nor wishes to understand the land he describes, preferring instead his borrowed conventions.

In the popular fiction written from 1850 through the first two decades of the next century—including adventure stories, juvenile tales, the Dime Novel, and religious polemics—the prairie as setting is typically buried beneath a mound of literary conventions. Only occasionally is it treated in any detail, and most frequently it serves as an exotic locale in which the action takes place, taking the form of a settlement with traces of the frontier (vast unsettled spaces and Indians) still evident. The author's focus is usually upon his characters and their actions; these plots, while not always as hackneyed as Murray's, are spun out with little reference to the landscape in which they take place.[37]

More representative of the popular prairie fiction of the late nineteenth century are the adventure romances written by such men as Sir William Francis Butler, R. M. Ballantyne, Gilbert Parker, and John Mackie, each of whom wrote works set in the prairie North West. Butler's *Red Cloud, The Solitary Sioux* (1882) draws upon his prairie experiences and his understanding of the methods of surviving there, but he simply grafted his romantic plot, involving hunts and escapades, on to those experiences. As a boy, Butler's favorite author was James Fenimore Cooper, and his plot in *Red Cloud* is certainly modelled on that source, even if his knowledge of the locale is not. Thus Butler, who reacted imaginatively to the prairie landscape—in both *The Great Lone Land* and *The Wild North Land*—resembles Murray and Ruxton in that he simply yokes the literary conventions of the popular romance to the landscape. Yet owing to his intimate acquaintance with the prairie, and his evident feelings for it, Butler differs from most other writers of adventure tales. His prairie in *Red Cloud* is a setting, not the convenient backdrop found in similar tales. His more detailed evocation of the land notwithstanding, Butler did not use the prairie in a manner radically different from other authors of the adventure romance. Although at one point in *Red Cloud* his protagonist "felt oppressed by this vague lonely waste," this feeling lasts only "a moment." Irving and Albert Pike reacted favorably to the prairie landscape initially but later reassessed the nature of that first reaction, seeing in the landscape some threatening quality. Butler, as his travel books record, also underwent this experience, yet it is significant that his most extended melancholy musings over the landscape are contained in his travel books, not in *Red Cloud.* Like other writers' works, Butler's novel celebrates the initially romantic reaction to the landscape, its vastness, pristine wildness, and lushness. This is wholly in keeping with the conventional form of the adventure romance, and Butler, intent on a depiction of Red Cloud as the last Sioux to live the nomadic life of his ancestors, does not press on, in fiction, to the more considered reaction to the landscape that prompted him to see in it a "terrible grandeur" as he does in his travel writing.[38]

Not all of the romantic adventure tales set on the prairie were written by Englishmen, however; the popular Canadian writer Sir Gilbert Parker used it in his tales of the Mounted Police. In *Pierre and His People: Tales of the Far North* (1892), Parker's use of the landscape generally lacks specifics; he is content simply to note that his setting is the prairie. In two separate stories, however, the landscape does function organically, though it is most evident in the opening of "A Sanctuary of the Plains." Father Corraine, a priest dwelling alone on the prairie, is staring at the setting winter sun:

> Where the prairie touched the sun it was responsive and radiant; but on
> either side of this red and golden tapestry there was a tawny glow and then a
> duskiness which, curving round to the north and east, became blue and
> cold—an impalpable but perceptible barrier rising from the earth, and shut-
> ting in Father Corraine like a prison wall. And this shadow crept stealthily
> on and invaded the whole circle, until, where radiance had been, there was
> one continuous wall of gloom, rising arc upon arc to invasion of the zenith,
> and pierced only by some intrusive wandering stars.[39]

This passage sets the tone of the story, which concerns Fr. Corraine's sheltering of an outlaw from the Mounted Police and, when discovered by a mountie, the love entanglement that keeps the constable from arresting the culprit. Parker's description of the sunset thus seems to provide both the setting for and the symbol of the moral dilemma about to be faced by the priest. Similarly, as the mountie and his girl ride away from Fr. Corraine, they see him "looking after them; his forehead bared to the clear inspiring wind, his grey hair blown back, his hands clasped. Before descending the trough of a great landwave, they turned for the last time, and saw him standing motionless, the one solitary being in all their wide horizon" (319). Though this is a romantic evocation after the fashion of Cooper, it is also one that is true to the facts of the environment.[40]

To complete this consideration of prairie in romantic formula fiction, nothing is better suited than a passage from that best known American western, Owen Wister's *The Virginian* (1902). Alighting from a train in Medicine Bow, Wyoming, after his trip across the prairie, Wister's eastern narrator comments:

> Town, as they called it, pleased me the less, the longer I saw it. . . . I have seen and slept in many like it since. Scattered wide, they littered the frontier from the Columbia to the Rio Grande, from the Missouri to the Sierras. They lay stark, dotted over a planet of treeless dust, like soiled packs of cards. Each was similar to the next, as one old five-spot of clubs resembles another. Houses, empty bottles, and garbage, they were forever of the same shapeless pattern. More forlorn they were than stale bones. They seemed to have been strewn there by the wind and to be waiting until the wind should come again and blow them away.

Despite the romanticism of the book, reality asserts itself here through the harshness of prairie conditions. Conversely, the general starkness of this passage is assuaged, since Wister seems reluctant to give up his romantic illusions and concludes that the starkness is a mirage, and that the town's true ambience is Edenic still: "Yet serene above their foulness swam a pure and quiet light, such as the East never sees; they might be bathing in the air of creation's first morning. Beneath sun and stars their days and nights were immaculate and wonderful."[41] Finally, Wister establishes the initial contrast between the towns and the plains through the application to the former of the very feature of the prairie that had disconcerted other travelers—"The same shapeless pattern."

With its curious tensions and reversals, therefore, this passage from *The Virginian* illuminates a key feature of nineteenth-century prairie fiction. Like the pioneers who came west, the writers on the prairie expected to find a new romantic country. What they found was frequently a landscape that, initially, they thought romantic, eventually coming to recognize it as dull, monotonous, or threatening. Similarly, in the development of prairie fiction there is a strain of the romantic existing side by side with an equally strong reaction that could be called the realistic—a duality that can be traced back to the first explorers: the French, by reason of their mode of travel, tended toward romantic wistfulness in viewing the landscape; traveling overland, the Spaniards—and to a lesser extent, the British—were inclined to see the prairie in a harsher light. Temperament very often governed reaction to the landscape, and those with romantic tendencies usually retained their favorable impressions until they were deflated by prolonged or particularly intense exposure to harsh conditions as with Brackenridge, Catlin, Albert Pike, Irving, and Parkman. *The Prairie* makes vivid the romantic conception of Natty Bumppo by the factuality of Edwin James's observations, though to be sure Cooper accomplishes this, in part, because of his lack of prairie experience. And the writers of the American Renaissance took solace in the prairie as a romantic, imaginative ideal. Later popular writers tend to see the landscape romantically, although in many of their works a darker, more realistic reaction to it is also evident. Conversely, as we shall now see, those writers who emphasized the realistic in their depictions of the prairie equally reveal a strong undercurrent of romanticism.

Before turning to these writers, however, some mention must be made of Mark Twain, whose *Roughing It* (1872) stands somewhere between the puerile sentimentality of the prairie romancers and the bitter melancholy of the realists. While the former revealed a superficial reaction to the prairie or ignored the landscape altogether, and the latter dwelt upon the harshness of life on the prairie, Twain struck a paradoxical middle course: he used realism to undercut his romanticism, but ultimately he took refuge in humor. And, as critics have recently argued, Twain's dilemma was caused by the landscape itself. Thus Stephen Fender writes: "To Samuel Clemens the geographical West was preeminently a place without history, with no integral culture, no roots—an absurd physical and social landscape," so "He lit out for the States." Similarly, Patricia Nelson Limerick says "When dust, heat, duration and monotony combined on the side of reality, romance had a few resources to draw on for its defense."[42] As such, Twain's problem in confronting the weird landscapes of the West—gravitating between romance and realism—suggests the inherent difficulty posed by the prairie landscape itself, and seen in first-person descriptions back to Castañeda.

Twain's book is based on his western trip, undertaken in July 1861 when he accompanied his brother Orion, who was taking up his post as Secretary of the Nevada Territory. Only the early parts deal with the prairie, since the protagonists travel by stage from western Missouri up the Platte Valley to the Black Hills and thence over the Rockies. The balance mainly deals with the Nevada Territory. For Twain's protagonists, who are traveling cross-country on a newly opened stage route, the Great Plains of Kansas lack all variety. Twain's narrator lends his particular deflating twist in his concluding exclamation: "But presently this sea upon dry ground was to lose its 'rolling' character and stretch away for seven hundred miles as level as a floor!"[43] Twain then alludes to this unromantic analogy repeatedly as his characters ride across the plains for several days and nights, their ride broken only occasionally by a sudden descent and then ascent of the banks of a watercourse.

At times, however, the narrator's reaction to the prairie is as positive and unqualified as Huckleberry Finn's response to nature, and gives us some idea of what Huck expected to find in "the Territories":

> It was another glad awakening to fresh breezes, vast expanses of level greens-ward, bright sunlight, an impressive solitude utterly without visible human beings or human habitations, and an atmosphere of such amazing magnify-ing properties that trees that seemed close at hand were more than three miles away.

And in retrospect the narrator concludes: "Even at this day it thrills me through and through to think of the life, the gladness, and the wild sense of freedom that used to make the blood dance in my veins on those fine overland mornings!" (66). Twain emphasizes here, as do the other romantic commenta-tors, the "uplifting" properties of the landscape as it is first seen, and the net result of such contact is similarly to make a sojourn in town "strange enough" after "such a long acquaintance with deep, still, almost lifeless and houseless solitude!" (75).

Prairie Realism

Twain's ambivalent reaction to the west and its landscapes reflects the growing force of literary realism in post–Civil War America. Though the role of western writers in this movement—Edward Eggleston, E. W. Howe, Joseph Kirkland, W. D. Howells, and Hamlin Garland—is well documented, critics have tended to concentrate on the shift in the depiction of character and mode of life—from the romantic yeoman living a rustic life to the actual farmer leading a hard life of isolation—without noting the extent to which this shift constituted the literary parallel to the individual's experience of the western landscape as seen in Irving, Albert Pike, and Francis Parkman, and others. Julie Roy Jeffrey has made the point succinctly:

> One of the differences between passing through the plains and settling there was visual. The traveler experienced the landscape as an ever-changing panorama. . . . The settler, fixed in one place, saw only the change of the season and the changes wrought by human hands. A view monotonous one

day would most likely be monotonous the next. What for some was a scenic backdrop for a journey became for others the stage for everyday activities. Involvement with nature replaced casual interest or romantic rhapsody.[44]

As the realists and their successors took up the prairie landscape as setting for their fiction, the ways in which characters' depicted "involvement with nature" became crucial as writers gravitated between the elation/deflation poles of prairie landscape response. Just as early travelers could not sustain their initial romantic reactions to the landscape, so too realistic writers could not sustain the informing pioneer myths that dictated the beneficent view of life in rural America, whether on the farm or in the small town; their own experience indicated otherwise, as did Irving's and Parkman's when they found themselves lost on the prairie.

The grimness that pervades E. W. Howe's *The Story of a Country Town* (1883) has since been echoed in numerous similar and more famous portrayals of life in a small prairie town; Howe's Fairview, Missouri, has had more famous successors in Gopher Prairie and Horizon, yet he was the first to depict the prairie as a settled landscape.[45] Early in the novel the narrator, Ned Westlock, comments: "Ours was the prairie district out West, where we had gone to grow up with the country" (7). This fact, which is repeated and alluded to throughout *The Story,* evokes the romance of pioneering, but it is opposed by the bleak picture of small-town prairie life that Ned Westlock presents. As indicated by the surname of the protagonist, Howe juxtaposes the romantic hope of the pioneer (the West) with the grim bleakness (lock) he finds on the prairie.

Early in the novel, Howe offers his central symbol, one highlighted by the flatness of the surrounding landscape:

> On the highest and bleakest point in the country, where the winds were plenty in winter because they were not needed, and scarce in summer for the opposite reason, the meeting-house was built, in a corner of my father's field. This was called Fairview, and so the neighborhood was known. There was a graveyard around it, and cornfields next to that, but not a tree or scrub attempted its ornament, and as the building stood on the main road where the movers' wagons passed, I thought that, next to their ambition to get away from the country which had been left by those in Fairview, the movers were anxious to get away from Fairview church, and avoid the possibility of being buried in its ugly shadow, for they always seemed to drive faster after passing it. (8–9)

Throughout the novel, and as an opening and closing symbol that is rooted in the book's theme of self-denial, the church's steeple looms over the populace in the same manner as its minister, John Westlock, looms over his son. After telling his tale of frustrated desire and unanswered opportunity, Howe closes the novel with this same symbol. So while Howe does not directly invoke the prairie landscape in *The Story of a Country Town,* his primary symbol stands above and encompasses all those whose empty lives are lived below, affected only by the wind. Unlike Alexander Henry's raised perspective from his oak tree, however, Howe's steeple reverses the effect of getting above the prairie landscape; whereas Henry's tree allowed him to dominate the prairie, the steeple dominates the lives of those below.

To a far greater degree than Howe's novel, Joseph Kirkland's *Zury: The Meanest Man in Spring County* (1887) juxtaposes the romantic hopes of the pioneer and the equally romantic view of the prairie as the garden of the world, against its realities. Kirkland, the son of Caroline Kirkland, continued his mother's work by depicting pioneer conditions, but his frontier was Illinois, where he settled in 1855. Not a farmer himself, Kirkland traveled widely throughout the state prior to the Civil War and saw the pioneer growth he would later depict in *Zury.*[46]

Kirkland's Zury (short for Usury) Prouder contrasts with Ned Westlock; the former lives the pioneer experience on the prairie—since his family depends on him from the time they arrive in Illinois. Ned, on the other hand, is an observer who lives in towns and merely watches others break and transform the prairie landscape. Forced by the harshness of the first prairie winter to take over the leadership of the family from his ineffectual father, Zury throws himself into a battle with the land—and succeeds by bending its elements to his purposes, eventually becoming the most prosperous resident of the district. This action becomes characteristic, for once he has subdued the land, Zury defies local corrupt politics and, later, the rapaciousness of his own character. Thus his initial confrontation with the land as a young man establishes Zury's mode of behavior throughout the novel until he is rejected by a woman he seeks; until then Zury approaches all affairs—as he did that first Illinois prairie winter—as confrontations.

The prairie landscape figures directly only in the very beginning of the book, however, where Kirkland contrasts its romantic potential with its harsh realities, suggesting, in the process, that its harshness produces noble men. Through his description of the Prouders and their prairie schooner, Kirkland presents the family as representative pioneers, a part of the larger migration. He also places considerable emphasis on the fecundity of the land, noting the various grasses and plants that flourish and trees that will flourish, once planted. Just before the family locates its claim on the edge of the "Grand Prairie," Kirkland comments that "Spring County is one of those highly-prized and early-sought-for localities where both prairie and timber awaited the settler."[47] With both wood and open land available, the Prouders appear to be entering a type of western Eden.

When the Prouders finally reach their land, Zury's mother, Selina "looked about her at forest and prairie and sky and solitude" and "heaved a deep, unconscious sigh" (11), over what she has seen:

> Under the warm afternoon sun, which was already sinking in the yellow western glow of a great, cloudless sky, lay an undulating ocean of grass and flowers. In places, where an inequality of the surface brought them into perspective range, the "prairie flowers" (blue gentian) gave to the whole sward a tinge of pale azure; here and there a tall "rosin weed" would raise its spike of bloom; and again, the golden-rod gave the needed "dash of color". . . .
> Among, between, and around them was the persistent, peculiar prairie grass, a hardy, seedless growth that spreads only by pushing out its intricate, interlacing roots; tenacious of life, and resisting drought and even fire with wonderful hardihood, but never deigning to reëstablish itself after its chosen place has been desecrated by the plow. (9–10)

Here is the prairie in the best romantic tradition: bathed in the golden light of a setting sun, an ocean of herbage, the apotheosis of fecundity: Eden. While Selina's is the usual reaction of the settler gazing upon a family homestead for the first time, and while this description is in keeping with previous literary presentations of the landscape, Kirkland is also employing point of view. He uses the normal first-person reaction to the landscape as a literary technique; Selina sighs over this vision of Eden, but the Prouders' actual experience on their new homestead is considerably less inviting. Zury's younger sister sickens, dies, and so begins a litany of misfortunes suffered by the family. Kirkland begins with the edenic archetype—which Annette Kolodny sees as a characteristic reaction of women to the prairie—only to destroy its pristine qualities by way of the Prouders' harsh experiences. His realistic method not only shows the influence of his mother, Caroline Kirkland—as Kolodny also argues—it bears out the usual elation/deflation reaction caused by the prairie landscape.

Just as Irving and Parkman were forced to reckon imaginatively with the prairie landscape when they were lost on it, realists like Howe and Kirkland were moved by first-hand experience to articulate a vision of the land and life on it which ran counter to the prevailing romantic myth of pioneering. They attempted to recreate for readers a pioneer's first exhilaration, followed by his ensuing deflation and struggles. Owing to his negative view of life in a small prairie town, Howe embodies the romantic view of the prairie in a single phrase—"we had gone to grow up with the country"—and even this refrain suggests a sense of wasted potential. Kirkland, less bleak but equally realistic, recreates for his readers Selina Prouder's golden first vision of their homestead, but follows this almost immediately with the death of her daughter. Still, the realists let go of their romantic image of the new prairie land only gradually. Their overall treatment of the landscape in fiction is like the individual's as seen in the travel and other first-person accounts: ambivalent, an alternation between imaginative ecstasy and caustic factuality—Edmund Flagg's reaction versus John Lambert's, or Brackenridges's versus Castañeda's, as it were.

Such is the case even with a writer as pessimistic as Hamlin Garland; however bitter, his writing has an undercurrent of nostalgia and, when writing of the Dakota prairie, it is informed as well with the image of the new land, once the home of buffalo and now the site of settlement. Garland characteristically uses realistic depiction, with little romanticizing, of the life of the western farmer. Lincoln, his protagonist in *Boy Life on the Prairie* (1899), for example, marvels at the surrounding prairie; upon moving there from Wisconsin, he "climbed to the roof of the house, and was still trying to comprehend this mighty stretch of grasses."[48] The nostalgic air of the book as a whole celebrates the pioneer experience, yet Garland's romantic vision is derived as much from his subject as it is his view of the land. Describing the experiences of a boy on the prairie his view of the land corresponds to the boy's innocence and delight of discovery. Lincoln—a name replete with pioneering connotations—is the archetypal American boy discovering the potential of the prairie West. Yet even in those works where Garland's subject does not dictate a romantic cast to the land, such a view persists.

The prairie often serves as the backdrop for his bitter polemics in the stories collected in *Main-Travelled Roads* (1891), *Prairie Folks* (1893), and *Other Main-Travelled Roads* (1910). Within these stories two opposing views of the prairie landscape predominate, both of which are seen in one of the original *Main-Travelled Roads* stories, "Among the Corn Rows." The tale concerns the determination of a young man from Wisconsin, who has taken a claim on the Dakota prairie, to return home to find and marry a wife within ten days. But before developing this plot, Garland introduces a local newspaper editor, Seagraves, who has a claim next to the protagonist's. Early in the story, Seagraves meditates on the landscape, noting in great detail its various qualities, and concludes: "No other climate, sky, plain could produce the same unnamable weird charm. No tree to wave, no grass to rustle, scarcely a sound of domestic life; only the faint melancholy soughing of the wind in the short grass, and the voices of the wild things of the prairie."[49] Seagraves's view of the landscape here is the prairie first glimpsed, seen in the most favorable light and season. And he is attracted to the land's "weird charm," a charm owing in large measure to the wildness of the land, the absence of man's domesticating nature. Though attracted by the landscape, however, Seagraves is aware that this same place, under a different guise, elicits a quite different reaction:

> The silence of the prairie at night was well-nigh terrible. Many a night, as Seagraves lay in his bunk against the side of his cabin, he would strain his ear to hear the slightest sound, and be listening thus sometimes for minutes before the squeak of a mouse or the step of a passing fox came as a relief to the aching sense. (87)

Seagraves is not central to the action of "Among the Corn Rows"; his role in the story is mainly to serve as a complement to the protagonist, apparently because Garland needed to justify his character's haste for a wife: to share the loneliness of the prairie. But the man's inarticulate character makes him an unfit consciousness for such musings; Seagraves, as a newspaperman, is more appropriate. A clumsy technique at best, Garland's use of a supporting character suggests his awareness that he had to account for the land's effect upon his protagonist, and that he felt a need to do so in some detail.

In *The Moccasin Ranch: A Story of Dakota* (1909), one of Garland's lesser-known works, he accords the prairie its most extensive and detailed treatment since Cooper. As in *The Prairie,* the setting is well articulated and symbolic. The book chronicles the settlers' excited reaction to their new habitat and, once they have stayed for a while, it charts their changed perception of the land as the excitement wears off. This transformation causes the central conflict which, in turn, is articulated by Garland's description of the prairie landscape.

The plot of Garland's story stretches from March to December, and primarily involves the relations of four people: Willard and Blanche Burke, newly removed from Illinois, who have come to Dakota to take up a claim far out on the prairie, accompanied by Rob Rivers and Jim Bailey, partners in a general store and land agents for the area in which the Burkes settle. Blanche Burke does not take to life in a shanty on the prairie and, responding to the attentions paid her by Bailey, she becomes pregnant by and runs off with him. Because they are forced to take refuge from a blizzard in the partners' store, Rivers learns of their resolve and attempts for a time to stop them; he drops his objections, however, after meditating over the hardships prairie life forces on women, though he subsequently resolves to bring his own sweetheart to the prairie.

Stripped thus to bare bones of plot, the story does not sound particularly promising; nor, as a story, is it. But at each point in the tale Garland makes his characters' relations and responses articulate through his use of the surrounding landscape. As the two wagons head west out of Boomtown, Dakota, at dawn, Garland describes the scene in a way that encapsulates and verifies 350 years of prairie description:

> As the sun rose, a kind of transformation-scene took place. The whole level land lifted at the horizon till the teams seemed crawling forever at the bottom of an enormous bowl. Mystical forms came into view—grotesquely elongated, unrecognizable. Hills twenty, thirty miles away rose like apparitions, astonishingly magnified. Willows became elms, a settler's shanty rose like a shot-tower—towns hitherto unseen swam and palpitated in the yellow flood of light like shaken banners low-hung on unseen flagstaffs.[50]

After the fashion of Cooper, Garland here introduces the landscape before the characters. Perhaps unknowingly, he also echoes James, Gregg, and Lambert on the prairie mirage, and Catlin's sense that traveling on the prairie makes one feel "like a squirrel in his cage." Garland's "enormous bowl" metaphor, moreover, is exactly that used by Castañeda when he spoke of looking at the prairie sky as if he were gazing up from the bottom of a "three-pint measure."

The response of Garland's characters to this scene is also of the kind encountered in previous accounts of the prairie:

> Burke marched with uplifted face. He was like one suddenly wakened into a new world, where nothing was familiar. Not a tree or scrub was in sight. Not a mark of plough or harrow—everything was wild, and to him mystical and glorious. His eyes were like those of a man who sees the world at its birth. (4)

Burke's amazed incredulity is the same as that seen in Castañeda and Kirkland's Selina, and, like Wister's evocation of the Eden archetype in *The Virginian,* Burke is presented as an Adamic figure. Later, as he and his wife prepare to sleep that evening, Burke senses, like Melville's Ishmael, the more terrifying side of this sublime setting: he "*felt* the silence and immensity of the plain outside. It was enormous, incredible in its wildness" (16–17). Accounting in part for this second reaction may have been the tedium of prairie travel:

> Hour after hour they moved across the swelling land. Hour after hour,
> while the yellow sun rolled up the slope, putting to flight the morning
> shapes on the horizon—striking the plain into level prose again, and warm-
> ing the air into genial March. Hour after hour the horses toiled on till the
> last cabin fell away to the east, like a sail at sea, till the road faded into a
> trail almost imperceptible on the firm sod. (4–5)

The technique and style of this passage stand in contrast to the poetic
description of early morning shadows and the prairie mirage that precedes it.
There the landscape presents a visage that piques the imagination. Here, on
the other hand, the grotesquely engaging shapes of early morning have given
way to the monotonous clarity of late morning, noon, and afternoon. Garland's descriptive technique defines the tedium of overland prairie travel in his
repetition of "Hour after hour," accentuated by an awareness that his characters are entering country where they will be isolated: the final cabin that "falls"
away "like a sail at sea" and later the road that fades away. His description of
the effect of the sun rising above the prairie—"striking the plain into level
prose"—is significant in that it suggests an organic relationship between style
and setting: the flat prairie at midday demands prose and a level style in
contrast to the more poetic and romantic style required to depict the morning.
This shift is, of course, the literary equivalent to the elation/deflation experiences of prairie explorers and travelers.

The Burkes, Garland's protagonists, are representative settlers in Dakota;
all around them others come to stake their claims and await the government
surveyors so that they may enter their deeds. In capturing the jubilant
expectation of the settlers Garland indulges in pathetic fallacy:

> And, then, all was so new and beautiful, and the sky was so clear. Oh,
> that marvellous, lofty sky with just cloud enough to make the blue more in-
> tense! Oh, the wonder of the wind from the wild, mysterious green sea to
> the west! With the change and sheen of the prairie, incessant and magical
> life was made marvellous and the winter put far away. (31–32)

On the one hand, as such a passage suggests, the season is responsible for
the negative response to the landscape; on the other hand, the setting has, in
fact, lost its freshness:

> By the first of November the wonder had gone out of the life of the set-
> tlers. One by one the novelties and beauties of the plain had passed away or
> grown familiar. The plover and blackbird fell silent. The prairie-chicken's

piping cry ceased as the flocks grew toward maturity, and the lark and
cricket alone possessed the russet plain, which seemed to snap and crackle in
the midnight frost, and to wither away in the bright midday sun. (67–68)

As he goes on to describe the increasing disaffection of the settlers, Garland
focuses the discontent in the reaction of women:

> The vast, treeless level, so alluring in May and June, had become an op-
> pressive weight to those most sensitive to the weather, and as the air grew
> chill and the skies overcast, the women turned with apprehensive faces to the
> untracked northwest, out of which the winds swept pitilessly cold and keen.
> (68–69)

By focusing upon women's reactions, Garland nicely interweaves his general
and specific concerns, for it is through Blanche Burke that the growing
aversion to the landscape is made particular.

Unlike her husband's reaction, Blanche's first impression of the prairie
landscape is not positive; she had consented to leave Illinois only reluctantly
and, after the party had traveled most of the day across the prairie, Will Burke
asks his wife what she thinks of the country they had traveled through that
day. "Not very much" (8) is her reply. Her aversion to a home on the prairie
becomes so acute by December, in fact, that she flees, as much from the prairie
landscape as from her husband. In charting Blanche's growing desperation,
Garland uses the landscape as a symbolic index to her state of mind, and he
makes it clear that Blanche is but one woman among many:

> Now the wind had dominion over the lonely women, wearing out their
> souls with its melancholy moanings and its vast and wordless sighs. Its
> voices seemed to enter Blanche Burke's soul, filling it with hunger never felt
> before. Day after day it moaned in her ears and wailed about the little cabin,
> rousing within her formless desires and bitter despairs. Obscure emotions,
> unused powers of reason and recollection came to her. (70–71)

Thus, Blanche is alone in her sod hut, spending "hours by the window
watching, waiting, gazing at the moveless sod, listening to the wind-voices,
companioned only by her memories." Not surprisingly Blanche rails at Will,
seeing their emigration as a "bitter mistake" (71).

Following a brief midwinter visit to town, Blanche is downcast when the
hour comes for their return journey. In its winter strangeness, the prairie is a

prison for the settlers, most of whom "were from the wooded lands of the East, and the sweep of the wind across this level sod had a terror which made them quake and cower" (86). As the winter deepens, each sod dugout becomes more and more cavelike:

> There were many days when the sun shone, but the snow slid across the plain with a menacing, hissing sound, and the sky was milky with flying frost, and the horizon looked cold and wild; but these were merely the pauses between storms. The utter dryness of the flakes and the never-resting progress of the winds kept the drifts shifting, shifting. (87–88)

Garland focuses the malaise engendered by the prairie landscape on Blanche, and she in turn manifests the primary reaction to prairie isolation, and especially to the never-ceasing wind. During an argument in December, Blanche exclaims "If I'd had any word to say about it, we never'd 'a' been out in this Godforsaken country" (88); immediately after, she punctuates this with "Oh, this wind will drive me crazy!" (89). As her husband prepares to go to a neighbor's because their supply of flour is low, his wife hears the wind,

> piping a high-keyed, mourning note on the chimney-top, a sound that rang echoing down through every hidden recess of her brain, shaking her, weakening her, till at last she turned to her husband with wild eyes. "Take me with you! I can't stay here any longer—I shall go crazy!" (89–90)

To be sure, Blanche's desperation is caused, in part, by her awareness that she is carrying a child fathered by Jim Bailey, who has been paying obvious attentions to her from her arrival on the prairie; but the wind, and the landscape that allows such wind, is the symbol of her plight. Blanche's desperation, indeed, lends ironic resonance to the prairie; before they went to sleep their first night on the prairie, Blanche had said "Isn't it wonderful . . . It's all so strange, like being out of the world, someway" (16). When she made this comment, Blanche defined an initial fascination with the prairie that exists side by side with her revulsion. In December, the reader sees, her earlier statement has become poignant: Blanche literally feels as if she is in an alien place.

Blanche Burke does not go to the neighbor's with her husband, however, and shortly after he leaves, Jim Bailey arrives. She tells him of her pregnancy and of her resolve to flee the prairie at once. Hearing this, he agrees to go with her. Their flight is delayed, though, by the bitterness of the storm, and they are forced to take refuge in Bailey and Rivers's store. Upon realizing what his partner intends, Rivers resolves not to allow him to undertake an immoral act. The point is moot, however, for the fury of the storm precludes traveling for two days—enough time for Rivers to reconsider—and time enough for Garland to use the raging storm as a symbolic counterpart of his characters' emotional struggles:

> Outside the warring winds howled on. The eye could not penetrate the veils of snow which streamed through the air on level lines. The powdered ice rose from the ground in waves which buffeted one another and fell in spray, only to rise again in ceaseless, tumultuous action. There was no sky and no earth. Everything slid, sifted, drifted, or madly swirled. (121–22)

More than simply a symbolic counterpart, however, the storm is also the factor that compounds the emotional situation and is, through its infuriating continuance, the cause of it.

At the same time, ironically, the analogous relation of the outside and inside enables Blanche to appreciate the sublimity of this prairie phenomenon:

> The strain upon her was twisting her toward insanity. The never-resting wind appalled her. It was like the iron resolution of the two men. She saw no end to this elemental strife. It was the cyclone of July frozen into snow, only more relentless, more persistent—a tornado of frost. It filled her with such awe as she had never felt before. (124)

Conversely, Rivers's contemplation of the storm enables him to see the morality of the human situation in a different light, a way that in turn occasions him to resolve not to impede the adulterous lovers. Notwithstanding the plot's melodrama, Garland uses the prairie quite effectively in *The Moccasin Ranch.* He is far more immediate in his treatment of his subject here than he is in many of his polemical *Main-Travelled Roads* stories. And in Blanche Burke's dissatisfaction with prairie isolation, Garland much more effectively treats one of the psychological results of rural western life—the very effects that concern him in his polemics.

A Canadian counterpart to Garland is Arthur Stringer, who from 1899 through 1940 wrote numerous popular romantic novels dealing mainly with crime and adventure. Among them is his prairie trilogy—*The Prairie Wife* (1915), *The Prairie Mother* (1920), and *The Prairie Child* (1922)—which grew out of his experiences as a rancher in southern Alberta. The narrator of the trilogy is Chaddie McKail, an American socialite who, through marriage to a

"Scotch-Canadian," Duncan Argyll McKail, is suddenly transported to his none-too-luxurious ranch on the Alberta prairie. Their relationship is tempestuous, and the various dislocations between husband and wife provide the substance of Stringer's plots, which are his main concern. As in *The Moccasin Ranch,* the contrast between Chaddie's previous life in the east and her life on the prairie—active society versus almost absolute isolation—accentuates the land's effect on women. Chaddie is, moreover, the first female protagonist in a prairie novel. Stringer's adoption of the female point of view suggests sympathy for pioneer wives similar to Garland; Chaddie, like Blanche, seems trapped between the walls of her homestead and, also like her, must adapt to radically new conditions. Her reactions to the landscape vary between romantic exhilaration and despondency. Upon arriving at the McKail's homestead and being summarily left by Duncan who has business in Calgary, Chaddie notes" "I became nervously conscious of the unbroken silence about me. . . ."[51] Yet shortly after, her reaction to the landscape is romantically effusive, after the fashion of Flagg or Bennett. Later, however, she and Duncan stop and look at their place from a distance: "I could see our shack from miles off, a little lonely dot of black against the sky-line. . . . It seemed so tiny, so lonely, so strange, in the middle of such miles and miles of emptiness, with a little rift of smoke going up from its desolate little pipe-end" (71). Though passages such as these establish Chaddie's various moods, they also serve to define the landscape which gives rise to them.

As the trilogy progresses and the relations between the McKails become more problematic, instances of Chaddie's enthusiasm for her surroundings become less frequent—she is busy raising her children and trying to keep her husband. Midway through *The Prairie Mother,* however, just as she is most uncertain of whether or not she will be able to entice Duncan to return, Chaddie climbs above her farm for perspective; having had her windmill repaired and reerected once more, Chaddie climbs it, and through its elevated view is able to renew something of her previous enthusiasm for the landscape. She feels "like an eagle poised giddily above the world."[52] The area around the base of the windmill, however, presents a less pleasing sight: "As I stared down at the roof of our shack it looked small and pitiful, tragically meager to house the tangled human destinies it was housing" (237–38). Like Garland, Stringer sees nature and human nature as related, and both suggest that the cause of tragedy is confinement. The contrast Chaddie sees here, between the glory of the far-distance and the grim pathos of the family's situation as reflected in the alien quality of their shack amid the surrounding fields, motivates her to take action. She resolves to effect Duncan's return to the family, and to improve their fortunes. Stringer uses the prairie landscape here as a catalyst. It presents Chaddie with a view of romantic potential and grim reality, and in the face of such a contrast Chaddie makes her choice. Her time on the windmill is an interlude from the world, and as she makes her way down, Stringer emphasizes her changed perspective. Before she found the golden prairie to be some distance from her; after weighing the two scenes, Chaddie looks down and comments that the world to which she has to return seems "a long way off" (244). In Stringer's *The Prairie Wife* and *The Prairie Mother,* as in much of Garland's work, and *The Moccasin Ranch* in particular, the prairie landscape operates as an informing presence; it serves to articulate both character and theme. Their techniques mix romance and realism, offering a dialectic that recapitulates individual reactions to the prairie itself.

Given the importance of gender-based differences to this study, Garland's apparent motives for focusing so sharply on Blanche need to be elaborated; they, in turn, apply equally well—if not as specifically—to Kirkland and Stringer. Among Garland critics, only Frances W. Kaye has taken up his depiction of women, and then without reference to *The Moccasin Ranch.* She suggests an Oedipal motivation on Garland's part, whereby as the man of culture—"woman's man,"—he triumphed over his farmer father—"man's man"—by being able to buy his mother a house in Wisconsin so that she no longer had to follow her husband's wanderings in search of better lands. This suggests that Garland was motivated primarily by a desire to prove himself, and his mother was an object of sympathy.[53]

Despite her moral transgressions, Blanche is portrayed in *The Moccasin Ranch* with considerable sympathy; except initially, when she calls Dakota "wonderful" and likens it to "being out of the world," Blanche does not share her husband's positive response to Dakota as Eden. As Annette Kolodny might put it, she is an unwilling Eve to his Adam. Here, it seems, is the salient gender difference: unlike the women writers discussed in *The Land Before Her,* Garland can only view pioneer women from the outside—as a man who watched his own mother's difficulties as his father moved the family throughout the west, Garland can only sympathize, he cannot empathize. Thus he views characters like Blanche as objects for his sympathy, and portrays them as such. Given the social roles of the times these women sometimes were, like his mother, pathetic figures yoked by marriage bonds to their husbands' wanderlust. Their men were driven to emigrate by social factors that inspired what historian John Mack Faragher has called an "archetypal nineteenth-century event . . ."; emigration was "infused and overlaid with male projections and identifications." At the same time, Faragher notes women's very different values as they accompanied their men:

> The analysis of the [trail] diary writing suggests again that essentially different social situations of men and women were associated with different cul-

tural phenomena. The men's world was made of the stuff of action, a world of closely shared identifications, expectations, and assumptions. In the standardized and even ritualized behavior of men lay the ability to communicate without verbal expression. . . . For women, however, articulation was at the very heart of their world, for verbal expression could achieve an interpersonal closeness that was socially denied by the exclusion of women from the public world and their isolation at home.[54]

Such personal needs were, of course, extremely difficult to meet during emigration and pioneering. The hardships women endured led, through the memories of their sons, Kirkland and Garland among them, to the creation of fictional characters like Blanche Burke and the far more well-known Beret Holm of O. E. Rölvaag's *Giants in the Earth.* Such portrayals have in turn fostered a stereotype of frontier women driven mad by the conditions of pioneering.

But despite Garland's articulate sympathy for women like his mother in *The Moccasin Ranch,* there appears to be little reason to accept the stereotype such writing created. Without question, the subordination of women's domestic values during the pioneering years—by rough living conditions in shack or dugout, lack of cultural amenities, and, most especially, infrequent contact with other women—was most evident on the prairie, to be sure, where each glance at the horizon reminded women of their isolation. Yet even so, such conditions did not persist as the years passed; as Sandra L. Myres has argued, the question of women's adaptation to the frontier—mountain and valley as well as prairie—is more complicated than fictional portrayals allow. In actual fact, she writes,

> usually women's isolation was more perceived than real. The physical isolation imposed by distance or weather soon came to an end; new settlers arrived; the comforting sight of smoke from a neighboring cabin could be seen on the horizon; the long winters ended; spring came again. But isolation and loneliness were not the same thing. Frontier women were rarely isolated from people; they were surrounded by husband, children, hired hands, often Indians or other native people; but they still were lonely. They missed their old companions and family members. They gazed out across the seemingly endless stretches of prairies and plains and recalled the green, well-watered valleys of the East; they stared at the great mountains and virgin forests and remembered the New England villages, the gentle rolling prairies of the Midwest. Without rejecting their new homes and new friends, they longed for the old and familiar. As one reads their letters and diaries, one is struck

by the frequency of comments about new friends, new delights in Western life juxtaposed with sad yearnings for home and family and bitter cries of loneliness, homesickness, and depression.[55]

Though quoted at length, Myres's historically based generalization lends necessary perspective on the prairie writings of the realist era. Men like Kirkland, Garland, and Stringer could only see the women's plight in prairie pioneering from the outside; they sympathized, and in Garland's case had other motives as well for besting his father, as Kaye has argued, but the stereotypical image of frontier wives as frightened drudges, left "twisting toward insanity" by the prairie landscape in isolated farmhouses, needs to be treated skeptically. Without question, these male writers were the first—after Cooper—to seize upon the dramatic possibilities of the prairie landscape in a sustained manner and, especially in *The Moccasin Ranch,* employ them effectively, yet the stereotypical treatment of women—however well motivated—leaves their fiction falling short of accomplished artistry.

Even so, the work of Garland and Stringer exemplifies a continuity in the literary depiction of the prairie beginning with James Fenimore Cooper. Throughout these works the prairie engendered certain imaginative effects and through them dictated the terms of its usage as a literary setting. As Cooper and Melville demonstrate, the landscape's allure was paradoxically (and inescapably) both attracting and repelling. And Albert Pike, through his rejection of the prairie as setting, confirms the difficulties posed by the prairie as a literary landscape, finding in it two coequal underlying qualities that could not be ignored. Romantic writers—once they had been there—could not deny the landscape's "power of throwing a man back upon himself" and, as literary fashions changed, their successors, the realists, were equally unable to deny its power to generate "a feeling of liberty and freedom from restraint" (Pike, 16). Thus, as a battleground of romance and realism in the nineteenth century, the prairie landscape dictated its terms by enforcing its peculiar imaginative demands—requirements that are rooted in descriptive writing from Castañeda on—and creative writers, like painters, were forced to adapt their artistic techniques as the vast space of the prairie landscape held its sway.

4

Luminous Landscape:
Prairie Pioneering

Toward the end of the first part of *O Pioneers!* (1913), in the process of describing Alexandra Bergson's newfound feelings for the "The Wild Land" of the Nebraska prairie, Willa Cather observes that "For the first time, perhaps, since that land emerged from the waters of geologic ages, a human face was set toward it with love and yearning."[1] As has often been suggested, this passage defines the essential relationship in the novel, that between Alexandra and the prairie. In a larger sense, however, it also defines the model tale of prairie fiction: pioneering, settling the land, inhabiting it, coming to terms with it. Throughout the nineteenth century, of course, writers from Cooper to Garland and Stringer were concerned with pioneering; it undergirds their fictions, even if they are not literally about settlement. Their stories about pioneering, often sentimental and melodramatic as in *The Moccasin Ranch* or *The Prairie Wife,* perhaps, define and detail pioneers' experiences, and reflect their sense of the new land. Not until Cather's *O Pioneers!* and the novels that follow in its wake, though, do we find a genuine prairie novel and see the potential of Cooper's first efforts fully realized. Throughout these fictions, further, as the authors strive to dramatize the landscape's various effects on their pioneers' imaginations, the prairie may be seen affecting their narratives as it had their predecessors', whether explorer, traveler, artist, or writer. Through twentieth-century fiction, the prairie was transformed from setting to an articulate landscape as, Cather wrote in *O Pioneers!,* "the great fact was the land itself" (15). Their works seize upon this "great fact," defining, shaping, and ultimately communicating through the fiction the way the land made a person feel at the time of pioneering.

Willa Cather's Prairie

Born in Virginia in 1873, Cather accompanied her parents on a move from their home there to the sparsely settled Nebraska prairie in 1883. Dorothy Canfield Fisher, who met Cather before she was twenty, has said that "an imaginative and emotional shift from Virginia to Nebraska is at the core of Willa Cather's fiction," and the extent to which personal experience of the prairie is crucial in Cather's work is suggested by her comments on her first impression of it in an interview following the publication of *O Pioneers!:* "As we drove further and further out into the country, I felt a good deal as if we had come to the end of everything—it was a kind of erasure of personality." She goes on to describe herself as a child "jerked away" from her familiar Virginia "woods and hills and meadows" and "thrown out into a country as bare as a piece of sheet iron." Similarly, Elizabeth Shepley Sergeant writes that Cather, while talking about the prairie, admonished her for her eastern sensibility, saying: "You could not understand. You have not seen those miles of fields. There is no place to hide in Nebraska."[2] In another interview, Cather commented that "Whenever I crossed the Missouri River coming into Nebraska the very smell of the soil tore me to pieces" and she spoke, probably only part facetiously, of her desire to throw over writing and take up a quarter section of land. Being in the West—with the multitude of feelings it occasioned—held for Cather some of her happiest moments, yet, at the same time, she feared the feeling of exposure the prairie offered, having—as E. K. Brown noted— recurrent worries "that sudden death would overtake her somewhere on the prairies. The feeling would come on her obsessively and darken her life for days" while she was visiting Red Cloud.[3]

As an artist, Cather wrote of the prairie in such polarized terms. She saw the landscape both "as open as an honest human face" and as "a country flat and featureless, without tones or shadows, without accent or emphasis of any kind to break its vast monotony." Critics have often discussed Cather's sense of the prairie landscape at considerable length, but none has thus far placed her reactions in the context of a history of the prairie landscape.[4] As a result, perhaps, we do not as yet appreciate fully the extent to which she made first-rate fiction of the prairies. Cather's personal reaction to the prairie landscape became—through the passage of time, the workings of memory, and above all the gradual perfection of her art—her paramount subject. Thus Fisher wrote in an evaluation published in 1933:

> I offer you a hypothesis about Willa Cather's work: that the only real subject
> of all her books is the effect a new country—our new country—has on peo-

ple transplanted to it from the old traditions of a stable, complex civilization. Such a hypothesis, if true, would show her as the only American author
who has concentrated on the only unique quality of our national life, on the
one element which is present more or less in every American life and unknown and unguessable to Europeans or European colonials. . . . Americans
have no choice but to accept the definite break with the past.

To accomplish this, as James Woodress has recently written in *Willa Cather: A
Literary Life* (1987), Cather had to struggle for many years:

> Jim Burden's memories [in *My Ántonia*], like Cather's, are set down many
> years after the fact. By then the ugliness of the prairie had been filtered out,
> leaving only a retouched mythic landscape. When Cather suggests that she
> and the country had it out together by the end of the first autumn [after she
> had moved to Nebraska in 1883], she is foreshortening considerably. There
> is ample evidence, especially in her early stories, to show that the glow that
> lights the country in *O Pioneers!* and *My Ántonia* was a good while in com-
> ing. Soon after her first collection of stories, *The Troll Garden,* was published
> in 1905, she wrote Witter Bynner to explain the bleak tone of her western
> tales. She guessed then that her early experiences had clung to her, for she
> had been pretty much depressed as a child by all the ugliness around her.
> The contrast with Virginia had been stark. One simply could not imagine
> anything so bleak and desolate as a Nebraska farm in the 1880s, and she re-
> membered coming as close to dying of homesickness as any healthy child
> could.

As such a personal history suggests, Willa Cather confronted in probably the
most direct and extended way the compositional problems caused by "the fear,
the physical strain and the cultural agoraphobia" of settling "an unplotted
wilderness." More than any other prairie writer, ultimately, she succeeded
most completely in bringing the muse into her country.[5]

As Woodress's overview suggests, Cather's early stories dealing with Nebraska demonstrate the process by which she came to master her pioneering
materials, and suggest something of the struggle she engaged in, characterized as they are by stark grimness and an almost cynical tone wholly absent
from her classic prairie fictions. In "On the Divide" (1896), for example,
which tells of a Norwegian homesteader's decision to take a neighbor's daughter and force her to marry him, Cather writes: "If it had not been for the few
stunted cottonwoods and elms that grew along a nearby river's banks," Canute
Canuteson "would have shot himself years ago."[6] The face the prairie presents

reflects desolation and something of the demonism which terrified Ishmael's Vermont colt:

> He knew by heart every individual clump of bunch grass in the miles of red shaggy prairie that stretched before his cabin. He knew it in all the deceitful loveliness of its early summer, in all the bitter barrenness of its autumn. He had seen it smitten by all the plagues of Egypt. He had seen it parched by drought, and sogged by rain, beaten by hail, and swept by fire, and in the grasshopper years he had seen it eaten as bare and clean as bones that vultures have left. After the great fires he had seen it stretch for miles and miles, black and smoking as the floor of hell. (494)

Canute, Cather says, "drank alone and in solitude not for pleasure or good cheer, but to forget the awful loneliness and level of the Divide" (496); in his loneliness, he seizes his neighbor's daughter. Cather's depiction of life on the Divide in her early tales is, like Garland's before her, unremittingly grim, but unlike his "Among the Corn Rows" and *The Moccasin Ranch,* she does not countenance a romantic vision of the new land. Instead, she finds only desperation:

> Insanity and suicide are very common things on the Divide. They come on like an epidemic in the hot wind season. Those scorching dusty winds that blow over the bluffs from Kansas seem to dry up the blood in men's veins as they do the sap in the corn leaves. Whenever the yellow scorch creeps down over the tender inside leaves about the ear, then the coroners prepare for active duty; for the oil of the country is burned out and it does not take long for the flame to eat up the wick. It causes no great sensation there when a Dane is found swinging from his own windmill tower, and most of the Poles after they have become too careless and discouraged to shave themselves keep their razors to cut their throats with. (495)

One might look as well at "Peter" (1892), "Lou, The Prophet" (1892), or "El Dorado: A Kansas Recessional" (1901), but throughout these stories Cather is both direct and, apparently, embittered, seeing the prairie landscape as destroying its homesteaders' spirit through its very vastness and the loneliness it occasions. Though Cather later called these stories "bald, clumsy, and emotional,"[7] in retrospect their very clumsiness attests to her struggle to come to terms with the prairie, to pioneer the prairie through her art.

Cather's first novel, *Alexander's Bridge* (1912), has nothing to do with the prairie West—it has often been seen as a Jamesian pastiche, a view she herself encouraged, but which she came to regret. Though she later tried to present her shift from the sitting-room novel to the pioneer novel as a sudden one, Cather's change was more gradual. She once held that her decision to write "came from 'an enthusiasm for a kind of country and a kind of people, rather than ambition,'" and "The Bohemian Girl" (1912), which appeared in *Mc-Clure's* only four months after the serialized version of *Alexander's Bridge* concluded there, reflects that enthusiasm by pointing in the direction of Cather's prairie novels.[8] She sets the story after the homesteading period has passed, thereby avoiding the effects of adjusting to the land. But her symbolic rendering of the prairie offers a changed authorial perspective as well—the caustic, dismissive commentary of "On the Divide" is replaced by a narrative voice which understands the esthetic pull the prairie exerts on Clara Vavrika and, what is more, is at ease with it; thus the landscape underscores both the conflict and the theme of the story.

Certainly this shift can be explained in part by Cather's growing skill as an artist—she had been writing seriously for twenty years between "Peter" and "The Bohemian Girl"—but it can also be accounted for by her perspective while she was writing. At the time of composition, she had been away from Nebraska, except for visits, for over fifteen years. Indeed, Cather wrote to Elizabeth Sergeant—after drafting a new scene for the story in Pittsburgh and continuing onto Nebraska to visit her parents—that (as Sergeant paraphrases): "the story seemed right when she again made human connection with the region. It was like the people and had taken the shape of the land." By defining her characters in relation to their place, of course, Cather was seeking authenticity but, as the whole of her fiction shows, she was also seeking critical images, environmental details which served to define her characters' essential imaginative qualities. These she got from the land itself, but with some considerable difficulty, for she had trouble writing about Nebraska when she was there. As Sergeant continues:

> But the general effect of the West had been overpowering—she had run into the same old shock she used to suffer at the mere size of it. When she was in the East, she forgot everything but the sharp, specific flavor. Once there, an unreasoning fear of being swallowed by the distances between herself and everything else jumped out at her—as in childhood, again.

Thus owing to the imaginative demands created by the prairie landscape, throughout Cather's fiction there is a movement away from the literal prairie and toward a symbolic one. By detaching herself from the prairie, ironically,

Cather was better able to define and communicate its qualities and better able to dramatize the feelings it evoked.[9]

With its dynasty of second-generation pioneers and the relationship between Nils Ericson and Clara Vavrika, "The Bohemian Girl" contains elements that Cather later used in *O Pioneers!*, *The Song of the Lark* (1915), and *My Ántonia* (1918). As he approaches the family home he left twelve years before, Nils's first glimpse of Clara Vavrika Ericson (now his brother's wife) is presented in the context of the landscape, with Cather employing the same technique of backlighting used by Cooper, symbolically tying Clara to the land. Late in the day against a hillside Nils sees a woman on horseback:

> Once in the main road, she let [the horse] out into a lope, and they soon emerged upon the crest of high land, where they moved along the skyline, silhouetted against the band of faint color that lingered in the west. This horse and rider, with their free, rhythmical gallop, were the only moving things to be seen on the face of the flat country. They seemed, in the last sad light of evening, not to be there accidentally, but as an inevitable detail of the landscape.[10]

Forced to choose between her present unhappy marriage to the most lumpish and materialistic of the Ericson brothers and a life in Europe with Nils, Clara dwells upon her attachment to the prairie as she contemplates her position:

> The great, silent country seemed to lay a spell upon her. The ground seemed to hold her as if by roots. Her knees were soft under her. She felt as if she could not bear separation from her old sorrows, from her old discontent. They were dear to her, they had kept her alive, they were a part of her. There would be nothing left of her if she were wrenched away from them. Never could she pass beyond that skyline against which her restlessness had beat so many times. She felt as if her soul had built itself a nest there on that horizon at which she looked every morning and every evening, and it was dear to her, inexpressibly dear. (37)

Clara's dilemma is not without precedent in Cather's writing—far better known is "The Sculptor's Funeral" (1905)—but her use of the individual's attachment to the western landscape as a means of symbolic expression is. Throughout the story Clara's dissatisfaction as a member of the Ericson family is evident; she finds solace in wit and sarcasm unnoticed by the family. Yet it is the land that holds Clara, and Cather's symbolic evocation of it lends greater depth to the love story, since Nils, too, is attracted to the prairie once again. But its major function is to symbolize Clara's sensitive character. Her "inevitable" relationship with the landscape predicates an equally inevitable clash of wills with the smug and insensitive Ericsons who farm the land.

The inevitability of Clara's relationship with the land in "The Bohemian Girl" and the backlighting technique Cather uses to express it recalls Cooper's *The Prairie,* of course, but it also looks forward into Cather's canon where, as Dorothy Canfield Fisher argued in 1933, the imaginary effects of a new country became the author's paramount concern. Central to this was Cather's need to express on the printed page the feelings engendered by the prairie landscape, so this first use of backlighting assumes added significance in view of the transformation in Cather's art that took place between *Alexander's Bridge* and *O Pioneers!.* Whereas Cooper's introduction of Natty Bumppo at the outset of *The Prairie* is spectacular and obvious, Cather's use of the same technique throughout her work would prove to be just as she expresses it here, inevitable. Cooper dramatizes abstractions by introducing Leatherstocking as he does, embodying them in a single character who represents his author's thinking. Cather's use of the same technique was to carry its effects much further, using the "inevitable" organic relationships between several characters and their landscapes to embody not just thinking but, and more especially, feeling. These emotions, which she was able to isolate through the prairie landscape, are essential to her characters' beings and, more importantly, define Cather's artistry.

Even though "The Bohemian Girl" lessens the abruptness of the shift from *Alexander's Bridge* to *O Pioneers!,* Cather's change was a dramatic one, as she explains in a flyleaf dedication of a friend's copy of *O Pioneers!:* "This was the first time I walked off on my own feet—everything before was half real and half an imitation of writers whom I admired. In this one I hit the home pasture and found that I was Yance Sorgensen and not Henry James."[11] By entering her "home pasture," of course, Cather knew she was taking a risk, since only Cooper and Garland, among writers of stature, had before depicted the prairie west, and neither had placed it at the center of his work. In "My First Novels [There Were Two]" Cather speaks of her choice of setting, noting that "Nebraska is distinctly déclassé as a literary background," and explaining that after the novel was published she was confronted with questions such as "How did you come to write about that flat part of the prairie west, Miss Cather, which not many people find interesting?" But she also claimed she wrote it for herself, and that she expected little interest in her tale of Nebraska, citing the New York critic who wrote: "I simply don't care a damn what happens in Nebraska, no matter who writes about it."[12]

That Cather was able to interest those who were negatively biased must be attributed to her art—an art that depends upon the recreation, as opposed to mere description, of prairie experience. Her material is not in itself different from that found in early descriptive accounts and later in second-rate fiction; nor can the images and motifs that she employs be described as original. What constitutes the advance made by Cather lies in the extent to which she *dramatizes* what others had merely observed. Her deliberateness can be seen in a letter she wrote to Sergeant just after she finished writing *O Pioneers!*, as Sharon O'Brien paraphrases: "it was the story she had always wanted to write, and she had written it without thinking about anybody else's opinion, without being afraid of anybody. She had let the country be the hero. . . ." Cather offers here a description of her intention in her prairie novels, certainly, but the final phrase reverberates throughout her canon as well, since landscape plays a paramount role: one protagonist after another is symbiotically entwined with her or his land, and has to be understood in relation to it. Indeed, after Sergeant had read and responded to *O Pioneers!*, saying that it "had no sharp skeleton," Cather conceded the point, adding that the prairie itself had no such skeleton, "no sculptured lines or features."[13] In so saying, Cather reveals the crucial role played by landscape in her growing esthetic.

Cather's dramatic techniques are in evidence from the beginning of *O Pioneers!* and begin with the novel's epigram, the poem "Prairie Spring," in which its two parts hinge on "The eternal, unresponsive sky. / Against all this, Youth." These lines define both the primacy of prairie space and human struggle within it. In the narrative proper, Cather continues this association by dwelling on the "unresponsive sky."[14] Like Cooper and Garland before her, she gives the prairie its due and introduces the land before presenting any signs of humanity; thus she begins: "One January day, thirty years ago, the little town of Hanover, anchored on a windy Nebraska tableland, was trying not to be blown away" (3). The absence of a definite historical date, together with organic imagery and diction, serves to accentuate the force of nature and the impermanence of man's dwellings in the face of such a force. Hanover is "anchored," (the word choice an echo of the prairie/sea analogy), and the word *trying* suggests that its attempts might not be successful.

Unlike Owen Wister's earlier presentation of Medicine Bow as an image only, Cather dramatically evokes Hanover's precarious hold on its location: "A mist of fine snowflakes was curling and eddying about the cluster of low drab buildings huddled on the grey prairie, under a grey sky" (3). The verb *huddled* in conjunction with the adjectives *low drab* suggests the human response to the power of the forces of nature on the prairie, just as *cluster* emphasizes again the possibility of the town being carried off by the wind. In this scene, too, there are no definite contours: not only are the buildings "drab" but the reader sees them against a "grey prairie" which is "under a grey sky." The effect of Cather's

description is thus vagueness rather than clarity, sameness rather than difference.

Similarly, the buildings themselves suggest no ordered arrangement:

> The dwelling-houses were set about haphazard on the tough prairie sod;
> some of them looked as if they had been moved in overnight, and others as if
> they were straying off by themselves, headed straight for the open plain.
> None had any appearance of permanence, and the howling wind blew under
> them as well as over them. (3)

One has a clear, sad sense of the pathetic and the impermanent and, to the
same effect, Cather uses the more impersonal and somewhat awkward "dwell-
ing-houses" to describe the homes of Hanover: these buildings, which appear
as uneasy initiates are not rooted, they are only "set about . . . on the tough
prairie sod." Hence, they seem to "stray" about aimlessly like animals that do
not wish to be domesticated, and they are buffeted by the prairie wind which,
owing to their seemingly casual construction, blows under them as well as
around them.

When Cather does describe the town, she emphasizes its relative insignificance; there is a single main street, and "On either side of this road straggled
two uneven rows of wooden buildings" (4), which she then goes on to
enumerate. Throughout, the scene is largely bare of people; the shopkeepers
are "keeping well behind their frosty windows," the children are in school,
and those who do venture forth are wrapped "in coarse overcoats, with their
long caps pulled down over their noses" (4). The protagonists, similarly, are
initially described merely as "a boy" and "a girl." Only later does the reader
learn they are Emil and Alexandra Bergson.

As Alexandra, Carl Linstrum, and Emil begin their journey home, after
finishing their errands in town, Cather moves to a consideration of the human
response to the landscape. Nevertheless the responses she notes fall within the
context of her opening descriptions. The three drive not toward home on the
distant prairie but "toward the streak of pale, watery light that glimmered in
the leaden sky" (14). In keeping with its precarious grip on its location, the
town "vanished as if it had never been, had fallen behind the swell of the
prairie, and the stern frozen country received them into its bosom" (15).
Creating here an atmosphere of forlorn isolation, Cather compounds it by
inverting the usual mother-earth image, for these characters are clasped
against the earth's frozen bosom. This atmosphere is heightened further by the
waning light in the "leaden" sky which, as suggested in the novel's first
paragraph, did not provide much illumination even at two o'clock.

"The homesteads were few and far apart; here and there a windmill gaunt against the sky, a sod house crouching in a hollow," Cather continues, and then goes on to articulate what her opening descriptions in the novel dramatize: the land's vastness dwarfs the puny efforts of man, making his windmills "gaunt" and forcing his dwellings to crouch. Specifically, she observes with the oft-quoted words "But the great fact was the land itself, which seemed to overwhelm the little beginnings of human society that struggled in its sombre wastes" (15). Indeed, the prairie exacts real respect from its inhabitants: "It was from facing this vast hardness that [Carl's] mouth had become so bitter; because he felt that men were too weak to make any mark here, that the land wanted to be let alone, to preserve its own fierce strength, its peculiar, savage kind of beauty, its uninterrupted mournfulness" (15). This is a place where "The roads were but faint tracks in the grass, and the fields were scarcely noticeable. The record of the plow was insignificant, like the feeble scratches on stone left by prehistoric races, so indeterminate that they may, after all, be only the markings of glaciers, and not a record of human strivings" (19–20). At the same time that Cather emphasizes man's lack of impact on the prairie, she also creates the impression of the antiquity of the land. "Of all the bewildering things about a new country, the absence of human landmarks is one of the most depressing and disheartening" (19), her narrator observes, echoing Castañeda's repeated "nothings" to emphasize the way in which man left no mark on the prairie to show of his passage, and commentators from his time on have agreed.

By calling attention to Carl's embittered appearance, Cather prepares the reader for her introduction of John Bergson, Alexandra and Emil's father who, after eleven years of struggling with the land, is about to die, leaving Alexandra (rather than his less imaginative sons) to carry on after him. By doing so, Cather introduces a gender-based approach to the prairie and to pioneering—*O Pioneers!* dramatizes a movement from the point of view of the male defeated in an attempted conquest of the land to that of the female, inviolate; this movement is one, as well, from a negative, defeated point of view to a positive, affirmative one. "A pioneer should have imagination," Cather writes, speaking of Alexandra after her father's death, "should be able to enjoy the idea of things more than the things themselves" (48). Similarly in *O Pioneers!* as a whole, John Bergson dies, a man defeated in his attempt to "tame" (20) the land, while Alexandra, his daughter, succeeds because she— unlike her brothers, who have no imagination—understands and affirms the land's strengths. [15]

Once introduced in the opening section of the novel as geographical setting in its own right, the prairie in *O Pioneers!* serves as a characterization device as the work progresses. The harsh and alienating image first presented reflects the values of those who like John Bergson "had come to tame" the land without understanding it. "Its genius was unfriendly to man" (20), he thinks; dying in his house, Bergson recalls his struggle, after which he still sees the land as "an enigma. It was like a horse that no one knows how to break to harness, that runs wild and kicks things to pieces. He had an idea that no one understood how to farm it properly, and this he often discussed with Alexandra" (22). In part because of her father's failure, his daughter eventually sees—like Francis Parkman—that one must seek to understand and adapt to the prairie. This vision is central to the development of her character in the novel's first part, "The Wild Land," and the understanding she achieves is foreshadowed in the description of her and Emil driving across the prairie toward their homestead: "The rattle of her wagon was lost in the howling of the wind, but her lantern, held firmly between her feet, made a moving point of light along the highway, going deeper and deeper into the dark country" (18). [16]

In addition to her narrative techniques, which accede to the land's imaginative primacy, Cather reverses the normal seasonal order used in conventional presentations of the land—conventional in the sense that most homesteaders took up claims in the spring so as to build and plant before winter. But instead of beginning at the usual time, as numerous accounts of prairie pioneering, such as *The Moccasin Ranch* do, Cather begins in winter. Garland begins in the spring and, in terms of his depiction of the prairie landscape, the movement is from the benign to the malignant. Perhaps aware of this, Cather reverses the order so that, roughly parallel to Alexandra's growing awareness of the land, the reader moves from a negative reaction—one owing, in part, to the general ignorance of the region Cather could assume in her readers—to an understanding, favorable one. [17] More personally, Cather's objective at the outset of *O Pioneers!* is rooted in her own experience of the prairie; she sought to create the same sort of "erasure of personality" for her reader that she experienced in 1883. Once this has been accomplished, largely in the first two sections of the novel's first part, "The Wild Land," Cather is able to concentrate on her characters' relations; yet Alexandra Bergson's story is not her own. *O Pioneers!* is about her relationship with the land she farms, about her role as pioneer.

When she visits Crazy Ivar early in the novel, Alexandra is seeking his knowledge, so she adopts a respectful attitude toward his reverence for nature. A fool-saint, Ivar stands at the other pole from John Bergson, who "knew every ridge and draw and gully between him and the horizon" (20), but was not able to employ his knowledge successfully. Ivar's knowledge is of a different order—transcendental rather than empirical—and ultimately Alexandra is influenced by Crazy Ivar's point of view, which she adopts in addition to the commonsense approach to farming her father tried to employ. During her inspection tour of neighboring farms some years later, a trip occasioned by her brothers' desire to abandon the farm for jobs in the city, Alexandra discovers a newfound understanding; the land

> seemed beautiful to her, rich and strong and glorious. Her eyes drank in the breadth of it, until her tears blinded her. Then the Genius of the Divide, the great, free spirit which breathes across it, must have bent lower than it ever bent to a human will before. The history of every country begins in the heart of a man or a woman. (65)

Immediately after this, Alexandra recognizes a transcendent attachment to the land in which "she felt the future stirring" (71).

Alexandra's relationship with the prairie's "personality"—for the landscape is to all intents and purposes a character within the novel—evolves from and relates to this "Genius of the Divide," and occasions a movement from realism to romance. In this way, furthermore, Cather introduces a new kind of "romance" element to prairie fiction; in *O Pioneers!* the romantic component is not something which occurs *on* the prairie, it consists of Alexandra's love *for* the prairie itself. Her relation with the land is personal, since it depends on her understanding of the "Genius of the Divide," and the timing of its advent is crucial: Alexandra comes to understand its beauty at the moment of pioneering. Afterwards, once the land is settled and developing, man's relation with the prairie is not the same; thus the tone of the novel once "The Wild Land" ends is that of nostalgic melancholy.

Thus Cather focuses on pioneering at its apogee, at a moment of what might be called romantic apprehension for, writing her novels of pioneering long after the pioneering period had passed, she knew well of the smug materialists who succeeded the pioneering generation. Indeed, she satirizes their lack of imagination and taste through Alexandra's brothers, grown affluent by way of her foresight. When Carl Linstrum returns for a visit sixteen years after Bergson's death he sees the many changes brought by rapid settlement and tells Alexandra "I even think I liked the old country better. This is all very splendid in its way, but there was something about this country when it was a wild old beast that has haunted me all these years. Now, when I come back to all this milk and honey, I feel like the old German song, 'Wo bist du, wo bist du, mein geliebtest Land?'" (118). Alexandra agrees readily.

Cather's most thematically central symbolic use of the landscape is to be found in the final pages of the novel. Having just agreed to marry, Alexandra and Carl walk about the field in the evening; they are lighted by the red rays of the setting sun: "They paused on the last ridge of the pasture, overlooking the house and the windmill and the stables that marked the site of John Bergson's homestead." They are described standing on the ridge overlooking the family's original homestead, with "brown waves of earth" rolling away "to meet the sky" (307). Although she does not backlight her characters here, Cather uses the interplay of light to dramatize their isolation and to symbolize their stature within *O Pioneers!;* they alone remember and value the experience of pioneering, which occurred when the prairie was still a "wild old beast." In turn, as she thinks of the dream in which she is carried off by a figure personifying death and the land itself—the "Genius of the Divide," the same "Genius" her father saw as unfriendly to man—Alexandra is described as "still gazing into the west, and in her face there was that exalted serenity that sometimes came to her at moments of deep feeling. The level rays of the sinking sun shone in her clear eyes" (308). This is how she looked when she first understood the "Genius of the Divide"; here she experiences again that same transcendence which made her feel "as if her heart were hiding down there" amid the "quail and plover and all the little wild things that crooned or buzzed in the sun" (71).

While not concerned with prairie pioneering, Cather's next novel, *The Song of the Lark,* offers material that both displays her growing artistry and, at the same time, defines the substantive difference in her handling of prairie landscape in *O Pioneers!* and her best-known prairie novel, *My Ántonia.* Taking up *The Song of the Lark* in her *The Voyage Perilous: Willa Cather's Romanticism* (1986), Susan J. Rosowski has noted Cather's well-known comments that *O Pioneers!*

> seemed to have written itself, with the country and the people telling their
> own story. As though Cather had erased her individual self, the book has an
> impersonal quality. The narrator speaks with a universal voice, and Alex-
> andra, one of Cather's few major characters not based on an identified model,
> seems more mythic than human. It was as if in writing this book Cather had
> become the impersonal, godlike creator she had long been writing about. [18]

Rosowski continues to argue that in *The Song of the Lark* Cather "explored what led to that experience" by turning to a story focused on the development of an artist, Thea Kronborg, who moves from her beginnings in Moonstone, Colorado, to acclaim as a world-renowned operatic star.

If in *O Pioneers* the land insisted on becoming the hero of the story, then in *The Song of the Lark* Cather left the impersonality of her first prairie novel behind, forging a commingling of place and voice for the first time, a symbiosis that would have its best expression in her second telling of prairie pioneering, *My Ántonia*. While focused on Thea's struggle and growth as an artist and taking place largely away from Moonstone, its story is one that, as Rosowski notes, "used a midwestern point of view and spoke with a midwestern narrative voice."[19] This distinction is key, for in so saying Rosowski points up the crucial difference between Cather and her prairie predecessors. While Cooper, Garland, and others were able to fashion prairie fiction that met the generic conventions of their day, Cather struggled until she devised forms that spoke to her readers through the voices of prairie people and, by way of their perspective, seemingly, through the voice of the prairie landscape itself. *O Pioneers!* depicts prairie pioneering impersonally and intellectually; *My Ántonia*, by contrast, makes its reader feel pioneering and, especially, the imaginative effects of prairie space. The difference between the two lies in *The Song of the Lark*.

Rosowski notes that when she sings the part of Sieglinde late in the novel,

> Thea Kronborg fulfills Cather's definition of art, "to keep an idea living, intact, tinged with all its original feeling . . . and transfer it on paper a living thing with color, odor, sound, life all in it."

Cather sets out to do this in *The Song of the Lark* by charting Thea's birth as an artist as a process separate from her literal birth; in doing so she—like her reader after her—seems to take Thea's tentative steps toward her (initially inchoate) goal with her. And likewise, while describing Cather's characteristic attitudes toward her art, James Woodress discusses the author's attitude toward her protagonists; that when Cather talked of feeling

> as if she had gotten into another person's skin, she was using a simile that describes accurately her creative process. Her creative imagination required total absorption in her fictional world. She used this figure more than once in letters and interviews, and when she had finished writing novels that created strong central characters . . . she always felt a sense of loss in parting with her protagonists.[20]

Like Cather's adoption of a midwestern voice, her imaginative projection of herself into her characters informs *The Song of the Lark* and its successors. What is more, this same projection explains Cather's transformation of the prairie landscape. Unlike her predecessors, she is able to render the prairie landscape luminous in a way unseen before by way of her own "gift of sympathy" with it and, more importantly, by the way in which her protagonists' "original

feeling[s]" for the landscape—especially Thea's, Jim Burden's, and Ántonia's—are made central to their very beings.

Thus in *The Song of the Lark,* as Thea progresses toward her own self-
realization as an artist, the western landscape around Moonstone plays a
crucial role, charting her own understanding of her feelings, direction, and
destiny. When she struggles for direction in Chicago—though she seems
herself largely unaware of her struggle—she visits the art institute "one bleak
day in February" and she returns repeatedly. Though she dutifully looks at the
whole of the collection, realizing "that she was missing a great deal," her
attention is captured by a single painting, Jules Breton's *The Song of the Lark:*

> But in that same room there was a picture—oh, that was the thing she
> ran upstairs so fast to see! That was her picture. She imagined that nobody
> cared for it but herself, and that it waited for her. It was a picture indeed.
> She liked the name of it, "The Song of the Lark." The flat country, the early
> morning light, the wet fields, the look in the girl's heavy face—well, they
> were all hers, anyhow, whatever was there. She told herself that the picture
> was "right." Just what she meant by this, it would take a clever person to ex-
> plain. But to her the word covered the almost boundless satisfaction she felt
> when she looked at the picture.[21]

Thea's identification with the painting, accompanied as it is by her inability to
really explain that identification because she does not herself fully understand
it, offers the first step in her artistic development and, at the same time,
reveals a writer working well within her character's skin. Just as Thea's
inarticulate identification with prairie space is evident in the passage, so too
the narrator's grasp of Thea's somewhat befuddled state of mind is clear. Thus
as Thea gropes toward self-understanding her feelings, attractions, and identifications are carefully dramatized.

The role played by the prairie landscape is central to this rendering, for its
recollection sparks Thea's epiphany; when she goes to hear a performance of
Dvořák's *New World Symphony* in April after her February visit to the gallery,
Thea's inarticulate reaction to the Breton painting becomes articulate—her
emotions flood to the fore:

> This was music she could understand, music from the New World indeed!
> Strange how, as the first movement went on, it brought back to her that
> high tableland above Laramie; the grass-grown wagon-trails, the far-away
> peaks of the snowy range, the wind and the eagles, that old man and the first
> telegraph message.

When the first movement ended, Thea's hands and feet were cold as ice. She was too much excited to know anything except that she wanted something desperately, and when the English horns gave out the theme of the Largo, she knew what she wanted was exactly that. Here were the sand hills, the grasshoppers and locusts, all the things that wakened and chirped in the early morning; the reaching and reaching of high plains, the immeasurable yearning of all flat lands. There was home in it, too; first memories, first mornings long ago; the amazement of a new soul in a new world; a soul new and yet old, that had dreamed something despairing, something glorious, in the dark before it was born; a soul obsessed by what it did not know, under the cloud of a past it did not recall. (251)

Seen in conjunction with Thea's reaction to the Breton painting and her subsequent realization in Panther canyon, this passage reveals Cather defining not only her character, but also her character's quest as an artist, in terms of western landscape. Yet Thea is not merely homesick; on the contrary, this flood of insight shows that her essence as a person is bound up inextricably in "the immeasurable yearning of all flat lands," and that her yearnings as an incipient artist find their counterpart in her western landscapes.

That this is so is confirmed by the Panther canyon scene when, summering at Fred Ottenburg's ranch and launched on the path that will lead her to operatic stardom, Thea meditates on some shards of ancient broken pottery while bathing. If Cather as an artist set out to get into the skin of her character, here she gets her character into the skin of the landscape, for Thea is bathing in a stream "at the bottom of the cañon":

One morning, as she was standing upright in the pool, splashing water between her shoulder–blades with a big sponge, something flashed through her mind that made her draw herself up and stand still until the water had quite dried upon her flushed skin. The stream and the broken pottery: what was any art but an effort to make a sheath, a mould in which to imprison for a moment the shining, elusive element which is life itself—life hurrying past us and running away, too strong to stop, too sweet to lose? The Indian women had held it in their jars. In the sculpture she had seen in the Art Institute, it had been caught in a flash of arrested motion. In singing, one made a vessel of one's throat and nostrils and held it on one's breath, caught the stream in a scale of natural intervals. (378)

Just as one can see a progression between these three passages—as well as increased self-consciousness on Thea's part—so too can a landscape progression be seen between Cather's three prairie novels of the 'teens. The impersonality of *O Pioneers!* that Rosowski notes gave way to the voice, self-consciousness, and self-assurance that comes to characterize Thea in the last section of *The Song of the Lark,* majestically entitled "Kronborg." These qualities, Cather makes clear, derive in significant measure from Thea's relation with her beginnings and, most especially in the *New World* passage, with her own western landscapes, "the immeasurable yearnings of all flat lands." What is more, Cather takes her reader not only under her character's skin, she takes her under the skin of the land itself. After writing *The Song of the Lark,* Cather was ready to turn her attention once more to her own landscape and another of her own themes, prairie pioneering. After Thea's midwestern voice had been found, Cather was ready to use a similar voice to create a luminous prairie landscape, to render it aglow with meaning and understanding in the "sheath" that is *My Ántonia.*

In *My Ántonia,* her most well-known and best-regarded novel, Cather again takes up prairie pioneering and shows a more refined technique in handling both character and landscape. In the earlier novel Alexandra is both objective character and subjective sensibility, but in *My Ántonia* Cather separates the two functions, so that Ántonia's character is seen symbolically by Jim Burden, the narrator; to him, she is a bridge between his present self and his pioneer Nebraska boyhood. Such a romantic perspective in a first-person narrator is crucial since, given the omniscient narration in *O Pioneers!,* Cather could be accused of romanticizing in her presentation of Alexandra as pioneer. Yet because of what we are told about Burden in the Introduction and his role as putative author of the narrative, romantic nostalgia functions as character, not narration. When *O Pioneers!* ends, the reader has difficulty believing Alexandra will find her future with Carl equal to her pioneering past. Ending *My Ántonia,* our misgivings over Burden's tangible link to pioneer days— through Ántonia and her family—focus either on Jim's romantic idealism or his self-delusions, but they are directed toward the character, not his creator.[22]

Using Burden as narrator also allowed Cather to develop the symbolic possibilities of the prairie landscape much further, since as reminiscing narrator, Burden presents objects—whether characters, things, or elements in landscape—subjectively. And because his tale is a reminiscence, Burden evaluates all of the various people, places, and events he has known in light of his subsequent knowledge and experience. Thus we are told that Burden lives in New York and works as "legal counsel for one of the great Western railways"; more significantly, apart from his work, he leads an empty life, married to a woman who is "temperamentally incapable of enthusiasm," one who "has her own fortune and lives her own life" playing "the patroness to a group of young poets and painters of advanced ideas and mediocre ability."[23] Burden's life is somewhat barren. As such, writing about Ántonia, whom he "had found again after long years" (iii), is a kind of antidote for his present, a romantic retreat into his past, and thereby, into prairie pioneering. *My Ántonia* is the title of his reminiscence. Distant in time and space from pioneering and Nebraska—as Cather herself was—Jim Burden sees his material romantically from the beginning of the novel, and Cather is at pains to develop this aspect of his character, initially and throughout.[24]

Burden and the speaker in the Introduction agree that growing up in "a little prairie town" "was a kind of freemasonry," and Ántonia, who "seemed to mean to us the country, the conditions, the whole adventure of our childhood," personifies their fellowship. At the same time, Burden offers comments in the Introduction and throughout the narrative which serve as Cather's directions to her narrative technique. Dropping his manuscript off one winter day at the speaker's New York apartment, Burden protests that his tale "hasn't any form"—he "simply wrote down pretty much all" Ántonia's "name recalls" for him (iv). Toward the end of novel, in Book V, "Cuzak's Boys," when Burden returns to find Ántonia "a battered woman now," but still "a rich mine of life" (353), he offers a passage defining Cather's narrative structure in *My Ántonia:*

> Antonia had always been one to leave images in the mind that did not
> fade—that grew stronger with time. In my memory there was a succession
> of such pictures, fixed there like the old woodcuts of one's first primer: Án-
> tonia kicking her bare legs against the sides of my pony when we came home
> in triumph with our snake; Ántonia in her black shawl and fur cap, as stood
> by her father's grave in the snowstorm; Ántonia coming in with her work
> team along the evening sky-line.

Burden sees in these images of Ántonia "immemorial human attitudes which we recognize by instinct as universal and true" (353). And without question, also, the prairie landscape as she invokes it plays a fundamental role in achieving the novel's impact; indeed, critics have often remarked Cather's use of the twinning technique, whereby Burden and Ántonia are presented as in a symbiotic relationship, yet her technique in *My Ántonia* is not one of twinning.[25] Rather, Cather offers us a triad, with Ántonia and Jim's shared experiences of pioneer prairie landscape as the third element.

A seldom-remarked passage in *My Ántonia* makes the centrality of the prairie and its organic relation to Cather's tale precise and vivid. Toward the end of the novel, when Burden visits Ántonia after the birth of her daughter, but before she marries Anton Cuzak, the two walk across the prairie; Burden continues:

> As we walked homeward across the fields, the sun dropped and lay like a great golden globe in the low west. While it hung there, the moon rose in the east, as big as a cart-wheel, pale silver and streaked with rose colour, thin as a bubble or ghost-moon. For five, perhaps ten minutes, the two luminaries confronted each other across the level land, resting on opposite edges of the world. (321–22)

Burden then goes on to tell Ántonia—in a passage frequently commented upon, since it has been interpreted as affirmation or equivocation—that he would have liked to have her "for a sweetheart, or a wife, or my mother or my sister—anything that a woman can be to a man" (321). However, as their relation is defined in the novel, each is a luminary, the polar opposite of the other, turning a bright being toward the other "across the level land." This third element in Cather's symbolic configuration is as necessary as the other two, for the characters are conjoined through their shared experience of and sympathy with the prairie.[26]

Jim and Ántonia arrive in Nebraska on the same night, and the land informs their relation from first to last. Describing his arrival in Nebraska at the age of ten, newly orphaned, to live with his grandparents, Jim sees "nothing but land: not a country at all, but the material out of which countries are made" and feels a sense of erasure, "the feeling that the world was left behind, that we had got over the edge of it, and were outside man's jurisdiction" (7). Young Jim's initial impression of the prairie, his feeling of being "blotted out" (8), is the first of Cather's prairie images, embodying the seeming emptiness of the land. In *O Pioneers!*, she had dramatized the relationship between land, sky, and man's structures through imagery and diction; here, the same impression is given an immediacy by reason of first-person narration. In *O Pioneers!* Cather presented the prairie in winter as an image, a scene. Here the emphasis is upon the felt quality of this landscape, seen in late summer or early autumn, and made articulate by Jim Burden's filtering sensibility. The omniscient narrative technique of *O Pioneers!* had the effect of objectifying the prairie, at least until Alexandra reaches her accord with the "Genius of the Divide," whereas Cather's use of the first-person point of view in *My Ántonia* has the effect of locating the reader *in* the landscape.

Rebounding from his initial loss of a sense of self in the face of the vast prairie, Burden adapts quickly—and in the process he recapitulates the sentiments and expressions of numerous travelers before him. Although his first view of the prairie from the back of the wagon was appalling, leading him to state that he had "never before looked up at the sky when there was not a familiar mountain ridge against it" (9), two days later he is mesmerized. Except for a few large broken fields, Jim sees "Everywhere, as far as the eye could reach . . . nothing but rough, shaggy, red grass, most of it as tall as" he is (14). Employing the recurrent phrase to suggest vastness, he also resorts to synecdoche and simile:

> As I looked about me I felt that the grass was the country, as the water is the sea. The red of the grass made all the great prairie the colour of wine-stains, or of certain seaweeds when they are first washed up. And there was so much motion in it; the whole country seemed, somehow, to be running. (15)

Shortly thereafter, as he and his grandmother walk off to visit her garden, Burden expands synecdoche to personification:

> I can remember exactly how the country looked to me as I walked beside my grandmother along the faint wagon-tracks on that early September morning. Perhaps the glide of long railway travel was still with me, for more than anything else I felt motion in the landscape; in the fresh, easy-blowing morning wind, and in the earth itself, as if the shaggy grass were a sort of loose hide, and underneath it herds of wild buffalo were galloping, galloping. . . . (16, Cather's ellipsis)

Hence only two days after his arrival, Burden had begun to shift the basis of his comparisons from his Virginia past to the prairie past—from mountain ridges to galloping buffalo.

Just after his sense of the past comes to him, Jim undergoes a mystical experience, which is almost the obverse of the sense of impermanence dramatized at the beginning of *O Pioneers!*:

> I wanted to walk straight on through the red grass and over the edge of the world, which could not be very far away. The light air about me told me that the world ended here: only the ground and sun and sky were left, and if one went a little farther there would be only sun and sky, and one would float off into them, like the tawny hawks which sailed over our heads making slow shadows on the grass. While grandmother took the pitchfork we found standing in one of the rows and dug potatoes, while I picked them up out of

the soft brown earth and put them into the bag, I kept looking up at the hawks that were doing what I might so easily do. (16–17)

Burden's sense of transcendence here is occasioned by the landscape. Cather has evoked a different sort of "erasure of personality." Staying behind in the garden, Jim leans against "a warm yellow pumpkin" and, having immersed himself in the minutiae of the surrounding scene, he observes:

> I was something that lay under the sun and felt it, like the pumpkins, and I did not want to be anything more. I was entirely happy. Perhaps we feel like that when we die and become a part of something entire, whether it is sun and air, or goodness and knowledge. At any rate, this is happiness; to be dissolved into something complete and great. (18)

Reminiscent of Alexandra's dream, here the "something" into which Jim has immersed himself is the new (for him) prairie, with its elemental simplicity of "ground and sun and sky."

Having presented Burden's initial romantic immersion in the landscape, Cather counters and tempers it with other views of the land and the various sufferings within Ántonia's family over the next year—their animal-like deprivation, cruel treatment at the hands of Peter Krajiek and, finally, Mr. Shimerda's suicide. Registered through Burden's eyes, Cather downplays their impact while, at the same time, she acknowledges the crushing effects of prairie isolation. Describing the afternoons he shared with Ántonia during his first autumn on the prairie, Jim says he "never got used to them. As far as we could see, the miles of copper-red grass were drenched in sunlight that was stronger and fiercer than at any other time of the day." "The whole prairie was like the bush that burned with fire and was not consumed. That hour always had the exultation of victory, of triumphant ending, like a hero's death— heroes who died young and gloriously. It was a sudden transfiguration, a lifting-up of day." Countering this romantic invocation of the prairie's "magnificence," are the images of "two long black shadows," flitting before Jim and Ántonia or following after, "dark spots on the ruddy grass." Just then, as "the edge of the sun sank nearer and nearer the prairie floor," the children espy the stooped figure of Mr. Shimerda "moving on the edge of the upland, a gun on his shoulder. . . . walking slowly, dragging his feet along as if he had no purpose." Just as Clara Vavrika was defined as a figure within the landscape in "The Bohemian Girl," so too is Shimerda here; he is alone on the prairie, illuminated by a fading light which holds no warmth for him—Ántonia tells

Jim " 'My papa sick all the time' " as they race to Shimerda. The group listens to the chirping of an insect Ántonia has made a nest for in her hair, a "feeble minstrel"; "The old man's smile," Jim says, "as he listened, was so full of sadness, of pity for things, that I never afterward forgot it." When the sun drops below the horizon, "a sudden coolness" follows it and the scene ends as Jim races his "shadow home" (40-43).

Viewed closely, this scene suggests the organic relationship between the prairie and the lives of Cather's protagonists. She contrasts Jim's romantic invocation of the land's "magnificence," the intimations of immortality it offers him, with the "dark shadows" of the children and the even darker shadow of Mr. Shimerda—a melancholy figure made visible by the landscape in which he seeks, half-heartedly, for game. A stranger in an even stranger land, he does not die the hero's death Burden envisions. On the contrary, in the midst of winter—a season which in Nebraska brooks no romance— Shimerda methodically blows the top of his head off.

In the same vein, the next summer Burden and Ántonia watch a "beautiful electric storm," perched Alexander Henry-like atop "the slanting roof of the chicken house":

> the lightning broke in great zigzags across the heavens, making everything stand out and come close to us for a moment. Half the sky was chequered with black thunderheads, but all the west was luminous and clear: in the lightning flashes it looked like deep blue water, with the sheen of moonlight on it; and the mottled part of the sky was like marble pavement, like the quay of some splendid seacoast city, doomed to destruction. Great warm splashes of rain fell on our upturned faces. One black cloud, no bigger than a little boat, drifted out into the clear space unattended, and kept moving westward.

Here are the recurrent elements in travelers' accounts: the optical illusions, an implicit prairie/sea analogy, and the vast space that allows one to see both clear weather and violent storm at once. The prairie, as presented here, serves as counterpoint to the relation between Jim and Ántonia, offering an image of romantic beauty and stark terror. Thus Ántonia responds to the storm by recalling the past winter, combining both an appreciation of its beauty and an awareness of its threatening aspect: " 'I wish my papa live to see this summer,' " she says, " 'I wish no winter ever come again.' " After her comment, Jim asks her why she cannot be herself more often, as she is then, rather than being—as she so often is—coarse like her brother Ambrosch; she responds:

"If I live here, like you, that is different. Things will be easy for you. But they will be hard for us" (139–40).

By drawing attention to the luminosity of the prairie sky and landscape in the midst of a thunderstorm, Cather offers a visual equivalent of Jim and Ántonia's relations, but also an equivalent to the kinship of pioneering which fostered their mutual dependency. No scene in *My Ántonia* makes this more apparent than the episode in which Cather pointedly refers to the prairie landscape tradition in which she is writing. Resting after a game with "The Hired Girls" while pinicking, Ántonia says to Jim: "I want you to tell the girls about how the Spanish first came here. . . ." Jim then recounts the apocryphal story, which he believes, that Coronado's expedition traveled beyond Kansas as far north as the Republican River in present-day Nebraska. The girls question him as to why Coronado had come so far, what the country was like then and why he had not gone back to Spain; Jim cannot answer their questions, saying he "only knew the schoolbooks said the Spaniard 'died in the wilderness, of a broken heart.'" Concurring, Ántonia recalls her father, and says "More than him has done that. . . ." Thinking this over, the group "sat looking off across the country, watching the sun go down. The curly grass about us was on fire now. The bark of the oaks turned red as copper. There was a shimmer of gold on the brown river." This description, which recalls the earlier passages when Jim lies—pumpkin-like—in his grandmother's garden and when he and Ántonia meet Mr. Shimerda, serves as preliminary to the novel's most famous image:

> Presently we saw a curious thing: There were no clouds, the sun was going down in a limpid, gold-washed sky. Just as the lower edge of the red disk rested on the high fields against the horizon, a great black figure suddenly appeared on the face of the sun. We sprang to our feet, straining our eyes toward it. In a moment we realized what it was. On some upland farm, a plough had been left standing in the field. The sun was sinking just behind it. Magnified across the distance by the horizontal light, it stood out against the sun, was exactly contained within the circle of the disk; the handles, the tongue, the share—black against the molten red. There it was, heroic in size, a picture writing on the sun.

Cather orchestrates this spectacle carefully: the refrain-like repetition of golden and glowing prairie description; the discussion of Coronado and the country's romantic past which sets the atmosphere; Coronado's strivings and tragedy as parallel to Mr. Shimerda's; finally, the whole is encompassed in the most evocative and effective use of prairie mirage to be found in fiction since Cooper's introduction of Natty Bumppo. The symbolic plough, rendered "heroic in size" by the prairie landscape, encapsulates Cather's vision of the pioneer spirit; although it soon fades—"the ball dropped and dropped" until "that forgotten plough had sunk back to its own littleness somewhere on the prairie" (243–45)—Cather's symbolic vision, embodied in an image made luminous by the landscape, powerfully lingers. It is, indeed, *the* image in the mind that does not fade, one that possesses the reader's mind.

Thus when placed in the context of the literature of the prairie, stretching back to the very Spaniard whom Cather evokes here, her prairie writings define a pattern of the ways in which the landscape forces literary adaptation. Other writers defined the practical adjustments required by the landscape, but Cather was the first to define the new strategies and to refine the old conventions in order to do justice to the prairie in fiction. Similarly, her view of the land, which commingles a romantic fancifulness—"the Genius of the Divide," Ántonia's unquenchable optimism, and Burden's sentiments—with its stark realities—the opening of *O Pioneers!* and Mr. Shimerda—recognizes both poles in the history of reaction to the landscape.

Not surprisingly, given the imaginative struggle implicit in her development of narrative techniques adapted to prairie spaces, Cather herself offers the best description of this process through Jim Burden. Like the whole of *My Ántonia,* his musings are delicately invoked through the agency of the prairie landscape. Away at the University of Nebraska at the opening of Book III, Jim contemplates his future as opened up to him by his teacher, Gaston Cleric: "I knew that I should never be a scholar. I could never lose myself for long among impersonal things. Mental excitement was apt to send me with a rush back to my own naked land and the figures scattered upon it." Continuing, Burden defines the pull the prairie exerts upon him, since even "in the very act of yearning toward the new forms that Cleric brought up before me, my mind plunged away from me, and I suddenly found myself thinking of the places and people of my own infinitesimal past. They stood out strengthened and simplified now, like the image of the plough against the sun." By having Jim recall the scene he and his friends saw on their picnic here, Cather's use of backlighting encapsulates the interplay of memory and present perception that is crucial in *My Ántonia.* Jim's recalled "plough against the sun" is an image that embodies the whole of pioneering and, as well, his personal past. Thus this use of backlighting moves well beyond the merely symbolic presentation of Natty Bumppo at the outset of *The Prairie* for, more than an idea represented by its dramatic presentation, this is Jim's plough and it represents an entire ideal created by the mixture of remembered thinking and feeling impinging upon the present moment. Instead of working with two real-

ities—the natural and the symbolic—Cather offers two points in time embodied by the plough; the past infuses the present and serves to help shape
Jim's, and so our, understanding of it.

Thus later, when looking out his window on the edge of Lincoln one March
evening, Jim notices that on

> the prairie, where the sun had gone down, the sky was turquoise blue, like a
> lake, with gold light trobbing in it. Higher up, in the utter clarity of the
> western slope, the evening star hung like a lamp suspended by silver
> chains—like the lamp engraved upon the title-page of old Latin texts, which
> is always appearing in new heavens, and waking new desires in men.

So reminded of work, Jim shuts his window and takes up his Latin text,
Virgil, two lines of whose *Georgics* Cather quotes; the first is directly relevant
to Jim's recollections of his pioneering boyhood, "the best days are the first to
flee," but the second is most relevant to Cather's art, and defines her position
in prairie writing as the author of both *O Pioneers!* and *My Ántonia*: "for I shall
be the first, if I live, to bring the Muse into my country" (262–64). Ántonia is
the novel's informing symbol, earth mother and muse—she is able to keep
Cuzak, a city man, on a farm "in one of the loneliest countries in the world"
(366) and she inspires Jim Burden to write of their shared experience. Yet it
was Willa Cather who emphatically brought the muse into her country by
creating them both, creating their shared "freemasonry"—crafting the succession of images which encapsulates their lives and defines their relation as
two luminaries, reflecting one another "across the level land." Willa Cather
transformed her own experience of the prairie into the substance of great art,
and it is seen at its apotheosis in *My Ántonia*.

When closing the novel, Jim returns again to the first road he traveled in
Nebraska—"which used to run like a wild thing across the open prairie"—
that he and Ántonia each traveled that first night, thinking "I had only to
close my eyes to hear the rumbling of the wagons in the dark, and to be again
overcome by that obliterating strangeness" (371). Cather's own sense of
erasure, of "obliterating strangeness," became her characters'—theirs defined,
described, and effected—communicable. And Cather's transference of her
personal reaction to her characters is the same action, intrinsically, as Francis
Parkman's embellishment of one entry in his journal—"Awkward feeling,
being lost on the prairie"—into an extended analytical passage in *The Oregon
Trail*. Both reactions were caused by the prairie landscape, but in Willa
Cather they reach and sustain their highest level of accomplished artistry.[27]

Though this discussion has been limited to Cather's most extended treatments of the prairie landscape, it could well have been extended to include the fiction she published during the 1920s and later. Though landscape, per se, never again played the crucial role in Cather's writing seen in the works just discussed, an argument can be made that her use of landscape after *My Ántonia* is far less overt, more subtly an element of character. That is, characters are defined by the landscapes they relish. Thus the lush beauty of the Forrester place with its stream, Lombardy poplars, meadows, and marshlands in *A Lost Lady* (1923) set the Forresters apart from the materialists of Sweet Water represented by Ivy Peters. Yet, as is well known, Cather's intention in that novel was to create the emotional effect of Mrs. Forrester, rather than her character itself—thus landscape in that novel is less a presence than the spatial context for an era, when the nobility of the Forresters has been replaced by the rapaciousness of men like Peters.[28] Similarly, Godfrey St. Peter in *The Professor's House* (1925) is drawn to Tom Outland's mesa in the southwest while Myra Henshawe in *My Mortal Enemy* (1926) takes herself out to a California headland and looks out at the ocean, seeing one final dawn before she dies.

But it is in *Death Comes for the Archbishop* (1927), that Cather most fully integrates character with landscape after *My Ántonia*. As in the earlier novel, the protagonist, Bishop Latour, removes to a new world and, like Jim and Ántonia too, he comes to love his new land—vitally, with feelings so strong for New Mexico that they become an essential part of his being. In Book III, "The Mass at Ácoma," Fr. Latour's feelings for the mesa plain between Laguna and Ácoma convey both his attraction and his mystification:

> This mesa plain had an appearance of great antiquity, and of incomplete-
> ness; as if, with all the materials for world-making assembled, the Creator
> had desisted, gone away and left everything on the point of being brought
> together, on the eve of being arranged into mountain, plain, plateau. The
> country was still waiting to be made into a landscape.[29]

Unlike Jim Burden's memories of pioneering years on the Nebraska when his new land was transformed into a country, Latour's New Mexico is transformed by the priest while we read; we follow as he makes this mesa plain into a landscape, his own landscape, preferred to his native France. Thus the integration of Latour and New Mexico is fully realized in the novel—they seem, as we read, mutually dependent. The process of taking New Mexico as his own had begun, Cather writes, while the priest was crossing "the vast plains of Kansas" "along the Santa Fé trail":

> Father Latour had found the sky more a desert than the land; a hard, empty
> blue, very monotonous to the eyes of a Frenchman. But west of the Pecos all

that changed; here there was always activity overhead, clouds forming and moving all day long. . . . The whole country seemed fluid to the eye under this constant change of accent, this ever-varying distribution of light. (95–96)

Cather's dramatization of the landscape as an essence of Latour's character is remarkably subtle, to be sure, but it is finally an integration borne of her experience with her own landscape, and of her experience in depicting the Nebraska prairies in fiction before she turned to the southwest.

Rölvaag, Grove, and Stegner: Pioneering the Prairie

Although Cather remains predominent as the writer who made prairie pioneering most thoroughly her own, and did so with such subtlety, there is also a second cadre of novels which, in a sense, are more directly about the processes of pioneering the prairie than Cather's are. Of these novels, O. E. Rölvaag's *Giants in the Earth* (1927) is the most widely known; in it he concentrates on defining precisely the immediate psychological effects of pioneering, focusing directly on the hardships involved.[30] Rölvaag's treatment of Beret Holm's growing insanity is far more excruciating than Cather's imagistic treatment of Mr. Shimerda's melancholy, and as with Garland's Blanche Burke, the reader senses her growing dismay early in the narrative. Because of her bizarre religious beliefs—including terror of divine retribution and other anxieties and repressions—Beret feels that the family should never have left Norway, the site of all she cherishes, and her worst fears are confirmed by the prairie landscape, which aggravates her already pronounced melancholy temperament. Per Hansa, on the other hand, is the natural pioneer; the move from Norway to the Dakota prairie is for him the necessary experience of a lifetime—he sees his homestead as his destiny and, despite several very bad years in which the settlers are visited by plagues of grasshoppers, he usually thrives through foresight and ingenuity. Thus husband and wife each represent a particular philosophical point of view, and the conflict that results strikes to the center of the psychological effect of the pioneer experience—if either party gains ascendancy over the other, the latter's essence will be denied.

While Beret's melancholy has its roots in her old-world upbringing, the prairie landscape appalls her, leading her ultimately to a state of agoraphobia, in which she covers the windows of their dugout. When she finally succumbs to her fears during the first plague of grasshoppers, they lead her to hide with her children in a large trunk, a cherished family heirloom. Beret's first thought upon their arrival at their homestead, after wandering lost on the prairie for several days, becomes her refrain in the novel: "here there was nothing even to hide behind."[31] Immediately following this, Rölvaag expands upon the nature of Beret's fears at greater length:

> The infinite surrounding her on every hand might not have been so oppressive, might even have brought her a measure of peace, if it had not been for the deep silence, which lay heavier here than in a church. Indeed, what was there to break it? She had passed beyond the outposts of civilization; the nearest dwelling places of men were far away. Here no warbling of birds rose on the air, no buzzing of insects sounded; even the wind had died away; the waving blades of grass that trembled to the faintest breath now stood erect and quiet, as if listening, in the great hush of the evening [. . . .] Had they travelled into some nameless, abandoned region? Could no living thing exist out here, in the empty, desolate, endless wastes of green and blue? . . . How *could* existence go on, she thought, desperately? If life is to thrive and endure, it must at least have something to hide behind! (37)

Like Irving in the Cross Timbers when he compares his surroundings to a Gothic cathedral, Beret is reminded of a church by the western landscape— yet Rölvaag's allusion ironically inverts Irving's, for Beret sees no splendor here, only an unfittingly somber silence which exceeds that of a church. She comes to believe in the prairie horizon as a magic circle. She interprets their New World home in terms based on Old World beliefs and feels that nothing good can come to them there. As a result, she grows increasingly strange, overcome by the enormity without; she is anxious and nervous whenever Per Hansa travels away from their house and, after he concocts a lime mixture to cheer her by whitening the walls of their sod hut, she resorts to staring at the dark floor—the bright walls inside being too like the brightness outdoors.

Before Per Hansa's party relocates the rest of the group in the early sections of *Giants in the Earth,* while they are still lost on the prairie, Beret inquires of her son whether or not those they are seeking have been located; when he replies negatively, her response is reminiscent of Blanche Burke's and Jim Burden's sense that the prairie is somehow out of the world: "This seems to be taking us to the end of the world . . . beyond the end of the world!" (8).

Like Cooper in *The Prairie* and Cather in *O Pioneers!,* to dramatize the idea that "the great fact was the land itself," Rölvaag introduces the landscape before introducing the characters:

> Bright, clear sky over a plain so wide that the rim of the heavens cut down
> on it around the entire horizon. . . . Bright, clear sky, to-day, to-morrow,
> and for all time to come. . . . And sun! And still more sun! It set the
> heavens afire every morning; it grew with the day to quivering golden
> light—then softened into all the shades of red and purple as evening
> fell. . . . It was late afternoon. A small caravan was pushing its way through
> the tall grass. The track that it left behind was like the wake of a boat—ex-
> cept that instead of widening out astern it closed in again. "Tish-ah!" said
> the grass. . . . "Tish-ah, tish-ah!" . . . Never had it said anything else—
> never would it say anything else. It bent resiliently under the trampling feet;
> it did not break, but it complained aloud every time—for nothing like this
> had ever happened to it before. (3)

The prairie is a magnificent object of visual apprehension here and Rölvaag
portrays the caravan from, as it were, the prairie's point of view; his personification of the grass introduces a new perspective—that of the resilient grass
which so vexed Castañeda. The grass's complaint, moreover, emphasizes man's
inability to have any impact on the landscape—"Tish-ah" is really a phonetic
equivalent of "hush, hush"—and in its bending without breaking implies the
return of each blade to its upright posture.

When Rölvaag does introduce Per Hansa and his family, one reason for his
choice of title becomes clear:

> The caravan seemed a miserably frail and Lilliputian thing as it crept over
> the boundless prairie toward the sky line. Of road or trail there lay not a
> trace ahead; as soon as the grass had straightened up again behind, no one
> could have told the direction from which it had come or whither it was
> bound. The whole train—Per Hansa with his wife and children, the oxen,
> the wagons, the cow, and all—might just as well have dropped down out of
> the sky. Nor was it at all impossible to imagine that there were trying to get
> back there again; their course was always the same—straight toward the
> west, straight toward the sky line. . . . (6)

By referring to *Gulliver's Travels* here, Rölvaag provides a familiar literary
analogue: like Gulliver, a giant in Lilliput, Per Hansa and his fellow pioneers
are metaphorical giants because of their confrontation with the prairie. But
just as clearly, they are metaphorical giants only: the land dwarfs them.
Similarly, by alluding to Swift's work of fantasy, Rölvaag implies the problems inherent in depicting an unfamiliar landscape as setting. As his opening

descriptions indicate, travel on the prairie has aspects of the fantastic about it—Per Hansa's party is lost when the novel opens, traveling to the accompaniment of the complaining prairie grass without the comfort of any Old World landmarks. So while Rölvaag's dominant mode is realism, by invoking *Gulliver's Travels* he suggests something of the fantastic as well—by doing so, he defines the same incredulity seen in Castañeda.

As in the case of Irving and Parkman, the impact of the prairie is the strongest when Per Hansa acknowledges that he is lost: "he literally did not know where he was, nor how to get to the place he had to reach" (6). Looking about for his rendezvous, Per Hansa thinks he should have been there "two or three days ago; but he hadn't seen anything that even looked like the place . . . Oh, my God! If something didn't turn up soon! . . . My God! . . . (7). As a result of this experience, Per Hansa is—like Albert Pike—thrown back upon himself; undaunted, he digs in and is determined to find their companions. True to the reaction of Alexander Henry, Per Hansa "swung over and held straight toward the highest part" of an elevation (9), and, immediately after, the party views the sunset. Like Cooper and Cather, Rölvaag uses the prairie sunset symbolically, but his usage emphasizes darkness as well as light:

> At the moment when the sun closed his eye, the vastness of the plain seemed to rise up on every hand—and suddenly the landscape had grown desolate; something bleak and cold had come into the silence, filling it with terror. . . . Behind them, along the way they had come, the plains lay dark green and lifeless, under gathering shadow of the dim, purple sky. (9)

Symbolically, the bright sunshine of the book's second paragraph ("And still more sun!") has its counterpart in Per Hansa; this image of desolation, bleakness, and silence—a terrifying landscape—has its counterpart in Beret Holm. This tension between the romantic and the realistic persists to the end of the novel. Per Hansa, after all, dies when he becomes lost while on a foolish errand made mainly to please Beret, and he is found months later, dead, with his eyes "set toward the west" (453). Thus the landscape is used throughout *Giants in the Earth* as a symbolic externalization of the philosophical and psychic differences between Per Hansa and Beret; it is the perfect symbol for a naturalistic universe against which Per Hansa struggles, armed only with his wits and his indomitable (and romantic) pioneer spirit.

While this symbolic opposition is readily apparent throughout the novel, Rölvaag lends complexity to his characterization by undercutting the ostensible symbolic values associated with Per Hansa and Beret Holm. Per Hansa is, in the main, associated with sunshine and elements that evoke the romance of pioneering while Beret, for her part, stands in opposition to these values, emphasizing the lost Old World, the starkness of the landscape, and the bleakness of their prospects. Yet in each case, Rölvaag makes it clear to the reader that the opposition is not this simple: Per Hansa's brightness is shown to be somewhat illusory and, ultimately in the subsequent volumes of Rölvaag's trilogy, *Peder Victorious* (1929) and *Their Father's God* (1931), Beret's melancholia passes—indeed, she emerges from the trilogy its truly heroic character.[32] Just before his crop is destroyed by grasshoppers, Per Hansa's brightness is counterpointed by the reader's awareness of a growing sense of impending disaster by his hubris:

> Per Hansa was in a rare mood that afternoon. Now he was binding his own wheat, his hands oily with the sap of the new-cut stems; a fine oil it was, too—he rubbed his hands together and felt a sensuous pleasure welling up within him. His body seemed to grow a little with every bundle he tied; he walked as if on springs; a strength the like of which he had never felt before ran through his muscles. How good it was to be alive! He had made a daring throw, and luck had smiled on him! . . . He tied the ripe, heavy bundles, gave them a twist, and there stood the shock! [. . .] How absurdly light-hearted and gay he felt today! . . . . (328)

Just after this, as they sit at supper, Per Hansa and his neighbor, Tönseten, engage in a good-humored conversation about how this first crop will make each of them rich (329). Per Hansa's self-congratulatory glee is undercut throughout the harvesting by the attention paid to his ongoing disagreements over farming methods with his neighbors and, most especially, by reminding the reader frequently of Beret's melancholy. Thus prepared by such loomings, the reader sees the plague of grasshoppers, especially in view of the biblical imagery that accompanies it, as retribution for Per Hansa's hubris.

Beret certainly sees the plague in this manner, for when her husband comes to her and finds her hiding in the "great chest" they brought with them from Norway, she advises him to hide too; distraught by the destruction of his crop, Hansa embraces her, crying, and Beret responds: " 'That's right!' she crooned. . . . 'Weep now, weep much and long because of your sin!' " (338). As husband and wife lie in one another's arms, Rölvaag moves the scene away from them, back to the grasshoppers and the prairie:

> Outside, the fiendish shapes flickered and danced in the dying glow of the day. The breeze had died down; the air seemed unaccountably lighter.
> . . . That night the Great Prairie stretched herself voluptuously; giantlike

and full of cunning, she laughed softly into the reddish moon. "Now we will
see what human might may avail against us! . . . . Now we'll see . . . (339)

By personifying the landscape as seductress, Rölvaag emphasizes its allure and
its deceptive charms—these attributes have seduced Per Hansa into relying
far too much on his own ability and prescience without reference to other
factors. Brought back to earth by the plague of grasshoppers—whose "fiend-
ish" cast nicely embodies the complex mixture of cultural, theological, and
philosophical assumptions Rölvaag brings to bear here—Per Hansa is both
romantic pioneer *and* struggling naturalistic victim, preyed upon by the
forces which beset him.

But if Rölvaag's personification of the landscape encapsulates the philosophical views *Giants in the Earth* presents, it also demonstrates that while Per
Hansa can be seen—even in a qualified way—as one of the "giants in the
earth" the real giant is the land itself, and in some ways the real tension in the
novel is between the mythic and the naturalistic, as the following description
of the prairie in winter suggests:

> An endless plain. From Kansas—Illinois, it stretched, far into the Cana-
> dian north, God alone knows how far; from the Mississippi River to the
> western Rockies, miles without number. . . . Endless. . . . beginningless.
> A grey waste . . . an empty silence . . . a boundless cold. Snow fell; snow
> flew, a universe of nothing but dead whiteness. Blizzards from out of the
> northwest raged, swooped down and stirred up a greyish-white fury, impene-
> trable to human eyes. As soon as these monsters tired, storms from the
> northeast were sure to come, bringing more snow. . . . "The Lord have
> mercy! This is awful!" said the folk, for lack of anything else to say.
> Monsterlike the Plain lay there—sucked in her breath one week, and the
> next week blew it out again. Man she scorned; his works she would not
> brook. . . . She would know, when the time came, how to guard herself and
> her own against him! (241)

What the mythic and the naturalistic have in common, finally, is an antago-
nism toward Christian ideology—Per Hansa, throughout, is as concerned
with trolls as he is with the Lord. But in facing the "giant" prairie, Hansa is a
character engaged in a mythic, and ultimately futile, struggle; he is out-
matched by the natural power of the prairie, certainly, but also by a sense that
it is a mysterious, cursed land. Thus the final chapter of the novel, in which
Per Hansa and Hans Olsa—the best men in the settlement—die as a result of

exposure to the elements is called "The Great Plain Drinks the Blood of Christian Men and Is Satisfied."

A more positive expression of the humbling effects of the prairie, one taking up their esthetic implications, is found in *Fruits of the Earth* by Frederick Philip Grove, the most eminent novelist of prairie pioneering in Canada. Grove's basis for his use of the prairie in his fiction, like Cather's, lay in his own experience of the landscape; thus in *Over Prairie Trails* (1922)—his first published work in English, a series of descriptive travel essays—Grove writes (and unknowingly echoes Alfred Jacob Miller and Albert Pike): "For a moment I thought that something after all was missing here on the prairies. But then I reflected again that this silence of the grave was still more perfect, still more uncanny and ghostly, because it left the imagination entirely free, without limiting it by even as much as a suggestion."[33] Grove's positive reaction to the silence and imaginative freedom occasioned by the landscape ironically echoes Irving's sense while lost that "there is something inexpressibly lonely in the solitude of a prairie. The Loneliness of a forest seems nothing to it" (100). While Irving is confounded because the prairie's open vista forces him to recognize his isolation, Grove delights in that same openness and the imaginative freedom it occasions.

At the beginning of *Fruits of the Earth* (1933), Grove's most direct treatment of prairie pioneering, his protagonist, Abe Spalding, is not much interested in understanding the prairie land he comes to settle and conquer.[34] Coming west from Brant County, Ontario in the summer of 1900, Spalding is seeking "a 'clear proposition' . . . a piece of land capable of being tilled from line to line, without waste areas, without rocky stretches, without deeply cut gullies which denied his horses a foothold." Or as Grove more pointedly observes: Spalding "wanted land, not landscape, all the landscape he cared for he would introduce himself." He dreams, moreover, of "a mansion dominating an extensive holding of land, imposed upon that holding as a sort of seigneurial sign-manual. Dominating this prairie."[35] Thus, Abe's attitude resembles that of Cather's John Bergson and Rölvaag's Per Hansa, for he seeks to dominate the prairie by enforcing his will upon it, shaping it to his needs and to his vision.

Grove underscores this theme of man against prairie by Abe's first dramatic, and symbolic action. Instead of spending the night in town upon his arrival, Spalding travels out to his claim and, though it is late afternoon, ploughs until sundown, cutting sixteen rounds. While doing so, Abe "had the peculiar feeling as though he were ploughing over an appreciable fraction of the curvature of the globe; for whenever he turned at the north end of his furrow, he could no longer see his wagon, as though it were hidden behind the shoulder of the earth" (25). Grove's basis for this scene had its source in personal experience—reminiscent of Cooper and Cather—as he explains in *In Search of Myself* (1946):

> Somewhere towards the end of my outward drive, to town, I saw a man; and what is more, he was ploughing straight over the crest of a hill to the west, coming, when I caught sight of him, towards my trail. The town which I was approaching lay on the railway, in the dry belt of the country; the general verdict was that the surrounding district was unfit for farming. The mere fact, therefore, that this man was ploughing as he came over the crest of the hill was sufficiently arresting and even startling. Besides, outlined as he was against a tilted and spoked sunset in the western sky, he looked like a giant.[36]

Running counter to his resolve to conquer the prairie as he rides out to his claim, however, is an inchoate attraction to the land as it is: "He would conquer! Yet, as he looked about, he was strangely impressed with this treeless prairie under the afternoon sun. . . . this prairie seemed suddenly a peculiar country, mysteriously endowed with a power of testing temper and character"; thus translating the attraction of the prairie into a challenge, Abe continues to assert his initial resolve: "But this immense and utter loneliness merely aroused him to protest and contradiction: he would change this prairie, would impose himself upon it, would conquer its spirit!" (22–23).

Throughout the first part of the novel, as the title of this section, "Abe Spalding," suggests, the landscape is a thing Abe molds to suit his desires. A man possessed, he thinks only of his ongoing battle with the soil and the elements, having no time for his family, nor any for his neighbors' discussions of metaphysical questions, nor any for relaxation. Abe dreams only of the time when he will put twelve hundred acres of wheat in; he does so and, through a last-minute decision to stack his wheat, turns probable ruin into his best crop ever. Flush with victory, Abe finally builds his mansion complete with electric power; seeing its lights blazing one night from miles away constitutes his "proudest moment" (119). The prairie seems to have its revenge, however, for a year later and as a result of Abe's haste, his favorite child, Charlie, is crushed to death beneath a wagonload of wheat.

The shock of Charlie's death, following so closely upon Abe's achievement of his dreams, effects a change in his character. Whereas before he has been an economic pragmatist, monomaniacally concerned only with subduing his land, Abe becomes in Part II a man motivated by selflessness and civic pride. Grove dramatizes this transformation through Abe's changing perception of the prairie landscape—but he does so in an overtly schematic manner far less satisfying than Cather's. In a chapter entitled "The Prairie," Abe notices that his dream mansion, which has existed for only five years, is already showing the wear of the prairie winds, as is his windbreak of trees. Gazing across the prairie, Abe realizes that "Whatever relieved the sky-line was man's work" (135), and like his house and windbreak, these too were in the process of being leveled by the force of natural elements. Thus he concludes that on the prairie, even after twenty years of continuous settlement "man remains distinctly an interloper" (137).

To balance this newfound realistic view of his position on the prairie, Abe also acquires another new viewpoint which, if not exactly romantic, at least involves an appreciation of the imaginative effects of the landscape, and which takes the form of an articulation of his earlier, inchoate sense of the peculiar and mysterious on the prairie. He appreciates the

> frequency of mirages. Often a distant strip of land was lifted above the hori-
> zon like a low-flung cloud; a town or a group of farmsteads, ordinarily hid-
> den behind the intervening shoulder of the world, stood up clearly against
> the whitish sky which only overhead shaded off into a pale blue. . . . On
> this prairie, near things often seemed to be distant—a haystack no more
> than a quarter of a mile away loomed gigantic as though separated from the
> eye by two or three miles. (135)

Throughout this chapter, it is as if after twenty years in the area Abe discovers the landscape for the first time—he who years earlier had wanted "land, not landscape." Although as Grove planned it, Abe also sees and understands the peculiarly characteristic traits of the prairie landscape that strangely impressed him as he rode out to plough his first furrow in the summer of 1900.

Significantly, one of the images Grove employs in articulating Abe's newfound understanding is the same as that used by Cather in Jim Burden's trip to the family's garden—the soaring hawk. Grove writes: "Altogether it is even to-day a landscape which in spite of the ever encroaching settlements of man, seems best to be appreciated by a low, soaring, flight, as by that of the marsh-hawk so commonly seen" (136). Similarly, in the midst of a description of various aspects of the landscape, Grove writes:

> The prevailing silence—for, apart from man's dwellings, not even the
> wind finds anything to play its tunes on—is accentuated rather than dis-
> turbed by the sibilant hum, in early summer, of the myriads of mosquitoes
> that haunt the air. . . . That silence, like the flat landscape itself, has some-

thing haunted about it, something almost furtive. . . . (final ellipsis Grove's, 138)

This seeming silence is the very same aspect of the land which so impressed Albert Pike and so disturbed Cather and Rölvaag's Beret Holm—the capacity of the prairie to seem, concurrently, both vacant and full of life, to both attract and repel.

Finally, when Abe's newfound knowledge is fully articulated, Grove resorts to the traditional prairie/ocean analogy:

> Abe, now that he was becoming conscious of this landscape at last, and of its significance, could at first hardly understand that he, of all men, should have chosen this district to settle in, though it suited him well enough now. But even that became clear. He had looked down at his feet; had seen nothing but the furrow; had considered the prairie only as a page to write the story of his life upon. His vision had been bounded by the lines of his farm; his farm had been floated on that prairie as the shipwright floats a vessel on the sea, looking not so much at the waves which are to batter it as at the fittings which secure the comfort of those within. But such a vessel may be engulfed by such a sea. (138)

Before Abe had been aware only of his farm, his "ship," but now he sees his metaphoric ship within the context of the wider sea in which it sails. Though a hackneyed analogy, Grove employs it here to interject a familiar parallel into a still largely unfamiliar landscape, just as Cather did through Burden's feeling that the prairie grass made the land feel as if it were in motion. The prairie landscape, moreover, is a fit symbol of Abe's transformation, since it provides him with an uninterrupted view—a long perspective—unequalled on earth. Although it takes him twenty years, Abe eventually obtains an understanding of himself and of his community that equals in imaginative breadth the physical vastness of the prairie. That vastness is "a landscape in which, to him who surrenders himself, the sense of one's life as a whole seems always present, birth and death being mere scansions in the flow of a some-what debilitated stream of vitality" (137).

In coming to conquer, Abe Spalding stands as a fictional analogue to such earlier commentators as Lewis and Clark, who failed to see the uniqueness of the prairie landscape in their adherence to contemporary esthetics, and to Washington Irving, who was equipped to see the landscape only in terms of his previously inculcated literary conventions. And just as the landscape forced itself upon Irving when he was lost, so the prairie asserted its peculiar impressiveness for Abe. Like those actual travelers and explorers who preceded him onto the prairie, Grove's Abe Spalding learns, as Cather's John Bergson does not, that man must adapt to the prairie and understand it—it will not adapt to him nor be conquered by him; it is implacable: "Man passes, they say; his work remains. Does it? It seemed vain in the face of the composure of this prairie" (262).

In Wallace Stegner's *On a Darkling Plain* (1939) the pioneering theme is treated from a slightly different perspective. Edwin Vickers, just released from the Princess Pats regiment because of lung damage from mustard gas suffered during the battle of Ypres, arrives in the spring of 1918 to take up a homestead in southern Saskatchewan near the American border. Like other pioneers, he is seeking a new life, but his reasons for taking up a homestead alone cluster about his desire to flee society: "He was a man upon the earth, anchored in the rind of a continent, as far from the fever and sickness of humanity as he could get; his own man, taking no orders and needing no support."[37] Seeking isolation on the prairie, Vickers learns—like his predecessors—that the landscape forces introspection. He soon discovers his need for humanity and so befriends his neighbor's daughter. Reminiscent of Garland's "Among the Corn Rows" and Cather's "On the Divide," Vickers is frightened, as well, when he meets another neighbor, Wilde, whose sod hut is filled with pictures of women appealing to his "perversion and starved lust" (90–91). Vickers is aware of his own sexual needs and, at the same time, acknowledges a neighbor's reasons for declining his invitation to share a meal, the same motives which concerned Garland and Stringer: "No. Wife's over home waitin'. Been alone four days. That's enough in this country. Drive you batty in a week" (113).

But while Stegner dissects the psychological effects of prairie isolation during Vickers's time on the prairie, much of his analysis defines the way the landscape makes a person feel:

> To kill some of the interminable time he began to keep a diary, putting into it whatever he saw or felt or thought. The way a hawk coasting in a long glide down an air current suddenly folded wings and dropped, a red-brown streak through the afternoon; the scuffle of dust where it struck, and the heavy launching again, the slow beating upward and southward with a gopher limp in the dragging talons.
>
> That, or the drift of the wind after sundown, always a west wind that blew directly out of the clean sky, trailing the roll of the eastward earth. A dozen times he tried to get into poetry that feeling of riding the naked back of a planet, but the thing was stubborn in his hands, an image too big for him. If he did get something down, it turned out next day when he read it

over to be a series of glib Tennysonian prettinesses that he ripped out of the tablet and threw at the wall. At times like those he hated the vast earth. It was too big and too impersonal; it dwarfed him, made his very consciousness seem sick, as if he were the one spot of corrupt tissue in a might health. (109–10)

Describing Vickers's attempt to describe the prairie, Stegner addresses the several esthetic problems raised by the prairie landscape. Vickers longs to capture the feeling of "riding," Pegasus like, "the naked back of a planet." But though, as here in the description of a hawk's kill, Vickers evidently has muse enough he does not have the means to articulate his scene and his sense of it. Instead, he scorns his inculcated literary conventions—such is his implication—for they are not suitable form for his feelings. The land's impersonality forces him to reckon with his own minuscule stature in relation to the larger world—it forces him to objectify, to recognize his own insignificance. And later, Vickers writes as much in a letter to a friend: "That is the magnificence of this country. It takes my breath sometimes, the sweep of it. But I can't get a flash of it into poetry that satisfies me. It's altogether too indifferent to my little human itches and urges and yearnings" (127). Vickers implies here that his difficulty arises from the land itself—it scorns subjectivity. A poet and critic who also scorned subjectively was, of course, Mathew Arnold, whose "Dover Beach" is the source of Stegner's title. Although the allusion relates mainly to Vickers's retreat from society—where "ignorant armies clash by night"—because of its alienating qualities, Stegner's Saskatchewan "darkling plain" provides also only a temporary retreat from subjectivity.

And Vickers's inability to write poetry that satisfies him, as he continues to explain in his letter, seems "to mean that poetry and art have to deal with people or there's no reason for their existing. There's no point in landscape for landscape's sake. My lines about wind and sun and moon and the motion of blowing grass are as asinine out here as silk parasol would be, or eau de Colgne" (127). Like Cather, Rölvaag, and Grove, Stegner raises esthetic issues here that are rooted in psychological responses to the landscape itself. As he says, by its very nature art must deal with humanity but the essence of the prairie landscape is the relative absence of humanity, even to the present. In this vein, too, is another comment in his letter, where he says that the land makes him feel as if he is "hanging on" to the earth "so tight that there isn't time to analyze" emotions (123). Vickers's dissatisfaction, like Abe Spalding's when he sees the prairie as a "peculiar country, mysteriously endowed" (23), echoes Albert Pike's view that the land has the power to throw "a man back upon himself"; that is, it enforces the very introspection and objectivity of which Vickers speaks.

Vickers's initial romantic exhilaration is followed by a sense of emptiness caused by his inability to capture his feelings in poetry. Though the landscape's qualities force him toward introspection, its seeming featurelessness makes articulate emotional analysis difficult. Responding to these frustrations, Vickers tries to control time by building a sundial and, through his various contacts with his neighbors, gradually recognizes his own need for human society. As he states in his letter, his art depends upon interaction within society. Vickers' resolve to return to society—forced upon him in part by the objectifying properties of the prairie landscape—is carried out when the town nearest his homestead is struck by the flu outbreak of 1918 where, recognizing his responsibility, he takes part in ministering to its victims.

In *On a Darkling Plain,* then, Stegner employs the landscape as a catalyst for Vickers's recuperation. The prairie's "magnificence" forces Vickers to rely on his personal abilities, and faced by such a bare and impersonal vista, he must rethink his relations with the rest of humanity and with the very earth itself as he rides "the naked back of a planet." And Edwin Vickers, though he is an unusual homesteader in that he is fleeing society, is nevertheless as much a pioneer as Per Hansa or Abe Spalding; each opened new land for settlement and reacted to the requirements of the land. Explorers and travelers attested to the ways in which the prairie landscape made them rethink their assumptions, but Wallace Stegner, like Cather, Rölvaag, and Grove before him, transformed an imaginative process into a major technical motif in fiction.

The representative works examined here—comprising only a small portion of the fiction treating prairie pioneering—show that the opening of the prairie to art through its use as setting required as much imaginative and technical adaptation from writers as the landscape did of its settlers. Stegner's overt analyses of Vickers's compositional problems are confirmed, explicitly and precisely, in Cather's subtle prairie novels and confirmed, more directly but equally emphatically, in Rölvaag and Grove's novels of pioneering. For artistic pioneers as well as literal pioneers on the prairie, clearly, "the great fact was the land itself."

Part **3**

Inhabitants

5

A Complex of Possibilities:

Prairie as Home Place

Because they came west to stay, prairie pioneers were responding to very different motivations than those that drove the explorers and travelers who preceded them. Yet even so, homesteaders shared a crucial perception with their predecessors: each group was struck, first and foremost, by the pristine newness and scope of the land—Henry Nash Smith's "virgin land" or Jim Burden's "not a country at all, but the material out of which countries are made" (7)—and so by extension struck by the potential the prairie offered to succeeding generations (though, to be sure, estimations of this potential waxed and waned over time). Explorer, traveler, and pioneer are united then by the enterprises of beginnings—seeing, describing, mapping, and finally, settling—each of which engendered, as has been seen, a concomitant fervor derived from being the first to grapple with the prairie landscape. But as the works of Howe, Stringer, and Cather have already demonstrated, inhabiting the prairie was quite a different matter altogether from settling it. Rather than excitement, the prairie as home place in fiction is characterized by a certain somnolence which Cather chose to see—in both *O Pioneers!* and *My Ántonia*, but most thoroughly in *One of Ours* and *A Lost Lady*—as complacency. Hers was a harsh view—and the degree to which she held it is still an arguable point—yet once the prairie was settled, the imaginative and practical problem became, quite simply, how to live there.

Beginning this consideration of the function of the prairie landscape in fiction written about postpioneering generations with what appears to be a ringing statement of the obvious is a way of getting at both the variety and complexity of the issues raised in the fiction. For the first time, attention is turned to the prairie, which is no longer viewed as "new land" but rather as "my land," and by extension, my place. As with Cather's criticisms of succeeding generations and her defensiveness at the hands of easterners who did not—and still do not—view the prairie as fictional setting as "interesting," the writers examined in this chapter display both harshness toward and defensiveness about the prairies but, also like Cather, they display equally a sense of single-minded identification and affirmation with the prairies as *their* home place. Almost all born there and schooled to see the East as cultural mecca, these writers are perhaps understandably ambivalent about their homes, yet their fiction not only affirms individual identity through their prairie roots, it also bears the stamp of the prairie as *their* landscape. Yet as their personal histories and the development of their fiction make clear—and here Willa Cather offers a major example of the western native ever struggling with the imaginative demands of western space—this process was neither very easy nor, really, ever complete.

The imaginative effects of prairie space have persisted in weighing heavily on the minds of native-born writers, so much so that allusions to the landscape are central to their comments touching upon the West as personal heritage. Thus Canadian Robert Kroetsch has written of "the consequence of the northern prairies to human definition: the diffusion of personality into a complex of possibilities rather than a concluded self" while Wright Morris has spoken in the same fashion of the Nebraska plains as having "conditioned what I see, what I look for, and what I find in the world to write about." Perhaps most pointedly, N. Scott Momaday has written of the west generally:

> The land itself seems to inspire artistic expression. In every season it is touched with clear and brilliant light; there are natural formations of every shape, color, and size—and these very dimensions seem to change with the time of day. So deeply involved with this landscape are those who live within it that it may be said to determine human thought and expression.

Demonstrating this feeling in *House Made of Dawn* (1966), Momaday recounts a Kiowa's description of his tribe's lands in the southern prairie:

> Loneliness is there as an aspect of the land. All things in the plain are isolate; there is no confusion of objects in the eye, but *one* hill or *one* tree or *one* man. At the slightest elevation you can see to the end of the world. To look upon that landscape in the early morning, with the sun at your back, is to lose the sense of proportion. Your imagination comes to life, and this, you think, is where Creation was begun.
>
> . . . .

The first man among them to stand on the edge of the Great Plains saw farther over land than he had ever seen before. There is something about the heart of the continent that resides always in the end of vision, some essence of the sun and wind. That man knew the possible quest. There was nothing to prevent his going out; he could enter upon the land and be alive, could bear at once the great hot weight of its silence. In a sense the question of survival had never been more imminent, for no land is more the measure of human strength. But neither had wonder been more accessible to the mind nor destiny to the will. [1]

In so describing the landscape's imaginative effects, and especially by saying that "no land is more the measure of human strength," Momaday defines the physical and imaginative tasks not only of the prairie pioneer, but also of the prairie inhabitant. They too have had to grapple—and indeed, grapple still—with the determinative effects of prairie space.

The imaginative task of the prairie-born writer is of a different order from that of those who chronicled pioneering, for after the pioneer period passed there is no longer "new land," only the land, settled, used and, to the degree possible, imaginatively digested. Within this scheme, the prairie landscape is no longer a strange new world that must be understood on its own terms; it is an overarching presence, seemingly understood, that has been incorporated into the prairie writer's very being yet, because it remains strange and daunting—it is a landscape ever at odds with conventional esthetics. The prairie offers only an uneasy solace. Momaday, writing from his Kiowa background, sees the prairie as the land of his people for generations—a heritage his protagonist, Abel, has rejected by leaving for the army and for Los Angeles. But the prairie writer of European descent, unable to so see the prairie settled by whites only a generation or two before, faces the problem of writing from what amounts to an alien landscape—alienated from his eastern audience and seemingly barren of human connections.

Robert Kroetsch poses the prairie writer's dilemma succinctly when he asks "How do you establish any sort of *close* relationship in a landscape—in a physical situation—whose primary characteristic is *distance?*" On another occasion, he defines the context of his question and, at the same time, points to the paradox of prairie fiction and to the contemporary writer's technical, esthetic, and perceptual problems in trying to contain prairie space within the covers of a book. In "On Being an Alberta Writer," Kroetsch asks "How do you write in a new country?" and goes on to say:

> Our inherited literature, the literature of our European past and of eastern
> North America, is emphatically the literature of a people who have *not* lived

on prairies. We had, and still have, difficulty finding names for the elements and characteristics of this landscape. The human response to this landscape is so new and ill-defined that our writers come back, uneasily but compulsively, to landscape writing. Like the homesteaders before us, we are compelled to adjust and invent, to remember and forget. We feel a profound ambiguity about the past—about both its contained stories and its modes of perception.[2]

A compulsion to write the landscape is rooted, as Kroetsch says, in the homesteading experience. Yet because that period has passed, he evinces both ambivalence and skepticism about such writing even as he acknowledges that it derives from an inescapable imaginative relationship with the land. Such a landscape demands of its writers, in Kroetsch's words, "a complex of possibilities rather than a concluded self." At the core of this complex is, as Momaday says, a deep involvement with the landscape, an integration so profound "that it may be said to determine human thought and expression." Cather communicates this feeling of an almost symbiotic integration between character and landscape in her postpioneering fiction of the 1920s, especially in *Death Comes for the Archbishop,* but it is also apparent in all her work after *My Ántonia.* Though Virginia-born, Cather's artistry presages the prairie writer's fundamental conundrum: coming to terms with the determinative effects and personal associations of prairie space and, in so doing, forging a relationship with the home place. Like Cather herself, many native-born writers have fled the prairies only to return in their fiction to their "home pasture."

Postpioneering Prairie

If, as previously argued, pioneering is the paradigmatic story of prairie fiction, then relations between pioneers and successive generations follows immediately after as a major motif. Social changes wrought in the Hanover and Black Hawk districts after the urgency of pioneering had passed are a backdrop to, respectively, *O Pioneers!* and *My Ántonia,* and Cather moves such concerns centerstage in *One of Ours* and *A Lost Lady.* Likewise, both Grove and Rölvaag offer relations between generations as a major concern, the latter in two sequels to *Giants in the Earth, Peder Victorious* and *Their Father's God.* Indeed, these concerns persist well into the modern era. Intergenerational relations—the prairie as heritage, as home—lie at the heart of Wright Morris's works—witness his *Plains Song: For Female Voices* (1980)—and, in

Canada, Margaret Laurence's Manawaka series. And as writers explored relations between pioneers and their children, the prairie small town as image and social structure assumed greater consequence and, like family ties to prairie place, lingers still in the fiction.

Martha Ostenso's *Wild Geese* (1925) is representative of the first treatments of postpioneering in its concern with a pioneer's relations with his children. Born in Norway and brought to the northern prairies as an infant, Ostenso uses the interlake and prairie regions of Manitoba as setting for *Wild Geese*. Thus the novel has been singled out from her works set in the U.S. and treated within the Canadian context. Ostenso uses the land deliberately to define her major antagonists, the pioneer Caleb Gare and his daughter Judith. While Gare tries to conquer his land, wringing from it all it will produce, Judith rebels against his domination and in doing so exhibits an understanding attitude toward the land that is, in some ways, reminiscent of Alexandra Bergson's.

Caleb is a pioneer who strives to dominate everything around him—the prairie, his family, and his community. Unlike Abe Spalding, Gare has no redeeming qualities whatsoever; he is able to manage feeling only for a prized field of flax and is, emphatically, a miner of the soil—he simply oversees the work done by his children. As Ostenso presents him, Gare's harshness is defined by the land itself: Caleb "could not be characterized in terms of human virtue or human vice," for he is "a spiritual counterpart of the land, as harsh, as demanding, as tyrannical as the very soil from which he drew his existence."[3] As a melodramatic villain, Gare's control over his family is in the same generic vein, since he maintains his sway by virtue of the "dark secret" he holds over his wife, who bore an illegitimate son by another man before their marriage; thus he succeeds in cowing all his children but Judith, who defies him. Relations within the Gare family are seen from the point of view of Lind Archer, a newly arrived teacher who boards with them.[4]

Daniel S. Lenoski has perceptively written that in *Wild Geese* "Ostenso is clearly attempting to synthesize voice and prairie space as completely as possible"; he continues to assert that "the land is not *merely* geography" to the novel's characters. "It is image. It *means*. It has value that gives their lives meaning."[5] Indeed, Ostenso's recreation of "prairie space" parallels Cather's, particularly in that the land is characterized as a living thing, and that Judith Gare—who like Alexandra has a "gift of sympathy"—perceives the land's being more thoroughly than others. Yet as Lenoski argues, the imaginative effects of prairie space unite all Ostenso's characters—it is a means of characterization. Even Gare cherishes a field of flax above all else ("There was a transcendent power in this blue field of flax that lifted a man above the petty artifices of birth, life, and death" [119]). In a heavy-handed discussion of the "spareness of both physical and spiritual life" on the northern prairies, Ostenso has Mark Jordan—Mrs. Gare's illegitimate son—articulate her technique in using prairie space as her major element of characterization:

> The silence is awful. You feel immense things going on, invisibly. There is that eternal sky—light and darkness—the endless plains of snow—a few fir trees, maybe a hill or a frozen stream. And the human beings are like totems—figures of wood with mysterious legends upon them that you can never make out. The austerity of nature reduces the outward expression of life, simply, I think, because there is not such an abundance of natural objects for the spirit to react to. We are, after all, only the mirror of our environment. Life here at Oeland, even, may seem a negation but it's only a reflection from so few objects that it has the semblance of negation. These people are thrown inward upon themselves, their passions are stored up, they are intensified figures of life with no outward expression—no releasing gesture. (78)

Like Laurence Ricou before him, Lenoski uses this passage to discuss the ways in which the prairie landscape enforces introspection—well they might. Yet when placed in the context established here, Ostenso's words eerily echo explorers and literary figures alike, particularly the phrase "thrown inward upon themselves," a sentiment almost identical to Albert Pike's "throwing a man back upon himself" of a century before.

Thus the major characters in *Wild Geese* are counterpointed by the landscape, and defined primarily in relation to it. Gare is described in images of landscape, although significantly not of the prairie: his head "loomed forward from the rest of his body like a rough projection of rock from the edge of a cliff . . ." (13). Looming over the others as malevolent presence and likened to a cliff, Gare may be seen analogous to Cooper's rock tower, which serves as Ishmael Bush's bastion in *The Prairie*. His role in the novel, furthermore, also is analogous to Bush's: he too is antagonist and catalyst for his book's action. After berating his family one evening—his usual practice—Gare emerges with his lantern to take his ritualistic walk through his fields. Here Ostenso draws upon the prairie setting in order to dramatize her protagonist's mania:

> Far out across the prairie a lantern was swinging low along the earth, and dimly visible was the squat, top-heavy form of a man. It was Caleb Gare. He walked like a man leaning forward against a strong wind. He frequently went outside alone so, with a lantern; no one knew where, nor why; no one asked. Judith had once told Amelia scornfully that it was to assure himself that his land was still all there. . . .

> Caleb pressed on through the half-dark, leaning forward as if against some
> invisible obstacle. Presently he came to a ridge from which he could look
> east and west, north and south, upon the land that was his; the two tame
> hayfields, separated from each other by a neck of timber belonging to Fusi
> Aronson (it would be well to own that timber, a fine stand it was) [. . . .]
> (18–19)

Two elements in the landscape are used to characterize Gare: seen from a
distance on the prairie, carrying his lantern (like Alexandra at the end of the
first chapter of *O Pioneers!*), Gare's symbolic stature is made imagistically vivid
to the reader. Similarly, Ostenso uses the view from an eminence—like
Howe's use of the church tower—as a means to delimit Caleb's position on the
prairie, the extent of his holdings, his desire for more land, and his distrust-
ing, acquisitive attitude toward his neighbors.

The wild geese, Ostenso's central symbol, are first seen flying north "to a
region beyond human warmth . . . beyond even human isolation . . ." (32).
Their flight symbolizes Judith Gare's movement away from her father's tyr-
anny. Despite Caleb's attempts to cow her by beating and stabling her, Judith
affirms her spirit, and rejoices in the child she conceives out of wedlock. Like
Cather's Alexandra, Judith is ultimately her father's opposite: he lacks all
feelings while she delights in her emotions and displays an Alexandra-like
sympathy with of the rhythms of the earth, as seen most clearly when she
removes her clothing and embraces the ground.[6] Thus when Judith serves as
central consciousness for a view of the prairie landscape, her personality and
history combine to present both its romance and its harshness:

> As she jogged along in the cart, her eyes idled across the flat, unsurprising
> earth that went on and on into the north with scarcely a perceptible undula-
> tion. Here was the bush land, without magnificence, without primitive re-
> dundance of growth: here was the prairie, spare as an empty platter—no,
> there was the solitary figure of a man upon it, like a meagre offering of earth
> to heaven. Here were the little wood trails and prairie trails that a few men
> had made on lonely journeyings, and here the crossings where they had met
> to exchange a word or two. The sky above it all was blue and tremendous, a
> vast country for proud birds that were ever on the wing, seeking, seeking.
> And a little delicate wind that was like a woman, Jude thought to herself,
> but could in a moment become a male giant violating the earth. (112–13)

While writers such as Willa Cather and others have noted the presence of birds
on the prairie, Ostenso highlights the animation their presence brings the

landscape. Describing her first impression of the prairie landscape, when she was ten years old, Cather recalls being impressed by "splendid notes" of the larks.[7] Ostenso also employs these birds to dramatize both poles of the prairie experience; the prairie is empty, the site of "lonely journeyings," but also arched over by a "tremendous" blue sky for "seeking" birds. Her final sentence, which lends symbolic weight to the omnipresent prairie winds, draws upon an element in the landscape to make a thematic point particular to *Wild Geese*—Judith is like the "delicate wind," in view of her understanding of the earth's rhythms while Caleb Gare, her polar opposite, is a "male giant violating the earth."

Wild Geese combines romance and realism in its depiction of pioneer prairie life, as do the works of Garland and Cather. Yet the way in which Ostenso went about her mixture is instructive: by reaching to the conventions of the melodrama for her depiction of Caleb Gare, who is a human equivalent to the landscape—a figure like Abe Spalding but who, unlike Grove's character, is melodramatically evil and so unable to learn—she posits a most extreme view of the land's harshness. As with Abe Spalding's overarching ambition and Rölvaag's reference to Gulliver's Lilliput, however, the exaggeration with which Caleb's character is drawn suggests the fantastic—the land seems to demand a man who is a tyrant, a harsh monomaniac, or perverse giant. To balance this view, though, Ostenso presents Judith with her sense of the land as a delicate creature, something to be understood and nurtured, and to be enveloped by the image of the ever "seeking" geese. Throughout, her characters display an almost symbiotic relation with the land, as Judith herself asserts: "The land was here, they were all rooted to it, like the hay, and the grain and the trees in the bush. Departure from it would only mean an end of growth" (283). In *Wild Geese,* then, the fantastic harshness of the land demands melodrama while, at the same time, its romantic qualities are equally evident—by organically defining their roles in the narrative, the landscape affects all Ostenso's characters, achieving the fusion of "voice and prairie space" she sought.

Another representative novel that concerns the relations between pioneers and those who came immediately after is Conrad Richter's *The Sea of Grass* (1937). Richter, born in Pennsylvania, went west to live in New Mexico and this novel draws upon his experiences there, depicting life on the West Texas–Eastern New Mexico plains during the period in which settlers took up land previously used for cattle ranching. The sea-of-grass image, an overt invocation of the prairie/sea analogy, is central to Richter's depiction because certain of his characters—most notably Lutie Brewton and the nesters who try to settle the land—seem to drown there.

The narrative technique is similar to that of *My Ántonia.* Told from the point of view of Hal, a nephew of the protagonist, Colonel Jim Brewton, the novel dramatizes Brewton's relations with the settlers, or nesters, and with his wife, Lutie Brewton. Like *My Ántonia,* too, Richter's use of a first-person narrator distances the work's inherent romanticism from its author. Hal, who was a boy when ranchers such as his uncle were at the height of their influence, tells a tale tinged with nostalgia for those days, since as he grows he watches his uncle's power progressively diminish.

Richter depicts this decline on two levels, the public and the personal, and in each realm the prairie counterpoints the decline Hal describes. Because ranchers like Brewton, who had a place "larger than Massachusetts with Connecticut thrown in,"[8] owned only a small portion of their holdings, the rest owned by the government, they are helpless to stop settlers from taking up claims on what had been "their" land. Upon being told that the army was there to protect the settlers' right to farm the land, Brewton sneers: "You can keep the nesters from being blown away but God himself can't [keep] the prairie" from being blown away (80). Brewton proves to be right, for the land that will support ranching on a large scale will not support farming on any scale at all.

The domestic plot, which runs parallel to the struggle between the ranchers and nesters, involves the relations between the Colonel and Lutie Cameron, a St. Louis belle who comes west to marry him. A person of great intensity, Lutie bears three children but, because she is not a frontier woman, she cannot bear the isolation of her ranch house and ultimately leaves the Colonel. Richter defines her dissatisfaction through her aversion to the prairie land-scape, apparent as soon as she arrives in Salt Fork from St. Louis, as Hal relates:

> But when we reached the top of the escarpment and, suddenly like com-ing on the ocean unaware, there in front of us stretched the vast, brown, empty plain, dipping and pitching endlessly like a parched sea, she stopped as if she had run into barbed wire. I tried to point out a remote, nearly in-distinguishable cloud shadow that marked the general location of the distant ranch house, but she didn't seem to hear me, chatting almost breathlessly about a traveling acquaintance on the Pullman palace car. . . . (13)

Upon her arrival in the house, Lutie has a wall of trees planted, ostensibly for shade, but actually because she cannot bear the open view. Describing occa-sions on which he drove his aunt into town, Hal realizes this:

> the moment we passed out through the dense wall of cottonwoods and tam-arisks, [Lutie] chatted incessantly, her sensitive face turned away from the

wide sea of grass as if it were the plague, so that I swore she never saw the road runner racing with the carriage wheel or the antelope moving among the cattle. And I thought that at last I begun to understand the reason for her wall of cottonwoods and tamarisks, which had not been planted for summer shade at all. (33)

Lutie's response to the landscape is like that of Blanche Burke in *The Moccasin Ranch,* Mr. Shimerda in *My Ántonia,* and Beret Holm in *Giants in the Earth;* each author sees some people as constitutionally ill-suited for life on the prairie which, as Washington Irving wrote, does not allow the individual to imagine "some livelier scene beyond."[9] As commentators like Brackenridge and Butler attest, too, the prairie vista makes one aware of his isolation, and as Stegner's Edwin Vickers realizes, this forces a person to objectify his situation. Taking such feelings to an extreme, Lutie cannot bear isolation and, at the same time, she has little sympathy with her husband's fight with the nesters who are, to her, the very social element she misses. Thus, she leaves both her husband and her children. Lutie's inability to cope with frontier conditions, however, has the effect of enhancing Richter's presentation of Colonel Brewton as a romantic pioneer—like Cather's Captain Forrester in *A Lost Lady*—a man of forthright morals and spartan endurance. Hal describes his qualities nostalgically in the novel's first paragraph, saying,

> That lusty pioneer blood is tamed now, broken and gelded like the wild horse and the frontier settlement. And I think I shall never see it flowing through human veins again as it did in my Uncle Jim Brewton riding a lathered horse across his shaggy range or standing in his massive ranch house, bare of furniture as a garret, and holding together his empire of grass and cattle by the fire in his eyes. (3)

By depicting Brewton romantically, as a massive figure bent on controlling the prairie, Richter offers a view consistent with that seen in Cather, Rölvaag, Grove, and Ostenso. John Bergson sought to dominate the land, and as he is dying recognizes the futility of his approach, since the land was like a horse no one could break. Per Hansa, Abe Spalding, and Caleb Gare also sought to control the prairie and bend it to their wills—yet each failed. Thus by evoking the romantic image of the new, scarcely touched land sullied by the nesters, Richter is within what might be called the romantic tradition of prairie writing, a tradition that includes the numerous elation-deflation reactions seen in earlier descriptions and depictions of the prairie as well as the stories of pioneering. Yet in *The Sea of Grass,* the transformation of the land is brought about not so much by a changing single point of view as by the collision of different points of view. The ranchers value the land in its semi-wild state while settlers, regardless of advice to the contrary, are determined to attempt farming. Equally, Lutie and the nesters value settlement and the society it brings, even as the land proves too arid for settlement. Without the "sea of grass" to cover the soil, the prairie blows away, leaving a land suitable for neither purpose. As such, Richter's novel depicts a prairie that has passed through the pioneer stage, and the issues it raises relate not to settlement but its proper usage once settled.

Small Town Ethos and the Dust Bowl 1930s

E. W. Howe's *The Story of a Country Town* began in 1883 a tradition of fictional treatment of the prairie small town that takes up the concerns of life after pioneering. Works by Garland, Cather, Edna Ferber, Ruth Suckow, and others define small-town American life and foster, further, "the revolt from the village." Such small towns were not exclusively prairie towns, of course, but they reach their apogee in Sinclair Lewis's *Main Street* (1920), which depicts Gopher Prairie, Minnesota, from the point of view of Carol Kennicott, newly married wife of the town's physician and newly arrived from Min-neapolis. Despite her attempts to improve life in the town through a literary association and similar cultural efforts, Gopher Prairie is unyielding: its residents will not alter their smug and intolerant ways. And while the landscape is of no particular importance to Lewis's dissection of small-town narrow-mindedness, its connotation of isolation from cultural centers is vital to the novel, since Lewis is drawing upon the same eastern prejudice as that articulated by Cather's New York critic: "I simply don't care a damn what happens in [the prairie West], no matter who writes about it." Thus, in *Main Street* the prairie connotes rural America after pioneering has passed, a place from which relatively cultured and enlightened people, like Carol Kennicott, are forced to flee.

In contrast, some of the best fiction depicting the prairie small town ethos also dramatizes its second crucial period, the dust bowl thirties. These were bad years for the region, yet the drought produced some of the finest prairie fiction—Sinclair Ross's *As For Me and My House* (1941) and W. O. Mitchell's *Who Has Seen the Wind* (1947), being two of the most notable examples.

Indeed, critics in Canada have long seen Ross's fiction as a sine qua non of Great Depression literature—coupled with Anne Marriott's *The Wind Our Enemy* and glossed by Barry Broadfoot's *Ten Lost Years,* Ross's stories and *As For Me and My House* define and dramatize the dust bowl years on the Canadian prairies.[10] Yet Ross's claim to preeminence rests on esthetic grounds only, since his fictions pale beside the actual sine qua non of depression fiction, John Steinbeck's *The Grapes of Wrath.* Its electric appeal from its publication two years before *As For Me and My House,* in 1939, is well-known, an appeal punctuated and amplified by the film version produced in 1940 featuring the young Henry Fonda as Tom Joad.

In fact, the prairie provides only a literal point of departure for the Joads in Steinbeck's *The Grapes of Wrath.* Evicted from their farm in Oklahoma, the Joads—like the throng of Okies they typify—set out for California to start a new life in what they hold to be a land of plenty. Hounded throughout their journey by authorities and stalked by want and starvation, the Joads represent Steinbeck's rejection of capitalism and other established norms, including Christianity. In their stead, he presents a vision based on the life cycle: people adapt—as do the Joads—to the conditions that confront them. They change, but they continue on. The role of the prairie in *The Grapes of Wrath* is that of a landscape at the bottom of the cycle during the dust bowl. Like humanity, which the Joads exemplify, it too will go on and renew itself.

For the Joads, being forced to leave constitutes an erasure of family history, of connection with a place of their own; on the eve of their departure to join 250,000 other Okies trekking toward the promised land in California, Grampa Joad expresses a wish to stay: "This country ain't no good, but its my country." In so saying, Grampa echoes an earlier sentiment expressed by the third-person narrator in one of the novel's inner chapters, who asks: "How can we live without our lives? How will we know it's us without our past?" Steinbeck's Okies—both the numberless throng and the Joads themselves—abandon such considerations to flee west, saying along with the narrator of their past: "No. Leave it. Burn it."[11]

North of the border, on the other hand, Ross's characters are entrapped by the land itself; they have no option to go, no promised land to which to flee, despite their very real motives for fleeing. Unlike Steinbeck's characters, they can neither "leave" their past nor "burn" it; they must confront it each day they live on the prairie in the throes of its drought. Ross, who was born on a Saskatchewan homestead, grew up there, and worked in several prairie small towns, offers his view most acutely in the stories collected in *The Lamp at Noon and Other Stories;* though published in 1968, it collects pieces which appeared separately between 1934 and 1952. Three of these, particularly, embody the tragic pathos of characters striving, continuing, in the face of a seemingly hostile landscape: "The Lamp at Noon," "Not By Rain Alone," and "A Field of Wheat." [12] This distinction is important here because Ross's writing is most like Steinbeck's not in *As For Me and My House,* but rather in his earlier stories. Like Steinbeck's *The Grapes of Wrath,* they dramatize the helplessness of farmers who, through no fault of their own, are unable to succeed at farming. Yet Ross seeks no recourse in politics, nor any in ideology; his characters hold out, plaintively seeking solace in a new born babe, a horse's neck, or a commitment to an unforgiving land. The agent of their destruction, always, is the prairie dust bowl itself. And both husband and wife are affected by their struggle. Indeed, the wife in "The Lamp at Noon" *is* driven mad, for she smothers her baby son trying to flee from the duststorm. But in Ross's depiction each demands a separate sympathy, she for being left alone, isolated, and unable to communicate with her husband, he because he cannot show her his fears and frustrations over the futility of his struggle with nature.

Thus for Steinbeck the dust bowl is a point of departure for a tale of epic heroism while, for Ross, it is human experience to be dramatized and, especially, detailed. Indeed, Ross's Bentleys, the protagonists of *As For Me and My House,* are the antithesis of Steinbeck's Joads: they find themselves in a dust bowl environment, one that punctuates their introspection just as its tedium encourages it. The Joads, conversely, have no time for introspection—they are perpetually up and doing, acting; as Ma Joad notices, late in the novel: "Funny, ain't it. All the time we was a-movin' an' shoven', I never thought none. An' now these here folks been nice to me, been awful nice; an' what's the first thing I do? I go right back over the sad things . . ." (357).

In *As For Me and My House* life on the prairie during the dust bowl thirties is depicted in excruciating detail and, from first to last, that detail is derived from the physical features of the prairie landscape. A sense of dispirited loneliness pervades the novel; at its outset, Philip and Mrs. Bentley—she is the narrator and has no first name—are newly arrived in Horizon where Philip is to be the local minister. Horizon is merely the latest in a succession of similar prairie towns in which they have lived since their marriage twelve years previously. The emptiness of the surrounding prairie reflects the barrenness of the Bentley's lives—the term "barren," (first used by Henry Kelsey to describe the prairie in the late seventeenth century), moreover, has several levels of meaning in the novel. A land without rain, the prairie is barren of trees; the Bentleys' marriage is spiritually barren just as it is physically barren, the latter owing to Mrs. Bentley's inability to have a child; and Philip, whom Mrs. Bentley claims to be an artist, is also seen to be artistically impotent.

Considering the implications of these factors and the ongoing critical debate over perspective in the novel, David Williams touches upon two points that are of supreme importance in assessing Ross's depiction of the dust bowl landscape:

> If Mrs. Bentley doesn't make things quite as clear to us [as other things are made to her], it is because she dare not acknowledge to herself how she projects her own spirit onto the landscape. No more desolate portrait of the Dust Bowl exists in the literature of North America because no other narrator is a barren woman, bent on blaming the earth for its infertility. [13]

Indeed, the bleak vision Ross offers in *As For Me and My House* is Mrs. Bentley's bleak vision—the novel presents the world as Mrs. Bentley is able to see it, so her own barrenness and the emptiness of her life finds its counterpart in the dust bowl landscape surrounding the Bentleys in Horizon.

The novel is narrated through Mrs. Bentley's diary entries, which are dated and cover little more than a year; there are frequent gaps of several days, which dramatize the uneventful character of her life, just as numerous repetitions dramatize the tedium of her situation. "The novel is less like a story," Warren Tallman observes, "than it is like a cumulative picture in which Ross, by a remarkable, almost *tour de force* repetition of detail, grains a central scene upon the reader's consciousness so that all other details and even the action of the novel achieve meaningful focus in relation to the one scene at the center, repeated some thirty times." [14] This central scene, repeated so many times in the novel, is Philip's retreat into his study in order to—Mrs. Bentley says— avoid her. There he sits, drawing or looking at his previous drawings, most of which depict false-fronted small-town buildings staring at one another along a prairie main street.

The source of Ross's "cumulative" picture technique is the landscape itself; his use of repetition and the diary form, moreover, constitute the culmination of a tradition in prairie writing. David Thompson commented that the journal form, "however dull, is the only method in my opinion, that can give the reader a clear idea of" the prairie landscape, and here Thompson confirmed the internal evidence provided by Henday's repetitions of "We are still in the Muscuty plains" and also Kelsey's implicit vexation with the vastness of the landscape. Thompson's observation was itself later confirmed in the writings of Edwin James, George Catlin, and John Lambert, among others, who noted the monotony of the landscape and the ways in which this monotony affects the imagination. As it is used by both Thompson and Ross, the journal format attempts to give suitable form to the land's monotony. Similarly, in his first

extended description of Horizon's locale and environs, Ross combines a series
of responses and techniques frequently found in prairie literature:

> It's an immense night out there, wheeling and windy. The lights on the
> street and in the houses are helpless against the black wetness, little unillu-
> minating glints that might be painted on it. The town seems huddled to-
> gether, cowering on a high, tiny perch, afraid to move lest it topple into the
> wind. Close to the parsonage is the church, black even against the darkness,
> towering ominously up through the night and merging with it. . . . Above,
> in the high cold night, the wind goes swinging past, indifferent, liplessly
> mournful. It frightens me, makes me feel lost, dropped on this little perch
> of town and abandoned. I wish Philip would waken. [15]

This passage has much in common with Wister's description of Medicine Bow
and Cather's opening paragraph in *O Pioneers!*—the town seen from a distance, the possibility that it might "topple in the wind," and the indifference
of the forces without. Mrs. Bentley's frightened reaction to the prairie also
echoes the sort of responses to the land seen in Butler's "terrible grandeur"
passage in *The Wild North Land* and his larger awareness of the loneliness and
isolation it engenders. And the wind, which ultimately drives Blanche Burke
from the prairie in Garland's *Moccasin Ranch,* similarly affects Mrs. Bentley;
because of its indifference—the same sense of the land perceived by Stegner's
Vickers—she feels as Beret Holm feels at the outset of *Giants in the Earth.*

Where Ross goes beyond his predecessors, where an originality equal to
Cather's lies, is in the extent to which "the outer situation mirrors the
inner"[16]—the landscape serving as the objective correlative of Mrs. Bentley's
feelings and state of mind. After the Bentleys spend a difficult evening with
Paul, the local school teacher who befriends them, for example, Mrs. Bentley
writes:

> There's a high, rocking wind that rattles the windows and creaks the walls.
> It's strong and steady like a great tide after the winter pouring north again,
> and I have a queer, helpless sense of being lost miles out in the middle of it,
> flattened against a little peak of rock. . . . The town, too, seems clinging to
> a little peak, the rays of light from lamps and windows like so many thin-
> drawn tentacles. The stars are out, up just above the wind. They light the
> sky a little, and leave it vast and dark down here. (35)

The disturbing wind punctures Mrs. Bentley's vulnerability, which derives
from Philip's hostility toward her, since she is certain he resents her inability

to bear them a child. Ross makes the prairie wind the agent of his exposition. Such use of the details of prairie space, which are repeated again and again, account far more for the novel's tedious dramatization of the Bentleys' relations than does Philip's retreat into his study.

Similarly, just after Mrs. Bentley has had to defend their decision to adopt Steve, the recently abandoned twelve-year-old son of a local Roman Catholic ne'r do well, she dwells upon the dust swirling through Horizon:

> It's been nearly dark today with dust. Everything's gritty, making you shiver and setting your teeth on edge. There's a crunch on the floor like sugar when you walk. We keep the doors and windows closed, and still it works in everywhere. I lay down for a little while after supper, and I could feel it even on the pillow. The air is so dry and choking with it that every few minutes a kind of panic seizes you, and you have an impulse to thresh out against it with your hands. (62)

In this instance, the seeping dust symbolizes the disapproval of the Protestant townsfolk—those with "Main Street minds"—who thoroughly disapprove of the Bentley's decision to adopt Steve, and Mrs. Bentley's panicked response reflects her suppressed anger.

On Christmas Eve, two weeks after the Bentleys learn that Judith West is expecting a child—putatively Philip's—Mrs. Bentley walks off into the snow-covered prairie, away from the town:

> The hollows and crests of the drifts made the walking hard, and half a mile from town I perched for a few minutes on a fence post that stood up about a foot above the snow. I sat so still that a rabbit sprinted past not twenty feet in front of me, and a minute later, right at my feet, there was the breathlike shadow of a pursuing owl. I had been climbing a little all the time I walked, so that I could see the dark straggle of Horizon now below me like an island in the snow. A rocky, treacherous island, I told myself, that had to have five lighthouses. (148)

The difficulty she experiences in walking is the externalization of her difficulty in knowing how to cope with Judith's pregnancy, while the owl pursuing the rabbit might well be seen as a forecast of how she will respond to the situation. What she sees from her raised perspective is similarly a reflection of her own feeling of betrayal and also of her own subsequent treacherousness.

Yet Ross's most impressive symbolic use of the elements of the landscape lies not with these continual parallels between the external landscape and the

Bentleys' inner one; rather, it lies in his depiction of Partridge Hill, a nearby community where Philip holds a weekly service. Describing their first meeting with the congregation there, Mrs. Bentley's observation reflects the community's relationship with the dust bowl prairie landscape:

> The last hymn was staidly orthodox, but through it there seemed to mount something primitive, something that was less a response to Philip's sermon and scripture reading than to the grim futility of their own lives. Five years in succession now they've been blown out, dried out, hailed out; and it was as if in the face of so blind and uncaring a universe they were trying to assert themselves, to insist upon their own meaning and importance. (19)

Ross cannot, like Steinbeck before him, see fit to hold out a promised land to these characters—he offers in vivid detail the "grim futility" of his characters entrapped in the dust bowl. At the root of Ross's description is the same perception of the prairie landscape that so affected Castañeda, Irving, Parkman, and others. While those men were concerned with finding their way through a land that enforced an awareness of their own loneliness, the residents of Partridge Hill, in the face of an equally impersonal landscape, are engaged in trying to assert their presence.

On another trip to Partridge Hill, Mrs. Bentley reports that the congregation was

> listening to the wind, not Philip, the whimpering and strumming through the eaves, and the dry hard crackle of sand against the windows. From the organ I could see their faces pinched and stiffened with anxiety. They sat in tense, bolt upright rows, most of the time their eyes on the ceiling, as if it were the sky and they were trying to read the weather. (37)

Here Ross implies a truth made evident by the landscape: that the weather has far more pertinence to the lives of these people than do Philip's sermons and scriptures. Indeed, through Mrs. Bentley's sense that there is "something primitive," followed as it is by Paul's etymological lecture ("That was what you heard this morning—pagans singing Christian hymns. . . ." [19]), Ross suggests that Christianity is as imported and inappropriate a form on the prairie as Washington Irving's literary conventions—and the people of Partridge Hill attest to that view. To accentuate this, when Peter Lawson, a young Partridge Hill boy whose illness Mrs. Bentley mentions throughout, dies, Ross describes the cemetery as "just a fenced-in acre or two on the prairie" where "There are dry, stalky weeds on the graves, and you can see where gophers and badgers have been burrowing." Later, his father stares off "across the hot burned fields" and, trying to steady himself, says "We aren't going to get even our seed this year. Maybe he's not missing such a lot" (109).

As Philip Bentley sees it, art and religion have much in common: they "are almost the same thing anyway. Just different ways of taking a man out of himself, bringing him to the emotional pitch that we call ecstasy or rapture. They're both a rejection of the material, common-sense world for one that's illusory, yet somehow more important" (112). Philip Bentley, however, has a problem in common with his wife. As David Stouck has pointed out, Philip's art is essentially narcissistic: he cannot escape the force of the prairie landscape and the small towns that dot its imperturbable surface. Thus when Mrs. Bentley describes Philip while he labors over his pictures, her diction emphasizes the fact that, for Philip as an artist, the prairie landscape is inescapable:

> Alone in there, hunched over his table, groping and struggling to fulfill himself—intent upon something that can only remind him of his failure, of the man he tried to be. I wish I could reach him, but it's like the wilderness outside of night and sky and prairie, with this one little spot of Horizon hung up lost in its immensity. He's as lost, and alone. (25)

Philip himself, however, argues that the personal has no place in an estimation of art; he tells Mrs. Bentley that, if she would decide whether or not a given picture is any good, she must "turn it upside down. That knocks all the sentiment out of it, leaves you with just the design and form" (154). Stouck points out that Ross, by whisking his characters off for a holiday in the foothills midway through the novel, is in effect fulfilling the requirements of Philip's esthetic observation; like Philip's picture, Ross's characters are for the time being turned "upside down."[17] At the same time, however, the trip also constitutes Ross's use of a raised perspective—going to the foothills allows the characters to "get above" their lives in Horizon. As a consequence, Philip paints with increased interest, accomplishment, and a genuine desire for appreciation. At the same time, Mrs. Bentley's raised perspective allows her a long-range view of their situation on the prairie, since throughout the interlude she weighs Philip's behavior there against life in Horizon.

Philip's inability as an artist to escape his own self-absorption suggests that as an artist he cannot escape the prairie landscape. Throughout the novel there are numerous examples of the dust bowl prairie environment providing Ross with images suitable to the psychological relations between his characters. This dynamic relation offers a wider perspective of the role of landscape in the novel, particularly as it relates to Philip's art—his repeated attempts to capture the essence of Horizon in his paintings and sketches. One of Mrs. Bentley's walks produces a response which illuminates Philip's, her own, and Ross's reliance on the prairie environment as subject matter:

> There was a hot dry wind that came in short, intermittent little puffs as if it were being blown out of a wheezy engine. All round the dust hung dark and heavy, the distance thickening it so that a mile or more away it made a blur of earth and sky; but overhead it was thin still, like a film of fog or smoke, and the light came through it filtered, mild and tawny.
>
> It was as if there were a lantern hung above you in a darkened and enormous room; or as if the day had turned out all its other lights, waiting for the actors to appear, and you by accident had found your way into the spotlight, like a little ant or beetle on the stage.
>
> I turned once and looked back at Horizon, the huddled little clutter of houses and stores, the five grain elevators, aloof and imperturbable, like ancient obelisks, and behind the dust clouds, lapping at the sky.
>
> It was like one of Philip's drawings. There was the same tension, the same vivid immobility, and behind it all somewhere the same sense of transience.
>
> I walked on, remembering how I used to think that only a great artist could ever paint the prairie, the vacancy and stillness of it, the bare essentials of a landscape, sky and earth, and how I used to look at Philip's work, and think to myself that the world would some day know of him. (59)

Looking back at Horizon, Mrs. Bentley compares life on the prairie to Philip's art and, in so doing, precisely articulates an esthetic reaction that lies not only at the core of *As For Me and My House,* but also at the core of this book. Philip's art, Mrs. Bentley asserts, is in a certain sense a transcription of the prairie landscape—Stouck has called it a mirror—and so is Sinclair Ross's and all those treated here. Similarly, Cather recognized the pull the land exerted on her imagination from the time of her arrival in Nebraska, saying that "by the end of the first autumn, that shaggy grass country had gripped me with a passion I have never been able to shake. It has been the happiness and the curse of my life." By seeing the land as both happiness and curse, Cather was acceding to the overriding imaginative pull the prairie exerts; this tension informs her depiction of Nebraska throughout her fiction. Though far less given to celebrating prairie life than she—such was his experience of the dust bowl—Sinclair Ross fashioned from the prairie narrative strategies that equal Cather's in *O Pioneers!* and *My Ántonia,* and that display the same fascination and revulsion. [18]

By writing about the problems inherent in depicting the landscape through his artist-protagonist, Ross, like Cather and Stegner before him, dramatizes the overwhelming imaginative force of the landscape especially on the artist but also on the people of Partridge Hill as well. Philip is able to paint different subjects, and in another manner altogether, only when he is away from the prairie; while living on it the land forces itself into his consciousness and dictates his subject matter. Were he a better and less self-absorbed artist, perhaps Philip could define his own aims—but he is not, and so submits to it. Like Vickers, Philip finds "the image too big for him," but like Stegner—though far more effectively—Ross has captured the unique qualities of the prairie through a discussion of the difficulties it poses. Moreover, while expressing some of this same frustration himself through both the Bentleys, Sinclair Ross has certainly overcome—to an almost astonishing degree—the difficulties of prairie depiction in *As For Me and My House*. [19]

While his story is about the relations between his characters, and particularly involves the narrowly self-conscious narrative point-of-view taken by Mrs. Bentley, Ross's novel does indeed, as Williams asserts, offer the most "desolate portrait of the Dust Bowl" in North American literature. It does this because of the excrutiating exactness of the detail Ross presents; though there is a faint hope that the Bentleys will prosper with their new bookstore and new son, few readers seem willing to bet on it. Unwilling because of Mrs. Bentley's character, to be sure, but also unwilling because the Bentleys seem so exactly suited to the dust bowl prairie. For Ross's characters in the stories, and for the Bentleys most emphatically, there is no promised land.

Late in the novel, Mrs. Bentley describes one of Philip's paintings featuring "two horses frozen on their feet," which he saw on his way to Partridge Hill. She describes the picture:

> The way the poor brutes stand with their hindquarters huddled up and their heads thrust over the wire, the tug and the swirl of the blizzard, the fence lost in it, only a post or two away—a good job, if it's good in a picture to make you feel terror and pity and desolation. (153)

This is, finally, exactly what Ross does through his evocation of the prairie landscape in both *The Lamp at Noon and Other Stories* and *As For Me and My House:* make us feel "terror and pity and desolation." And this passage, like Cooper's introduction of Natty Bumppo or Cather's "two luminaries" image in *My Ántonia* or Grove's description of Abe Spalding plowing his first rounds, encapsulates its author's essential intention, offering us, as it were, Ross's version of a "picture writing on the sun" (MA, 245). In conjunction with Mrs. Bentley's feelings of "terror and pity," Philip Bentley's horses, frozen on their feet, attest to Sinclair Ross's artistry—this image embodies the essence of his accomplishment in *As For Me and My House.* Integrated as it is within the landscape that defines its characters, Ross's novel shows that, indeed, it does "take a great artist" to depict "the prairie, the vacancy and stillness of it, the bare essentials of a landscape, sky and earth . . ." (59).

It is fitting that W. O. Mitchell's *Who Has Seen the Wind* (1947) should be discussed in conjunction with Ross's first novel because the two works, though they have a great deal in common are, at the same time, vastly different. If Ross's prairie makes the reader feel "terror and pity and desolation," then Mitchell's prairie has his readers feeling growth and beauty and transcendence—and this despite the fact that he too is depicting the Canadian prairie during the dust bowl thirties. The differences lie in the interpretation accorded the prairie landscape by each writer and the strain of prairie landscape response to which each adheres, although both techniques have their beginnings in the traditions of prairie landscape depiction. Ross relies upon those elements in the landscape that produced the feelings of monotony registered in the accounts of James, Catlin, Lambert, and others. Mitchell, on the other hand, recreates the first romantic exhilaration seen in the non-fictional account of writers such as Brackenridge, Irving, or Flagg. He single-mindedly accentuates a romantic, positive view of the prairie by emphasizing his character's growing understanding of and relationship to the land; this is not to say that details of the dust bowl depression are ignored, but that they are in the story's background rather than, as in Ross's novel, its foreground. The novel is a romantic *Bildungsroman,* and the prairie landscape is the focal point for Brian O'Connal's education. Whenever Brian experiences a crisis he finds solace and understanding in the natural workings of prairie nature. The "dirty thirties" have their spokesman in Brian's Uncle Sean, a farmer who is plagued by the very natural occurrences starkly dealt with by Ross in his *Lamp At Noon* stories and in his depiction of Partridge Hill in *As For Me and My House;* though subordinated, Sean and his sometimes comic outbursts against nature serve as counterpoint to Brian's growing consciousness.

Mitchell's depiction of life in a small prairie town during the thirties is similar to Ross's, however, since in each novel the "Main Street" mentality prevails. Mitchell's depiction of small-town bigotry is like his treatment of Uncle Sean's problems on the farm: it counterbalances the prevailing romantic view of life the novel presents. Although Ross is more subtle, his realism is also balanced by romanticism—much of Mrs. Bentley's dissatisfaction with Philip's feelings for her are a reflection of her perspective. She is hopelessly romantic, and longs to be fussed and fawned over like a young belle; when she is asked by a cowboy to dance, while on their holiday, she agrees, "hoping absurdly Philip might see" her (97).

In *Who Has Seen the Wind,* Mitchell—like Garland, Cather, and Rölvaag before him—introduces the prairie landscape before focusing on his characters; yet whereas his precursors opted to dramatize the land's appearance, Mitchell describes it with matter-of-fact directness:

> Here was the least common denominator of nature, the skeleton requirements simply, of land and sky—Saskatchewan prairie. It lay wide around the town, stretching tan to the far line of the sky, shimmering under the June sun and waiting for the unfailing visitation of wind, gentle at first, barely stroking the long grasses and giving them life; later, a long hot gusting that would lift the black topsoil and pile it in barrow pits along the roads, or in deep banks against the fences. [20]

Thus like Cather, Mitchell emphasizes the land first, only gradually moving to the town. There, four-year-old Brian O'Connal wanders about, having been told by his grandmother to play outside; while doing so, he visits the local minister's wife to ask her about God, whom, with childish irritation over being so banished, he wants to "get after" his grandmother. Without receiving a satisfactory answer, Brian continues his wanderings until he finds that "Ahead lay the sudden emptiness of the prairie. For the first time in his four years of life he was alone on the prairie" (10–11). Like Irving when he was lost, Brian here sees the prairie comprehensively for the first time, noticing the steady wind, gophers, and grasshoppers: "And all about him was the wind now, a pervasive sighing through great emptiness, unhampered by the buildings of the town, warm and living against his face and in his hair" (11).

Brian's education takes the form of testing things learned in the town against the natural forces that he finds on the prairie. The Young Ben, whom he notices at the edge of town at the same time as his first glimpse of the prairie, is a character analogous to Cather's Crazy Ivar in his natural correspondence with the cycles of nature; throughout Brian associates Ben with the prairie. Brian experiences a series of deaths among creatures and people around him; as he tries to understand each one in turn, he draws upon his appreciation of the natural cycle made manifest by the prairie. When his baby pigeon dies, Brian's father asks where he would like to bury it; instinctively, Brian replies: "The prairie—dig a hole for it in the prairie. . . . Where the [Young Ben] is." This decision made, Brian "was aware of a sudden relief; the sadness over the death of the baby pigeon lifted from him" (58). Likewise, when his dog dies some years later Brian buries it on the prairie himself: "He knew that a lifeless thing was under the earth. His dog was dead." Just after this the Young Ben appears and helps Brian cover the grave with rocks to keep coyotes away. Within Brian as he looks at the grave is "an emptiness that wasn't to be believed" (178). And some time later, when his father dies, Brian again seeks tranquility in the prairie, which he visits after the funeral; there, he realizes:

> Forever for the prairie; never for his father—never again.
> People were forever born; people forever died, and never were again. Fathers died and sons were born; the prairie was forever, with its wind whispering in through the long dead grasses, through the long and endless silence. (241)

Thus in the novel Brian recognizes the cyclical nature of life—made manifest by the prairie—and, contemplating his loss, he sees "the dark well of his mother's loneliness" (242) as much more important; so he leaves the prairie abruptly to go home and help assuage her grief. When, just prior to the novel's end, Brian's grandmother dies, he sees her death in light of those that came before, and so takes it maturely, recognizing it as the proper end to her long life.

In *Who Has Seen the Wind,* Mitchell uses the natural cycles of the prairie as an index to Brian's growth, integrating his knowledge with the prairie landscape, so the boy matures to an understanding very like that found in Steinbeck's *The Grapes of Wrath.* Yet unlike Steinbeck, Mitchell offers his character's transformation as one with the prairie; its symbiotic connection— of his growth in concert with his perception of the prairie landscape encapsulated by his decision to become "a dirt doctor" as the novel closes. Like Steinbeck, Mitchell sees the dust bowl thirties as a low point in the life cycle and, as well, a failure of man's knowledge—hence Brian's resolve to minister to the land, which his Uncle Sean has described as "sick" throughout the novel.

Finally, Mitchell's dramatization of Brian's developing understanding, like Cather's depiction of Alexandra Bergson and Jim Burden, suggests that the prairie must be understood on its own terms—that man must adapt to its cycles. Michael Peterman has compared Mitchell's novel to *My Ántonia,* and he notes that "the emotional responsiveness of Jim and Brian to the landscape of the open Prairie is remarkably similar."[21] In so saying, Peterman has made a point necessary to this study. When placed side by side, the parallels between the novels seem striking but, because each falls within the prairie novel tradition, they are not so very surprising. Placed within the context provided here, Mitchell's novel shares with Cather's (as well as other examples of the form) the salient features of the prairie novel—the commingling of realism with romance occasioned by the landscape itself, and the epistemological process involved in adapting to its features.

Indeed, a distinction more relevant than that between countries is that between the sexes. Central to the romantic tradition of prairie writing is a person's reaction to the landscape, and the differences based on gender are instructive, even if not yet conclusive. The clash of points of view in both *Wild Geese* and *The Sea of Grass* suggests a gender basis for scrutinizing the imaginative impact of the prairie landscape. In Garland, Stringer, Rölvaag, Richter, Ross, and numerous lesser writers, women are those most negatively affected by removal to the prairies—as they may have been in actual fact—and their reactions stand in opposition to their husbands' romantic domination of the lands they pioneered. Yet Willa Cather in *O Pioneers!* and Martha Ostenso in *Wild Geese,* taking the next step while still subscribing to a romantic vision of the land, acknowledged the romantic attractions of pioneering but insisted that through their sympathy, women were better able to adapt to its imaginative demands. In contrast to their view, the work of male writers offers the image of the isolated farm wife driven mad by loneliness and the inattentions of her driven husband. Garland, Richter, and Ross, apparently writing from genuine sympathy, stand in opposition to Cather and Ostenso's more empathtic rendering. The landscape, in any case, remains the salient feature in immediate postpioneering fiction as writers struggle with the physical and imaginative demands of prairie life.

The Modern Era: "The Home Place"

An incident from one of Mitchell's later prairie novels is an apt beginning for a discussion of contemporary prairie fiction, for it suggests that the reactions occasioned by the landscape throughout prairie writing remain yet. At the same time, it points toward the sometimes begrudging attitude seen in native writers toward their home place, and to the techniques they have devised and are devising to deal with prairie space. In *The Vanishing Point* (1973), Mitchell moves from lyric romanticism to irony in treating the prairie landscape; his protagonist, Carlyle Sinclair, an Indian agent on a Stony Indian reservation, recalls an exercise he undertook as an eleven year old in grammar school art class. The students were instructed in the geometric depiction of the vanishing point in a prairie scene, the final meeting place of roads, telephone poles, and fences at the distant horizon line, a line which provides perspective. Having accomplished his exercise, Carlyle is dissatisfied with the result:

it was shocking; his eye travelled straight and unerring down the great prairie harp of telephone wires strung along tiny glass nipples of insulators on the cross-bars, down the barbed-wire fence lines on the other side of the highway. And as the posts and poles marched to the horizon, they shrank and crowded up to each other, closer and closer together till they all were finally sucked down into the vanishing point.[22]

After looking at and analyzing it for a time, Carlyle decides that "The drawing had to have something more—some gophers, like tent pegs—clump of wild roses—buck brush. That was it! A tree!" (319).

He begins putting trees in his picture—pines and poplars—and is discovered shortly after by his teacher, who straps him for his disobedience. This notwithstanding, Carlyle is unrepentant—he actually longed to put in a tiger. Carlyle's action suggests his need, as Dick Harrison has written, to "go beyond the imposed perspective"[23] of his teacher to a more natural, and comfortable one—one at odds with the prairie landscape. At the same time, however, Carlyle's action encapsulates the white man's means of understanding the prairie. Looking at his drawing of a prairie scene, one which creates a sense of prairie vastness accurately, if mechanistically, Carlyle is shocked. Like Catlin, Alfred Jacob Miller, Paul Kane, and other painters, Carlyle feels compelled to fill the space, even though he is prairie born, for it seems to need something. Washington Irving, likewise, filled the space through his literary conventions, and many commentators back to Castañeda confirm their own shock at the land's emptiness while others delighted in it—for a time. Mitchell's *The Vanishing Point* suggests that while the prairie has been settled and, to a certain extent, controlled, its basic elements—land and sky, stretching to the horizon—still attract and even haunt its writers today in the same manner as it did then. Like those who preceded them, contemporary writers have felt the need to fill prairie space—they are still drawn to landscape writing, as Kroetsch asserts—and so have been and are effecting techniques that adjust to the landscape.

No single contemporary prairie writer has confirmed this more than Wright Morris who, though spending only his adolescence in Nebraska, has written and rewritten the prairie's effects on his imagination throughout a massive body of work: novels, stories, essays, critical writings, and "photo-texts"—*The Home Place* is one such book—which combine his prose with his photographs. In an essay published during the 1950s, entitled "Our Endless Plains," Morris defines the relationship between the prairie landscape and its inhabitants which his work addresses: "the plain is a metaphysical landscape. . . . Where there is almost nothing to see, there man sees the most."[24]

Using two characters, "the Grandmother" and "the Grandfather"—original pioneers, whose plains experience dated from the 1880s through the 1950s—Morris pokes at and probes the human connections to the plains which fascinate him still—unceasing dust, houses which sit "on the plain as if [they] had been ordered by mail and delivered," "the mood of space and loneliness with which the plainsman must come to terms," and "what draws some men to the plains, and what drives some women crazy" (139). Placed in the context established here, these very factors, which Morris finds so obsessive, are the very same "metaphysical" reactions which are traceable to Castañeda. Indeed, the sense of wonder, of puzzlement, with which Morris concludes his essay might be reasonably seen as Castañeda's "Who could believe?"; thus Morris writes:

> On the other hand I have spent most of my life puzzling over the lines on the map of my childhood. In what sense, it might be asked, have I been away? The high plain lies within me. It is something I no longer try to escape. If I stand at the window where the Grandfather stood, I see what he saw. The dream that appealed to him still appeals to me. The tall corn still flowers, the golden grain still waves, skyscrapers now rise where the dust blows and the Oklahoma Sooners won forty-seven consecutive games.
>
> But the prevailing temper, the dominant note, is not struck by these triumphs, however deserved, but by the seat of the harrow that lies buried like a shield in the stormcave mound. The enduring mood is pathos, the smallness of man and the vanity of his passing triumphs in the face of the mindless forces of the plains. . . . There is more than room enough for a man both to find and lose himself. There is neither shelter from the passions of nature, nor the nature of man. (142)

Although critics have seen such passages as this as romantic or nostalgic—the term used is "destructive nostalgia"—Morris's fiction is more concerned with valuing past motives and mores, as his *Plains Song* suggests in its depiction of several generations of women in a single family. His pioneer women, unlike Garland's, Rölvaag's, or Ross's, are not cowed by the prairie; they may not like it, but they adapt to it. The prairies themselves play a crucial role in that, as G. B. Crump has written,

> In the nineteenth century, the pioneer projected on the plains his vision of American promise; in the twentieth, they became the wasteland where the dream turned to dust. On a metaphysical level, their empty expanses suggest

the void of reality before it has been processed and given shape by the consciousness of the perceiver.[25]

Throughout Morris' fiction the image of prairie flatness is never far distant and, as he himself suggests above, he is always probing its significances—personal, fictional, cultural, and metaphysical. In *The Works of Love* (1952), for example, Morris begins: "In the dry places, men begin to dream. Where the rivers run sand, there is something in man that begins to flow. West of the 98th Meridian—where it sometimes rains and it sometimes doesn't—towns, like weeds, spring up when it rains, dry up when it stops." But as he goes on to describe the dreaming thus engendered in a sod hut on the Nebraska prairie, where the protagonist's father, Adam Brady, lived in the 1880s, Morris makes it clear that it is not dryness alone that fosters dreams. Seeking to woo a wife to share his dugout, Brady has a romantic photograph of himself made to send to prospective wives who answer his ad. In the photo he is standing against the backdrop image of a "virgin forest," so that in the picture:

> there was no indication, anywhere in it, of the landscape through the window that Adam Brady faced. There was not an inkling of the desolation of the empty plain. No hint of the sky, immense and faded, such as one might see in a landscape of China—but without the monuments that indicated men had passed, and might still be there. In that place, remote as it was, men at least had found time to carve a few idols, and others had passed either in order to worship, or to mutilate them. But in this place—this desolation out the window—what was there? Nothing but the sky that pressed on the earth with the dead weight of the sea, and here and there a house such as a prairie dog might have made.[26]

Brady is suffering from the same isolation and loneliness which motivated a similar search for a wife in Garland's "Among the Corn Rows," the isolation that is seen in Cather's early stories and is also a factor in Vickers's eventual return to civilization in *On a Darkling Plain.* Morris holds up Brady's photograph as a sham, and he does so by invoking the prairie landscape directly; on the prairie there are no landmarks which show of a man's passage—as there are even in remote China—and Morris's contrast here echoes the inability of man to make his presence, or even his passage, apparent in the prairie landscape, as witnessed in Castañeda's comments or in Rölvaag's complaining prairie grass. In his description of Brady's house, too, Morris suggests Brady's dugout is a part of his desolate environment, for he is living like a prairie dog; this also troubled Beret Holm, for she felt that living in a prairie dugout debased humans. Nebraska prairie and Brady's sod hut represent "reality"—as indeed they were to many—a reality that forces Brady into dreams and misrepresentation, lying in order to obtain a wife who, upon her arrival, is kept from running away immediately—in the manner of Blanche Burke—only by the intersession of the same act of God that held Blanche: a snowstorm. Though "This desolate place, this rim of the world, had been God's country to Adam Brady, but to his wife, Caroline Clayton" Nebraska is "a godforsaken hole." Caroline remains only because their marriage has been consummated. Brady, for his part, combines "these two points of view. He could leave" the prairie "but he would never get over it" (12–13).

In *Ceremony in Lone Tree* (1960), Morris gives the impalpable landscape—which fills the eyes yet makes one wonder—specific attention:

> Waves of plain seem to roll up, then break like a surf. Is it a flaw in the eye, or in the window, that transforms a dry place into a wet one? Above it towers a sky, like the sky at sea, a wind blows like the wind at sea, and like the sea it has no shade. There is no place to hide. One thing it is that the sea is not: it is dry, not wet. [27]

Writing in the second half of the twentieth century, Morris here is equally reacting to, being overwhelmed by, those elements in the landscape that so affected Coronado, Castañeda, and virtually every other commentator or writer who described the prairie. He notes the sea-like qualities of the landscape, the absence of "human" landmarks—of the sort he missed in *The Works of Love*—on the prairie and, like Beret's refrain and Cather's flat statement, sees "no place to hide" on the prairies.

Yet in Morris's works there is a crucial difference that attests to his role as inhabitant: the prairies seem to ooze from his very pores, not only as space but also in time. This is a quality his work shares with the others treated in this chapter, and his comment that "Where there is almost nothing to see, there man sees the most" defines their approach to the prairie as home place, as heritage. Their sense of prairie space, too, contrasts with that of their predecessors—explorer, traveler, or pioneer—who expected newness and, almost always, adapted to the new conditions they found. Inhabitants see the landscape as very dear, demanding of its people, perhaps because the prairie is an alienating landscape, feelings held very close to the heart. Thus to Morris, to the late Margaret Laurence, and to Robert Kroetsch, the prairie is home;

when they look at the prairie—its features, buildings, and people—it is with acknowledgement and identification, even longing.

Morris's work shows this perhaps most directly in his "photo-texts," which offer images of the 1930s and 1940s, focusing starkly with black-and-white directness on the farmhouses, towns, possessions and, occasionally, people of the prairies. In *God's Country and My People* (1968), for example, Morris offers an abandoned farmhouse as his first photograph and writes:

> Is it a house or an ark? A scud seems to blow on the sea of grass and the land falls away like the sea from a swell. On the receding horizon waves of plain break like a surf. . . . Little wonder this house resembles an ark. The porch is gone from the front, shingles from the roof, and the last tenants went thataway with the Okies—except for those who stand, immaterial, at the windows, or move about with the creak of hinges. The land has tired of the house but it will not soon be free of the inhabitants.[28]

Morris's description recapitulates reactions to prairie space since Castañeda, of course, and his description of the house recalls the opening of *O Pioneers!*, but what is most significant is his elegiac tone: Morris sees this house as a romantic icon, one that symbolizes his plains heritage. This knowledge haunts his works, and haunts him still.

A recent novel, *Plains Song,* treats relations throughout successive generations of a pioneering family, and is especially effective in its handling of the feminine point of view. Equally, in "The Origin of Sadness" (1986), Morris offers a precise paragraph that succinctly evokes prairie space as it relates to his protagonist, though setting is of little importance to the story beyond "the home place":

> From Oklahoma he drove north to his birthplace, the winter landscape bleak and sunless. The stands of trees planted by the settlers were dying. In the sweep of his car lights the barkless branches rose up before him like tongues of flame. All of his anguish and suppressed grief chose this moment to overwhelm him. On a road of gravel, under threatening skies, the sight of a patch of road weeds, that blew to no purpose, just to be blowing, filled him with a tearful and burning despair. He had to slow the car and pull to the side of the road. Low sweeping black clouds seemed intent on clearing the plain of all living creatures, and Schuler sat in wonderment at the deep satisfaction this spectacle gives him. Whose side, in the name of God, was he on? He did not know.[29]

Though Schuler's plight has little to do with landscape—he is a geologist home in the midst of personal crisis—Morris's precise invocation of prairie space—wind that blows "to no purpose," clouds that seem to wish to clear the plain "of all living creatures"—attest to the commonality between him and his prairie predecessors. At the same time, such references suggest the degree to which the impact of prairie winds and spaces are integrated with character; for an inhabitant, the feelings engendered by prairie space are, like Schuler's, ingrown and inescapable. Though Morris is here deep in his character's angst, the inhabitant's relationship with prairie space, its felt pull on both character's and, by extension, author's imagination is never far distant.

Just as Wright Morris analyzes and dramatizes the effect of the Nebraska prairie on his imagination and writing, so too authors of contemporary Canadian prairie fiction continue to assess man's relation to the land, and to its landscape. Indeed, as mentioned at the outset of this study, the Canadian prairie region has been seen by its critics as far more of a formulative environment than Americans have seen their own prairies, with three major critical overviews in print—two of which, Laurence Ricou's *Vertical Man/Horizontal World* (1973) and Dick Harrison's *Unnamed Country* (1977) were published within five years of each other. In addition, numerous individual-author monographs, collections of essays, and dozens of articles on prairie writing have appeared since Ricou and Harrison's studies were published.

To confirm that scrutiny of Canadian prairie writing proceeds unabated, 1986 saw the publication of two separate collections of essays intent on defining the ongoing interest: *Trace: Prairie Writers on Writing* and *Essays on Saskatchewan Writing*.[30] Not surprisingly, each collection reprints Henry Kreisel's essay "The Prairie: A State of Mind," which offers the quotation with which this study began and now, fittingly enough, makes an appearance as it is about to end: "All discussion of the literature produced in the Canadian west must of necessity begin with the impact of the landscape upon the mind."[31] Originally published in 1968, Kreisel's essay has been reprinted at least six times since, testifying to its influence and to the continuing critical interest in defining man's relation to the land on the Canadian prairies. This surge of activity is a part of the larger concern for understanding Canadian literature as an emerging body of work generally. But, as this book has endeavored to show, Kreisel's thesis is partial only, one which exists in too narrow a sphere— in this case the somewhat arbitrary division of a national boundary which bisects the prairie's topography. The boundary does not, however, alter the landscape's effect on the writing, nor does it preclude consideration of all prairie fiction as something of a closed system, one defined by landscape. "Prairie writing" as descriptive phrase has thus had greater currency north of the forty-ninth parallel than it has south of it, reflecting both the greater urgency of understanding an emerging literature, as well as the more finite boundaries of the prairies as a distinct region within Canada, itself a very regionalized country.

To a far greater extent, therefore, than seen in contemporary American writing, the Canadian prairie writers yet to be examined have been engaged in an urgent process of self-definition and self-analysis as prairie writers. In contemporary Canadian writing, "the home place" has been defined in terms of the new land and the prairie landscape itself. In a 1970 interview, also reprinted in *Trace,* Robert Kroetsch and Margaret Laurence discuss their personal need, when younger, to get out of the prairies where they were born, only to find once successfully away (like Cather), that they were drawn back, inexorably, to the prairies through their fiction. Each concluded, in a phrase of Kroetsch's that has become a truism of Canadian prairie writing that "In a sense, we haven't got an identity until somebody tells our story. The fiction makes us real."[32]

Similarly, Kroetsch has spoken of his experiences in using his prairie inheritance as "a kind of archaeology that makes *this place,* with all its implications, available to us for literary purposes." Within this process is his constant awareness that:

> we both, and at once, record and invent these new places called Alberta and Saskatchewan. That pattern of contraries, all the possibilities implied in *record* and *invent,* for me finds its focus in the model suggested by the phrase: a local pride.
>
> The phrase is from William Carlos Williams—indeed those three words are the opening of his great poem *Patterson,* about Patterson, New Jersy: *a local pride.*
>
> The feeling must come from an awareness of the authenticity of our own lives. People who feel invisible try to borrow visibility from those who are visible. To understand others is surely difficult. But to understand ourselves becomes impossible if we do not see images of ourselves in the mirror—be that mirror theatre or literature or historical writing. A local pride does not exclude the rest of the world, or other experiences; rather, it makes them possible. It creates an organizing centre. Or as Williams put it, more radically: the acquiring of a local pride enables us to create our own culture— "by lifting an environment to expression."

Kroetsch continues to discuss the oral tradition on the Canadian prairies and its relation to prairie writing, seeing that tradition as a foundation for much contemporary fiction from the region. His comment is offered at some length because Kroetsch articulates—both as prairie writer and as critic—a concern central to Margaret Laurence's and his own writing, to be sure, but also to this entire book: the need to lift "an environment to expression." This has been an imaginative process—whether one looks at Castañeda, Cooper, Catlin, or Cather—of both recording and inventing. And in so doing, the literature reveals that the imaginative effects of prairie space have been paramount in this process since, as Kroetsch says earlier in this essay, prairie writers have found themselves forced back—again, like Castañeda—"uneasily but compulsively, to landscape writing," "compelled to adjust and invent, to remember and forget."[33]

In Margaret Laurence's fiction, on the one hand, and Robert Kroetsch's, on the other, then, the two modes of recording and inventing of which Kroetsch speaks are readily evident. Born in Manitoba, Laurence chronicles life on the prairie in the 1940s, and deals with the ways in which the land continues to haunt those who have left it. Like Cather, though, Laurence wrote first of another place—in her case, Africa, where she lived for several years before she hit her own "home pasture," the mythical town of Manawaka, Manitoba, which is based on Laurence's own Neepawa.[34] Indeed, Laurence's Manawaka Series—*The Stone Angel* (1964), *A Jest of God* (1966), *The Fire-Dwellers* (1969), *A Bird in the House* (1970), and *The Diviners* (1974)—is in large measure a working out of the heritage of the present generation of prairie Canadians, the result of the polyglot mixture of Indian, French, English, Scots, Germans, Poles, Scandinavians, and Ukrainians who make up the prairie provinces. Through the series, Laurence was "lifting an environment to expression," since each protagonist's coming to terms with her beginnings, her ancestry and her place is central to every book in it. She described her intentions in her essay, "A Place to Stand On," saying:

> the people were more important than the place. Hagar in *The Stone Angel* was not drawn from life, but she incorporates many of the qualities of my grandparents' generation. Her speech is their speech, and her gods their gods. I think I never recognized until I wrote that novel just how mixed my own feelings were towards that whole generation of pioneers—how difficult they were to live with, how authoritarian, how unbending, how afraid to show love, many of them, and how willing to show anger. And yet, they had inhabited a wilderness and made it fruitful. They were, in the end, great survivors, and for that I love and value them.

This is not to say that Laurence's fiction sidesteps the imaginative effects of prairie space; rather like Cather in *One of Ours* or in *A Lost Lady,* such concerns are wholly integrated within—and thus a function of—her characters. In the series, as Cathy N. Davidson has argued, each protagonist's being and destiny are so integrated with Manawaka that "geography becomes psychology."[35] Though little concerned with the overt effects of prairie space, per se, Laurence never forgets the prairie as personal identification, as heritage, as "home place." Indeed, in the same interview quoted above, Laurence speaks of the powerful impact *As For Me and My House* had upon her, for in it she saw the possibility of writing from her own background. Thus she writes, at some length in "A Place to Stand On," of Manitoba in her writing, echoing similar descriptions by both Cather and Morris:

> When one thinks of the influence of a place on one's writing, two aspects come to mind. First, the physical presence of the place itself—its geography, its appearance. Second, the people. For me, the second aspect of environment is the most important, although in everything I have written which is set in Canada, whether or not actually set in Manitoba, somewhere some of my memories of the physical appearance of the prairies come in. I had, as a child and as an adolescent, ambiguous feelings about the prairies. I still have them, although they no longer bother me. I wanted then to get out of the small town and go far away, and yet I felt the protectiveness of that atmosphere, too. I felt the loneliness and the isolation of the land itself, and yet I always considered southern Manitoba to be very beautiful, and I still do. I doubt if I will ever live there again, but those poplar bluffs and the blackness of that soil and the way in which the sky is open from one side of the horizon to the other—these are things I will carry inside my skull for as long as I live, with the vividness of recall that only our first home can have for us.[36]

Early in *The Stone Angel,* Hagar Shipley recognizes that in the Manawaka cemetery "a person walking there could catch the faint, musky dust-tinged smell of things that grew untended and had grown always, before the portly peonies and the angels with rigid wings, when the prairie bluffs were walked through only by Cree with enigmatic faces and greasy hair." Throughout the novel, as background to Hagar's eighty-year memories of her life, Laurence depicts the interrelations of four generations, deftly touching, as here, on Manawaka's relation with the surrounding land; by so doing, she chronicles pioneering, postpioneering growth, the dust bowl, and the modern era. These concerns are not foregrounded, but are embodied by Hagar's mystifications over changes in mores, dress, language, and her need to understand her life— she is a person "rampant with memory"—before she dies.[37]

Another such passage born of the prairie landscape appears in one of the short stories in *A Bird in the House*, "To Set Our House in Order." It is told retrospectively by Vanessa MacLeod, an adolescent, whose mother has just borne a baby boy after a difficult delivery. Feeling strange, not understanding all she has heard said around the house about the birth, Vanessa retreats—à la Brian O'Connel—into the prairie landscape surrounding Manawaka:

> It was late summer, and the wheat had changed colour, but instead of being high and bronzed in the fields, it was stunted and desiccated, for there had been no rain again this year. But in the bluff where I stopped and crawled under the barbed wire fence and lay stretched out on the grass, the plentiful poplar leaves were turning to a luminous yellow and shone like church windows in the sun. I put my head down very close to the earth and looked at what was going on there. Grasshoppers with enormous eyes ticked and twitched around me, as though the dry air were perfect for their purposes. A ladybird laboured mightily to climb a blade of grass, fell off, and started all over again, seeming to be unaware that she possessed wings and could have flown up.[38]

Given the context established by prairie fiction, Vanessa's awareness of nature echoes not only *Who Has Seen the Wind,* but also *O Pioneers!*, *My Antonia* and other works. Laurence's romanticism is, of course, derived from landscape itself and, moreover, her description of the prairie bluff suggests another passage from her work, from *The Diviners.* There, the protagonist, Morag Gunn, looks out the window of a train traveling from Toronto to Vancouver, not stopping in Manawaka to visit her stepfather, and notices "The small bluffs of scrub oak and poplar"; she thinks,

> In Ontario, *bluff* means something else—a ravine, a small precipice? She's never really understood that other meaning; her own is so clear. A gathering of trees, not the great hardwoods of Down East, or forests of the North, but thin tough-fibred trees that could survive on open grassland, that could live against the wind and the winter here. That was a kind of tree worth having; that was a determined kind of tree, all right.

Laurence's concern with self-understanding in the Manawaka series is perhaps best suggested by passages such as this, where a character considers the very texture of her own prairie language for, as Kroetsch indicates in his concern for "visibility" in literature, prairie Canadians are defining their own perspective. Central to that perspective is language and, at the same time, their relationship with the prairie landscape. So as if to dramatize Morris's observation that where there is little to see man sees most, Morag continues her musing, meditating over "The grain elevators, like stark strange towers," of the prairies, thinking that "People who'd never lived hereabouts always imagined" that it "was dull, bleak, hundreds of miles of nothing. They didn't know. They didn't know the renewal that came out of the dead cold."[39]

But if Margaret Laurence has mainly recorded prairie history on a personal level, Robert Kroetsch has been urged on by the desire to invent. In a conversation with Shirley Neuman and Robert Wilson, Kroetsch has seen "Where is the Voice Coming From?"—the title of a story by Rudy Wiebe, another prairie writer bent on both recording and inventing—as "the prototypical question of Canadian poetics."[40] Each writer, Kroetsch says, is engaged in answering that question. He himself began by recording, compulsively drawn to landscape writing, as he concedes. In "That Yellow Prairie Sky," his first full-length published story, Kroetsch intended to write about the north—where he had just been working—but found himself drawn to western memories; the story has much in common with Ross's *The Lamp at Noon* stories, for after a ruinous summer hailstorm the narrator's brother, a farmer, "scooped up a handful of hailstones, and . . . flung them back at the sky."[41] Even when he did write about the north, in his first novel, *But We Are Exiles* (1965), he describes the prairie in a way that confirms his familiarity; as his characters cross the country by car, traveling east, Kroetsch writes:

> And the flat country then. Dusty and dry. Dry and dusty and hot. Wheat country. And the first elevator. There at Dufresne, alone and reaching, like a great damned phallus, like one perpetual hard-on, Mike said, trying to make eternity. They laughed and the sky was so big that Peter couldn't breathe. He hadn't believed there was so much sky. And trees looking self-important and a little scared. The high piercing whine of gravel trucks. And little gas-station cafés that looked like boxes that fell off the roaring semi's that shook the trees and the telephone-poles.[42]

Though not an especially important passage in the novel, this is one derived from the relationship between prairie space and the human imagination— Kroetsch's phallus-like grain elevator is reminiscent of Cooper's rock tower, itself suggestive of the need for a raised perspective; his final sentence is an updated version of Cather's opening description of Hanover at the beginning of *O Pioneers!*.

A postmodern novelist, critic, and poet, Kroetsch has rejected formal realism, in effect "writing himself into existence" through the self-referential worlds created in the fiction. As Peter Thomas has noted, he has been drawn to figures like Grove and Grey Owl precisely because they "created" themselves by defining their own stories, making themselves real through their fiction, or, if one prefers and Kroetsch readily concedes, their lies. Yet as he says in "On Being an Alberta Writer," the western landscape is central to the writer's imaginative problem. On another occasion, he told an interviewer that "The Western landscape is one without boundaries quite often. So you have the experience within a kind of chaos, yet you have to order it somehow to survive."[43] Kroetsch's "chaos" in the western landscape has been a process of inventing to, in effect, fill prairie space. And like Cather and others, Kroetsch has found that he too has had trouble writing about his home place while there; he wrote in an unpublished journal, "For me, the imagined Alberta begins to be a place through which I can say all the things I want to say. Living there, I find the design becomes lost in detail." Yet at the same time, the place Alberta beckons him: he wrote a descriptive account of his home province, *Alberta*, he has said, "as a literal account of a world which I then treated imaginatively in *The Studhorse Man*."[44]

It was in his second novel, *The Words of My Roaring* (1966), that Kroetsch first used the recorded history of his native Alberta to head off on his path of invention. Like Ross and Mitchell, Kroetsch uses the dust bowl thirties, but his mode is unlike theirs—neither realistic nor romantic—rather, his story is underlaid by classical myth. The lack of rain is likened to the Old Testament plagues, and prairie man suffers at the hands of a wrathful God. Johnnie Backstrom, Kroetsch's narrator and protagonist (and also the local under-taker), runs for the provincial assembly on the promise of rain against the incumbent, Doc Murdoch, who owns a lush garden despite the drought. Murdoch also has a daughter who is a love goddess who attracts Johnnie. Thus Kroetsch translates the period's troubles into mythic terms, adapting the myth of Hades's abduction of Persephone, but retains the actual history of Alberta, since Johnnie runs as a candidate for John George Applecart, radio preacher turned politician, who inveighs against the "scarlet Who-er of Babylon"—as he describes eastern interests.[45] Applecart is modelled closely on the actual winner of the 1935 Alberta election, William Aberhart. While Kroetsch's concern in the novel is not the prairie landscape per se, the dust bowl conditions versus Doc Murdoch's lush garden (he is the candidate of the "Who-er") form the basis of its conflict.

Kroetsch has also spoken about a need in the West to engage in a process of "demythologizing the systems that threaten to define" prairie Canadians—American, British, and eastern-Canadian paradigms—and in practice his fiction, beginning especially with *The Words of My Roaring*, has deliberately overturned conventional expectations about the experience he describes.[46] This movement is readily seen in *Words*, but it is in his next novel, *The*

Studhorse Man (1969), that the inventive use of myth dominates the literal realism in the story. Kroetsch's technique is metafictional, and his story is comic and surreal, both recalling and parodying the Odyssey. During the Second World War, Hazard LePage wanders the prairies looking for the perfect mare for his stud-horse, Poseidon, despite the fact that the days of horsepower on farms were fleeting. His next novel, *Gone Indian* (1973), is characterized by Indian myths as well as classical, used in much the same manner.

But it is Kroetsch's 1975 novel, *Badlands,* which best offers his inventive spirit as a prairie novelist. A paleontologist, William Dawe, rafted through the Alberta badlands in search of dinosaur bones. His story is pieced together from his field notes by his daughter, Anna Dawe; the novel concludes when Anna finds her father's final entry, "I have come to the end of words." Earlier she had realized that "There are no truths, only correspondences," and another character, Web, is informed by his prairie past and offers—by the imagery associated with him—Kroetsch's desire to fill the prairie space through his invented correspondences. Thus when Web—emphatically a drinker—is attracted to a woman giving a temperance lecture, Kroetsch's images reflect his prairie being, and are drawn, as ever so, from the landscape itself:

> A great and tearing lump of drought worked in Web's throat. All the
> prairie winds of his growing up awakened in his mind, the dust so dry in his
> nostrils it stung like alkali, the dust pinching shut his eyes, binding his
> throat. A lifetime of trying to grow free on these open prairies. And yet he
> must be closer to that woman; he eased his way between two listeners,
> stepped across the open space. [47]

Though seemingly only an incidental passage in *Badlands,* here Kroetsch offers an image that encapsulates the prairie writer perfectly. Intent as he is with mythologizing his place—probing its "complex of possibilities"—he is nevertheless ever aware that he is stepping "across the open space" of the prairies. This recognition and the others found throughout his fiction and particularly in his critical comments reveal Kroetsch's concomitant knowledge that, on the prairies, "the great fact is the land itself." The crucial, never waning problem faced by the native-born prairie writer is devising strategies to enclose prairie space, somehow, within the covers of a book without just offering what Kroetsch calls "landscape writing." Yet despite his own attempts to fill the void of prairie space with history, myth, tall-tales, and tricksters, Kroetsch has never, himself, been able to elude the press of the prairie landscape.

On the prairie, the great fact *is* the land itself and it has ever been so since Castañeda's first European incursion. Intersection by the Canadian-American border has made minimal difference, despite the attempts of Canadian critics to see the prairie as distinctively their own landscape. Writers who took up the postpioneering prairie and native-born writers, whether American or Canadian, have continued to testify to the land's inexorable influence through their works; the modernist and postmodernist strategies they have attempted to write of the prairie have in no way circumvented the imaginative effects of prairie space. Indeed, Kroetsch's metafictionalized mythologizing is but another way of dealing with the effects of the landscape on the imagination, of filling what he calls the "chaos" of western space. On the North American prairie, as in the Russia of "Gogel, Turgenev, Lermontov," of which Willa Cather spoke, "the earth speaks louder than the people."[48] This process of imaginative adaptation to the prairie is ongoing, probably never ending; it can be seen wherever one looks in prairie writing.

A final and randomly chosen example is by Saskatchewan writer Sharon Butula, whose second novel, *The Gates of the Sun* (1986), offers a western story of Andrew, who is variously a cowboy, outlaw, and rancher. Butula begins with Andrew's recalled initial reactions to the prairie—he is being brought there, like Jim Burden—and his first memory concludes:

> He had felt himself being drawn into the boundless, ringing space between the stars as though something in the complicated, secret interior of his body was a part of the night sky, yearned to break out of the hard prison of his bones, to go back to where it had come from.
>
> But most of all there was the sun filling the sky. Molten light, thundering above them. For days they crossed the prairie under its blaze, until it came to him that he was in the sun's land now, that the sun was lord here, that the sun, perhaps, was the God he had heard of.[49]

Responding to all the strange sights he saw in what became Kansas, Castañeda wrote, "Who could believe . . . ," and the correspondence between his amazement over prairie space and Butula's over three hundred years later is exact; that correspondence has been confirmed and amplified by the numerous deeply felt and precise analyses considered here. From Castañeda's sixteenth-century exploration narrative to contemporary writers, prairie writing attests, that the land does, without question, speak louder than the people. It is, from Castañeda to Butula, the great fact.

Notes

Introduction

1. Wallace Stegner, *Wolf Willow: A History, a Story, and a Memory of the Last Plains Frontier* (1962; rpt. New York: Viking, 1966), p. 3. Subsequent references are to this edition. Pedro de Castañeda, of Najera, *The Narrative of the Expedition of Coronado by Castañeda*, trans. George Parker Winship (1896), rpt. *Spanish Explorers in the Southern United States, 1528–1543*, ed. Frederick W. Hodge and Theodore H. Lewis (1907; rpt. Austin: The Texas State Historical Association, 1984), p. 383.

2. Sir William Francis Butler, *The Wild North Land: Being the Story of a Winter Journey, with Dogs, Across Northern North America* (1873; rpt. London: Sampson Low, Marston, Low & Searle, 1874), p. 30. Willa Cather, *O Pioneers!* (1913; rpt. Boston: Houghton Mifflin, 1941), p. 15.

3. Henry Kreisel, "The Prairie: A State of Mind," *Transactions of the Royal Society of Canada*, 4th ser., 6 (June 1968), 171–80; rpt. *Contexts of Canadian Criticism*, ed. Eli Mandel (Chicago: Univ. of Chicago Press, 1971), p. 257. Robert Kroetsch, "On Being an Alberta Writer," in *Robert Kroetsch: Essays, Open Letter*, p. 74.

There are three book-length studies of Canadian prairie fiction, as well as several collections of essays and scores of single essays; they survey too narrow a field. Prairie fiction, properly so called, does not stop at the forty-ninth parallel, whether one is looking north or south. Harrison's *Unnamed Country* purports to be a developmental study, and it is: he traces *Canadian* prairie fiction, beginning with the first explorer to visit what is now the Canadian prairie, Henry Kelsey. But Harrison does not accord any work of non-fiction major treatment until Sir William Francis Butler's *The Great Lone Land*. Butler was writing at a time when a prairie landscape tradition was over three hundred years old and, besides, he was influenced by the writings of his major non-Canadian predecessor, James Fenimore Cooper, who wrote *The Prairie* (1827) over forty years before *The Great Lone Land*.

Critics of American literature, concentrating on the Turner thesis, have largely ignored the field of prairie fiction, as such, subsuming it into the long-time, and still ongoing, analysis of the role of the frontier and that of the West. By striking a balance between the American and Canadian approaches, and by incorporating materials from each, this book attempts an analysis derived from and focused upon the prairie itself, irrespective of the border.

See Edward McCourt, *The Canadian West in Fiction;* Laurence Ricou, *Vertical Man/Horizontal World: Man and Landscape in Canadian Prairie Fiction;* Dick Harrison, *Unnamed Country: The Struggle for a Canadian Prairie Fiction*. See also W. H. New, *Articulating West: Essays on Purpose and Form in Modern Canadian Literature;* and *Writers of the Prairies*.

4. Henry Nash Smith, *Virgin Land: The American West in Symbol and Myth*, p. 187. Richard Slotkin, *Regeneration Through Violence: The Mythology of the American Frontier, 1600–1860*, pp. 26, 19. Subsequent references are to this edition. Stephen Fender, *Plotting the Golden West: American Literature and the Rhetoric of the California Trail*, p. 8.

A succinct summary of European esthetic reactions to the prairie-plains landscape, both positive and negative, is available in Ray Allen Billington, *Land of Savagery, Land of Promise: The*

European Image of the American Frontier in the Nineteenth Century, pp. 90–95; Henry Nash Smith treats some of the same concerns in *Virgin Land,* pp. 123–260, as does Howard Mumford Jones, *O Strange New World: American Culture: The Formative Years.* And, though offering a different emphasis, a work which treats the Canadian prairies in similar fashion is Doug Owram, *Promise of Eden: The Canadian Expansionist Movement and the Idea of the West, 1856–1900.*

5. David Lowenthal, "The American Scene," 61. J. Wreford Watson, "The Role of Illusion in North American Geography: A Note on the Geography of North American Settlement," 10. See Yi-Fu Tuan, *Topophilia: A Study of Environmental Perception, Attitudes, and Values* and his *Space and Place: The Perspective of Experience.* More generally, see also *Geographies of the Mind: Essays in Historical Geosophy in Honor of John Kirtland Wright,* ed. David Lowenthal and Martyn J. Bowden (New York: Oxford, 1976), Jay Appleton, *The Experience of Landscape* and *Environmental Aesthetics: Essays in Interpretation,* ed. Barry Sadler and Allen Carlson (Victoria: Univ. of Victoria, 1982). See also Catherine Elizabeth Raymond, "Down to Earth: Sense of Place in Midwestern Literature," Ph.D. diss. Univ. of Pennsylvania 1979), pp. 32–84. Raymond provides an excellent overview of environmental perception theory and its relation to literary analysis.

6. Glenda Riley, *The Female Frontier: A Comparative View of Women on the Prairie and the Plains,* p. 2; Sandra L. Myres, *Westering Women and the Frontier Experience, 1800–1915,* p. 98. These two books are much the best introduction to women on the frontier, but the literature on the subject is growing rapidly. See also John Mack Faragher, *Women and Men on the Overland Trail;* Julie Roy Jeffrey, *Frontier Women: The Trans-Mississippi West, 1840–1880;* Lillian Schlissel, *Women's Diaries of the Westward Journey;* Joanna Stratton, *Pioneer Women: Voices From the Kansas Frontier;* Glenda Riley, *Frontierswoman: The Iowa Experience* and *Women and Indians on the Frontier, 1825–1915;* Elaine Leslau Silverman, *The Last Best West: Women on the Alberta Frontier, 1880–1930;* Elizabeth Hampsten, *Read This Only to Yourself: The Private Writings of Midwestern Women, 1880–1910;* and, while more of a collection of quotations and images than a work of analysis, Linda Rasmussen et al, *A Harvest Yet To Reap: A History of Prairie Women.* For a synthetic discussion of the perceptions of "ordinary women" of the prairie landscape, see Julie Roy Jeffrey, " 'There Is Some Splendid Scenery': Women's Responses to the Great Plains Landscape."

7. Martha Mitten Allen, *Traveling West: 19th Century Women on the Overland Routes,* p. 12; Annette Kolodny, *The Land Before Her: Fantasy and Experience of the American Frontiers, 1630–1860,* pp. 12, 6. R. W. B. Lewis, *The American Adam: Innocence, Tragedy, and Tradition in the Nineteenth Century.*

8. Perhaps with poetic justice, any attempt to trace the development of prairie landscape depiction seems fraught with as many complications as the actual confrontation with this area itself. For example, the region is variously called "prairie," "plains," and "Great Plains," depending on individual background and local usage. The situation is compounded further by the fact that the northern extension of the area referred to by geographers as "The Great Plains"—that is, the Canadian section—is called "the prairies" by Canadians. Conversely, Americans frequently refer to the Dakotas as "The Great Plains." Accordingly, for the sake of consistency the term "prairie" is used here, and it is taken to mean the area described above. For what it is worth, most of the writers considered here—Cooper, Irving, Garland and Cather, as well as the Canadians—used "prairie" far more often than "plains."

9. Walter Prescott Webb, *The Great Plains,* pp. 7–8. For a discussion of changing attitudes toward regionalism on the Great Plains, including a discussion of Webb, see Frederick C. Luebke, "Regionalism and the Great Plains: Problems of Concept and Method." *Canada: A Geographical Interpretation,* and Gerald Friesen, *The Canadian Prairies: A History,* pp. 3–10.

10. The major surveys of Canadian prairie fiction are cited above. Critical overviews of American prairie materials include Dorothy Dondore, *The Prairie and the Making of Middle*

America; Henry Nash Smith, *Virgin Land;* Roy W. Meyer, *The Middle Western Farm Novel in the Twentieth Century;* and Carol Fairbanks, *Prairie Women: Images in American and Canadian Fiction.*

Chapter 1

1. Alvar Nuñez Cabeza de Vaca, *The Narrative of Alvar Nuñez Cabeça de Vaca,* trans. (Thomas) Buckingham Smith (1851), rpt. in *Spanish Explorers in the Southern United States 1528–1543,* pp. 1–126. The standard history of exploration in North America is still John Bartlet Brebner, *The Explorers of North America 1492–1806;* Brebner treats Cabeza de Vaca pp. 57–62. Another account, more recent and equally factual but more readable, is Bernard DeVoto, *The Course of Empire,* pp. 9–21.

2. Pedro de Castañeda, of Najera, *The Narrative of the Expedition of Coronado by Castañeda,* trans. George Parker Winship (1896), rpt. *Spanish Explorers in the Southern United States,* p. 331. Subsequent references are to this edition. Another translation has appeared since Winship: George P. Hammond and Agapito Rey, *Narratives of the Coronado Expedition, 1540–1542* (Albuquerque: Univ. of New Mexico Press, 1940). The latter is a more literal translation than Winship's; but his is preferable for its superior literary quality, and so has been used, though both renderings for all cited passages have been compared.

3. Francisco Vazquez Coronado, "Translation of a Letter from Coronado to the King, October 20, 1541," in *The Journey of Coronado 1540–1542,* trans. and ed. George Parker Winship (New York: A. S. Barnes, 1904), pp. 214–15. For another translation of the same letter, see Hammond and Rey, pp. 185–90.

4. Coronado, p. 216.

5. "The Latest Account of Cibola, and of More than Four Hundred Leagues Beyond," in *The Journey of Coronado 1540–1542,* pp. 195–96; commenting on the document from which this passage was translated, Winship says "This appears to be a transcript from letters written, probably at Tiguex, on the Rio Grande, during the late summer or early fall of 1541"; Winship, *Journey,* p. 190, n. 1. See also *Narratives of the Coronado Expedition,* pp. 308–12, for another translation of the same document.

6. Herbert E. Bolton, *Coronado: Knight of Pueblos and Plains,* p. 255. Bolton also suggests that Castañeda may have been waiting for someone's death before he wrote of the true nature of the environment. He may also have been simply dissatisfied with his earlier chapter, and so rewrote the plains material to sharpen it; the earlier chapter contains no account of the buffalo.

7. Hammond and Rey's translation of the final sentence is "This was because the earth was so round, for, wherever a man stood, it seemed as if he were on the top and saw the sky around him within a crossbow shot. No matter how small an object was placed in front of him, it deprived him of the view of the land" (*Narratives of the Coronado Expedition,* p. 280). It is not clear here what a man is "on top" of; the "three-pint measure," however, appears to be Winship's metaphor. There is no question, though, that the comparison of buffalo to pine trees is Castañeda's metaphor.

8. In addition to Castañeda's *Narrative,* there are eleven letters and reports which relate to the Coronado expedition, of which nine are translated and included in Winship's volume. Their extent and histories are recounted in the introduction to *Spanish Explorers* by Hodge and Lewis, pp. 275–80. They are also translated and included in *Narratives of the Coronado Expedition.* Of the four commentators who deal directly with the plains region (those cited above plus Captain Juan Jaramillo's *Narrative* [Winship, pp. 222–40]) only Jaramillo does not discuss the disorientating effect of the landscape. Bolton quotes an unidentified member of Coronado's expedition

who agreed with his general's estimation of the plains: "Traveling in these plains is like voyaging at sea . . . for there are no roads other than cattle trails. Since the land is so level, without a mountain or a hill, it was dangerous to travel alone or become separated from the army, for on losing sight of it one disappeared" (Bolton, pp. 254–55).

The Spanish impression of the plains does not rest entirely with Coronado's expedition. Two other expeditions visited the prairie, one under Vincente Zalidivar Mendoza in 1598 and another under Juan de Oñate in 1601; their impressions and evaluations corroborate those left by Coronado and his men. See "Discovery of the Buffalo" and "Expedition to the North, 1601," in *Don Juan de Oñate: Colonizer of New Mexico, 1595–1628,* pp. 405, 750–51.

9. DeVoto, p. 45.

10. Raymond, p. 392. She is quoting Henry Glassie, "Meaningful Things and Appropriate Myths: The Artifact's Place in American Studies," *Prospects,* vol. 3, ed. Jack Salzman (New York: Burt Franklin, 1977), p. 33.

11. See, for example, Fr. Jolliet's misgivings about the prairie prior to seeing it himself, and his impressions upon being there; *Jesuit Relations and Allied Documents,* ed. Reuben Gold Thwaites (1899; rpt. New York: Pagent, 1959), 58: 105, 107. See also "The Mississippi Voyage of Jolliet and Marquette, 1673," *Jesuit Relations and Allied Documents,* 59: 87–163.

12. Fr. Claude Jean Allouez "Narrative of a 3rd Voyage to the Illinois, Made by Fr. Claude Allois," in *Jesuit Relations,* 60: 157. For other French reactions to the Mississippi valley, see "Memoir of La Salle's Discoveries, by Tonty, 1678–1690 [1693]," *On the Discovery of the Mississippi, etc.,* trans. Thomas Falconer (London, 1844); rpt. *Early Narratives of the Northwest, 1634–1699,* ed. Louise Phelps Kellogg (New York: Scribner's, 1917), pp. 283–322; Fr. Louis Hennepin, *A New Discovery of a Vast Country in America,* 2 vols., ed. Reuben Gold Thwaites (1903; rpt. Toronto: Coles, 1974). For overview interpretation, see John Logan Allen, *Passage Through the Garden: Lewis and Clark and the Image of the American Northwest,* pp. 1–48; Dorothy Dondore, *The Prairie and the Making of Middle America,* chapters one and two; and DeVoto, pp. 131–56. The best discussion of varying imaginative conceptions of the American West is to be found in Smith, *Virgin Land;* he considers the relationship thought to exist between trees and fertility, pp. 174–80, and discusses the Great American Desert and the search for the Great River of the West. Regarding these opposing views, see W. Eugene Hollon, *The Great American Desert: Then and Now*; the Great River of the West is treated in Allen, *passim,* in the chapter just cited. DeVoto treats at some length the various misconceptions that brought explorers into the West, and a passage by water to the Pacific is foremost among them.

The single exception to my generalization among the French explorers was Pierre Gaultier de Varennes de La Verendrye; he and his sons traveled up the Assiniboine River—in what is now Manitoba—in 1738 and then overland to the Mandan Indian villages on the Missouri; his reactions to the prairie landscape are consistent with those of Castañeda and the other overland travelers. See G. Hubert Smith, *The Explorations of the La Verendryes in the Northern Plains, 1738–43,* pp. 44–45.

13. Henry Kelsey, *The Kelsey Papers,* ed. Arthur G. Doughty and Chester Martin (Ottawa: Public Archives of Canada and The Public Record Office of Northern Ireland, 1929), p. 3. The slashes indicate the endings of lines in the transcript copy of the papers held by the Public Record Office of Northern Ireland; Kelsey wrote some of his journal in verse. Doughty and Martin maintain, in their introduction to the *Papers,* that these documents are transcript copies, "and the probable inference is that they were copied by Kelsey for his own private use, the originals going into the files of the Hudson's Bay Company" (p. x).

In another instance, however, Kelsey seems to have more in common with the French explorers. Thus while traveling through—in all likelihood—the park country west of the upper Assiniboine in present-day Saskatchewan, he describes both wooded and unwooded areas together: "August ye 12th Now we pitcht again & about noon ye ground/ begins to grow *barren* heathy & barren in fields of about/ half a Mile over Just as if they had been Artificially/ made with fine groves of Poplo growing round ym we/ went to day by Estimation 10 Miles/" (p. 11). Here Kelsey marvels over the relationship between the wooded areas and those without wood; and like the French he wonders over the symmetry of the scene: "Artifically/made."

But there is also something both original and uniquely English in Kelsey's observation here, since he first calls the grasslands "barren," then, crossing the word out, substitutes "heathy & barren." John Warkentin, remarking on this passage, maintains that Kelsey "used barren in the sense of the plains being without trees, not a lifeless wasteland," but by 1690 the connotation of "barren," when applied to land, was "not fertile, sterile, unproductive" and "bare." Kelsey, moreover, compounded this impression by adding to his description the "English" word "heathy," replete with its connotations of "waste land." Thus, just as Coronado looked in vain for some landmark of the sort found in Europe, so Kelsey's use of this "English" word also suggests the way in which his attitude toward the prairie is conditioned here by his previous European background. See *The Western Interior of Canada: A Record of Geographical Discovery, 1612–1917,* ed. John Warkentin (Toronto: McClelland and Stewart, 1964), p. 27. Here Warkentin reprints those passages of Kelsey's journal that deal with landscape. Regarding the meaning of "barren" as "not fertile, unproductive, bare," the *Oxford English Dictionary* lists this as a literal meaning applying to land as established in 1377; likewise its figurative meanings, "Bare of intellectual wealth" and "unproductive of results," were established by 1549. The meaning to which Warkentin alludes, "A tract of barren land; spec. applied in N. America to: a. elevated plains on which grow small trees and shrubs, but no timber, classes as *oak-barrens, pine-barrens,* etc., according to the trees growing on them," is not cited as current until 1784 when used by Thomas Jefferson (*OED,* 1933 ed. 1: 681). Similarly, because Kelsey uses "barren" as a parallel term for "heathy," a word whose English meaning as "waste land, or marginal land" was equally well established at the time he was writing, it appears most likely that he meant the word barren to mean "sterile."

14. Anthony Henday, "York Factory to the Blackfeet Country; The Journal of Anthony Hendry [sic], 1754–55," Lawrence J. Burpee, ed., *Proceedings and Transactions of the Royal Society of Canada,* 3rd ser., 1 (Ottawa, 1907), sec. 2, p. 328. Subsequent references are to this edition. Not until after the publication of this journal was it decided that the man's name was Henday, not Hendry.

Another Hudson's Bay man sent inland some seventeen years later concurred with both Kelsey and Henday, for he too called the Saskatchewan prairie country barren. See Matthew Cocking, "An Adventurer from Hudson Bay: Journal of Matthew Cocking, from York Factory to the Blackfeet Country, 1772–73," sec. 2, pp. 104–07. It was during the latter half of the eighteenth century that the interior portions of the North American continent were described in English in print for the first time. Jonathan Carver believed the area west of the Mississippi to be one promising to "produce a sufficient supply of all the necessaries of life for any number of inhabitants," though he was not particularly descriptive; *Travels through the Interior Parts of North American in the Years 1766, 1767, and 1768,* 3rd ed. (London: C. Dilly, 1781), p. 536. Edward Umfreville, another former Hudson's Bay employee, in 1790 published a book highly critical of the company; in it he describes the country in which he worked. Having been in charge of one of the westernmost posts on the Saskatchewan River, Umfreville describes the "boundless" country bordering the river, its weather, buffalo, and open spaces. His descriptions, however, are matter-of-fact and not very detailed; see Edward Umfreville, *The Present State of Hudson's Bay, Containing a Full Description of that Settlement, and the Adjacent Country; and Likewise of the Fur Trade, with Hints for its Improvement.*

15. T. D. MacLulich, "The Explorer as Sage: David Thompson's *Narrative*," *JCF*, No. 16 (1976), pp. 97, 98.

16. David Thompson, *David Thompson's Narrative, 1784–1812,* ed. Richard Glover (Toronto: Champlain Society, 1962), p. 141. Subsequent references are to this edition.

17. Alexander Henry, *New Light on the Early History of the Greater Northwest, the Manuscript Journals of Alexander Henry, Fur Trader of the Northwest Company, and of David Thompson, Official Geographer and Explorer of the Same Company, 1799–1814,* ed. Elliot Coues (New York: Francis P. Harper, 1897), 1: 94. Subsequent references are to this edition. It should be noted that, despite the title of Coues's volume, the text of the whole is made up of Henry's journals alone; Coues felt the need to give equal credit to Thompson because his papers, which had not yet been edited and published at the time Coues was working, lent a great deal of information to Henry's journals.

18. The literature describing the range, extent of herds, and other facts of buffalo lore are well known and need not be repeated here; suffice it to say that virtually every explorer or traveler who came upon large herds of buffalo found it necessary to comment on the experience; witness, for example, Castañeda and the other men who accompanied Coronado, as well as the Spanish explorer himself. There has been little comment, however, on the means by which such impressions were obtained. The flat expanse of prairie allowed those who traveled across it to glimpse vast numbers of buffalo in a manner that other landscapes did not, and the two entities—land and buffalo—become intertwined in the various accounts. Numerous commentators, moreover, complained of the animals as an impediment; their numbers were such that travelers had to detour around, since they could seldom prevail upon the beasts to move. See, for example, Henday, p. 333.

19. Two other passages from Henry's journals illustrate the shock experienced by Europeans upon witnessing the cruelty of the forces of nature on the prairie. After noting the first breakup of ice on the Red River, for example, he writes:

> *Wednesday, Apr. 1st.* The river clear of ice, but drowned buffalo continue to drift by entire herds. Several are lodged in the banks near the fort. The [Indian] women cut up some of the fattest for their own use; the flesh appeared to be fresh and good. It is really astonishing what vast numbers have perished; they formed one continuous line in the current for two days and nights. One of my men found a herd that had fallen through the ice in Park River and all been drowned; they were sticking in the ice, which had not yet moved in that part. The women had excellent sport in raising the back fat and tongues. (1: 174)

Even Henry, whose store of descriptive adjectives does not extend much beyond "delightful" and "beautiful," is moved to pronounce the scene "astonishing."

Here Coues cites another account which corroborates Henry's: in 1795 John McDonnell, on a journey down the Qu'Appelle River, spent an entire day counting buffalo carcasses in the river and mired along the banks. By the end of the day he had counted 7,360 (1: 174, n. 39). In perhaps the most imagistically striking scene described in the Lewis and Clark journals prior to reaching the Great Falls of the Missouri River, Clark describes the Indians "jumping from one cake of ice to another, for the purpose of Catching the buffalow as they float down" while the prairie on either side of the river is on fire. Clark treats the scene, however, in a matter-of-fact manner. See Meriwether Lewis and William Clark, *Original Journals of the Lewis and Clark*

Expedition, 1804–1806, ed. Reuben Gold Thwaites (1904–05; rpt. [intro. Bernard DeVoto] New York: Arno Press, 1969), 1: 278–79.

20. Warkentin, p. 106.

21. *Original Journals,* 1: 45–46. Here and throughout, the 1969 reprint of the *Original Journals* has been used; they retain the same pagination as Thwaites' 1904–05 edition. Clark is using "barren" here in its particularly eastern North American sense, as with "pine-barrens" and "oak-barrens."

The first version of the expedition's descriptions was published in Philadelphia in 1814, edited by Nicholas Biddle. See Meriwether Lewis and William Clark, *History of the Expedition Under the Command of Lewis and Clark,* ed. Elliott Coues, 4 vols. (1893; rpt. New York: Dover, 1965). The story of the publication of the materials collected on the expedition is a complex one; see Paul Russell Cutright, *A History of the Lewis and Clark Journals* (Norman: Univ. of Oklahoma Press, 1976).

22. Allen, *Passage Through the Garden,* p. 188. The notion of the West as garden, of course, is recurrent throughout American history and literature. The countervailing view, that the plains were sterile—the Great American Desert—is usually attributed to Zebulon Montgomery Pike's observations, published in 1810. Such opinions, however, were actually common prior to Pike; in 1796, for example, a French-Canadian *voyageur,* Jean Baptiste Truteau, wrote of the upper Missouri: "These large prairies, or great waste lands are completely sterile; scarcely grass grows there." *Before Lewis and Clark: Documents Illustrating the History of the Missouri 1785– 1804,* ed. A. P. Nasatir (St. Louis: St. Louis Historical Documents Foundation, 1952), 2: 377.

23. Neither explorer uses the terms "Prairie" or "plains" with any exactness. At times they are used interchangeably, while other contexts suggest that "plain" was used in its generic, European sense, the same sense in which Kelsey, for example, used it; that is, as a flat area of relatively small size, perhaps enclosed by higher land or trees. More frequently, "prairie" seems to suggest country which is not enclosed, the higher country above the river banks, dotted here and there by clumps of trees—the French use of prairie as "meadow."

24. For discussions of contemporary esthetic conventions, see Samuel H. Monk, *The Sublime: A Study of Critical Theories in XVIII-Century England,* pp. 164–232; *The Genius of the Place: the English Landscape Garden, 1620–1820,* ed. John Dixon Hunt and Peter Willis (London: Paul Elek, 1975); Christopher Tunnard, *A World with a View: an Inquiry into the Nature of Scenic Values.* The latter is useful for the overview it provides. A perceptive and succinct summary of dominant esthetic values in relation to landscape may be found in I. S. MacLaren, "Retaining Captaincy of the Soul: Response to Nature in the First Franklin Expedition."

25. Zebulon Montgomery Pike, *An Account of Expeditions to the Sources of the Mississippi, and through the Western Parts of Louisiana, to the Sources of the Arkansaw, Kans, La Platte, and Pierre Juan, Rivers; Performed by Order of the Government of the United States during the Years 1805, 1806, and 1807. And a Tour through the Interior Parts of New Spain, when Conducted through these Provinces by order of the Captain-General in the Year 1807* (Philadelphia, 1810). For a discussion of Pike and the Great American Desert see Hollon, *The Great American Desert,* and Smith, *Virgin Land,* especially Chapter XVI: "The Garden and the Desert," pp. 174–83. The most recent treatment of the desert/garden controversy, which summarizes and details the various views while establishing the degree to which each was believed, is John L. Allen's "The Garden-Desert Continuum: Competing Views of the Great Plains in the Nineteenth Century."

26. *The Journals of Zebulon Montgomery Pike with Letters and Related Documents,* ed. Donald Jackson, 2 vols. (Norman: Univ. of Oklahoma Press, 1966), 1: 78–79. Subsequent references are to this edition.

For an account of the critical attention accorded Pike's book on first publication, see W. Eugene Hollon, *The Lost Pathfinder: Zebulon Montgomery Pike,* pp. 176–78. A British edition was published in 1811, and French and Dutch translations appeared during the next two years; Hollon claims there was a German translation as well, but Jackson (2: 406) does not list one.

27. Pike has the distinction of publishing what was probably the first extended description of the black-tailed prairie dog, and his accounts of buffalo and wild horses, while not unlike those written by others, were among the first to be published and to achieve a wide audience. Just downstream from the site of Dodge City, Kansas, Pike describes his first glimpse of a large herd of buffalo. Though the party had seen and killed individual animals throughout their trip from St. Louis, and Pike had seen individual buffalo on his previous western trip, as they moved west into Kansas they came upon large herds:

> In the afternoon discovered the north side of the river [the Arkansas] to be covered with animals; which, when we came to them proved to be buffalo cows and calves. I do not think it an exaggeration to say there were 3,000 in one view. It is worthy of remark, that in all the extent of country yet crossed, we never saw one cow, and that now the face of the earth appeared to be covered with them. (1: 343)

Here Pike moves in his description from the general and the already known (the river, then versus now) to the unknown and the new—the view of thousands of calves and cows when hitherto they had seen none. Pike presents the buffalo, indeed, as if they had appeared out of nowhere. And like Castañeda over 250 years earlier, Pike marvels over the numbers and habits of the buffalo, noting that the bulls would ring the great herds of cows and calves. His incredulous tone also echoes Castañeda's "Who could believe . . .": "I will not attempt to describe the droves of animals we now saw on our route," he concludes; "suffice it to say, that the face of the prairie was covered with them, on each side of the river; their numbers exceeded imagination" (1: 343).

As these passages show, although Pike does not focus upon the way these sights made him feel, his emphasis upon the magnitude of such scenes reflects their impact. The reader is called upon to imagine a vast expanse, black with movement, like that described by Henry at his post on the Park and Red Rivers. Pike may have refrained from more exact description out of a fear of inability—like Lewis above the Great Falls—to do the sight justice, or he may have thought embellishments like Castañeda's unnecessary, or he may have simply been disinclined. Or he may have felt that the phrase, "exceeded imagination," was all that could be said.

28. Yet even so, it is quite possible to hold that Lewis's application of "sublime" is confused. William Gilpin, for example, wrote that "When the landscape approaches nearer *simplicity,* it approaches nearer the *sublime;* and when variety prevails, it tends more to the *beautiful.* A vast range of mountains, the lines of which are simple; and the surfaces broad, grand, and extensive, is rather *sublime* than *beautiful.*" Given the variety which Lewis sees, "beautiful" may be the more appropriate term, although both his and Pike's contexts suggest their need for a stronger term than beautiful, so strong were their feelings. According to Gilpin's dictum, a prairie viewed alone should be the height of the sublime. William Gilpin, *Observations Relative Chiefly to Picturesque Beauty, Made in the Year 1716, On Several Parts of Great Britain, Particularly the High-lands of Scotland* (London, 1789), I, 122; as quoted by Monk, *The Sublime,* p. 225.

29. The literature of westward migration is vast; see Bernard DeVoto, *The Year of Decision: 1846;* Ray Allen Billington, *The Far Western Frontier: 1830–1860;* John D. Unruh, Jr., *The Plains Across: The Overland Emigrants and the Trans-Mississippi West, 1840–60;* Faragher, *Women and Men on the Oregon Trail;* Jeffrey, *Frontier Women;* Myres, *Westering Women and the Frontier*

Experience, especially chapters 1, 3, and 5; and Allen, *Traveling West.* Fender adopts a literary point of view toward the subject and, while not explicitly focused on overland travel, Kolodny's *The Land Before Her* offers a great deal of discussion of women's accounts. For a succinct overview account of the overland migration, see Faragher's first two chapters, though Unruh's book is generally regarded as the exhaustive treatment of the subject. He cites a report in the St. Louis *Missouri Gazette* of 1813 asserting the ease with which wagons could be taken across the plains to the Columbia river (1), and 300,000 is his total number of emigrants (84–85).

30. H. M. Brackenridge, *Journal of a Voyage up the river Missouri; performed in Eighteen Hundred and Eleven,* 2nd. Ed. (Baltimore, 1816), rpt. *Early Western Travels, 1748–1846,* ed. Reuben Gold Thwaites, VI (Cleveland: Arthur H. Clark, 1904), 75, 89. Subsequent references are to this edition. Hereafter the multivolume *Early Western Travels* series, which reprinted all of the significant narratives and accounts written during the period it surveys, will be abbreviated *EWT.*

This journal was originally published in Brackenridge's *Views of Louisiana* (Pittsburgh, 1814); thus while the title page of the Baltimore edition states that it is a second edition, the book published in 1816 constitutes the first publication of the Missouri journal as a separate volume. Between the separate editions Brackenridge revised and expanded the work.

31. See John Bradbury, *Travels in the Interior of America in the Years 1809, 1810, and 1811 . . . ,* 189–90. Here Bradbury describes the same scene in much the same terms; the two had met and were traveling together. Such sights as this, the prairie black with buffalo, bulls bumping and rutting about (especially if a traveler happened upon the herd, as here, during mating season), are common in this literature; such is the case with Henry, Brackenridge, Bradbury, and later, with James and De Smet. The animals animate the landscape and lend an air of strangeness, of mysteriousness, to it by their presence and by their numbers. At the end of his description of this scene, for example, Bradbury agrees that an immense herd was seen running at least a mile from them; the sound of their feet resembled, he says, "distant thunder" (190).

Pierre-Jean De Smet, S. J., a longtime missionary among the Indians of the upper Missouri, once noted the tormented bellowings of a herd which had been accosted by droves of mosquitoes: "During a whole week we heard their bellowings like the noise of distant thunder, or like the murmers of the ocean-waves beating against the shore." These descriptions, and others like them, show that travelers and explorers were attracted to the buffalo for their numbers (since many depended on them for food), and also by the way in which most plains Indian tribes revered the animal. They were also attracted to the animals by their size, mannerisms, and the sounds they made—the buffalo made the land exotic, at times almost unreal by their stampings and snortings. Indeed, it is virtually impossible to discuss the imaginative impression the prairie landscape had on white travelers without considering the buffalo—imaginatively, the two were often seen as symbiotic elements of that landscape. See P. J. De Smet, S. J., *Western Missions and Missionaries: A Series of Letters* (New York, 1859; rpt. [introd. William L. Davis, S. J.] Shannon: Irish Univ. Press, 1972), p. 83.

32. Brackenridge's attitudes are consistent with other travelers from the same period; I have dealt with his writings because they are the most articulate and detailed example. John Bradbury, for example, was an English naturalist who notes the relationship between the prairie and the convexity of the earth's surface and also finds "sublimity" in a prairie scene, viewed from above, including grazing buffalo. See Bradbury, *EWT,* V, 149, 239, 240–41. Gabriel Franchère's *Narrative,* which describes Franchère's visit to the prairie in Saskatchewan as he returned from the northwest coast of the pacific in 1814, offers a view colored by a "literary" style, since Franchère's descriptions were embellished by the poet Michel Bibaud. These three narratives

are significant, further, because they served as major sources for Washington Irving's *Astoria*. See Gabriel Franchère, *Narrative of a Voyage to the Northwest Coast of America in the years 1811, 1812, 1813, and 1814*, 372–73. In his preface, Thwaites describes Franchère's need for a collaborator, p. 15; see also Edgeley W. Todd, Introd. *Astoria, or Anecdotes of an Enterprise Beyond the Rocky Mountains*, by Washington Irving, pp. xxvii–xxxii, and *passim*.

33. Edmund Flagg, *The Far West; or a Tour Beyond the Mountains*, 2 vols. (New York, 1838), rpt. *EWT*, 26: 214. Subsequent references are to this edition.

34. John Palliser, *Solitary Rambles and Adventures of a Hunter in the Prairies* (London, 1853; rpt. Rutland, VT: Charles E. Tuttle, 1969), p. 106. Subsequent references are to this edition. Palliser's was one of numerous books of hunting lore concerned with the North American West; another, for example, is James C. Southesk's *Saskatchewan and the Rocky Mountains: A Diary and Narrative of Travel, sport, and Adventure, During a Journey Through the Hudson's Bay Company's Territories, in 1859 and 1860* (Toronto: James Campbell and Son, 1875). Perhaps the most well-known of prairie hunters during the prewar period was William Drummond Stewart, a British nobleman who hired artist Alfred Jacob Miller to, in effect, illustrate a hunting trip he took to the prairies in 1837. For a recent overview of these figures, see John I. Merritt, *Baronets and Buffalo: the British Sportsman in the American West* (Missoula: Mountain Press, 1985).

35. For an excellent discussion of Palliser's mixed esthetic assumptions and reactions, here and in his subsequent Canadian expedition, see I. S. MacLaren, "Aesthetic Mappings of the West by the Palliser and Hind Expeditions, 1857–59." MacLaren's article offers a particularly fine differentiation between the esthetic preferred by British observers, the picturesque, and that offered by the open prairie, the sublime.

Reactions like Palliser's to the wild prairie landscape were ubiquitous; in addition to those commentators discussed here, see also Victor Tixier, *Travels on the Osage Prairies*, pp. 158–59 and *passim*. This work was originally published in French in 1844 as *Voyage aux prairies osages, Louisiane et Missouri, 1839–40*. Viewing the prairie, Tixier writes that "A vague, sad emotion filled my heart at the sight of this solitude" (158). Another European traveler came to the prairie about this time and also found them to be lonely, but Maximilian, Prince of Wied-Neuwied, was unique in that he compared the region to the jungles of Brazil; there, he says, "nature is so infinitely rich and grand" and he heard "from the lofty, thick, primeval forests on the banks of the rivers, the varied voices of the parrots, the macaws, and many other birds, as well as of the monkeys, and other creatures. . . ." On the prairie, conversely, he notices that "the silence of the bare, dead, lonely wilderness is but seldom interrupted by the howling of the wolves, the bellowing of the buffaloes, or the screaming of the crows. . . ." It is a landscape which "scarcely offers a living creature, except now and then, herds of buffaloes and antelopes, or a few deer and wolves." *Travels in the Interior of North America in the Years 1832, 1833, and 1834*, trans. H. Evans Lloyd (London, 1843), rpt. *EWT*, 22–25; 23: 42.

36. See Fender. Another traveler who offers many of the same views as Flagg was Thomas J. Farnham, in his *Travels in the Great Western Prairies, the Anahuac and Rocky Mountains, and in the Oregon Territory*.

37. Edwin James, *Account of an Expedition from Pittsburgh to the Rocky Mountains, Performed in the Years 1819, 1820. By Order of the Hon. J. C. Calhoun, Secretary of War, Under the Command of Maj. S. H. Long, of the U. S. Top. Engineers*, 3 vols. (London, 1823), rpt. *EWT*, 14–17. Subsequent references are to this edition.

38. When Coronado's party was caught in a hailstorm before they entered the plains, Castañeda could only remark that the extensive damage the storm exacted would have been far greater had it struck them while they were on the plain. Indeed, he suggests that they would

have lost all of their horses. See Castañeda's *Narrative,* in *Spanish Explorers in the Southern United States, 1528–1543,* p. 333.

39. [John Lambert], *United States: Pacific Railroad Reports.* 33rd Cong., 2nd Sess., Senate Exec. doc. 78, 1855, 1, Papers Accompanying governor I. I. Stevens' Reports, pp. 166–67; rpt. Warkentin, *The Western Interior of Canada,* pp. 151–52.

40. Smith, *Virgin Land,* p. 175. Horace Greeley, perhaps the most well-known commentator to enter the debate on prairie prospects during the 1850s, also had an opinion regarding the Great American Desert: he held resoundingly in the affirmative. His letters, written during his "overland journey" to California in the summer of 1859, were published in the newspaper he edited, the New York *Tribune.* Writing from somewhere in Western Kansas, at station 18 on the Pike's Peak Express stagecoach line (which had only just begun operations), Greeley states:

> I would match this station and its surroundings against any other scene on our continent for desolation. From the high prairie over which we approach it, you overlook a grand sweep of treeless desert, through the middle of which flows the Republican [River], usually in several shallow streams separated by sandbars or islets—its whole volume being less than that of the Mohawk at Utica though it has drained above this point an area equal to that of Connecticut.

Thus utilizing comparison to the East, Greeley holds that his impression of the land is not dependent on local or seasonal variations in rainfall: "We have not passed a drop of living water in all our morning's ride. . . . Yet there has been much rain here this season, some of it not long ago. But this is a region of sterility and thirst. If utterly unfed, the grass of a season whould hardly suffice, when dry, to nourish a prairie fire." Following this, Greeley sardonically encapsulates his impression of the land with the sentence "Even the animals have deserted us." See Horace Greeley, *An Overland Journey From New York to San Francisco in the Summer of 1859* (1860; rpt. [ed. Charles T. Duncan] New York: Knopf, 1964), p. 82.

41. For an excellent overview of Frémont's publicizing role, see Patricia Nelson Limerick, *Desert Passages: Encounters with the American Deserts,* pp. 25–44. Frémont was especially vexed by the lack of wood in the region, and notes in his journal each time his party was forced to use dried buffalo dung as a substitute; this he always calls *"bois de vache."* Regarding the prairie itself, he notes that its uniformity is "never sameness" and whenever an object breaks the distant horizon "There is always the suspense of the interval needed to verify the strange object" as the eyesight seems to play tricks. He too climbs the nearest eminence in order to encompass the prairie visually, and his descriptions of the number and extent of buffalo along the Platte River are like those of Henry and James, among others. See *The Expeditions of John Charles Frémont,* ed. Donald Jackson and Mary Lee Spence (Urbana: Univ. of Illinois Press, 1970), 1: 56–57, 191, 195.

42. Josiah Gregg, *Commerce of the Prairies; or, the Journal of a Santa Fe Trader, during Eight Expeditions Across the Great Western Prairies and a Residence of Nearly Nine Years in Northern Mexico,* 2 vols., 2nd Ed. (New York, 1845), rpt. *EWT,* 19–20; 19: 189, 162. Subsequent references are to this edition. For printing history, see Max L. Moorhead, introd, *Commerce of the Prairies,* by Josiah Gregg (1841; rpt. [ed. Max L. Moorhead] Norman: Univ. of Oklahoma Press, 1954), p. xxxii.

43. Another who had extensive prairie experience, and whose writings offer views parallel to Gregg's was Fr. De Smet, since he traveled and lived throughout the West from 1838 until his death in 1873. See his *Life Letters and Travels of Father Pierre-Jean De Smet, S. J., 1801–1873.*

44. For an important analysis of women's roles in the fur trade, see Sylvia Van Kirk, *"Many*

Tender Ties": Women in Fur Trade Society, 1670–1870. Van Kirk notes, for example, that "In 1692, when Henry Kelsey returned from the first inland voyage ever undertaken by a Hudson's Bay Company man, he was accompanied by a Cree women whom he called his wife and insisted that she be allowed to enter the fort" (64).

45. Jeffrey, *Frontier Women,* p. 203. Writing in *Women and Men on the Overland Trail,* John Mack Faragher states that "Not one wife initiated the idea; it was always the husband. Less than a quarter of the women writers recorded agreeing with their restless husbands, most of them accepted it as a husband-made decision to which they could only acquiesce," though he goes on to say that nearly a third wrote of their objections. Similarly, Jeffrey in *Frontier Women* notes that most westward emigrants between 1840–80 emigrated for economic reasons, and that, since men " 'make decisions,' especially about economic matters . . .":

> the evidence suggests a pattern in which men brought up the subject of emigrating. Some women were taken by surprise, for, as one said, "the thought of becoming a pioneer's wife had never entered my mind." But this did not mean that women were passive spectators. Their style was to respond, to influence, even to argue. (30)

Jeffrey and others go on to detail the understandable fears and frustrations of those who emigrated—Lillian Schlissel, for example, writes that "When women wrote of the decision to leave their homes, it was almost always with anguish, a note conspicuously absent from the diaries of men" (14). Once on the Overland trail, Jeffrey analyzes women's social connections, though most were so busy, as one wrote, *"we have no time for sociability.* But as the trip wore on, and the rolling prairies receded and gave way to harsh deserts and mountains, it became clear that women would be unable to keep the world they valued intact" (41). There is also the straightforward matter of personal constitution and individual temperament to consider: Jeffrey notes a pioneer woman who wrote "A woman that cannot endure almost as much as a horse has no business here, as there is no such thing as getting help!" (77). Thus pioneering was not, obviously, for the faint-hearted, but recent research has demonstrated that the women were probably not opposed to the move generally. Sandra Myres, for example, notes "A survey of 159 women's trail diaries and reminiscences showed that only a small number, about 18 percent, were strongly opposed to the westward journey while 32 percent were strongly in favor of the trip" (102).

46. Faragher, p. 183, Kolodny, p. 7.

47. Myres, p. 6. See particularly Myres's first two chapters, which offer extensive context for understanding the social roles of women on the frontier.

48. Faragher, pp. 12, 14–15; Myres, pp. 25–26. This is not to suggest, however, that men's and women's trail diaries were essentially alike; they were different in all sorts of ways relative to each sex's social role. As regards response to landscape, however, men and women saw the new land in much the same ways, and used much the same vocabulary to describe it.

49. Myres, pp. 21, 28. Eliza W. Farnham, *Life in Prairie Land* (1846; rpt. New York: Arno Press, 1972, p. 236.

50. Allen, p. 13; Myres, p. 36.

51. For a discussion of the changing views of the Canadian North West, see Doug Owram, *Promise of Eden.*

52. Henry Youle Hind, *Narrative of the Canadian Red River Exploring Expedition of 1857 and of the Assinniboine and Saskatchewan Exploring Expedition of 1858,* 2 vols. (London: Longman, Green, Longman, and Roberts, 1860), 1: 147, 134–35. MacLaren, "Aesthetic Mappings,"

pp. 44, 36. For the record of the Palliser expedition see *The Papers of the Palliser Expedition, 1857–1860,* ed. Irene M. Spry (Toronto: Champlain Society, 1968).

53. Sanford Fleming, *England and Canada: A Summer Tour Between Old and New Wesminster* (Montreal: Dawson Brothers, 1884), pp. 216–17. Several progress reports were published under Fleming's name; each of which dealt with a certain part of the country surrounding the projected route. See, for example, Sanford Fleming, *Report on Surveys and Preliminary Operations on the Canadian Pacific Railway up to January 1877* (Ottawa: MacLean, Roger & Co., 1877).

54. George Munro Grant's *Ocean to Ocean* (1873) was one of the first traveler's accounts published which included a European's reaction to the Canadian prairie landscape. Grant was attached to Fleming's first exploratory journey for what became the Canadian Pacific Railway, accomplished in 1872 by way of an entirely Canadian route from Toronto to Vancouver Island. Like many others, who came to the Canadian west both before and after him, Grant is primarily concerned with the future of the country, not its topography. Thus he concentrates, while describing the prairie, on its agricultural and settlement prospects—for he was anxious to encourage Canadian settlement to fill the "great lone land" since American designs on British territory were generally feared. And like many others before him, Grant is specific about the prairie landscape only when he is able to climb some hill and encompass it within his sight. Together with James and Flagg, Grant is struck by the sheer spectacle of a thunderstorm on the prairie. But, apart from corroborating the impressions of others, Grant's book yields little that has not been noted previously; his observations are of the same order as those of Brackenridge, Bradbury, and other travelers who visited the American prairie. Both *Ocean to Ocean* and *Picturesque Canada* (1882) are significant mainly in that they were among the first to articulate a vision of Canada as another nation stretching from the Atlantic to the Pacific. See George M. Grant, *Ocean to Ocean: Sanford Fleming's Expedition Through Canada in 1872.*

55. William Francis Butler, *The Great Lone Land: A Narrative Tale of Travel and Adventure in the North-West of America* (London: Sampson Low, Marston, Low, & Searle, 1872), pp. 92–93, 94. Subsequent references are to this edition.

56. Sir William Francis Butler, *The Wild North Land,* pp. 30–31. De Smet, *Western Missions,* p. 73.

Chapter 2

1. William H. Goetzmann, "The West as Romantic Horizon," in *The West as Romantic Horizon* (Omaha: Center for Western Studies, Joslyn Art Museum, 1981), p. 12. This book provides an excellent, if brief, overview of American painters of the frontier, but Goetzmann—along with William N. Goetzmann—has followed with a more extensive treatment, *The West of the Imagination.* Howard R. Lamar discusses Seymour in his introduction to Edwin James, *Account of an Expedition from Pittsburgh to the Rocky Mountains* (Barre, MA: Imprint Society, 1972), pp. xv–xxxvi.

Some comment should be made about the way in which these artists are being used here. None of the figures treated saw himself as a landscape painter, so landscapes per se are of secondary concern in their works. Even so, their depiction of prairie space represents a confrontation between their inculcated esthetic assumption of what constitutes a pleasing landscape and the place they found in the North American west.

2. These terms are taken from M. H. Abrams, *The Mirror and the Lamp: Romantic Theory and the Critical Tradition.*

3. Bernard DeVoto maintained that Catlin "was the first painter of the West who had any effect," in *Across the Wide Missouri,* p. 373. DeVoto could not call Catlin the first without qualification because of the presence in the West of Seymour and also Peter Rindisbacher, who lived for five years in the Red River settlement before heading south for St. Louis. Karl Bodmer and Prince Maximilian saw works by both artists in 1833 before they ascended the Missouri, and Bodmer met Rindisbacher at that time in St. Louis. See *150 Years of Art in Manitoba: Struggle for a Visual Civilization* (Winnipeg, Manitoba: The Winnipeg Art Gallery, 1970) and Alvin M. Josephy, Jr., *The Artist Was a Young Man: The Life Story of Peter Rindisbacher.*

4. Schlissel, *Women's Diaries of the Westward Journey,* p. 105. In addition, DeVoto makes the point that through *Letters and Notes* and *North American Indian Portfolio* (1844), as well as his Indian gallery, which was widely seen in the eastern United States and in England, Catlin established "the first set of conventions of Western painting" (DeVoto, *Across,* 392).

5. George Catlin, *Letters and Notes on the Manners, Customs, and Conditions of the North American Indians,* 2 vols. (1841; rpt. New York: Dover, 1973), 1: 2. Subsequent references are to this edition. Biographical material is from William H. Truettner, *The Natural Man Observed: A Study of Catlin's Indian Gallery,* pp. 12, 69–73, 82.

6. See, for example, *Letters and Notes,* 1: 15.

7. William H. Truettner observes that Catlin "ascended the Missouri with the full vocabulary of the picturesque at his command, noting ruins, the gentle conformation of the green hills, and the sublime aspect of prairie fires." Truettner, *The Natural Man Observed,* p. 105.

8. William H. Truettner summarizes the issue, saying that Catlin's "interests were too broad to perfect any one of his talents, and such uneven results leave one at a loss, finally, to account for his ability. Energy and devotion made him a brilliant interpreter of savage life, but expediency often robbed him of ultimate artistic success." This is seen particularly in Catlin's landscapes, which reveal, in the main, very little depth or sense of perspective and hence fail to do justice to the definitive feature of the prairie. Another commentator, perhaps a bit too harshly, nevertheless offers the critical consensus when he says that "Catlin had failed badly in his attempts at landscape painting despite his love for it. He was too literal and explicit, even diagrammatical, in his portrayal of the scenes of Indian life." Truettner, p. 105. See also William H. Goetzmann, "The Man Who Stopped to Paint America," in *Karl Bodmer's America,* pp. 4, 21.

9. It is less problematic to observe the way in which these same techniques are used in other types of scenes. Catlin's portrait of a Crow chief, *He Who Jumps Over Everyone* (fig. 8), is a good example. The chief is pictured in profile on a horse which is standing on its hind legs, and the scene is depicted from eye level. The chief is situated in the foreground with, apparently, an unvaried prairie, dotted here and there with orange wildflowers, behind and around him. Looking behind the chief to the extreme background, it is impossible to tell where the land ends and the sky begins, although there is a definite cloudbank on the right edge of the background, and there may be either another cloudbank or a line of hills directly behind the chief, appearing beneath his right foot. All of these various elements prompt the viewer to focus on the mounted Indian and tend to obscure the nature of the surrounding landscape. Indeed, the clouds both behind the chief and those on the horizon (which cannot be distinguished from the far-distant prairie) preclude precise and direct treatment of the prairie landscape. Had Catlin pictured the chief against a cloudless prairie sky there would have been no obscuring the nature of the landscape. This is not to suggest that Catlin should have so pictured the chief; the conventions of portraiture were well established and, certainly, the obscured background helps to make Catlin's painting a more effective portrait. Apart from such considerations, however,

this portrait can be described as providing another instance in which he deferred in his painting from presenting prairie landscapes as directly as he described them in his book.

10. Truettner, p. 105. Here Truettner describes Catlin's usual manner of working while on his upper Missouri trip. Regarding Catlin's landscapes, Truettner writes: "Time and interest often determined finish, there was no consistent attempt to improve his style, and the results are uneven" (111).

11. Paul Kane, *Wanderings of an Artist among the Indians of North American From Canada Vancouver's Island and Oregon Through the Hudson's Bay Company's Territory and Back Again* (London, 1859), rpt. in *Paul Kane's Frontier*, ed. introd., and *catalogue raisonné*, by J. Russell Harper (Austin: Univ. of Texas Press, 1971). Subsequent references are to this edition. For further discussions of Catlin and Kane, see Ann Davis, *A Distant Harmony: Comparisons Between the Painting of Canada and the United States of America* and Ann Davis and Robert Thacker, "Pictures and Prose: Romantic Sensibility and the Great Plains in Catlin, Kane, and Miller."

12. In his entry for this painting in his *catalogue raisonné*, Harper writes: "As in other cases, the composition for this canvas would appear to have a European prototype (or possibly to be after a painting by George Catlin)," entry IV–105, p. 284.

13. J. Russell Harper's *catalogue raisonné* (287–88) lists some thirteen sketches and paintings in which Kane depicted the buffalo, all of which, significantly, feature individual studies of two or three buffalo. In addition, there are also works done on the buffalo hunt and at a buffalo pound. But there are no depictions of extensive buffalo herds. This is remarkable because Kane himself at one point described a prairie black with buffalo "as far as the eye could reach, and so numerous were they, that at times they impeded our progress, filling the air with dust almost to suffocation" (82). Given Kane's vexation over these buffalo, it is surprising that he did not attempt to depict such a scene. In *Métis Chasing a Buffalo Herd*, which depicts the greatest buffalo population in Kane's works, scarcely more than one hundred are visible.

While Kane did not paint or sketch this scene, described by so many travelers and explorers from Castañeda on, another illustrator of the West, John Mix Stanley, did. Stanley traveled throughout the West from the late 1830s and was a friend of Kane's; the two may have met again at Fort Vancouver in 1847. Stanley later accompanied the I. I. Stevens expedition (that described by John Lambert) which explored the possibility of a northern route to the Pacific during the early 1850s. Stanley's illustrations were published (in color) in the government's *Reports* (pub. 1855–61). Stanley's scene is taken from an eminence, and presents the sort of depiction that Edwin James described in his *Account* of the Long expedition, buffalo as far as the eye can see, winking in and out of view at the farthest horizon (James, 15: 239).

Governor Stevens, writing in the *Report* of the scene, stresses the need both for the visual aid and, in fact, for Stanley's illustration:

> we ascended the top of a big hill, and for a great distance ahead every square mile seemed to have a herd of buffalo upon it. Their number was variously estimated by the members of the party—some as high as half a million. I do not think it any exaggeration to set it down at 200,000. I had heard of the myriads of these animals inhabiting these plains, but I could not realize the truth of these accounts till today, when they surpassed anything I could have imagined from the accounts which I had received. The reader will form a better idea of this scene from the accompanying sketch, taken by Mr. Stanley on the ground, than from any description.

As for Stanley himself, he later talked to a writer, who recorded his comments in the following manner:

> The artist in sketching this scene, stood on an elevation in advance of the foreground, whence, with a spyglass, he could see fifteen miles in any direction, and yet he saw not the limit of the herd.
>
> Who can count the multitude? You may only look and wonder! Or, if you seek to estimate the "numbers without number," what sum will you name, except "hundreds of thousands"?

Hence Stanley's technique in getting above this scene corresponds to that of other painters and, moreover, to that of most Europeans on the prairie, whatever their purpose. He needed to get above the landscape. See Stanley's *Herd of Bison, Near Lake Jessie* (fig. 10). Quotations from Stevens and from *Stanley's Western Wilds* are from Robert Taft's *Artists and Illustrators of the Old West, 1850–1900*, p. 16.

14. J. Russell Harper, *Painting in Canada: A History*, p. 123. Commenting on Kane's first showing of his western work, mounted immediately upon his return to Toronto in late 1848 and so containing only his immediate sketches and watercolors, Harper writes in *Paul Kane's Frontier* that these "Landscapes bloom with the glow of the clear Canadian atmosphere":

> All of the sketches in the exhibition were painted with a factual and objective approach which could not fail to speak directly to those who saw them. By contrast, a similar show of Catlin's works would have revealed a nervous, romantic air. Curiously, when Kane painted up his sketches into canvases, he altered his approach, losing the lucid freshness of his first impressions by introducing subjective overtones. These were intended to make his canvases into more profound works of art, but by present-day standards they quite failed to do so. (28)

See Harper's Fig. 106 in *Paul Kane's Frontier* for a reproduction of Kane's putative Italian source for *Assiniboine Hunting Buffalo*.

15. William J. Orr, "Karl Bodmer: The Artist's Life," in *Karl Bodmer's America*, p. 359 and *passim*.

16. DeVoto, pp. 404–06; Goetzmann, "The Man Who Stopped to Paint America," pp. 21, 18; James Thomas Flexner, *That Wilder Image: The Painting of America's Native School from Thomas Cole to Winslow Homer* (Boston: Little, Brown, 1962), p. 89. Goetzmann makes substantially the same point as Flexner, based on far more Maximillan-Bodmer materials than DeVoto and Flexner had available to them: "But in the upper Missouri country [Bodmer] began to realize that he was in a wholly new land of awesome space, immense distances, infinite horizons, and mountainous rock formations like none he had ever seen before" (20). Another recent work on Bodmer is John C. Ewers et al, *Views of a Vanishing Frontier*.

17. Flexner, p. 91. DeVoto, p. 405. Biographical information on Miller has been taken from: DeVoto, pp. 302–39, 406–15; *The West of Alfred Jacob Miller*, Marvin C. Ross, ed., rev. ed. (Norman: Univ. of Oklahoma Press, 1968), pp. xiii–xxxvi; and *Alfred Jacob Miller: Artist on the Oregon Trail*, ed. Ron Tyler, *catalogue raisonné*.

18. Given the variety which Miller incorporates in his scenes—foreground eminence, prairie, and background hill or mountain—his paintings must be described as "beautiful" only, in terms of Gilpin's definitions. See Monk, *The Sublime*, p. 225.

19. Quoted by Carol Clark, "A Romantic Painter in the American West," in *Alfred Jacob Miller: Artist on the Oregon Trail*, pp. 51–52.

20. In this painting Miller places his mounted "Green-Horn" against a large cloudbank overhanging the prairie, using a convention employed by Catlin in his portrait of *He Who Jumps Over Everyone*, the Crow chief. In both cases this device lessens the viewer's sense of vast distance behind the central figure.

21. *The West of Alfred Jacob Miller,* n. facing Plate 149. Subsequent references to Miller's descriptive notes are to this edition.

22. There is evidence, moreover, that Miller continued to adjust his technical presentation of the prairie landscape. As indicated above, Miller painted numerous versions of western work throughout his lifetime, repeating the same scenes. The body of *The West of Alfred Jacob Miller* is made up of a set of water-color copies of his on-the-spot sketches which he made for William T. Walters from July 1858 through August 1860. Several years later Miller made another set for Sir Alexander Hargreaves Brown. While I do not intend to embark on protracted comparisons of the various versions of each subject, it should be noted that in nine selected scenes Miller's subsequent treatment has altered the view of the prairie landscape. The changes he made, usually by lowering the angle of vision and moving a foreground knoll out of the picture, do not have any effect, really, on the subject—only upon its context. Thus it seems that long after he visited the prairie Miller was still experimenting with alternative methods of depicting its vast spaces.

The water colors painted for Sir Alexander Hargreaves Brown were published in *Braves and Buffalo: Plains Indian Life in 1837,* introd. Michael Bell (Toronto: Univ. of Toronto Press, 1973) along with Miller's notes. The nine subjects I have selected for comparison are:

The West of Alfred Jacob Miller (Plate Number)	Title of Painting	*Braves and Buffalo* (Page Number)
76	*Pawnee Indians on Warpath*	149
84	*Approaching Buffalo*	145
106	*Approaching the Buffalo*	19
117	*Medicine Circles*	77
142	*Breaking Camp at Sunrise*	121
151	*Yell of Triumph*	133
190	*Buffalo Rift*	23
198	*Prairie on Fire*	141
200	*A "Surround"*	160

23. Goetzmann, "The Man Who Stopped to Paint America," p. 21.

24. For a discussion of the various illustrators and artists to depict the west apart from those considered, see Taft's *Artists and Illustrators of the Old West, 1850–1900,* which can be augmented by Larry Curry's *The American West: Painters from Catlin to Russell.* Regarding those who painted the prairie in Canada during the nineteenth century, see *Painters in a New Land,* ed. Michael Bell (Toronto: McClelland and Stewart, 1973) and Ronald Rees, *Land of Earth and Sky: Landscape Painting of Western Canada* (Saskatoon: Western Producer Prairie Books, 1985).

25. Washington Irving, *Letters: Vol. II, 1823–1838,* ed. Ralph M. Aderman, et al (Boston: Twayne, 1979), pp. 733–34. Subsequent references are to this edition.

26. See particularly [Edward Everett], "The Crayon Miscellany, by the Author of the Sketch Book, No. 1—A Tour on the Prairies," rev. of *The Crayon Miscellany,* Vol. 1, by Washington Irving, *North American Review,* 41 (July 1835); rpt. *The Native Muse: Theories of American Literature,* ed. Richard Ruland, 2 vols. (New York: E. P. Dutton, 1976), 1: 263–69. For a descriptive summary, with extensive quotation, of the contemporary response to *A Tour,* see

Martha Dula, "Audience Response to *A Tour on the Prairies.*" See also Edgeley W. Todd, "Washington Irving Discovers the Frontier."

27. Not surprisingly, criticism of *A Tour* has concentrated on Irving's ability to portray the West realistically, or on his ability to lend to this material the aura of romance found in *The Sketch Book* and his other works. See Henry Seidel Canby, "Washington Irving," in *Classic Americans* (1931); rpt. *A Century of Commentary on the Works of Washington Irving,* ed. Andrew B. Myers (Tarrytown, New York: Sleepy Hollow Restorations, 1976), pp. 181–82. Writing fifty years ago, Canby presented an evaluation of *A Tour* which is still valid: "But here Irving is too close to his subject. . . . There is a camp scene, firelight flickering on wild faces, psalm-singing, alarms, rough humor of the frontier, which is Irving at his best, but he could not sustain it."

Similarly, Kathryn Whitford argues that Irving found the materials he used in *A Tour* to be "intractable": "The reader watches Irving trying one literary device after another and then abandon each, until the last quarter of the book becomes an increasingly matter of fact narrative and he condenses the arduous week of the return journey into three brief chapters which represent one fourth of the entire time of the expedition." Kathryn Whitford, "Romantic Matamorphosis in Irving's Western Tour," p. 31.

While some critics have argued that his falling off is a matter of style reflecting a personal transformation, that Irving becomes acclimatized to the prairie, Witford's assertion is the more tenable one; there is a noticeable trailing off toward the end of *A Tour,* as well as the various inconsistencies she discusses. But the intractability of Irving's material is as much a function of the landscape as it is, as Whitford suggests, one of Irving's inability to find a unifying technique or motif. He could not adapt it to his conventions, so he largely ignores it. Wayne R. Kime, in 'The Completeness of Washington Irving's *A Tour on the Prairies, WAL,* 8 (1973), 55–65, notes that "The notion that Irving was unable to perceive or portray the West except in false terms is virtually universal . . ." (56, n. 2). In the same note, Kime summarizes the sources of this negative evaluation, although he omits Whitford. Kime rejects these readings and argues that the "carefully shaped narrative framework of the book" presents Irving "as abandoning his naively conventional preconceptions about Western life and gradually achieving a clearer awareness of the West as reality" (55). Without question, there is something of this in *A Tour;* Irving had to know more of "the West as reality" after he had been there, but that is axiomatic. Whitford's reading, that Irving was simply daunted by his material, and so brought it to a hasty conclusion, offers my sense of the book; there are also, as she points out, too many elements and characters introduced with a flourish and then dropped for the book to be considered artistically accomplished. Two other critics who defend *A Tour* are William Bedford Clark, "How the West Won: Irving's Comic Inversion of The Westering Myth in *A Tour on the Prairies,*" and William J. Schieck, "Frontier Robin Hood: Wilderness, Civilization and the Half-Breed in Irving's *A Tour on the Prairies:*"

28. Washington Irving, *Journals and Notebooks, Volume V, 1832–1859,* ed. Sue Field Ross (Boston: Twayne, 1986), p. 78. Subsequent references are to this edition. For the most recent account of Irving's trip, his journals, and the writing of *A Tour,* see Ross's introduction, especially her discussion of the published editions of Irving's *Journals* that preceded the Twayne version. One of these, moreover, is particularly useful for its introduction; see also *The Western Journals of Washington Irving,* ed. John Francis McDermott (Norman: Univ. of Oklahoma Press, 1944).

29. Washington Irving, *A Tour on the Prairies* in *The Crayon Miscellany* (1835; rpt. [ed. Dahlia Kirby Terrell] New York: Twayne, 1979), p. 9. Subsequent references are to this edition.

30. See Dahlia Kirby Terrell, Introd., *The Crayon Miscellany* by Washington Irving, p. xx, n. 13. Terrell mentions Irving's admission that he had read only *The Pioneers* prior to his western tour, although he was doubtlessly aware of the reputation of the other two Leatherstocking Tales in print at the time. And while critics have considered the sources consulted by Irving before writing *A Tour*, none has mentioned either Cooper's *The Prairie* or Bryant's "The Prairies." It seems nevertheless quite likely that Irving would have availed himself of both his literary precursors before writing up his *Tour*; thus his use of "verdant waste," which is used by Bryant as well as Cooper. So while it cannot be argued that Irving arrived on the prairie without literary preconceptions, *A Tour* does contain echoes which might be attributed to Irving's consultation of sources after his trip but prior to writing his book. He refers to one of the rangers, old Ryan, for example, as a "real old Leatherstocking." See Stanley T. Williams, *The Life of Washington Irving*, 2: 72–91.

31. Henry Leavitt Ellsworth, *Washington Irving on the Prairie, or a Narrative of a Tour of the Southwest in the Year 1832*, ed. Stanley T. Williams and Barbara D. Simison (New York: American Book Co., 1937), p. 88. Irving's tour was abundantly recorded; in addition to his works and Ellsworth's *Narrative* there are two other first-person accounts. See Charles Joseph Latrobe, *The Rambler in North America*, 2 vols. (New York: Harper, 1835) and Count Albert-Alexandre de Portales, *On the Western Tour with Washington Irving* (Norman: Univ. of Oklahoma Press, 1968).

32. Irving's journal for this period, which covered Chapters 16–22 inclusive in *A Tour* is not extant, so cannot be compared to the finished passages in *A Tour*. In fact, scholars are uncertain as to whether such a journal was even written but, owing to the existing journals—which chronicle virtually all of the rest of the trip—and Ellsworth's comments as to the regularity with which Irving attended to such writing (Ellsworth, 70–71), it appears likely that such a journal was kept. See John Francis McDermott, introd., *The Western Journals of Washington Irving* for an explanation of the circumstances surrounding Irving's journals. In addition, such are the correspondences between the extant journals and the passages derived from them in *A Tour*, and such is the degree of correspondence regarding the daily incidents of the journey between *A Tour* and the narratives by Latrobe and Ellsworth (both of whom note the buffalo hunt on which Irving became lost, though not his separation), however, it is doubtful that Irving invented this incident.

33. See Donald A. Ringe, *The Pictorial Mode: Space and Time in the Art of Bryant, Irving, and Cooper*, pp. 48–49. Ringe selected quotations from these two paragraphs of *A Tour* to support his contention that "Irving is obviously deeply impressed with the expansiveness of the prairie landscape, and . . . he has a strong feeling of a loneness amidst the vast sweep of prairie and sky." Such is accurate within these two paragraphs only—not, as Ringe implies, to *A Tour* as a whole.

34. As I have argued here, the prairie which Irving saw and communicated through *A Tour* was predetermined by his style and cultural assumptions. The same can be said of both of his subsequent western books, *Astoria* and *The Adventures of Captain Bonneville, U. S. A.*, where the prairie landscape figures only occasionally.

35. Margaret Fuller, *Summer on the Lakes* (1844), in *The Writings of Margaret Fuller*, ed. Mason Wade (New York: Viking, 1941), p. 26. Subsequent references are to this edition.

Though not as completely steeped in western writing as Francis Parkman was when he traveled onto the prairies a few years later, Fuller had read Irving's western books and generally finds them wanting. Thus she writes toward the beginning of *Summer on the Lakes* that, "with the exception of the *Tour to the Prairies*," Irving's books have a stereotype, secondhand air. They lack the breath, the glow, the charming minute traits of living presence. His scenery is only fit to be glanced at from dioramic distance; his Indians are academic figures only. He would have made the best of pictures, if he could have used his own eyes for studies and sketches; as it is, his success is wonderful but inadequate. (25)

36. Myres, p. 30. Myres offers an excellent discussion of women's attitudes toward wilderness from a historical perspective in her second chapter, appropriately entitled "The Pleasing Awfulness." In addition see also Jeffrey, *Frontier Women, passim,* and her " 'There Is Some Splendid Scenery': Women's Responses to the Great Plains Landscape" as well as Schlissel, pp. 10–18.

37. Kolodny, *The Land Before Her: Fantasy and Experience of the American Frontiers, 1630–1860* (Chapel Hill: Univ. of North Carolina Press, 1984), pp. xii, xi, 8–9, xii. Subsequent references are to this edition. It should be noted that Kolodny is not using *prairie* in the same sense it is offered here. She is referring to the American usage of the term, where the prairie stretches from western Ohio to the beginning of the plains. As such, her prairie is better watered and more lush than the landscape farther west, the plains area in American usage.

At the same time, by ending with 1860, Kolodny has not examined the writings of women who settled the plains, so her argument cannot be extrapolated into the plains. She is apparently planning a subsequent volume, however, to include the plains and Rocky mountains.

38. Mason Wade, *Francis Parkman: Heroic Historian,* pp. 220–25; Mason Wade, Introd., 'The Oregon Trail Journal, 1846," in *The Journals of Francis Parkman,* ed. Mason Wade (New York: Harper, 1947), 2: 385–95. Here Wade details his rationale for seeing *The Oregon Trail* as severely diluted history, both because of the background and age of its author and the circumstances of its composition. As history, he much prefers the journals. As literature, however, the finished book is preferable, Wade's objections notwithstanding. See also Bernard DeVoto, *The Year of Decision: 1846, passim.* At one point DeVoto describes a moment in *The Oregon Trail* when Parkman almost rises above his class prejudices and understands a party of migrants he was viewing; but his prejudice proves too strong. Says DeVoto: "The historian succumbed to a parochialism of his class and we lost a great book" (176).

39. See E. N. Feltskog's editorial notes to his scholarly edition of *The Oregon Trail* for an account of Parkman's reading prior to his western trip: Francis Parkman, *The Oregon Trail* (1849; rpt. [ed. E. N. Feltskog] Madison: Univ. of Wisconsin Press, 1969), pp. 460–61, n. 16. The phrase "almost by heart" is Feltskog's. Unless noted otherwise, subsequent references are to this edition. Mason Wade also discusses Parkman's reading in *Journals,* 2: 397.

40. Some comment must be made regarding the circumstances surrounding the composition of *The Oregon Trail,* which Wade describes as having been composed under "singular difficulties," (*Journals,* 2: 385). Parkman's eyes, which were to trouble him for the rest of his life, were adversely affected by his western trip; so much so that he dictated *The Oregon Trail* to others; they would read a journal entry to him and, once Parkman had framed his passage, copy that one down. Wade, however, speaks of the composition of the book as "triple distillation," (*Francis Parkman,* 295). The third element he attributes to "the revision of the manuscript by the staid and proper Charles Eliot Norton—of all people!" (287); Wade claims that Norton bowdlerized Parkman's text while reading proof for the first book publication by revising it in accordance with his notion of literary decorum. Wade's thesis is disputed and effectively rebuffed by Feltskog (57a–64a), who thinks it more likely that the differences between the serial version and the 1849 edition are attributable to Parkman himself.

41. Francis Parkman, *Letters of Francis Parkman,* ed. Wilbur R. Jacobs, 2 vols. (Norman:

Univ. of Oklahoma Press, 1960), 1: 48. *Journals,* 2: 417. Subsequent references are to this edition.

42. Here too Parkman changed his emphasis, giving his feelings over being lost greater emphasis. While in his journal entry he notes the local fauna before mentioning his "Awkward feeling," in *The Oregon Trail* he inverts the presentation, so that he discusses the animals and vegetation only after he has presented his analysis of his feelings.

Parkman's use and evaluation of prairie phenomena is of a similar order. For example, in two instances he employs the setting sun (and its resulting mirage effect of making objects look larger) as a descriptive tool; in the first of these he describes a boy who was traveling with an emigrant group. The boy, Parkman says, "was short and stout, but his legs were of disproportioned and appalling length. I observed him at sunset, breasting the hill with gigantic strides, and standing against the sky on the summit, like a colossal pair of tongs" (76). This combination of back-lighting and the mirage illusion, increasing the figure's apparent size, is directly the result of the prairie landscape. Similarly, while leaving an Arapahoe Indian camp, Parkman views it against a glowing western sky: "When about a mile from the village, I turned and looked back over the undulating ocean of grass. The sun was just set; the western sky was all in a glow, and sharply defined against it, on the extreme verge of the plain, stood the clustered lodges of the Arapahoe camp" (352).

In addition to providing strikingly visual details made possible by the prairie landscape, these descriptions are also a verification of a preconceived expectation created in Parkman by Cooper's *The Prairie.* Since Parkman knew Cooper's Leatherstocking Tales well, he could not have missed the author's use of the figure against the setting sun as his means of introducing Natty Bumppo in *The Prairie.* Hence Parkman's use of this phenomenon is different from its discussion in Gregg's *Commerce of the Prairie* or James's *Account* of the Long expedition. When each of these men discussed the mirage effect on the prairie, they were simply describing a natural phenomenon and providing examples. When Parkman uses the same phenomenon here, however, he is using it as a literary device, at least in some sense, one appropriated from Cooper, who had himself appropriated it from the James *Account.* In the latter regard, see Orm Överland, *The Making and Meaning of an American Classic: James Fenimore Cooper's* The Prairie (Oslo: Universitetsforlaget, and New York: Humanities Press, 1973), pp. 76–77.

43. Francis Parkman, *The Oregon Trail* (1849; rpt. [ed. David Levin] New York: Penguin, 1982), p. 106. Feltskog's edition reprints the final edition of *The Oregon Trail* which, in David Levin's words, should be seen "as Parkman's most mature judgment of what he wanted to survive him." His changes for the 1872 and 1892 editions include "substantive and stylistic departures from the romantic judgment of his youth." Levin, however, opts for the 1849 edition "because students of American literature and of the Westward Movement will prefer to see how the young man wrote, and what he believed, at the time his book might have an immediate influence." ("A Note on the Text," 30). Except for punctuation and contemporary references which were no longer appropriate in the latter decades of the century (such as an allusion to the Great American Desert), this deletion is the only authorial change which bears on Parkman's reactions to the landscape.

Chapter 3

1. [Edward Everett], "The Crayon Miscellany, by the Author of the Sketch Book, No. 1—A Tour on the Prairies," rev. of *The Crayon Miscellany,* Vol. I, by Washington Irving, *North American Review,* 41 (July 1835); rpt. *The Native Muse,* 1: 266, 269.

2. [Herman Melville], "Mr. Parkman's Tour," rev. of *The California and Oregon Trail,* by Francis Parkman, *Literary World* (March 31, 1849), 291–93.

3. Several critics have explored this situation, but Edwin Fussell's *Frontier: American Literature and the American West* is the most thorough treatment of the subject as it applies to the writers of the American Renaissance. Because he is concerned with the entire West, however, Fussell's treatment of the prairie is incidental, and he does not attempt to define its use as a particular landscape in the writing he examines. And while more concerned with violence, myth, and the psychological effects of European man's passage through the land, Richard Slotkin, in *Regeneration Through Violence* devotes his two final chapters to Leatherstocking and the American Renaissance writers. In addition to these and Smith's *Virgin Land,* other notable works on the Westward Movement in American literature are Ralph Leslie Rusk, *The Literature of the Middle Western Frontier;* Dorothy Ann Dondore, *The Prairie and the Making of Middle America;* Lucy Lockwood Hazard, *The Frontier in American Literature;* and Robert Edson Lee's *From West to East: Studies in the Literature of the American West.*

4. Henry David Thoreau, *The Journal of Henry D. Thoreau,* ed. Bradford Torrey and Francis H. Allen (1906; rpt. Boston: Houghton Mifflin, 1949), 1: 473–74. Thoreau's landscape esthetics were more complex than had been generally supposed; see Richard J. Schneider, "Thoreau and Nineteenth-Century American Landscape Painting," *ESQ,* 31, no. 2 (1985), pp. 67–88. Ralph Waldo Emerson, *Nature,* in *Selections from Ralph Waldo Emerson,* ed. Stephen E. Whicher (Boston: Houghton Mifflin, 1957), p. 27.

5. While not dealing specifically with the prairie landscape, Smith and Slotkin—two of the preeminent analysts of American western myths—speak most directly to the attraction offered by the west to imaginative writers. Slotkin, for example, while discussing Thoreau's *A Week on the Concord and Merrimack Rivers,* writes: "The new frontiers are within the present geographical bounds of American society, within the mind of man. They must be approached as the frontier hunter approaches the wilderness: not in terms of civilized conventions, but as an unknown reality to be plumbed by total self-immersion in direct, simple, and unanticipated experience" (*Regeneration Through Violence,* 521). In just this fashion, Cooper, Melville and to a lesser extent, Thoreau himself, approached the prairie, "fronting"—to borrow a verb from Thoreau's *A Week*—its essential qualities directly.

6. Speaking of Ishmael Bush's intrusion west of the Mississippi, D. H. Lawrence saw "Great Wings of vengeful doom . . . spread over the west, grim against the intruder"; Richard Chase comments that in the book "We are always aware of the dark, foreboding panorama that surrounds us." There are also numerous discussions of the pictorial in Cooper, both in *The Prairie* and his other work, beginning with Henry Nash Smith's comment that setting in this novel is treated "as if it were an Elizabethan stage, a neutral space where any character may be brought at a moment's notice," and extending to the work of such critics as Donald A. Ringe, Blake Nevius, and H. Daniel Peck. These critics elaborate on Cooper's visual mode of presentation: his connection with the Hudson River school of painters, his use of eighteenth-century esthetic terms, and his use of space, light, and shadow. See D. H. Lawrence, *Studies in Classic American Literature;* Richard Chase, *The American Novel and its Tradition,* p. 57. Henry Nash Smith, Introd., *The Prairie: A Tale,* p. ix; Howard Mumford Jones, "Prose and Pictures: James Fenimore Cooper"; Donald A. Ringe, "James Fenimore Cooper and Thomas Cole: An Analogous Technique"; Donald A. Ringe, "Chiaroscuro as an Artistic Device in Cooper's Fiction"; Donald A. Ringe, *The Pictorial Mode: Space and Time in the Art of Bryant, Irving, and Cooper;* Blake Nevius, *Cooper's Landscapes: An Essay on the Picturesque Vision;* and H. Daniel Peck, *A World By Itself: the Pastoral Moment in Cooper's Fiction.*

7. James Franklin Beard, "Cooper and his Artistic Contemporaries," 492. Or as Donald A.

Ringe states, "the degree to which the various characters perceive that relation determines their moral standing in the tale" ("Man and Nature in Cooper's *The Prairie*," 316). A good overview of Cooper, the pictorial, and his use of eighteenth-century esthetics is provided by Ernest H. Redekop, "Picturesque and Pastoral: Two Views of Cooper's Landscapes," 184–205.

8. For the best single discussion of the novel's gestation and reception, see Orm Överland, *The Making and Meaning of an American Classic: James Fenimore Cooper's The Prairie*. Överland summarizes contemporary criticism of *The Prairie* leveled by Governor Lewis Cass of Michigan, Flint, and Drake on the grounds that Cooper knew nothing of the West (142). For a more recent version of the same argument, see Robert Edson Lee, *From West to East*. His title notwithstanding, Lee dismisses *The Prairie* as having no place in his study. Regarding the inaccuracy of Cooper's depiction of the west, see John T. Flanagan, "The Authenticity of Cooper's *The Prairie*"; and E. Soteris Muszynska-Wallace, "The Sources of *The Prairie*."

9. William P. Kelly, *Plotting America's Past: Fenimore Cooper and the Leatherstocking Tales*, p. 92. See also in this regard Folsom, *The American Western Novel*, pp. 37–58; Wayne Franklin, *The New World of James Fenimore Cooper*, pp. 213–48.

10. Regarding the overall influence of the James *Account* on Cooper, an extended passage from William H. Goetzmann's essay, "James Fenimore Cooper: *The Prairie*," in *Landmarks of American Writing*, is useful; summarizing the explorers' experiences, he writes:

> On the march, [they] passed through Indian lands, including the dangerous village of the "Bad Hearts," through buffalo herds strung out for miles, climbed towering Pikes Peak for the first time, and gazed with scientific detachment on the weirdly contrasting topography of the High Plains—where rising out of nowhere, like a ship on the sea, stand Scott's Bluff, Court-house Rock, and other strange eminences. They saw rivers that cut suddenly into the rolling plains, raging fires on the sea of grass, thickets of willows and dwarf trees in the river bottoms that afforded oases for Indian nomads, and the Cross Timbers—a forest standing for no apparent reason out on the bald prairie. Most of all, they were struck with the fact that this fantastic country resembled nothing so much as a "Great American Desert." To them it was a moonscape. The "lost pathfinder," Zebulon Pike, had been right when, ten years earlier in his own pub-lished account, he had described it in this exotic fashion. Any would-be settler who ventured out of the familiar forests of the Mississippi Valley, across the infinite and terrible spaces of the High Plains, clearly left most of the possibilities for civilization behind. In their view, he was entering upon what could only be a somber and disheartening enterprise. (67)

Goetzmann's tone—in concert with his detail—captures those elements Cooper seized upon in the James *Account* and developed in his novel.

11. James D. Wallace, *Early Cooper and His Audience*, p. 161.

12. William P. Kelly's discussion of *The Prairie* points up—in considerable detail and persuasively—Cooper's difficulties in achieving coherence in the novel. In trying to encapsulate American history—through characters representing all classes, as well as through the relation between this novel and its two Leatherstocking predecessors—Cooper attempts to offer a meliorist view of his country's future: "America's past has been ordered and its future made secure. With a resounding sense of closure, Cooper brings the Leatherstocking series to completion" (112). But, citing Bush's self-appointed role as judge, jury, and executioner of Abiram White as well as Middleton's "unpersuasive" (123) reconciliation of the novel's tensions, Kelly notes that "A novel which begins as an attempt to contain American experience becomes a self-deconstructing work in which Cooper's historiographic intentions are frustrated by his inability to enact them" (117). He ultimately concludes:

By setting *The Prairie* in the New West, Cooper necessarily predicated the novel's dialectical structure on faith rather than extrapolation. At a time in which the specter of national disruption loomed very large indeed, Cooper reaffirms his vision of American history and assures his readers of the constancy of national tradition. But like Jefferson, Cooper too heard a firebell in the night. (127)

13. James Fenimore Cooper, *The Prairie: A Tale* (1827; rpt. [ed. James P. Elliott] Albany: State Univ. of New York Press, 1985), pp. 9, 24, 76. Subsequent references are to this edition.

14. Thus when Middleton approaches the trapper, Paul Hover, and Dr. Bat while they are feasting on a buffalo, Cooper comments that "The meeting of two hunters on the American desert . . . was, consequently, somewhat in the suspicious and wary manner in which two vessels draw together in a sea, that is known to be infested with pirates" (107). Similarly, as Natty, Paul, Middleton, and Dr. Bat make their escape from Bush's rock citadel, along with Inez and Ellen, whom they have liberated, Cooper contrasts the trapper's assurance with the disorientation of the rest of his party by using the ocean/prairie analogy: "To most of the fugitives their situation was as entirely unknown, as is that of a ship in the middle of the ocean to the uninstructed voyager, but the old man proceeded at every turn, and through every bottom with a decision that inspired as followers with confidence . . ." (178). Cooper also keeps this association alive through light, passing references of this order.

15. *Överland*, p. 76.

16. For a more detailed discussion of this point, see James P. Elliott, "Historical Introd.," *The Prairie: A Tale*, pp. xv–xxxiii. Elliott takes up *Överland* and argues convincingly that Cooper's source "did not confine his imagination but gave it free reign," and concludes: "though Long's *Expedition* supplies many details for the world of *The Prairie*, the novel stands on its own as a metaphorical reconstitution of man's interaction with nature" (xix; xxiii–xxiv).

17. Cooper's use of Natty at the beginning of the *The Prairie* or of White at the end are not the sole instances of his use of the mirage effect in the novel. In chapter six he uses the phenomenon as a basis of comedy, since Dr. Bat assumes he has seen a horrible, uncatalogued, monster of the prairie when in fact the animal is his own jackass. Later, too, Natty comments on the optical and aural effects of the prairie landscape himself; speaking to Middleton, the trapper admonishes him that he may think his eyes and ears are keen:

"they may be good to see across a church or to hear a town bell, but afore you had passed a year in these Prairies you would find yourself mistaking a turkey for a horse or conceiting fifty times that the roar of a buffaloe bull was the thunder of the Lord. There is a deception of natur' in these naked plains, which the air throws up the images like water, and then it is hard to tell the prairies from a sea." (196)

18. Cooper borrowed not only landscape descriptions from the James *Account*, he also used the Seymour illustrations which accompanied James's text. His description of the Sioux camp seen from a distance, which opens chapter twenty-five, is almost exactly the same as Seymour's *Oto Encampment* in James. See *Överland*, pp. 83–87, and the relevant passages in James: *EWT*, 15: 183–84.

19. Speaking of Cooper's use of the rock tower, Blake Nevius has remarked that through its use Cooper decided "to play fast and loose with geological probability," and also attributes its role to the author's need for a "base of operations" (16, 14). Neither claim shows familiarity with Cooper's sources, nor with his use of them.

James describes Castle Rock, which is also marked on the map published in the *Account* (15: 306–07). But a more precise descriptive overview of the "rock towers" of the plains is found in a section entitled "Observations on the Mineralogy and Geology of a Part of the United States west of the Mississippi," by Augustus Edward Jessup (a geologist on the expedition), appended to the narrative of the expedition. Jessup writes, after describing the strata along the Platte,

> Behind these, occur lofty but uninterrupted ranges of naked rocks, destitute of any covering of earthy or vegetable matter, and standing nearly perpendicular. At a distant view, they present to the eye the forms of walls, towers, pyramids, and columns, seeming rather the effects of the most laborious efforts of art, than the productions of nature. (17: 195)

Given such descriptions, Cooper had a firm basis for the novel's naked rock tower in his source.

20. William Cullen Bryant, *Prose Writings,* ed. Parke Godwin (1884; rpt. New York: Russell & Russell, 1964), 2: 16.

21. [William Cullen Bryant], rev. of *The Prairie,* by James Fenimore Cooper, in *United States Review and Literary Gazette,* 2 (July 1827), 306–07; as quoted by Överland, p. 140.

22. William Cullen Bryant, "The Prairies," in *The Poetical Works of William Cullen Bryant,* ed. Parke Godwin (1883; rpt. New York: Russell & Russell, 1967), 1: 228–32. Another of Bryant's poems, "The Hunter of the Prairies," uses the prairie as setting; here the speaker is the hunter, and the prairie, "the green desert," is where he is free. The setting is Eden-like and not treated specifically; see *Poetical Works,* 1: 235–37.

23. For discussions of Poe's plagiarism, see John J. Teunissen and Evelyn J. Hinz, "Poe's *Journal of Julius Rodman* as Parody," Fussell, pp. 155–62; Wayne R. Kime, "Poe's Use of Irving's *Astoria* in 'The Journal of Julius Rodman.' " And while not addressed to *Julius Rodman* specifically, a good discussion of Poe's landscape esthetics is Catherine Rainwater, "Poe's Landscape Tales and the 'Picturesque' Tradition."

24. Edgar Allan Poe, *The Journal of Julius Rodman,* in *The Imaginary Voyages, Collected Writings of Edgar Allan Poe,* ed. Burton R. Pollin (Boston: Twayne, 1981), 1: 537. The *Journal* was serially published in *Burton's Gentleman's Magazine,* January to June, 1840. See Pollin's introduction for an overview of the *Journal,* pp. 508–15.

Similarly, Rodman remarks over "beautiful prairies" (542), notes a prairie stretching off "as far as the eye could reach" (553), sees buffalo swimming and drowning in the river (567–68), and describes "an immense and magnificent country spreading out on every side into a vast plain, waving with glorious verdure, and alive with countless herds of buffaloes and wolves, intermingled with occasional elk and antelope" (575). Rodman's vantage point for this latter description, of course, is from the "high grounds."

25. Although in "Roger Malvin's Burial" and *The Scarlet Letter* Hawthorne drew upon the West as frontier and wilderness more than as prairie, "The Great Carbunkle" (1836) does include a setting suggestive of the prairie—it is barren. And in "Earth's Holocaust" (1844) he actually uses the prairie as a setting. Emerson's use of the prairie is even less pronounced, but he does refer to it briefly, in four of his poems: "Boston," "Ode Inscribed to Ellery Channing," "The Titmouse," and "The World Soul." As Fussell suggests, the use of the prairie landscape in "Earth's Holocaust" probably owes more to the unreality of Hawthorne's parable than to any attraction to landscape. See Fussell, pp. 69–131, especially 85–88. In addition, while Fussell provides no sustained discussion of Emerson in relation to the West, one is available in Lee's *From West to East,* pp. 153–56. Dickinson refers to the prairie twice, once in "My Period Had Come for Prayer—" and again in "To Make a Prairie it Takes a Clover and One Bee."

26. Henry D. Thoreau, *Walden,* in *The Writings of Henry D. Thoreau* (1854; rpt. [ed. J. Lyndon Stanley] Princeton: Princeton Univ. Press, 1971), p. 4.

In *Walden,* as in the what might be called pre-Parkman Melville, the prairie is a source of syntactical allusion only; it is not accorded any of the thematic importance found in *Moby-Dick*. Discussing food at the beginning of "Economy," for example, Thoreau comments that all the "bison of the prairie" require is "a few inches of palatable grass, with water to drink" (12). Most of his prairie allusions are of this type.

In two instances, however, the prairie landscape is presented as symbolic of aspects central to the Walden experiment. Describing the immediate area around Walden Pond in "Where I Lived, and What I Lived For," Thoreau writes:

> There was pasture enough for my imagination. The low shrub-oak plateau to which the opposite shore arose, stretched away toward the prairies of the West and the steppes of Tartary, affording ample room for all the roving families of men. "There are none happy in the world but beings who enjoy freely a vast horizon"—said Damodara, when his herds required new and larger pastures. (87)

Here the prairie is invoked as an imaginative symbol of space and distance suitable for the habitation of man. Later, in "Solitude," Thoreau describes the neighborhood of Walden Pond and concludes: "But for the most part it is as solitary where I live as on the prairies" (130). Here again the prairie is alluded to in order to provide a landscape that symbolizes an idea; in this case, solitude. Fussell comments that "*Walden* rests firmly on the outrageous proposition that a man can live 'at the West' or 'on the frontier' without going near either" (201). It should, however, be pointed out that Thoreau's use of the prairie, like his use of the West, is metaphoric. His concern in the above instances is with what the prairie symbolizes, not with where or what it is.

27. While he alludes to the prairie on numerous occasions throughout *Leaves of Grass* (1855; revised through 1891–92), Whitman does not directly confront landscape until *Specimen Days* (1882), when he recounts his trip through the west. For example, he wrote "Night on the Prairies" (1860) before he had seen the landscape. In the poem the speaker imagines himself among a group of westward-bound emigrants; stepping away from their campfire, he muses upon the stars and death, saying nothing about the land. Walt Whitman, "The Prairie States," in *Leaves of Grass,* ed. Harold W. Blodgett and Sculley Bradley (New York: Norton, 1965), p. 402. Significantly, when he did visit the prairie west, he finds the landscape to be confirmation of his idea of it:

> Grand as the thought that doubtless the child is already born who will·see a hundred millions of people, the most prosperous and advanced of the world, inhabitating these prairies, the Great Plains, and the valley of Mississippi, I could not help thinking it would grander still to see all those inimitable American areas fused in the alembic of a perfect poem, or other esthetic work, entirely western, fresh, and limitless—altogether our own. . . .

See Walt Whitman, *Specimen Days,* ed. Lance Hidy (1882; rpt. Boston: G. R. Godine, 1971), p. 93. He then goes on to catalog the various sights he sees along the rail line for the purposes of such a poem. And though Whitman's outpouring of sentiment here might be discounted since, at the age of sixty he was here seeing for the first time the American west of which he had sung for so long, his use of the prairie in poetry is not radically different than that of others who were enamored of the idea of the west. It is ever a representative landscape in a catalog of American scenes. A poem which resulted from his trip, "The Prairie States" (1881) expressed the same sentiments as the prose passage; a "newer garden of creation" becomes home for "joyeous, modern, populous millions."

A representative example of Whitman's use of the prairie in poems that are not ostensibly set there is found in "When Lilacs Last in the Dooryard Bloom'd" (1865–66). In the tenth section of the poem, he uses the prairie to symbolize the center of the country: "Sea-winds blown from east and west, / Blown from the Eastern sea and blown from the Western sea, till / there on the prairies meeting . . . perfume the grave of him" he loves (332, ll. 74–77). Here the prairie is invoked so that Whitman may unify Lincoln, the "great star early droop'd in the western sky" (328, l. 2), with the entire mourning nation. Two other references to the prairie in the poem occur during Whitman's panoramic view of the whole nation. He refers to "the far-spreading prairies cover'd with grass and corn" (333, l. 92) as the day's light passes over the whole nation, and, later, the bird's song rises *"over the myriad fields and the prairies wide"* (355, l. 160). Though the effect of the westward movement is far more apparent in Whitman than in others, his references to the prairie are more promiscuous than Thoreau's and their casualness contrasts with Melville's pointed allusions.

28. Herman Melville, "Hawthorne and His Mosses," *Literary World,* (August 17 and 24, 1850); rpt. in Herman Melville, *Moby-Dick: An Authoritative Text,* ed. Harrison Hayford and Hershal Parker (New York: Norton, 1967), p. 546. Subsequent references to *Moby-Dick* are from this edition. Herman Melville, *Selected Poems of Herman Melville,* ed. Henning Cohen (Carbondale: Southern Illinois Univ. Press, 1964), pp. 96–101.

29. Edwin Fussell, *Frontier,* p. 259. Fussell provides a compelling argument about Melville's use of the West in this book, too; he sees a correspondence in the author's mind between "ocean" and "West," so that the two terms are interchangeable. The West, moreover, helps to make Melville's tale American, as does his central drama of the hunt: "an American hunting story, regardless of ostensible locale, was inevitably a story about the West" (257). See also John W. Nichol, "Melville and the Midwest, 613–25 and, more recently, Jack Scherting, "Tracking the *Pequod* Along *The Oregon Trail.*" The latter is curious, in a way, for while it considers the Parkman/Melville parallel in some considerable detail, Scherting makes no mention of Fussell, does not take up the image of wild horses in both books, and misses other important correspondences.

30. Melville's sources for the "White Steed of the Prairies" were various. James Hall, *The Wilderness and the Warpath* (New York: Wiley and Putnam, 1846), pp. 169–70, discusses the tale of this horse as a gloss to his story, "The Black Steed of the Prairies." See Herman Melville, *Moby-Dick or, The Whale,* ed. Luther S. Mansfield and Howard P. Vincent (New York: Hendricks House, 1952), p. 711 for a discussion of Hall's text and Melville's steed. Another, more indirect, source was in all likelihood Parkman's *The Oregon Trail.* Though Parkman makes no mention of white horses, at several different points he notes both white buffalo and white wolves on the prairie. Melville may also have consulted some contemporary source that informed him that a "white buffalo—that is, an albino or unusually blond one—was about the most valuable object in the world to the Plains Indians, who regarded it as having great magical power." Mason Wade, in *The Journals of Francis Parkman,* II: 619, n. 76. Parkman's references to white animals are to be found in *The Oregon Trail,* pp. 126, 367, 390, and 393.

In addition, contemporary descriptions of wild horses on the prairie were also available to Melville; one is found in Pike, and Irving devotes a chapter to them in *A Tour* ("Ringing the wild horses," 83–86) as well as alluding to them frequently throughout. Irving's description of a captive horse, moreover, is similar to Melville's: "From being a denizen of these vast pastures, ranging at will from plain to plain and mead to mead, cropping every herb and flower and drinking of every stream," the wild horse "was suddenly reduced to perpetual and painful servitude . . ." (*A Tour,* 70). Given his interest in the prairie, it seems likely that Melville

251

availed himself of *A Tour;* his library contained a set of Irving's *Works,* but he did not acquire these volumes until June 1853. See Merton M. Sealts, Jr., *Melville's Reading: A Checklist of Books Owned and Borrowed,* p. 70, entry 292a.

31. George William Curtis, *Lotus Eating: A Summer Book* (1852) in *Prue and I, Lotus Eating* (London: J. M. Dent, n.d.), p. 214.

32. Albert Pike, *Prose Sketches and Poems, Written in the Western Country* (1834; rpt. [ed. David J. Weber] College Station: Texas A & M Univ. Press, 1987), p. 9. Subsequent references are to this edition.

33. Rev. of *A Tour on the Prairies,* by Washington Irving, *Southern Literary Messenger,* I (1835), 456; as quoted by Fussell, *Frontier,* p. 158.

34. Charles Augustus Murray, *The Prairie-Bird* (1844; rpt. London: Richard Bentley, 1845). Another sportsman turned romancer was William George Drummond Stewart, who employed Alfred Jacob Miller in 1837; he wrote *Altowan; or Incidents of Life and Adventure in the Rocky Mountains,* ed. J. Watson Webb, 2 vols. (New York: Harper, 1846), a work very like Murray's, and *Edward Warren* (1854; rpt. [ed. Bart Barbour] Missoula: Mountain Press, 1986).

35. George Frederick Ruxton, *Life in the Far West,* (1848; rpt. [ed. Leroy R. Hafen] Norman: Univ. of Oklahoma Press), p. 57. Stewart, Murray, and Ruxton are discussed in De Voto's *Across the Wide Missouri,* where De Voto maintains that Ruxton was a spy and alleges that Stewart was. Because of his numerous trips into the west, moreover, Stewart receives considerable attention (20–21, *passim*). For a more recent discussion of these figures, see Merritt, *Baronets and Buffalo.*

Some works set on the Canadian prairie are, like Ruxton's, mainly descriptive accounts with a fictional plot appended, as in the case of Alexander Begg's *Dot It Down: A Story of Life in the Northwest* (1871). Begg describes the Red River settlement in great detail, and pays considerable attention to its social structures, but the plot is little more than a pretext for his descriptive asides. Similarly, the prairie landscape, while frequently alluded to as surrounding the settlement, is not evoked in any direct manner.

36. A representative illustration from Emerson Bennett, *Prairie Flower: or, Adventure in the Far West* (1849; rpt. New York: G. W. Carleton, 1881):

> The prairie! the mighty, rolling, and seemingly boundless prairie! With what singular emotions I beheld it for the first time! I could compare it with nothing but a vast sea, changed suddenly to earth, with all its heaving, rolling billows. Thousands upon thousands of acres lay spread before me like a map, bounded by nothing but the deep, blue sky. What a magnificent sight! A sight that made my soul expand with lofty thought, and its frail tenement sink into utter nothingness before it. Talk of man—his power, his knowledge, his *greatness*—what is he? A mere worm, an insect, a mote, a nothing, when brought in compare with the grand, the sublime, in nature. Go, take the mighty one of earth—the crimson-robed, diamond-decked monarch whose nod is law. . . . (45–47)

As this passage indicates, instead of proving his point Bennett simply highlights the fact that he has never seen the prairie. His initial description and diction seem to have been borrowed directly from Bryant's "The Prairies," and his expanding soul might be attributed to Brackenridge, Pike, Irving, or others. Bennett simply included what he had read about the prairie without incorporating it at all; he quickly moves on to other considerations.

37. This survey of the popular romance literature set on the prairie is intended to be representative rather than exhaustive. See especially Dorothy Dondore's *The Prairie and the Making of Middle America,* which details the prairie western romance in nineteenth-century America, pp. 210–87, 345–92. See also Henry Nash Smith, *Virgin Land,* pp. 123–260, and Roy W. Meyer, *The Middle Western Farm Novel in the Twentieth Century,* pp. 13–34. The only

extensive treatments of the Canadian popular romance are by Dick Harrison; see *Unnamed Country*, Chapters II and III for a broad overview and "Popular Fiction of the Canadian Prairies: Autopsy on a Small Corpus." Regarding Dime Novels, which very often featured an exotic—if hazy—prairie-plains setting for heroes such as Buffalo Bill, see *Virgin Land*, pp. 90–120, and Albert Johannsen, *The House of Beadle and Adams and Its Dime and Nickel Novels: The Story of a Vanishing Literature*.

38. Sir William Francis Butler, *Red Cloud, The Solitary Sioux: A Tale of the Great Prairie* (1882; rpt. Toronto: Macmillan, 1910), p. 33 and *The Wild North Land*, p. 30. For a biography of Butler, see Edward McCourt, *Remember Butler: The Story of Sir William Butler*.

R. M. Ballantyne, a Scottish author of over eight juvenile adventure romances set in exotic locales, drew upon his experiences as a Hudson's Bay clerk in Canada for several of these tales, and in works such as *The Red Man's Revenge* (1880) he employed a prairie setting. His presentation of the landscape is incidental, the only extended passage occurring as the protagonists chase an Indian who has kidnapped a young child in revenge for a slight. Like Emerson Bennett's landscape description, Ballantyne's owes more, one suspects, to his reading than to his personal experiences:

> Over the prairie waves they sped, with growing excitement as their hopes of success increased; now thundering down into the hollows, anon mounting the gentle slopes at full swing, or rounding the clumps of trees that here and there dotted the prairie like islets in an interminable sea of green; and ever, as they rounded an islet or topped a prairie wave, they strained their eyes in earnest expectation of seeing the objects of their pursuit on the horizon, but for several days they raced, and gazed, and hoped in vain.

Ballantyne's characters could be rushing through landscape as described by James Fenimore Cooper, so much does this passage owe to *The Prairie*. The reader is required to imagine only the conventionally "literary" prairie defined by Cooper. It conveys the initial reaction so often drawn by the sensitively romantic soul, the person who relishes the prairie's vastness but does not, for one reason or another, wait around for monotony—reality—to set in. R. M. Ballantyne, *The Red Man's Revenge: A Tale of the Red River Flood* (New York: Thomas Nelson and Sons, 1881), p. 74.

39. Gilbert Parker, "A Sanctuary of the Plains," in *Pierre and His People: Tales of the Far North*, in *The Works of Gilbert Parker*, (1892; rpt. New York: Scribner's, 1912), I: 319. Subsequent reference is to this edition.

40. Much the same could be said of the following description, from John Mackie's *The Prodigal's Brother* (1899), of a sleigh ride on the prairie:

> It filled one with an overpowering sense of the immensity and loneliness of that vast prairieland; and had it not been for the subdued hiss of the runners over the crisp snow, resembling the steady seething of water past a ship's side, and the jangling of bells, one would have felt that the silence of this land was something appalling—a veritable presence that weighed on the soul like a nightmare, till the victim was fain to cry out to free himself from the spell.

To the extent that *The Prodigal's Brother* is a conventional romance concerning the rivalry between two brothers—one responsible, the other dissolute—in their love for the same woman, the realistic character of this passage could also be described as yet another example of the prairie overpowering literary propriety. John Mackie, *The Prodigal's Brother, A Story of Western Life*, pp. 117–18. Mackie was for several years a N.W.M.P. constable and, having noted this and his familiarity with Butler's *The Great Lone Land*, Harrison argues that "This [passage] could be straight Butler, but even so, it is one of the most vivid reactions to the land in the early fiction" (*Unnamed Country,* 55). Strictly speaking, Harrison is correct, since he is referring to early Canadian fiction, but Mackie (and Butler) had numerous precursors in their reaction to the prairie landscape, and this passage could be straight Irving or perhaps straight Parkman, just as well. A figure analogous to Mackie is Harold Bindloss. Harrison discusses his work in *Unnamed Country* (83), and notes the writer's direct presentation of the prairie landscape in the numerous novels he set on the prairie, but concludes correctly that Bindloss "never seemed to find in the prairie any distinctive spirit of place."

A final group of works set—nominally, at least—on the prairie are the didactic novels of Nellie McClung and Ralph Connor, and the stories of John MacLean. Because polemics supercede any organic use of the prairie landscape, they are not significant to this study. (For a discussion of these works see Ricou and Harrison.)

41. Owen Wister, *The Virginian: A Horseman of the Plains* (1902; rpt. [ed. Philip Durham] Boston: Houghton Mifflin, 1968), p. 14.

42. Fender, pp. 157, 158. Fender offers the most extended—and best—discussion of the effects of the western spaces on style, stressing the clash between romantic ("plotting") and realistic ("unplotted") depiction. Patrica Nelson Limerick, *Desert Passages,* p. 65. Limerick discusses *Roughing It* from the vantage point of the effect of desert landscape on travel; the entire summary conclusion bears quoting:

> "Truly and seriously," Twain declared, "the romance had all faded far away and disappeared, and left the desert trip nothing but a harsh reality—a thirsty, sweltering, longing, hateful reality!" The desert crossing was a battle in the war between romance and reality, a battle in which reality gained total victory, and romance made an undignified retreat. Romance was impossible where physical reality intruded so aggressively on bodily comfort, and where visual reality refused to provide interest or amusement. When dust, heat, duration, and monotony combined on the side of reality, romance had a few resources to draw on for its defense. (65)

43. Mark Twain, *Roughing It* (1872; rpt. [introd. Franklin R. Rogers, ed. Paul Baender] Berkeley: Univ. of California Press, 1972), p. 47. Subsequent references are to this edition.

44. Jeffrey, "There Is Some Splendid Scenery," p. 70. See Vernon L. Parrington, *Main Currents in American Thought;* Alfred Kazin, *On Native Grounds: An Interpretation of American Prose Literature,* pp. 3–50; Smith, *Virgin Land,* pp. 224–49; Meyer, *The Middle Western Farm Novel in the Twentieth Century,* pp. 13–34; Walter Berthoff, *The Ferment of Realism: American Literature, 1884–1919;* Donald Pizer, *Realism and Naturalism in Nineteenth-Century American Literature;* Edwin W. Cady, *The Light of Common Day: Realism in American Fiction.*

45. Born in Indiana and reared in Missouri and Nebraska, Howe was for over thirty years editor and proprietor of the *Daily Globe* of Atchison, Kansas. He wrote this, his most significant novel, in the evenings after work and, when his manuscript was rejected by several publishers, had it printed on his own press. This edition of some 1,500 copies was virtually sold out within six months. Howe sent copies of the book to both W. D. Howells and Mark Twain, and each author gave it a careful and positive reading; Howe used excerpts from Twain's letter to help promote its sales. See Claude M. Simpson, Introd., *The Story of a Country Town,* by E. W. Howe (Cambridge: Harvard Univ. Press, 1961), pp. vii–xxvii. Subsequent references are to this edition.

46. Clyde E. Henson, *Joseph Kirkland* (New Haven: College and University Press, 1962), pp. 11–42. In an extended and excellent chapter in *The Land Before Her,* entitled "The Literary Legacy of Caroline Kirkland: Emigrants' Guide to a Failed Eden," Annette Kolodny points up the mother's influence on her son, and on his commitment to realism:

Caroline Kirkland was the direct progenitor of that bold new direction in American letters. For, in attempting to follow the "path marked out by his mother," emulating *A New Home* and parts of *Forest Life* in his desire to tell "the truth, unadorned and unvarnished," Joseph Kirkland composed *Zury*. . . . It was a portrait of the harshness of western life that was to have no little impact on Howells, just as it was the power of what he had learned from his mother that gave Joseph Kirkland the authority to urge Hamlin Garland to leave off journalism and take up the cause of realism in fiction. (155–56)

Kolodny is quoting Henson's study of Kirkland here (89), where Henson quotes from a letter from Joseph Kirkland to Louise C. Schuler. Kolodny's discussion is an excellent companion to this consideration of literary realism on the prairie, since she asserts the influence of figures like Caroline Kirkland and, at the same time, notes the gender basis of the prairie as Eden. Kirkland begins *Zury* with just such an image, only to have his characters find hardship and heartache on the Illinois prairie.

47. Joseph Kirkland, *Zury: The Meanest Man in Spring County, A Novel of Western Life* (1887; rpt. [introd. John T. Flanagan] Urbana: Univ. of Illinois Press, 1956), p. 8. Subsequent reference is to this edition.

48. Hamlin Garland, *Boy Life on the Prairie* (1899; rpt. [introd. B. R. McElderry, Jr.] Lincoln: Univ. of Nebraska Press, 1961), p. 5.

49. Hamlin Garland, "Among the Corn Rows," in *Main-Travelled Roads,* introd. William Dean Howells, Authorized ed. (1920; rpt. [afterword B. R. McElderry] New York: Harper & Row, 1956), p. 86. Subsequent references are to this edition.

50. Hamlin Garland, *The Moccasin Ranch: A Story of Dakota* (New York: Harper & Brothers, 1909), pp. 3–4. Subsequent references are to this edition. *The Moccasin Ranch* was first published serially in the *Chap-Book,* November 15, 1894–February 15, 1895, as "The Land of the Straddle-Bug," and is set outside the same Dakota "Boomtown" Garland wrote about as early as 1887.

51. Arthur Stringer, *The Prairie Wife* (New York: A. L. Burt, 1915), p. 29. Subsequent references are to this edition. Regarding Stringer's background and his prairie trilogy, see Victor Lauriston, *Authur Stringer: Son of the North, Biography and Anthology.*

52. Arthur Stringer, *The Prairie Mother* (New York: A. L. Burt, 1920), p. 237. Subsequent reference is to this edition.

53. Frances W. Kaye, "Hamlin Garland's Feminism," in *Women and Western American Literature,* pp. 135–61. Carol Fairbanks echos Kaye's point in *Prairie Women,* when she briefly discusses male writers in her first chapter.

54. Faragher, pp. 183, 132–33.

55. Myres, pp. 167–68.

Chapter 4

1. Willa Cather, *O Pioneers!* (1913; rpt. Boston: Houghton Mifflin, 1941), p. 65. Subsequent references are to this edition; to avoid confusion, the title will occasionally be abbreviated as OP.

2. E. K. Brown, *Willa Cather: A Critical Biography,* pp. vi–vii; "Willa Cather Talks of Work," The Philadelphia *Record,* August 9 1913; rpt. *The Kingdom of Art: Willa Cather's First Principles and Critical Statements, 1893–1896,* ed. Bernice Slote (Lincoln: Univ. of Nebraska Press, 1966), p. 448. Elizabeth Shepley Sergeant, *Willa Cather: A Memoir,* p. 49.

3. Interview by Eva Mahoney, Omaha *Sunday World-Herald,* Nov. 27, 1921; quoted by

Mildred R. Bennett in *The World of Willa Cather,* p. 138. Cather's happiness over being in the West is also seen in a letter to Dorothy Canfield Fisher (ca. 1933), Dorothy Canfield Fisher papers, University of Vermont. Brown, p. 164. Sharon O'Brien, in her recent feminist biography of Cather's life up to the publication of *O Pioneers!,* discusses the importance of Cather's sense of "erasure of personality" at some length; it is, indeed, central to her analysis. See Sharon O'Brien, *Willa Cather: The Emerging Voice;* see also the book that may well become the standard biography, James Woodress, *Willa Cather: A Literary Life.*

4. Respectively, Willa Sibert Cather, "Nebraska: The End of the First Cycle," *Nation,* 117 (Sept. 5, 1923), p. 238, and Willa Cather, "El Dorado: A Kansas Recessional," *New England Magazine,* 24 (June, 1901), pp. 357–69; rpt. in *Willa Cather's Collected Short Fiction, 1892–1912,* introd. Mildred R. Bennett, ed. Virginia Faulkner, rev. ed. (Lincoln: Univ. of Nebraska Press, 1970), p. 293–94. Hereafter this edition will be abbreviated CSF.

See John H. Randall, III, *The Landscape and the Looking Glass: Willa Cather's Search for Value;* Edward A. Bloom and Lilian D. Bloom, *Willa Cather's Gift of Sympathy;* Don D. Walker, "The Western Humanism of Willa Cather"; Evelyn J. Hinz, "Willa Cather's Technique and the Ideology of Populism."

The Blooms, for example, wrote that Cather's "principal symbol is the vast panorama of an untamed land. But it is a functionally complex symbol, accomodating several thematic levels, all inherently united" (27). Similarly, Mildred R. Bennett, in *The World of Willa Cather,* writes that Cather's

> mixed feelings toward this world of bleak, wild prairie, where she lived from 1883 to 1896, her love and hatred of it, were the feelings of a sensitive child to a parent: she blessed what it gave her, in life-long friendships, in emotional release, and, in a more material sense, in subject matter for her greatest writing; she hated it for the hold it had on her, for the acute longing she felt for it wherever in the world she happened to find herself. Employ it she did, magnificently; overcome it, never. (xii)

See also James A. Miller, Jr., "The Nebraska Encounter: Willa Cather and Wright Morris." Speaking of Cather and Wright Morris, Miller has written that "Few modern American writers have been so *stuck* with their material—and yet have so completely escaped the suffocation of mere local color" (165). Miller also takes up Cather's depiction of the pioneer experience in *"My Ántonia* and the American Dream," *PrS,* 48 (1974), 112–23. See also Bernice Slote, "Writer in Nebraska" and "The Kingdom of Art," in *The Kingdom of Art,* pp. 3–112.

Of current critics, Susan J. Rosowski has taken up Cather's use of the prairie landscape most effectively and persuasively; see particularly her "Willa Cather—A Pioneer in Art: *O Pioneers!* and *My Ántonia*"; "Willa Cather and the Fatality of Place: *O Pioneers!, My Ántonia,* and *A Lost Lady*"; and "Willa Cather's *A Lost Lady:* Art Versus the Closing Frontier." The second essay, which uses Cather's 1895 remark that "Geography is a terribly fatal thing sometimes" as basis for its thesis, offers a particularly cogent reading of Cather's relationship with the prairie. See also her *The Voyage Perilous: Willa Cather's Romanticism.* Rosowski's influence on the readings offered here has been critical—without question, she was the first to break the sod.

5. Dorothy Canfield Fisher, "Daughter of the Frontier," *New York Herald-Tribune Books,* May 28, 1933; as quoted by Woodress, pp. 452–53; Woodress, p. 42; Fender, p. 12. This is not to say that critics have ignored the central importance of pioneering and the pioneer's relationship to the new land; on the contrary. See, for example, Roy W. Meyer, *The Middle Western Farm Novel in the Twentieth Century,* pp. 13–78; James K. Folsom, *The American Western Novel, passim,* but especially chapters 2, 3, and 6; and John Milton "Plains Landscapes and

Changing Visions," 55–62. What is more significant is the extent to which the fiction recapitulates the individual's perception of the landscape—that is, the land seems, given its vastness and influence, to dictate its own story.

6. Willa Cather, "On the Divide," *Overland Monthly,* 37 (January 1896); rpt. in CSF, p. 493. Subsequent references are to this edition.

James Woodress has noted that in considering the early stories, "there is a paradox . . . for her stories and letters of this period are not of a piece." Though the stories "of Nebraska farmers are all tales of hardship, failure, deprivation," in her letters Cather revealed considerable enjoyment of farm prairie life while she was at home, writing enthusiastically to friends of her activities while in Red Cloud. Woodress continues to "speculate that Cather as a college freshman thought the proper tone for a story of farmers on the prairie should be Garland's," as seen in his *Main-Travelled Roads.* See Woodress, p. 78 and Chapter 4, *passim.* Though Cather disparaged her early stories and strictly controlled their republication during her lifetime, critics have seen them as both impressive on their own and as useful in understanding Cather's novels, since they lend continuity to the whole canon. Cather wrote stories from the time she was at the University of Nebraska until the last years of her life, so despite her reservations, they do reflect the range of her professional life. See "Publisher's Preface" (vii–ix), for an account of Cather's judgment of her stories, and Mildred R. Bennett, Introd., in CSF, (xiii–xli), for an account of their composition and publication. For a critical interpretation of the stories within the context of the canon, see Marilyn Arnold, *Willa Cather's Short Fiction.*

7. Latrobe Carroll, "Willa Sibert Cather," *The Bookman,* 53 (May 1921); as quoted by Mildred R. Bennett, Introd., CSF, p. xxvi. Cather said much the same thing in her 1913 Philadelphia *Record* interview; see *The Kingdom of Art,* p. 449.

8. Cather discusses her changed approach in "My First Novels [There Were Two]," in *On Writing: Critical Studies of Writing as an Art;* E. K. Brown, in *Willa Cather: A Critical Biography,* pp. 160–61 suggests the shift was more gradual; Bennett, introd., CSF, p. xxvi.

9. Sergeant, p. 79.

10. Willa Cather, "The Bohemian Girl," *McClure's,* 39 (August 1912); rpt. CSF, pp. 6–7. Subsequent references are to this edition.

11. As quoted by Bennett, *The World of Willa Cather,* pp. 200–01. Yance Sorgensen was a person from Red Cloud.

12. Cather, "My First Two Novels [There Were Two]," p. 94; "Willa Cather Talks of Work," rpt. *The Kingdom of Art,* p. 448.

13. O'Brien, p. 421. Sergeant, p. 97. Sergeant offers her own account of the letter O'Brien summarizes, alluding also to the imaginative effect on Cather of Dvořák's *New World Symphony,* p. 92.

14. For a discussion of "Prairie Spring" and *O Pioneers!,* as well as the development of Cather's poetry, see Mary R. Ryder, "Prosodic Variations in Willa Cather's Prairie Poems."

15. Recent criticism has exposed the commonplace image of the pioneer prairie wife, cowering indoors in fear of the vast western spaces outside while her husband pioneers, the sort seen in Blanche Burke in Garland's *The Moccasin Ranch,* to be a male myth. Clearly, its veracity is open to question and is undergoing revision, and Cather's Alexandra and Ántonia were two of the first fictional characters to stand in opposition to Garland's more usual (and more genteel) version. Feminist historians, too, in looking at nineteenth-century women—both on the western migration in the United States and the fur trade and western settlement in Canada— have played a key role in understanding this image which, while not wholly eroneous, has less of a basis in fact that had been earlier thought. Regarding Cather's feminist view of pioneering, see Susan J. Rosowski, "Willa Cather's Pioneer Women: A Feminist Interpretation" and "Willa

Cather's Women"; Kolodny, *The Land Before Her*, 131–58; and Fairbanks, *Prairie Women*. A good example of revisionist history is Glenda Riley's *Women and Indians on the Frontier, 1825–1915*.

16. This passage is reminiscent of Queequeg's lantern in *Moby-Dick*, discussed above, with reference to Melville's prairie analogy in "The First Lowering"; where each lantern is a symbol of hope made minuscule by nature's vast sweep. Certainly, a conscious parallel is possible, since Cather's novel takes its title from Whitman. For a discussion of *O Pioneers!* and nineteenth-century American literature, see John J. Murphy, "A Comprehensive View of Cather's *O Pioneers!*."

17. Stuart B. James, in "Western American Space and the Human Imagination" (149), has written that Cather's use of the landscape in her prairie novels is such that it emerges "as metaphor for the infinite, and the pioneers who enter those prairies are like people undergoing denudation; they are stripped to their spiritual bones." Indeed, but he fails to notice that her techniques are based on the recreation of the prairie pioneering experience. James's view is extrapolated by Fender.

18. Rosowski, p. 62. Sergeant discusses Cather's ease of composing *O Pioneers!* as does the author herself; see Sergeant, p. 92, and Cather, "My First Novels [There Were Two]," pp. 92–93.

19. Rosowski, p. 74.

20. Rosowski, p. 72. She is quoting Cather, "A Mighty Craft," *Nebraska State Journal*, March 1, 1896; rpt. *The Kingdom of Art*, p. 417. Woodress, p. 39.

21. Willa Cather, *The Song of the Lark* (1915; rpt. Boston: Houghton Mifflin, 1983), pp. 247–48. Subsequent references are to this edition. This edition contains revisions Cather made in 1937.

22. Although Burden's relationship with Ántonia has been perhaps the central issue addressed by critics, Susan J. Rosowski's recent lucid discussion of their relation in *The Voyage Perilous*, in terms of subject and object, is much the best yet seen—particularly in view of her contexts: romanticism and the whole of Cather's canon. Indeed, Rosowski begins by saying "It was as if everything Cather had written until now had been in preparation for *My Ántonia*" and, while her view is more encompassing than that offered here, this statement is emphatically true as regards Cather's use of landscape. See Rosowski, pp. 75–91.

23. Willa Cather, *My Ántonia* (1918; rpt. Boston: Houghton Mifflin, 1954), p. iii. Subsequent references are to this edition; to avoid confusion, the title will occasionally be abbreviated as MA.

Though the emptiness of Burden's present life—when he writes of Ántonia after rediscovering her—is apparent enough in the Introduction found in editions of the novel in print, the version published in the original 1918 edition, about twice the length of the revised Introduction, confirms the point. There, Cather goes into greater detail about Jim's wife and the circumstances of their marriage—"his career was suddenly advanced by a brilliant marriage"—as well as into greater detail about Jim's job and his appearance—"Though he is over forty now, he meets new people and new enterprises with the impulsiveness by which his boyhood friends remember him. He never seems to me to grow older." Yet his narrative reveals that he has grown older, and he looks back in romantic nostalgia at his pioneering boyhood from the emptiness of his present, a man who championed values—embodied in Ántonia and the west—that, many readers feel, he never acted upon. His marriage, for example, seems to suggest the same "respect for respectability" (202) he sneers at in Black Hawk. See Willa Cather, *My Ántonia* (Boston: Houghton Mifflin, 1918), pp. x, xi–xii.

24. Defining Burden's motives for, reticences throughout, and accomplishments in, his

reminiscence has been a major critical question in understanding the novel. Particularly significant in this regard is Blanche H. Gelfant's "The Forgotten Reaping-Hook: Sex in *My Ántonia.*" See also James E. Miller, Jr., *"My Ántonia:* A Frontier Drama of Time," and his *"My Ántonia* and the American Dream"; Terence Martin, "The Drama of Memory in *My Ántonia*"; David Stouck, "Perspective as Structure and Theme in *My Ántonia*"; Mary E. Rucker, "Prospective Focus in *My Ántonia*"; Robert Kroetsch, "The Fear of Women in Prairie Fiction: An Erotics of Space," in *Robert Kroetsch: Essays,* pp. 47–55; and Rosowski, 'Willa Cather—A Pioneer in Art," and "Willa Cather and the Fatality of Place."

25. Both James E. Miller, Jr., in *"My Ántonia* and the American Dream," and Michael Peterman have discussed the novel's imaginative impact, seeing its images as somehow exerting effects which exceed the narrative. See the latter's " 'The Good Game': The Charm of Willa Cather's *My Ántonia* and W. O. Mitchell's *Who Has Seen the Wind," Mosiac,* 14, No. 2 (1981), pp. 93–106.

26. Cather's most well-known critical comments on the novel as a form are in her essay, "The Novel Démeublé"; there, she rejects the "over-furnished" novel in favor of one pared down to essences—the sort *My Ántonia* is—saying: "Whatever is felt upon the page without being specifically named there—that, one might say, is created. It is the inexplicable presence of the thing not named, of the overtone divined by the ear but not heard by it, the verbal mood, the emotional aura of the fact or the thing or the deed, that gives high quality to the novel or the drama, as well as to poetry itself." Ántonia and Jim's shared prairie experience creates such tones in *My Ántonia,* and Cather's careful attention to the nuance of prairie landscape—leading her to use several prairie-based images on the order of the "two luminaries" "across the level land" passage"—make their fellowship visual, leaving images that "do not fade." See Willa Cather, "The Novel Démeublé," *On Writing,* pp. 35, 41–42.

It is worth noting that Cather thought sufficiently of this prairie-induced configuration to repeat it in *One of Ours* (1922). There, her luminaries are Claude Wheeler and Ernest Havel, and they meet along a road during harvest time, 1914, to share opinions on the war, newly broken out in Europe. Claude recognizes "the Havels' team a long way off" and pauses to wait the other's arrival:

> The sun was already low. It hung above the stubble, all milky and rosy with the heat, like the image of a sun reflected in grey water. In the east the full moon had just risen, and its silver surface was flushed with pink until it looked exactly like the setting sun. Except for the place each occupied in the heavens, Claude could not have told which was which. They rested upon opposite rims of the world, two bright shields, and regarded each other,—as if they, too, had met by appointment.

Focused as it is on two other characters from "opposite rims of the world," this passage defines their relation in the same way as its predecessor does Jim and Ántonia's; yet, given the different directions of the two novels—Claude's movement away from America toward the war and Europe versus Jim's movement back to Ántonia and their shared freemasonry—the passage in the later novel seems much less important, more a striking image of exposition. In *My Ántonia,* the passage offers a critical configuration which lies at the novel's core. Willa Cather, *One of Ours* (1922; rpt: New York: Vintage, 1971), pp. 140–41.

27. This discussion has been limited to the role of the landscape in the whole of *My Ántonia,* of course, but the notion of "luminosity" in the novel is broader than has been suggested here. For example, Cather offers other examples of the luminous beauty of the prairie landscape, aglow with life and noted by Jim, which relate more directly to his character and his motives for

writing than to his relations with Ántonia. When Jim kills a snake, which follows immediately after Jim and Ántonia's meeting with Mr. Shimerda, for example, he says at one point "The great land had never looked to me so big and free" (48). And, as well, the scene in which the tramp throws himself in a thresher—Ántonia cannot understand why anyone would want to kill himself in summer.

A more direct use of the luminous landscape is found in Jim's recurrent dream of Lena Lingard, first described in Book II, "The Hired Girls," and which Jim mentions again just after Lena's visit, that had interrupted his musings on Virgil at the beginning of Book III. When Lena comes to him he is lying against a shock of wheat, and she

> came across the stubble barefoot, in a short skirt, with a curved reaping-hook in her hand, and she was flushed like the dawn, with a kind of luminous rosiness all about her. She sat down beside me, turned to me with a soft sigh and said, "Now they are all gone, and I can kiss you as much as I like."

Though Jim wishes he could have had "this flattering dream about Ántonia," he never did (225–26, 270–71). Blanche H. Gelfant has treated the sexual imagery in these scenes, as well as Lena's role as seductress—tempting Jim away from his intellectual vocations—in considerable detail in "The Forgotten Reaping-Hook," but the role of the luminous landscape in these concerns needs further analysis. Cather's uses of "luminous"—in the thunderstorm passage, in the "two luminaries" passage, and here—seem tied to the romantic cast of pioneering, "the best days are the first to flee," and so are tied to the landscape.

28. Susan J. Rosowski, in "Willa Cather and the Fatality of Place," sees *O Pioneers!*, *My Ántonia*, and *A Lost Lady* as a "trilogy of place," noting that after the latter Cather used Nebraska as setting for only one other novel, *Lucy Gayheart* (1935): "The land was a magical hero of *O Pioneers!*, transforming the material world into a rich kingdom; by *My Ántonia* it had taken on human form, but with its vulnerability. Finally, in *A Lost Lady*, that land had suffered beneath the very race it had given rise to" (92). In so saying and throughout her essay, Rosowski sees the same movement away from landscape, as landscape, toward using the land as an element of character and, in *A Lost Lady*, as social analysis. By draining the Forresters' marsh after he acquires it, Peters is like the Bushes when they chop down trees at the outset of *The Prairie*. For a discussion of Cather's intentions in *A Lost Lady*, see Rosowski, *The Voyage Perilous*, pp. 114–29.

29. Willa Cather, *Death Comes for the Archbishop* (1927; rpt. New York: Vintage, 1971), p. 95. Subsequent reference is to this edition. For an excellent discussion of Latour's character and motivations, see Rosowski, *The Voyage Perilous*, pp. 159–74.

30. Quite by design, the novels treated in the balance of the chapter were selected to analyze the masculine point of view, since it contrasts with Cather's feminine perspective and, despite the superior artistry and fame of her prairie works, is usually taken as the normative view of prairie pioneering. To reject or belittle works on the basis of an author's gender, as Carol Fairbanks has in *Prairie Women*, seems to substitute one form of chauvinism for another. At the same time her approach—looking at successive "waves" of women who settled the prairie, defining common concerns, motifs, and the like—is defensible as a first step, perhaps; yet in the case of Cather, Margaret Laurence, and others, Fairbanks eschews the subtleties of artistry for sociological generalizations based on literary texts.

Despite this fundamental problem, Fairbanks does offer readings of individual works which correct long-standing misconceptions of female characters. Her discussion of both *Giants in the*

Earth and *Fruits of the Earth* (17–23) offers needed balance to understanding Beret Holm and Ruth Spalding. Even so, the needed even-handed, and scholarly view of pioneering women in fiction has yet to appear.

31. O. E. Rölvaag, *Giants in the Earth: A Saga of the Prairie.* trans. Lincoln Colcord and O. E. Rölvaag (1927; rpt. New York: Harper & Row, 1955), p. 36. Subsequent references are to this edition. *Giants in the Earth* was first published in Norwegian as *I de dage,* 1924, 1925. Rölvaag used ellipses as a stylistic device; unless they appear in brackets, they are his.

Giants in the Earth was followed by *Peder Victorious* (1929), which continues Rölvaag's story of the family into the second generation, and *Their Father's God* (1931). The most extended treatment of *Giants in the Earth* with reference to Rölvaag's life and other works is Paul Reigstad's *Rölvaag: His Life and Art.* Critics have debated a variety of questions, most particularly the role of nature in the novel and Beret's madness, for some time; see Joseph E. Baker, "Western Man Against Nature in *Giants in the Earth*"; Ann Moseley, "The Land as Metaphor in Two Scandinavian Immigrant Novels"; Curtis D. Rudd, "Beret and the Prairie in *Giants in the Earth*"; Steve Hahn, "Vision and Reality in *Giants in the Earth*"; Susan Grider, "Madness and Personification in *Giants in the Earth*"; and Dick Harrison, "Rölvaag, Grove, and Pioneering on the American and Canadian Plains."

32. Carol Fairbanks has recently argued in *Prairie Women* that the stereotypical reading of Beret Holm as a person incapacitated by the prairie landscape is erroneous, based as it has been only on *Giants in the Earth*—she concludes, after a reading of Beret's character in *Giants* and *Peder Victorious,* that she is "a powerful fictional character, multifaceted, subtle in her reactions, and believable in the changes she undergoes" and so "deserves full status as a pioneer hero" (18). This is a necessary corrective.

33. Frederick Philip Grove, *Over Prairie Trails* (1922; rpt. [introd. Malcolm Ross] Toronto: McClelland and Stewart, 1957), p. 33. Born Felix Paul Greve in 1879, Grove was a minor poet, novelist, translator, and dramatist in Germany before he fled in 1909 to North America to escape personal and financial problems. Where he arrived is uncertain, but in 1912 he turned up in Manitoba as Frederick Philip Grove and pursued a teaching career in rural towns. For Grove's background, and the controversy surrounding it, see Douglas O. Spettigue, *FPG: The European Years.*

Grove's works have received considerable criticism; see, for example, Edward McCourt, *The Canadian West in Fiction,* 56–69; Laurence Ricou, *Vertical Man/Horizontal World,* pp. 38–64; Dick Harrison, *Unnamed Country, passim;* for a discussion of Grove's intellectual underpinnings, see Stanley E. McMullin, "Grove and the Promised Land," pp. 10–19, and "Evolution versus Revolution: Grove's Perception of History." For a discussion of Grove's depiction of the pioneer along with Garland's, see Francis W. Kaye, "Hamlin Garland and Frederick Philip Grove: Self-Conscious Chroniclers of the Pioneers."

34. Although not as sure of Grove's biographical details as we are other figures, it is fairly certain that Grove—like Cather—wrote best about the prairie when he was not there; *Fruits* appears to have been written after he had moved to Simcoe, Ontario.

35. Frederick Philip Grove, *Fruits of the Earth* (1933; rpt. [introd. M. G. Parks] Toronto: McClelland and Stewart, 1965), p. 23. Subsequent references are to this edition.

36. Frederick Philip Grove, *In Search of Myself* (1946; rpt. [introd. D. O. Spettigue] Toronto: McClelland and Stewart, 1974), p. 259.

37. Wallace Stegner, *On A Darkling Plain* (New York: Harcourt, Brace and Co., 1939), p. 17. Subsequent references are to this edition. Born in Iowa in 1909, Stegner moved with his family to a homestead in southern Saskatchewan where he spent his boyhood summers,

alternating winters in Montana; his experiences during this time form the basis of *Wolf Willow,* a personal reminiscence and key prairie text, where he treats the frontier prairie, a landscape he first used in *On a Darkling Plain.*

Stegner now sees the novel as something of an embarrassment, an apprentice piece. See Wallace Stegner and Richard W. Etulain, *Conversations with Wallace Stegner on Western History and Literature,* pp. 31–37; see also Forest Robinson and Margaret Robinson, *Wallace Stegner.*

Chapter 5

1. Robert Kroetsch, *Gone Indian* (Toronto: New Press, 1973), p. 152. Wright Morris, as quoted by David Madden, "The Great Plains in the Novels of Wright Morris," *Critique,* 4 (1961–62), 5. N. Scott Momaday, "The Land Inspired the Artist," review of *American Indian Painting of the Southwest and Plains Area,* by Dorothy Dunn, *New York Times Book Review,* 28 July 1968, pp. 6–7; as quoted by Matthias Schubnell, *N. Scott Momaday: The Cultural and Literary Background* (Norman: Univ. of Oklahoma Press, 1985), p. 85. N. Scott Momaday, *House Made of Dawn* (New York: Harper & Row, 1966), pp. 117, 121. The phrase, "the home place" is taken from Wright Morris' 1948 novel of the same name.

2. Robert Kroetsch, "The Fear of Women in Prairie Fiction: an Erotics of Space," and "On Being an Alberta Writer," in *Robert Kroetsch: Essays,* pp. 47, 74.

3. Martha Ostenso, *Wild Geese* (1925; rpt. [introd. Carlyle King] Toronto: McClelland and Stewart, 1961), p. 33. Subsequent references are to this edition. Like Rölvaag, Ostenso uses ellipses as a stylistic device; unless they appear in brackets they are hers.

4. Critical discussion of the novel has emphasized the characters' alienation from the prairie landscape within some definition of the novel's generic implications, since it combines melodrama, romanticism, realism, and perhaps naturalism. Laurence Ricou, in *Vertical Man/Horizontal World* sees Ostenso offering a "serious and comprehensive vision of man on the prairie," presenting "man's overwhelming loneliness in a barren, empty land" (74). In addition to Ricou, see Dick Harrison, *Unnamed Country,* pp. 107–13, for a discussion of Ostenso's debt to the romantic melodrama, and David Arnason's unpublished dissertation, "The Development of Prairie Realism," (Univ. of New Brunswick, 1980) for a discussion of realism. Regarding naturalism, see Rosalie Murphy Baum, "Martha Ostenso's *Wild Geese:* More Insight into the Naturalistic Sensibility."

5. Daniel S. Lenoski, "Martha Ostenso's *Wild Geese:* The Language of Silence," pp. 279, 282. Lenoski provides much the best overview of the novel's criticism as well as a most persuasive reading.

6. Lenoski discusses Judith's "organic relation" with the earth in terms of the Great Mother archetype, offering a convincing rationale for her seemingly bizarre act. See Lenoski, *passim.*

7. "Willa Cather Talks of Work," in *The Kingdom of Art,* p. 448.

8. Conrad Richter, *The Sea of Grass* (New York: Knopf, 1937), p. 4. Subsequent references are to this edition. This novel is regarded as a classic of southwestern fiction, since its depiction of cattlemen and nester suggests the conflict between differing visions of the west. Richter's fiction is mainly historical, and is derived from his eastern background as well as from his time in the southwest. He is perhaps best known for his pioneering trilogy, *The Trees* (1940), *The Fields,* and *The Town* (1950; Pulitzer Prize), which takes a pioneer Ohio family from the 18th century through the Civil War era and beyond. Works which are similar to *The Sea of Grass* include *The Lady* (1957) and *The Rawhide Knot* (1978), a collection of stories which is also

concerned with the theme of marriage on the frontier. For overviews of Richter's work, see Edwin W. Gaston, *Conrad Richter* and Marvin J. LaHood, *Conrad Richter's America;* see also Barbara Meldrum, "Conrad Richter's Southwestern Ladies," in *Women, Women Writers, and the West,* pp. 119–29.

9. This is not to suggest, as some critics seem to have, that only women had great psychological difficulty adjusting to prairie spaces. Indeed, the historical record suggests that both men and women responded positively and negatively to the prairie landscape and, what is more, each came to feel comfortable there. But the preponderance of fictional women characters deeply affected by prairie isolation—mainly, it must be conceded, in works written by men— suggests that this motif is not simply a matter of incomplete understanding of what conditions actually were. The case of Garland, discussed above, suggests that a writer's motives for portraying women in a certain light—whether positively or negatively—are personal and complicated. And given the frequent concern for relations between husband and wife— particularly in Garland, Ross, Richter, and Morris, where the agent of tension is the prairie landscape—this question, like many other gender-related issues in prairie studies, needs more scrutiny; such studies, moreover, should reflect a relatively equal balance for both female and male writers. See Fairbanks, *Prairie Women* and also Barbara Howard Meldrum, "Women in Western American Fiction: Images, or Real Women?" in *Women and Western American Literature,* pp. 55–69.

10. Anne Marriott, "The Wind Our Enemy," in *The Wind, Our Enemy* (Toronto: Ryerson, 1939); rpt. in *Horizon: Writings of the Canadian Prairie,* pp. 100–05. The poem tells the story of the dustbowl years on the prairie, as does Barry Broadfoot's *Ten Lost Years: Memories of Canadians Who Survived the Depression.*

11. John Steinbeck, *The Grapes of Wrath* (1939; rpt. New York: Bantam, 1972), pp. 121, 96. Subsequent references are to this edition.

12. Paul Comeau has written, concerning "Not By Rain Alone," that: "plaintiveness and protest repeat themselves in conjunction with the seasons, as Ross's characters continue to hold out against a hostile environment. Their individual miseries are highlighted by the tragic mode in which these stories are written, a mode whereby nature assumes the personality of an angry, vengeful presence bent on destruction."

Comeau holds that Ross began in the tragic mode with these stories, continued into irony with *As For Me and My House,* and moved finally to comedy with *Sawbones Memorial* (1974). "Ultimately," he writes, Ross's "interpretation of the pioneer experience represents a detailed study in narrative perspective and fictional mode," and throughout Ross emphasizes the very precariousness of being. Paul Comeau, "Sinclair Ross's Pioneer Fiction," p. 183. See also Keith Fraser, "Futility at the Pump: The Short Stories of Sinclair Ross."

13. David Williams, "The 'Scarlet' Rompers: Toward a New Perspective in *As For Me and My House,*" p. 165.

14. Warren Tallman, "Wolf in the Snow," *Contexts of Canadian Criticism,* p. 239. Critical studies of *As For Me and My House* are numerous. For general considerations, see Lorraine McMullen's *Sinclair Ross* and Ken Mitchell's *Sinclair Ross: A Reader's Guide.* For more specific discussions, see Morton Ross's "The Canonization of *As For Me and My House:* A Case Study," and Robert Kroetsch's "The Fear of Women in Prairie Fiction: An Erotics of Space," in *Robert Kroetsch: Essays.* For consideration of Mrs. Bentley's character and her perspective as narrator— two concerns of primary importance, see Wilfred Cude, "Beyond Mrs. Bentley: A Case Study of *As For Me and My House,*" pp. 3–18 and also his "Turn It Upside Down: The Right Perspective on *As For Me and My House,* 469–88, which have been reprinted in Cude's *A Due Sense of Differences: An Evaluative Approach to Canadian Literature;* and also Paul Denham's "Narrative

Technique in Sinclair Ross's *As For Me and My House*. Critical discussion of Ross does not appear to be waning, certainly, since the Comeau and Williams articles, cited above, are but two of four articles on his work published in a single issue of *CanL*. and a recent issue of the same journal includes a response to Williams' article, Evelyn J. Hinz and John J. Teunissen, "Who's the Father of Mrs. Bentley's Child?: 'As For Me and My House' and the Conventions of Dramatic Monologue." Several others, not cited here, have been published on other aspects of the novel.

15. Sinclair Ross, *As For Me and My House* (1941; rpt. [introd. David Stouck] Lincoln: Univ. of Nebraska Press, 1978), p. 5. Subsequent references are to this edition.

16. Margaret Laurence, Introd., *The Lamp at Noon and Other Stories* by Sinclair Ross (Toronto: McClelland and Stewart, 1968), p. 7.

17. David Stouck, "The Mirror and the Lamp in Sinclair Ross's *As for Me and My House*," pp. 148–49.

18. Bennett, *The World of Willa Cather*, p. 140.

19. The recurrent question of a writer's physical location, vis-à-vis the prairie, while actually writing about the landscape is an intriguing one. As discussed above, Willa Cather wrote her prairie fictions far removed from the prairie—and had trouble writing about the landscape while there. Indeed, there is considerable irony in Cather's classic prairie fictions being written largely in her Manhattan apartment, just off Washington Square—but so they were. Ross wrote *As For Me and My House* while living in Winnipeg and Grove's *Fruits of the Earth* was likely composed while he was living in Ontario. Given this, prairie space seems to require suitable esthetic distance—emotions recalled in tranquility, as it were. This is, of course, consistent with the experiences of those who wrote the early accounts—Castañeda and the other explorers, Catlin, Kane, Bryant, Parkman and Irving—and might be used to argue that Cooper's choice of setting in *The Prairie* was not so audacious after all.

20. W. O. Mitchell, *Who Has Seen the Wind* (1947; rpt. Macmillan, 1972), p. 3. Subsequent references are to this edition. Born and raised in Weyburn, Saskatchewan, Mitchell has become something of a Mark Twain figure in Canadian writing in recent years, owing to his comic perspective and, at the rostrum, a marvelously funny declamatory style. After training as a teacher and, for a time, teaching, Mitchell determined to be a full-time writer. He served as fiction editor of *Maclean's* and wrote scripts for CBC radio, including thirteen which had originally been written as short stories and were published as *Jake and the Kid* (1962). Published the same year was *The Kite* (1962) and, in 1973, *The Vanishing Point*. The present decade has seen greater output, with the publication of a darker companion piece to *Who*, *How I Spent My Summer Holidays* (1981), *The Dramatic W. O. Mitchell* (1982), which collects his plays, and *Since Daisy Creek* (1984), a mature, dark novel which received widespread praise. Though somewhat dated, Laurence Ricou's discussion of Mitchell's work in *Vertical Man/ Horizontal World* (95–110) is excellent.

21. Peterman, p. 97.

22. W. O. Mitchell, *The Vanishing Point* (Toronto: Macmillan, 1973), p. 318. Subsequent reference is to this edition.

23. Harrison, *Unnamed Country*, p. 198.

24. Wright Morris, "Our Endless Plains," *Holiday*, 24 (July 1958), pp. 138, 140. Subsequent references are to this version.

25. G. B. Crump, "Wright Morris," in *A Literary History of the American West* (Fort Worth: Texas Christian Univ. Press, 1987), p. 778. See also David Madden, *Wright Morris*; G. B. Crump, *The Novels of Wright Morris: A Critical Interpretation*, and Raymond L. Neinstein, "Wright Morris: The Metaphysics of Home."

26. Wright Morris, *The Works of Love* (1952; rpt. Lincoln: Univ. of Nebraska Press, 1972), pp. 3, 5–6. For an excellent discussion of this novel, see Wayne C. Booth, "Form in *The Works of Love*," in *Conversations with Wright Morris: Critical Views and Responses,* ed. Robert E. Knoll (Lincoln: Univ. of Nebraska Press, 1977), pp. 35–73.

27. Wright Morris, *Ceremony in Lone Tree* (1960; rpt. Lincoln: Univ. of Nebraska Press, 1973), p. 3. Morris uses much the same language in "Our Endless Plains," p. 138.

28. Wright Morris, *God's Country and My People* (1968; rpt. Lincoln: Univ. of Nebraska Press, 1981), n. p. [p. 2].

29. Wright Morris, "The Origin of Sadness," in *Collected Stories, 1948–1986.* (New York: Harper & Row, 1986), p. 270. Wright Morris, *Plains Song: For Female Voices* (New York: Harper and Row, 1980). This novel received prompt critical attention, not surprisingly, since Morris had previously been criticized for his handling of female characters. See Joseph J. Wydeven, "Wright Morris, Women, and American Culture," in *Women and Western American Literature,* pp. 212–27, and Lynne Waldeland, *"Plains Song:* Women's Voices in the Fiction of Wright Morris," 7–19. Fairbanks also discusses the novel briefly in *Prairie Women,* p. 27.

30. Respectively, ed. Birk Sproxton (Winnipeg: Turnstone, 1986) and ed. E. F. Dyck (Regina: Saskatchewan Writers Guild, 1986).

31. Henry Kreisel, "The Prairie: A State of Mind," in *Contexts of Canadian Criticism,* p. 257.

32. Robert Kroetsch, "A Conversation with Margaret Laurence," in *Creation,* ed. Robert Kroetsch (Toronto: New Press, 1970); rpt. in *Trace,* p. 30. For a more general discussion of contemporary Western-Canadian writing, see my review essay " 'Where is the Voice Coming From?': Toward a Western-Canadian Aesthetic."

33. Kroetsch, "On Being an Alberta Writer," pp. 76, 75, 74.

34. Two Canadian critics have argued parallel treatment for Cather and Margaret Laurence. See Clara Thomas, "Proud Lineage: Willa Cather and Margaret Laurence" and Susan J. Warwick. "Telling Tales: Voice, Time and Image in the Fiction of Margaret Laurence and Willa Cather."

Clara Thomas has been a leading critic of Laurence's works; her *Margaret Laurence* (Toronto: McClelland and Stewart, 1969) was followed by *The Manawaka World of Margaret Laurence,* probably the standard work to date. At the same time, Laurence has received extensive attention from other critics. See also Patricia Morley, *Margaret Laurence* (Boston: Twayne, 1981) and Helen M. Buss, *Mother and Daughter Relationships in the Manawaka Works of Margaret Laurence* (Victoria: Univ. of Victoria, 1985). Another useful work which collects many previously published essays is *A Place to Stand On: Essays By and About Margaret Laurence.* With the exception of Thomas's first book, each of these offers a good bibliography to the extensive article literature on Laurence's works.

35. Cathy N. Davidson, "Geography as Psychology in the Writings of Margaret Laurence," p. 137. Davidson's essay nicely focuses on the ways in which Manawaka's geography informs the characters' understandings of themselves and their lives. Thus it adumbrates a view which is commonplace in Laurence criticism: that her vision has been formed by her prairie roots; this view is treated most extensively by Clara Thomas in *The Manawaka World of Margaret Laurence.* As to the prairie landscape, per se, Davidson notes that Laurence Ricou, in "Empty as Nightmare: Man and Landscape in Recent Canadian Prairie Fiction," "emphasizes that Manawaka sits only on the edge of the prairies. It lacks the uninterrupted flatness that makes the prairie landscape a 'perfect metaphor for existential, universal meaninglessness' " (Davidson, 137, n. 1). Ricou offers much the same interpretation of Laurence in his final chapter of *Vertical Man/Horizontal World,* entitled "The Bewildering Prairie: Recent Fiction."

Though Ricou's point is accurate—insofar as Manawaka/Neepawa's is not a prairie flatness equivalent to Cather's Hanover or Ross's Horizon—his concern for the landscape's ability to induce feelings of alienation (the landscape as metaphor) causes him to sidestep Laurence's positive integration of her characters with prairie space, seeing "the ultimate response" to the prairie landscape in the first four works of the series "is ambiguous" (*Vertical Man/Horizontal World,* 120). Laurence's women are not oppressed by the prairie, they celebrate it.

36. This and the previous quotation from Laurence's "A Place to Stand On," are from *Heart of a Stranger* (1976; rpt. Toronto: Seal, 1980), pp. 4–5.

37. Margaret Laurence, *The Stone Angel* (1964, rpt. [introd. William H. New] Toronto: McClelland and Stewart, 1968), p. 5.

38. Margaret Laurence, "To Set Our House in Order," in *A Bird in the House* (1970; rpt. [introd. Robert Gibbs] Toronto: McClelland and Stewart, 1974), pp. 58–59.

39. Margaret Laurence, *The Diviners* (1974; rpt. Toronto: Bantam, 1975), p. 282.

40. Shirley Neuman and Robert Wilson, *Labyrinths of Voice: Conversations with Robert Kroetsch,* p. 155. Wiebe's story, "Where is the Voice Coming From?", which focuses on Almighty Voice, a Cree Indian killed by the Mounted Police in 1897 after killing a cow and eluding them for eighteen months, should be seen as something of a primer of Wiebe's method of recording, as W. J. Keith has written in his *Epic Fiction:*

> It is, ultimately, a story about writing a story. . . . the governing image of the story—and, I would argue, by extension, the whole of Wiebe's work—is "[Almighty Voice's] death chant no less incredible in its beauty than in its incomprehensible happiness."
>
> . . . .
>
> The narrator focuses on his own difficulty in coming to terms with the story. He examines the tangible remains, the police-court facts: part of the skull of Almighty Voice, still preserved in a museum; a cannon said to have been used in the final encounter; the guardroom from which Almighty Voice once escaped; an enigmatic photograph identified as that of Almighty Voice. But what haunts the narrator, because he knows that within it lies the secret, is the voice that he cannot understand. (11–12)

A Mennonite born in Saskatchewan of parents who came to Canada from the Soviet Union, Wiebe's first three novels, *Peace Shall Destroy Many* (1962), *First and Vital Candle* (1966), and *The Blue Mountains of China* (1970), are concerned with moral issues and record much of Wiebe's Mennonite heritage, especially *Blue Mountains.* With his next novel, *The Temptations of Big Bear* (1973), Wiebe turned his attention to his native west and, through a complex narrative structure based on multiple points of view, tells the story of Big Bear, the Plains Cree chief who participated in the Northwest Rebellion of 1885 and was executed for his actions. His next novel, *The Scorched-Wood People* (1977), arguably his best work, also deals with the Rebellion using these techniques, but it tells the stories of its principal instigators, the métis leader Louis Riel and his general, Gabriel Dumont. In both of these novels, Wiebe draws upon documentary sources—recording—but then strives to create the human truth which his sources imply. The latter is a process of invention, whereby he departs from recorded history in order to obtain the essences which he sees lying beneath it. His is an epic task, and he is engaged in the very process of "demythologizing" of which Kroetsch speaks, probing the complex details of his prairie past which are, even among professional historians, still being digested. No better figure exists for Wiebe's approach than Riel, but he has also taken up Albert Johnson in his novel *The Mad Trapper* (1980); Johnson is an enigmatic and mythic figure from the history of the Canadian north of the same order as Big Bear and Riel. See "Where is the Voice Coming From?," in *Where is the Voice Coming From?* (Toronto: McClelland and Stewart, 1974), pp. 135–43. For critical overview, see W. J. Keith's *Epic Fiction: The Art of Rudy Wiebe* and also *A Voice in the Land: Essays By and About Rudy Wiebe*.

41. Robert Kroetsch, "That Yellow Prairie Sky," *Maclean's*, 30 April 1955, pp. 28–29, 48–50; rpt. *Modern Canadian Stories*, ed. John Stevens (New York: Bantam, 1975), p. 115. Kroetsch describes the writing of this story in his conversation with Margaret Laurence, reprinted in *Trace*, p. 20. The Ross-Kroetsch parallel has gotten some attention; see Jeanette Seim, "Horses & Houses: Further Readings in Kroetsch's *Badlands* and Sinclair Ross's *As For Me and My House*."

42. Robert Kroetsch, *But We Are Exiles* (Toronto: Macmillan, 1965), p. 135.

43. Russell M. Brown, "An Interview with Robert Kroetsch," *University of Windsor Review*, 7, no. 2 (Spring 1972), p. 2; as quoted by Peter Thomas, *Robert Kroetsch*, p. 12. Thomas discusses Grove and Grey Owl throughout his introduction, pp. 1–15. The phrase "writing himself into existence," a commonplace in Kroetsch criticism, has been taken from Robert Lecker, "An Annotated Bibliography of Works By and About Robert Kroetsch," p. 74. Lecker, who sees Kroetsch's fictive world as a "borderline" one, offers in this introduction to his bibliography a succinct statement of Kroetsch's work which still holds true: "Like their author (like the reader) Kroetsch's characters are not only products of experience, they produce it. Physically and emotionally they are explorers hovering on the brink of discovery, investing the world with their uncertainties of the moment. This is imagination—romance, not novel—a response to the actually and metaphorically 'undefined vastness' which constitutes Kroetsch's borderline universe. The milieu is voice, the message expression" (75). See also Lecker's *Robert Kroetsch*.

In addition to the works discussed here, Kroetsch has published two more novels, *What the Crow Said* (1978) and *Alibi* (1983), and several volumes of poetry, which offer an emphasis on the autobiographical not evident in the fiction. See particularly *Field Notes: a Continuing Poem* (Don Mills, Ontario: General, 1981) and *Advice to My Friends: a Continuing Poem* (Don Mills: Stoddard, 1985). The first volume collects much of Kroetsch's previously published poetry.

44. Robert Kroetsch, unpublished journal, 15 Dec. 1972; as quoted by Thomas, p. 128, n. 30. Brown interview, as quoted by Thomas, p. 128, n. 34. See Robert Kroetsch, *Alberta* (Toronto: Macmillan, 1968).

45. Robert Kroetsch, *The Word of My Roaring* (Toronto: Macmillan, 1966), p. 32.

46. Robert Kroetsch, "Unhiding the Hidden: Recent Canadian Fiction," p. 43.

47. Robert Kroetsch, *Badlands*, (1975; rpt. Toronto: General, 1982), pp. 269, 45, 66.

48. Cather, "On the Novel," in *Willa Cather In Person: Interviews, Speeches, and Letters*, p. 170.

49. Sharon Butula, *The Gates of the Sun* (Saskatoon: Fifth House, 1986), p. 4. For a discussion of Butula and the works which precede this novel, see David Arnason, "Leaving the Farm: Contemporary Saskatchewan Fiction," in *Essays on Saskatchewan Writing*, pp. 113–25.

Bibliography

Primary Material

Aldrich, Bess Streeter. *The Rim of the Prairie.* 1925. Lincoln: University of Nebraska Press, 1966.

———. *Spring Came on Forever.* 1935. Lincoln: University of Nebraska Press, 1985.

Audubon's America: The Experiences of John James Audubon. Donald Culross Peattie. Boston: Houghton Mifflin, 1940.

Ballantyne, R. M. *The Red Man's Revenge: A Tale of the Red River Flood.* New York: Thomas Nelson and Sons, 1881.

Begg, Alexander. *Dot It Down: A Story of Life in the North-West.* 1871. Toronto: University of Toronto Press, 1973.

Bennett, Emerson. *Prairie Flower: or, Adventures in the Far West.* 1849. New York: G. W. Carleton, 1881.

Binnie-Clark, Georgina. *Wheat & Woman.* Introduction Susan Jackel. 1914. Toronto: University of Toronto Press, 1979.

Brackenridge, H. M. *Journal of a Voyage up the River Missouri: performed in Eighteen Hundred and Eleven.* 2nd ed. Baltimore, 1816. Rpt. in *Early Western Travels, 1748–1846.* Ed. Reuben Gold Thwaites. Vol. VI. Cleveland: Arthur H. Clark, 1904, pp. 19–166.

Bradbury, John. *Travels in the Interior of America in the Years 1809, 1810, and 1811; including a description of Upper Louisiana, together with the States of Ohio, Kentucky, Indiana, and Tennessee, with Illinois and Western Territories, and Containing Remarks and Observations Useful to Persons Emigrating to those Countries.* 2nd ed. London, 1819. Rpt. in *Early Western Travels, 1748–1846.* Ed. Reuben Gold Thwaites. Vol. V. Cleveland: Arthur H. Clark, 1904.

Bryant, William Cullen. *Poetical Works.* Ed. Park Godwin. 2 vols. 1883. New York: Russell & Russell, 1967.

———. *Prose Writings.* Ed. Parke Godwin. 2 vols. 1884. New York: Russell & Russell, 1964.

Butler, Sir William Francis. *The Great Lone Land: A Narrative of Travel and Adventure in the North-West of America.* London: Sampson Low, Marston, Low & Searle, 1872.

———. *Red Cloud, The Solitary Sioux: A Tale of the Great Prairie.* London, 1882. Toronto: Macmillan, 1910.

———. *The Wild North Land: The Story of a Winter Journey, with Dogs, Across Northern North America.* 1873. London: Sampson Low, Marston, Low & Searle, 1874.

Butula, Sharon. *Country of the Heart.* Saskatoon: Fifth House, 1984.

———. *The Gates of the Sun.* Saskatoon: Fifth House, 1986.

———. *Queen of the Headaches.* Moose Jaw: Coteau, 1985.

Cabeza de Vaca, Alvar Nuñez. *The Narrative of Alvar Nuñez Cabeça de Vaca.* Trans. (Thomas) Buckingham Smith, 1851. Rpt. in *Spanish Explorers in The Southern United States, 1528–1543.* Ed. Frederick W. Hodge and Theodore H. Lewis. 1907. Austin: Texas State Historical Association, 1984, pp. 1–126.

Carver, Jonathan. *Travels through the Interior Parts of North America in the Years 1766, 1767, and 1768.* 3rd ed. London: C. Dilly, 1781.

Castañeda, Pedro de, of Najera. *The Narrative of the Expedition of Coronado by Castañeda.* Trans. George Parker Winship, 1896. Rpt. in *Spanish Explorers in the Southern United States, 1528–1543.* Ed. Frederick W. Hodge and Theodore H. Lewis. 1907. Austin: Texas State Historical Association, 1984, pp. 273–387.

Cather, Willa. *Alexander's Bridge.* Boston: Houghton Mifflin, 1912.

———. *Death Comes for the Archbishop.* New York: Knopf, 1927.

———. *Five Stories.* 1948. New York: Vintage, 1956.

———. *The Kingdom of Art: Willa Cather's First Principles and Critical Statements, 1893–1896.* Ed. Bernice Slote. Lincoln: University of Nebraska Press, 1966.

———. *A Lost Lady.* 1923. New York: Vintage, 1972.

———. *My Ántonia.* Boston: Houghton Mifflin, 1918.

———. *My Ántonia.* 1918. Boston: Houghton Mifflin, 1954.

———. "Nebraska: The End of the First Cycle." *Nation,* 117 (Sept. 5, 1923), pp. 236–38.

———. *O Pioneers!.* 1913. Boston: Houghton Mifflin, 1941.

———. *The Professor's House.* 1925. New York: Vintage, 1973.

———. *On Writing: Critical Studies of Writing as an Art.* Foreword Stephen Tennant. New York: Alfred A. Knopf, 1949.

———. *One of Ours.* 1922. New York: Vintage, 1971.

———. *The Song of the Lark.* 1915. Boston: Houghton Mifflin, 1983.

———. *Willa Cather's Collected Short Fiction, 1892–1912.* Introduction Mildred R. Bennett. Ed. Virginia Faulkner. Rev. ed. Lincoln: University of Nebraska Press, 1970.

———. *Willa Cather In Person: Interviews, Speeches, and Letters.* Ed. L. Brent Bohlke. Lincoln: University of Nebraska Press, 1986.

Catlin, George. *Illustrations of the Manners, Customs, and Conditions of the North American Indians with Letters and Notes.* 2 vols. 1841. New York: Dover, 1973.

Chateaubriand's Travels in America. Trans. Richard Switzer. Lexington: University of Kentucky Press, 1969.

Cocking, Matthew. "An Adventurer from Hudson's Bay: Journal of Matthew Cocking, from York Factory to the Blackfeet Country, 1772–73." Ed. Lawrence J. Burpee. *Proceedings and Transactions of the Royal Society of Canada,* 3rd. ser., 2, Ottawa, 1908, sec. 2, pp. 89–121.

Connor, Ralph. *Black Rock: A Tale of the Selkirks.* Toronto: Westminster, 1905.

———. *Corporal Cameron of the North West Mounted Police.* Toronto: Westminister, 1912.

———. *The Sky Pilot: A Tale of the Foothills.* Toronto: Westminster, 1899.

Cooper, James Fenimore. *Last of the Mohicans: A Narrative of 1757.* Introduction James Franklin Beard. Ed. James A. Sappenfield and E. N. Feltskog. 1826. Albany: State University Press of New York, 1983.

———. *The Pioneers, or the Sources of the Susquehanna; A Descriptive Tale.* Introduction James Franklin Beard. Ed. Lance Schachterle and Kenneth M. Andersen, Jr. 1823. Albany: State University Press of New York, 1980.

———. *The Prairie: A Tale.* Ed. and Introduction James P. Elliott. 1827. Albany: State University Press of New York, 1985.

Coronado, Francisco. "Translation of a Letter from Coronado to the King, October 20, 1541." In *The Journey of Coronado 1540–1542.* Trans. and ed. George Parker Winship. New York: A. S. Barnes, 1904, pp. 213–21.

Curtis, George William. *Prue and I, Lotus Eating.* London: J. M. Dent, n.d.

De Smet, Pierre-Jean, S. J. *Life Letters and Travels of Father Pierre-Jean De Smet, S. J., 1801–*

1873. Ed. Hiram Martin Chittenden and Alfred Talbot Richardson. 4 vols. New York: Francis P. Harper, 1905.

———. *Western Missions and Missionaries: A Series of Letters.* New York, 1859. Introduction William L. Davis, S. J. Shannon: Irish University Press, 1972.

de Tocqueville, Alexis. *Democracy in America.* 2 vols. 1835. New York: Vintage, 1945.

Dickinson, Emily. *The Complete Poems of Emily Dickinson.* Ed. Thomas H. Johnson. Boston: Little, Brown, 1951.

Early Narratives of the Northwest, 1634–1699. Ed. Louise Phelps Kellogg. New York: Scribner's, 1917.

Emerson, Ralph Waldo. *Poems of Ralph Waldo Emerson.* London: Oxford, 1921.

———. *Selections from Ralph Waldo Emerson: An Organic Anthology.* Ed. Stephen E. Whicher, Jr. Boston: Houghton Mifflin, 1957.

The Expeditions of John Charles Frémont. Ed. Donald Jackson and Mary Lee Spence. Urbana: University of Illinois Press, 1970.

Farnham, Eliza W. *Life in Prairie Land.* 1846. New York: Arno Press, 1972.

Farnham, Thomas J. *Travels in the Great Western Prairies, the Anahuac and Rocky Mountains, and in the Oregon Territory.* London, 1843. New York: De Capo Press, 1973.

Feikema, Feike. *This is the Year.* Garden City, New York: Doubleday, 1947.

Flagg, Edmund. *The Far West; or A Tour Beyond the Mountains.* 2 vols. New York, 1838. Rpt. in *Early Western Travels, 1748–1846.* Ed. Reuben Gold Thwaites. Vol. XXVI. Cleveland: Arthur H. Clark, 1906.

Fleming, Sandford. *England and Canada: A Summer Tour Between Old and New Westminster.* Montreal: Dawson Brothers, 1884.

———. *Report on Surveys and Preliminary Operations on the Canadian Pacific Railway up to January 1877.* Ottawa: Maclean, Roger & Co., 1877.

Franchère, Gabriel. *Narrative of a Voyage to the Northwest Coast of America in the years 1811, 1812, 1813, and 1814; or the First American Settlement on the Pacific.* Trans. and ed. J. V. Huntington. New York, 1854. Rpt. in *Early Western Travels, 1748–1846.* Ed. Reuben Gold Thwaites. Vol. VI. Cleveland: Arthur H. Clark, 1905, pp. 173–410.

Fuller, Margaret. *The Writings of Margaret Fuller.* Ed. Mason Wade. New York: Viking, 1941.

Garland, Hamlin. *Boy Life on the Prairie.* 1889. Introduction B. R. McElderry, Jr. Lincoln: University of Nebraska Press, 1961.

———. *Main-Travelled Roads.* Introduction William Dean Howells. Authorized ed. 1930. Afterword B. R. McElderry, Jr. New York: Harper & Row, 1956.

———. *The Moccasin Ranch: A Story of Dakota.* New York: Harper & Brothers, 1909.

———. *A Son of the Middle Border.* New York: Grosset & Dunlap, 1917.

Grant, George Munro. *Ocean to Ocean: Sandford Fleming's Expedition Through Canada in 1872.* Rev. ed. Toronto: The Radisson Society, 1925.

———. *Picturesque Canada.* 2 vols. Toronto: Belden Brothers, 1892.

Greeley, Horace. *An Overland Journey from New York to San Francisco in the Summer of 1859.* 1860. Ed. Charles T. Duncan. New York: Knopf, 1964.

Greenwood, Grace [Sarah J. Lippencott]. *New Life in New Lands: Notes of Travel.* New York: J. B. Ford, 1873.

Gregg, Josiah. *Commerce of the Prairies; or the Journal of a Santa Fe Trader, during Eight Expeditions Across the Great Western Prairies and a Residence of Nearly Nine Years in Northern Mexico.* 2 vols. 2nd ed. New York, 1845. Rpt. in *Early Western Travels, 1748–1846.* Ed. Reuben Gold Thwaites. Vols. XIX–XX. Cleveland: Arthur H. Clark, 1905.

Grove, Frederick Philip. *Fruits of the Earth.* 1933. Introduction M. G. Parks. Toronto: McClelland and Stewart, 1965.

————. *In Search of Myself.* 1946. Introduction D. O. Spettigue. Toronto: McClelland and Stewart, 1974.

————. *Our Daily Bread.* 1928. Introduction D. O. Spettigue. Toronto: McClelland and Stewart, 1975.

————. *Over Prairie Trails.* 1922. Introduction Malcolm Ross. Toronto: McClelland and Stewart, 1957.

————. *A Search for America.* 1927. Introduction Stanley E. McMullin. Toronto: McClelland and Stewart, 1971.

Guthrie, A. B. *The Big Sky.* New York: Sloane, 1947.

————. *The Way West.* Toronto: George J. McLeod, 1949.

Hawthorne, Nathaniel. *The Complete Novels and Selected Tales of Nathaniel Hawthorne.* Ed. Norman Holmes Pearson. New York: The Modern Library, 1937.

Henday, Anthony. "York Factory to the Blackfeet Country; The Journal of Anthony Hendry [sic], 1754–55." Ed. Lawrence J. Burpee. *Proceedings and Translations of the Royal Society of Canada,* 3rd ser., 1, Ottawa, 1907, sec. 2, pp. 307–64.

Hennepin, Fr. Louis. *A New Discovery of Vast Country in America.* Ed. Reuben Gold Thwaites. 2 vols. 1903. Toronto: Coles, 1973.

Henry, Alexander. *New Light on the Early History of the Greater Northwest, the Manuscript Journals of Alexander Henry, Fur Trader of the Northwest Company, and of David Thompson, Official Geographer and Explorer of the Same Company, 1799–1814.* Ed. Elliot Coues. 3 vols. New York: Francis P. Harper, 1897.

Hind, Henry Youle. *Narrative of the Canadian Red River Exploring Expedition of 1857 and of the Assinniboine and Saskatchewan Exploring Expedition of 1858.* 2 vols. London: Longman, Green, Longman and Roberts, 1860.

Howe, E. W. *The Story of a Country Town.* 1883. Ed. Claude M. Simpson. Cambridge: Harvard University Press, 1961.

Irving, Washington. *The Adventures of Captain Bonneville, U. S. A. in the Rocky Mountains and the Far West; Digested from his Journal by Washington Irving.* 1837. Ed. Edgeley W. Todd. Norman: University of Oklahoma Press, 1961.

————. *Astoria, or Anecdotes of an Enterprise Beyond the Rocky Mountains.* 1836. Ed. Edgeley W. Todd. Norman: University of Oklahoma Press, 1964.

————. *The Complete Works of Washington Irving.* Gen. ed. Richard Dilworth Rust. Vol. 5: *Journals and Notebooks, 1832–1859.* Ed. Sue Field Ross. Boston: Twayne, 1986. Vol. 22: *The Crayon Miscellany.* (1835). Ed. Dahlia Kirby Terrell. New York: Twayne, 1979. Vol. 24: *Letters: Vol. II, 1823–1838.* Ed. Ralph M. Aderman et al. New York: Twayne, 1979.

————. *The Western Journals of Washington Irving.* Ed. John Francis McDermott. Norman: University of Oklahoma Press, 1944.

Jackson, Helen Hunt. *Bits of Travel at Home.* Boston: Roberts Brothers, 1890.

James, Ewin. *Account of an Expedition from Pittsburgh to the Rocky Mountains, performed in the Years 1819, 1820. By Order of the Hon. J. C. Calhoun, Secretary of War, Under the Command of Maj. S. H. Long, of the U. S. Top. Engineers.* 3 vols. London, 1823. Rpt. in *Early Western Travels, 1748–1846.* Ed. Reuben Gold Thwaites. Vols. XIV–XVII. Cleveland: Arthur H. Clark, 1905.

Jaramillo, Juan. *The Narrative of Jaramillo.* In *The Journey of Coronado.* Trans. and ed. George Parker Winship. New York: A. S. Barnes, 1904, pp. 222–40.

Jesuit Relations and Allied Documents. Ed. Reuben Gold Thwaites. Vols. LVIII–LIX. Cleveland: Burrows Brothers, 1899.

Kane, Paul. *Wanderings of an Artist among the Indians of North America From Canada to Vancouver's Island and Oregon Through the Hudson's Bay Company's Territory and Back Again.* London, 1859. Rpt. in *Paul Kane's Frontier.* Ed., introduction and *catalogue raisonné* J. Russell Harper. Austin: University of Texas Press, 1971.

Kelsey, Henry. *The Kelsey Papers.* Ed. Arthur G. Doughty and Chester Martin. Ottawa: Public Archives of Canada and the Public Records Office of Northern Ireland, 1929.

Kirkland, Joseph. *Zury: The Meanest Man in Spring County, A Novel of Western Life.* 1887. Introduction John T. Flanagan. Urbana: University of Illinois Press, 1956.

Kroetsch, Robert. *Advice to My Friends: a Continuing Poem.* Don Mills, Ontario: Stoddard, 1985.

———. *Alberta.* Toronto: Macmillan, 1968.

———. *Alibi.* Toronto: Stoddard, 1983.

———. *Badlands.* 1975. Toronto: General, 1982.

———. *But We Are Exiles.* Toronto: Macmillan, 1965.

———. *Field Notes: 1–8 a Continuing Poem.* Don Mills: General, 1981.

———. *Gone Indian.* Toronto: New Press, 1973.

———. *Robert Kroetsch: Essays. Open Letter,* 5th series, no. 4 (Spring 1983).

———. *The Studhorse Man.* New York: Simon and Schuster, 1970.

———. "That Yellow Prairie Sky." *Maclean's,* 30 April 1955, pp. 28–29, 48–50. Rpt. in *Modern Canadian Stories.* Ed. John Stevens. New York: Bantam, 1975, pp. 106–15.

———. *What the Crow Said.* Don Mills: General, 1978.

———. *The Words of My Roaring.* Toronto: Macmillan, 1966.

[Lambert, John]. *United States: Pacific Railroad Reports.* 33rd Cong., 2nd. ses., Senate Executive Doc. 78, 1855, I, Papers Accompanying Governor I. I. Stevens' Reports, pp. 166–67. Rpt. in *The Western Interior of Canada: A Record of Geographical Discovery, 1612–1917.* Ed. John Warkentin. Toronto: McClelland and Stewart, 1964, pp. 161–62.

Laurence, Margaret. *A Bird in the House.* 1970. Introduction Robert Gibbs. Toronto: McClelland and Stewart, 1974.

———. *The Diviners.* 1974. Toronto: Bantam, 1975.

———. *The Fire-Dwellers.* Toronto: McClelland and Stewart, 1969.

———. *Heart of a Stranger.* 1976. Toronto: Seal, 1980.

———. *A Jest of God.* Toronto: McClelland and Stewart, 1966.

———. *The Stone Angel.* 1964. Introduction William H. New. Toronto: McClelland and Stewart, 1968.

Letters of the Lewis and Clark Expedition with Related Documents, 1783–1854. Ed. Donald Jackson. Urbana: University of Illinois Press, 1962.

Lewis, Meriwether and William Clark. *Original Journals of the Lewis and Clark Expedition, 1804–1806.* Ed. Reuben Gold Thwaites. 8 vols. 1904–05. Introduction Bernard DeVoto. New York: Arno Press, 1969.

Lewis, Sinclair. *Main Street.* 1920. Afterword Mark Schorer. New York: New American Library, 1964.

McCourt, Edward. *Home is the Stranger.* Toronto: Macmillan, 1950.

———. *Music at the Close.* Toronto: Ryerson, 1947.

McClung, Nellie. *Sowing Seeds in Danny.* 1911. Toronto: Ryerson, 1926.

Mackenzie, Alexander. *Voyages from Montreal, on the River St. Lawrence, through the Continent of North America to the Frozen and Pacific Oceans in the Years 1789 and 1793. With a Preliminary Account of the Rise, Progress, and Present State of the Fur Trade of that Country.* London: T. Cadell, 1801.

Mackie, John. *The Prodigal's Brother, A Story of Western Life.* London: Jarrold and Sons, 1899.

MacLean, John. *The Warden of the Plains and Other Stories of Life in the Canadian North-west.* Toronto: William Briggs, 1896.

Manfred, Frederick. *The Golden Bowl.* 1944. Albuquerque: University of New Mexico Press, 1971.

Maximilian, Prince of Wied-Neuwied. *Travels in the Interior of North America in the Years 1832, 1833, and 1834.* Trans. H. Evans Lloyd. London, 1843. Rpt. in *Early Western Travels, 1748–1846.* Ed. Reuben Gold Thwaites. Vols. XXII–XXV. Cleveland: Arthur H. Clark, 1906.

Melville, Herman. "Hawthorne and His Mosses." *Literary World,* August 17 and 24, 1850. Rpt. in Herman Melville. *Moby-Dick.* Ed. Harrison Hayford and Hershal Parker. New York: Norton, 1967, pp. 535–51.

———. *Moby-Dick, or The Whale.* 1851. Ed. Luther S. Mansfield and Howard P. Vincent. New York: Hendricks House, 1952.

———. *Moby-Dick: An Authoritative Text.* 1851. Ed. Harrison Hayford and Hershel Parker. New York: Norton, 1967.

[———]. "Mr. Parkman's Tour." Rev. of *The California and Oregon Trail,* by Francis Parkman. *Literary World,* March 31, 1849, pp. 291–93.

———. *Selected Poems of Herman Melville.* Ed. Henning Cohen. Carbondale: Southern Illinois University Press, 1964.

Miller, Alfred Jacob. *Braves and Buffalo: Plains Indian Life in 1837.* Introduction Michael Bell. Toronto: University of Toronto Press, 1973.

———. *The West of Alfred Jacob Miller.* Ed. Marvin C. Ross. Rev. ed. Norman: University of Oklahoma Press, 1968.

Mitchell, W. O. *The Dramatic W. O. Mitchell.* Toronto: Macmillan, 1982.

———. *How I Spent My Summer Holidays.* Toronto: MacMillan, 1981.

———. *Jake and the Kid.* 1962. Toronto: Macmillan, 1974.

———. *The Kite.* 1962. Toronto: Macmillan, 1974.

———. *The Vanishing Point.* Toronto: Macmillan, 1973.

———. *Who Has Seen the Wind.* 1947. Toronto: Macmillan, 1972.

Momaday, N. Scott. *House Made of Dawn.* 1969. Harper & Row, 1969.

———. *The Way to Rainy Mountain.* Albuquerque: University of New Mexico Press, 1969.

Morris, Wright. *Ceremony in Lone Tree.* 1960. Lincoln: University of Nebraska Press, 1973.

———. *Collected Stories, 1948–1986.* New York: Harper & Row, 1986.

———. *God's Country and My People.* 1968. Lincoln: University of Nebraska Press, 1981.

———. *The Home Place.* 1948. Lincoln: University of Nebraska Press, 1972.

———. "Our Endless Plains." *Holiday,* 24 (July 1958), pp. 68–69, 138–42.

———. *Plains Song: For Female Voices.* New York: Harper and Row, 1980.

———. *The Works of Love.* 1952. Lincoln: University of Nebraska Press, 1972.

Murray, Charles Augustus. *The Prairie-Bird.* 1844. London: Richard Bentley, 1845.

———. *Travels in North America During the Years 1834, 1835, & 1836.* 2 vols. London: Richard Bentley, 1839.

Oñate, Don Juan de. *Don Juan de Oñate: Colonizer of New Mexico.* Trans. and ed. George P. Hammond and Agapito Rey. Albuquerque: University of New Mexico Press, 1953.

150 Years of Art in Manitoba: Struggle for a Visual Civilization. Winnipeg: Winnipeg Art Gallery, 1970.

Ostenso, Martha. *Wild Geese.* 1925. Introduction Carlyle King. Toronto: McClelland and Stewart, 1961.

Palliser, John. *Solitary Rambles and Adventures of a Hunter in the Prairies.* London, 1853. Rutland, VT: Charles E. Tuttle, 1969.

Parker, Gilbert. *Pierre and His People: Tales of the Far North.* In *The Works of Gilbert Parker, Vol. I.* 1892. New York: Scribner's, 1912.

Parkman, Francis. *The Journals of Francis Parkman.* Ed. Mason Wade. 2 vols. New York: Harper and Brothers, 1947.

―――. *Letters of Francis Parkman.* Ed. Wilbur R. Jacobs. 2 vols. Norman: University of Oklahoma Press, 1960.

―――. *The Oregon Trail.* 1849. Ed. E. N. Feltskog. Madison: University of Wisconsin Press, 1969.

―――. *The Oregon Trail.* 1849. Ed. David Levin. New York: Penguin, 1982.

―――. *Vassall Morton: A Novel.* Boston: Phillips, Sampson, 1856.

Paul Kane's Frontier. Ed. J. Russell Harper. Austin: University of Texas Press, 1971.

Pike, Albert. *Prose Sketches and Poems, Written in the Western Country.* 1834. Ed. David J. Weber. College Station: Texas A & M University Press, 1987.

Pike, Z. M. *An Account of Expeditions to the Sources of the Mississippi, and through the Western parts of Louisiana, to the Sources of the Arkansaw, Kans, La Platte, and Pierre Jaun, Rivers; Performed by Order of the Government of the United States during the Years 1805, 1806, and 1807. And a Tour through the Interior Parts of New Spain, when Conducted through these Provinces by order of the Captain-General in the Year 1807.* Philadelphia: C. & A. Conrad, 1810.

―――. *The Journals of Zebulon Montgomery Pike.* Ed. Donald Jackson. 2 vols. Norman: University of Oklahoma Press, 1966.

Poe, Edgar Allan. *The Journal of Julius Rodman.* In *Collected Writings of Edgar Allan Poe.* Vol. I: *The Imaginary Voyages.* Ed. Burton R. Pollin. Boston: Twayne, 1981.

Quick, Herbert. *Vandemark's Folly.* Indianapolis: Bobbs-Merrill, 1922.

Richter, Conrad. *The Fields.* New York: Alfred A. Knopf, 1946.

―――. *The Lady.* 1957. Lincoln: University of Nebraska Press, 1984.

―――. *The Rawhide Knot.* 1978. Lincoln: University of Nebraska Press, 1984.

―――. *The Sea of Grass.* New York: Alfred A. Knopf, 1940.

―――. *The Town.* New York: Alfred A. Knopf, 1950.

―――. *The Trees.* New York: Alfred A. Knopf, 1940.

Rölvaag, O. E. *Giants in the Earth: A Saga of the Prairie.* Trans. Lincoln Colcord and O. E. Rölvaag. 1927. New York: Harper & Row, 1955.

―――. *Peder Victorious.* Trans. Nara O. Solum and O. E. Rölvaag. 1929. Introduction Gudrun Hovde Gvale. Lincoln: University of Nebraska Press, 1982.

―――. *Their Fathers' God.* Trans. Trygve M. Ager. 1931. Lincoln: University of Nebraska Press, 1983.

Ross, Sinclair. *As For Me and My House.* 1941. Introduction David Stouck. Lincoln: University of Nebraska Press, 1978.

―――. *The Lamp at Noon and Other Stories.* Introduction Margaret Laurence. Toronto: McClelland and Stewart, 1968.

―――. *Sawbones Memorial.* Toronto: McClelland and Stewart, 1974.

Ruxton, George Frederick. *Life in the Far West.* Edinburgh, 1848. Ed. Leroy R. Hafen. Norman: University of Oklahoma Press, 1951.

Scarborough, Dorothy. *The Wind.* 1925. Foreword Sylvia Ann Grider. Austin: University of Texas Press, 1979.

Smith, G. Hubert. *The Explorations of the La Vérendryes in the Northern Plains, 1738–43*. Ed. W. Raymond Wood. Lincoln: University of Nebraska Press, 1980.

Southesk, James C. *Saskatchewan and the Rocky Mountains: A Diary and Narrative of Travel, Sport, and Adventure, During a Journey Through the Hudson's Bay Company's Territories, in 1859 and 1860*. Toronto: James Campbell and Son, 1875.

Stead, Robert J. C. *Grain*. 1926. Introduction Thomas Saunders. Toronto: McClelland and Stewart, 1969.

———. *The Homesteaders: A Novel of the Canadian West*. 1916. Introduction Susan Wood Glicksohn. Toronto: University of Toronto Press, 1973.

Steele, Eliza. *A Summer Journey in the West*. New York: John S. Taylor, 1841.

Stegner, Wallace. *On a Darkling Plain*. New York: Harcourt, Brace, 1939.

———. *Wolf Willow: A History, a Story and a Memory of the Last Plains Frontier*. 1962. New York: Viking, 1966.

Steinbeck, John. *The Grapes of Wrath*. 1939. New York: Bantam, 1972.

Stewart, Sir William George Drummond. *Altowan; or Incidents of Life and Adventure in the Rocky Mountains. By an Amateur Traveler*. Ed. J. Watson Webb. 2 vols. New York: Harper & Brothers, 1846.

Stringer, Arthur. *The Mud Lark*. Indianapolis: Bobbs-Merrill, 1931.

———. *The Prairie Child*. New York: A. L. Burt, 1922.

———. *The Prairie Mother*. New York: A. L. Burt, 1920.

———. *The Prairie Wife*. New York: A. L. Burt, 1915.

Thompson, David. *David Thompson's Narrative, 1784–1812*. Ed. Richard Glover. Toronto: The Champlain Society, 1962.

Thoreau, Henry D. *Walden*. Ed. J. Lyndon Stanley. In *The Writings of Henry D. Thoreau*. 1854. Princeton: Princeton University Press, 1971.

———. *The Journal of Henry D. Thoreau*. Ed. Bradford Torrey and Francis H. Allen. Vol. I. 1906. Boston: Houghton Mifflin, 1949.

Tixier, Victor. *Travels on the Osage Prairies*. Trans. Albert J. Salvan. Ed. John Francis McDermott. Norman: University of Oklahoma Press, 1940.

Twain, Mark [Samuel L. Clemens]. *The Adventures of Huckleberry Finn*. 1884. Toronto: Oxford University Press, 1971.

———. *Roughing It*. 1872. Introduction Franklin R. Rogers. Ed. Paul Baender. Berkeley: University of California Press, 1972.

Umfreville, Edward. *The Present State of Hudson's Bay, Containing a Full Description of that Settlement, and the Adjacent Country; and Likewise of the Fur Trade, with Hints for its Improvement*. London, 1790. Ed. W. Stewart Wallace. Toronto: Ryerson, 1954.

Whitman Walt. *Leaves of Grass*. Ed. Harold W. Blodgett and Sculley Bradley. New York: Norton, 1965.

———. *Specimen Days*. 1882. Ed. Lance Hidy. Boston: D. R. Godine, 1971.

Wiebe, Rudy. *The Blue Mountains of China*. McClelland and Stewart, 1970.

———. *First and Vital Candle*. McClelland and Stewart, 1966.

———. *Peace Shall Destroy Many*. McClelland and Stewart, 1962.

———. *The Scorched-Wood People*. Toronto: McClelland and Stewart, 1977.

———. *The Temptations of Big Bear*. Toronto: McClelland and Stewart, 1977.

———. *Where is the Voice Coming From?*. Toronto: McClelland and Stewart, 1974.

Wister, Owen. *The Virginian*. 1902. Ed. Philip Durham. Boston: Houghton Mifflin, 1968.

Secondary Material

Books and Dissertations

Abrams, M. H. *The Mirror and the Lamp: Romantic Theory and the Critical Tradition.* New York: Oxford University Press, 1953.

Alfred Jacob Miller: Artist on the Oregon Trail. Ed. Ron Tyler. Fort Worth, Texas: Amon Carter Museum, 1982.

Allen, John Logan. *Passage Through the Garden: Lewis and Clark and the American Northwest.* Urbana: University of Illinois Press, 1975.

Allen, Martha Mitten. *Traveling West: 19th Century Women on the Overland Routes.* El Paso: Texas Western Press, 1987.

Appleton, Jay. *The Experience of Landscape.* London: John Wiley, 1975.

Arnason, David. "The Development of Prairie Realism." Ph.D. diss. University of New Brunswick, 1980.

Arnold, Marilyn. *Willa Cather's Short Fiction.* Athens: Ohio University Press, 1984.

Atherton, Lewis. *Main Street on the Middle Border.* Bloomington: University of Indiana Press, 1954.

Before Lewis and Clark: Documents Illustrating the History of the Missouri, 1785–1804. Ed. Abraham P. Nasatir. 2 vols. St. Louis: St. Louis Historical Documents Foundation, 1952.

Bennett, Mildred R. *The World of Willa Cather.* New ed. Lincoln: University of Nebraska Press, 1961.

Berthoff, Walter. *The Ferment of Realism: American Literature, 1884–1919.* New York: Free Press, 1965.

Billington, Ray Allen. *The Far Western Frontier, 1830–1860.* New York: Harper, 1956.

———. *Land of Savagery, Land of Promise: The European Image of the American Frontier in the Nineteenth Century.* 1981. Norman: University of Oklahoma Press, 1985.

Bloom, Edward A. and Lilian D. *Willa Cather's Gift of Sympathy.* Preface Harry T. Moore. Carbondale: Southern Illinois University Press, 1962.

Bolton, Herbert E. *Coronado: Knight of Pueblos and Plains.* Albuquerque: University of New Mexico Press, 1949.

Brebner, John Bartlet. *The Explorers of North America, 1492–1806.* 1933. New York: Double-day Anchor, 1955.

Broadfoot, Barry. *Ten Lost Years: Memories of Canadians Who Survived the Depression.* 1973. Markham, Ontario: Paperjacks, 1975.

Brown, Charles H. *William Cullen Bryant.* New York: Scribner's, 1971.

Brown, E. K. *Willia Cather: A Critical Biography.* Completed by Leon Edel. New York: Alfred A. Knopf, 1953.

Buss, Helen M. *Mother and Daughter Relationships in the Manawaka Works of Margaret Laurence.* Victoria: University of Victoria, 1985.

Butler, Michael Douglas. "The Literary Landscape of the Trans-Mississippi West, 1826–1902." Ph.D. diss. University of Illinois-Urbana 1970.

Cady, Edwin W. *The Light of Common Day: Realism in American Fiction.* Bloomington: Indiana University Press, 1971.

Canada: A Geographical Interpretation. Ed. John Warkentin. Toronto: Methuen, 1968.

A Century of Commentary on the Works of Washington Irving. Ed. Andrew B. Myers. Tarrytown, New York: Sleepy Hollow Restorations, 1976.

Chase, Richard. *The American Novel and its Tradition.* New York: Doubleday, 1957.

Clough, Wilson O. *The Necessary Earth: Nature and Solitude in American Literature.* Austin: University of Texas Press, 1964.

Contexts of Canadian Criticism. Ed. Eli Mandel. Chicago: University of Chicago Press, 1973.

Conversations with Wright Morris: Critical Views and Responses. Ed. Robert E. Knoll. Lincoln: University of Nebraska Press, 1977.

Crossing Frontiers: Papers in American and Canadian Western Literature. Ed. Dick Harrison. Edmonton: University of Alberta Press, 1979.

Crump, G. B. *The Novels of Wright Morris: A Critical Interpretation.* Lincoln: University of Nebraska Press, 1978.

Cude, Wilfred. *A Due Sense of Differences: An Evaluative Approach to Canadian Literature.* Landam, MD: University Press of America, 1980.

Curry, Larry. *The American West: Painters from Catlin to Russell.* Foreword Archibald Hanna. New York: Viking, 1972.

Cutright, Paul Russell. *A History of the Lewis and Clark Journals.* Norman: University of Oklahoma Press, 1976.

Davis, Ann. *A Distant Harmony: Comparisons Between the Painting of Canada and the United States of America* (Exhibition catalog). Winnipeg, Manitoba: Winnipeg Art Gallery, 1982.

DeVoto, Bernard, *Across the Wide Missouri.* Boston: Houghton Mifflin, 1947.

———. *The Course of Empire.* Boston: Houghton Mifflin, 1952.

———. *The Year of Decision: 1846.* Boston: Houghton Mifflin, 1943.

Dondore, Dorothy. *The Prairie and the Making of Middle America.* Cedar Rapids, Iowa: The Torch Press, 1926.

Ellsworth, Henry Leavitt. *Washington Irving on the Prairie or a Narrative of a Tour of the Southwest in the Year 1832.* Ed. Stanley T. Williams and Barbara D. Simison. New York: American Book Co., 1937.

Environmental Aesthetics: Essays in Interpretation. Ed. Barry Sadler and Allen Carlson. Victoria: University of Victoria, 1982.

Essays on Saskatchewan Writing. Ed. E. F. Dyck. Regina: Saskatchewan Writers Guild, 1986.

Ewers, John C., et al. *Views of a Vanishing Frontier.* Omaha: Joslyn Art Museum, 1984.

Fairbanks, Carol. *Prairie Women: Images in American and Canadian Fiction.* New Haven: Yale University Press, 1986.

Faragher, John Mack. *Women and Men on the Overland Trail.* New Haven: Yale University Press, 1979.

Fender, Stephen. *Plotting the Golden West: American Literature and the Rhetoric of the California Trail.* Cambridge: Cambridge University Press, 1981.

Flexner, James Thomas. *That Wilder Image: The Painting of America's Native School from Thomas Cole to Winslow Homer.* Boston: Little, and Company, 1962.

Folsom, James K. *The American Western Novel.* New Haven: College and University Press, 1966.

Franklin, Wayne. *Discoverers, Explorers, Settlers: The Diligent Writers of Early America.* Chicago: University of Chicago Press, 1979.

———. *The New World of James Fenimore Cooper.* Chicago: University of Chicago Press, 1982.

Friesen, Gerald. *The Canadian Prairies: A History.* Toronto: University of Toronto Press, 1984.

Fryer, Judith. *Felicitous Space: Imaginative Structures of Edith Wharton and Willa Cather.* Chapel Hill: University of North Carolina Press, 1986.

Fussell, Edwin. *Frontier: American Literature and the American West.* Princeton: Princeton University Press, 1965.

Gaston, Edwin W. *Conrad Richter.* New York: Twayne, 1965.

The Genius of the Place: the English Landscape Garden, 1620–1820. Ed. John Dixon Hunt and Peter Willis. London: Paul Elek, 1975.

Geographies of the Mind: Essays in Historical Geosophy in Honor of John Kirtland Wright. Ed. David Lowenthal and Martyn J. Bowden. New York: Oxford, 1976.

Goetzmann, William H. *Exploration and Empire: The Explorer and the Coronado Expedition, 1540–1542.* Alburquerque: University of New Mexico Press, 1940.

———— and Joseph C. Porter. *The West As Romantic Horizon.* Omaha: Center for Western Studies, Joslyn Art Museum, 1981.

———— and William N. Goetzmann. *The West of the Imagination.* New York: Norton, 1986.

Hafer, John William. "The Sea of Grass: The Image of the Great Plains in the American Novel." Ph.D. diss. University of Northern Illinois, 1975.

Hampsten, Elizabeth. *Read This Only to Yourself: The Private Writings of Midwestern Women, 1880–1910.* Bloomington: Indiana University Press, 1986.

Harper, J. Russell. *Painting in Canada: A History.* 2nd. ed. Toronto: University of Toronto Press, 1977.

Harrison, Dick. *Unnamed Country: The Struggle for a Canadian Prairie Fiction.* Edmonton: University of Alberta Press, 1977.

Hart, James D. *The Popular Book: A History of America's Literary Taste.* New York: Oxford, 1950.

Hazard, Lucy Lockwood. *The Frontier in American Literature.* New York: Croswell, 1927.

Henson, Clyde E. *Joseph Kirkland.* New Haven: College and University Press, 1961.

Hill, Douglas. *The Opening of the Canadian West.* London: Heinemann [1967].

Hipple, Walter J. *The Beautiful, the Sublime, and the Picturesque.* Carbondale: Southern Illinois University Press, 1957.

Hollon, W. Eugene. *The Great American Desert: Then and Now.* New York: Oxford, 1966.

————. *The Lost Pathfinder: Zebulon Montgomery Pike.* Norman: University of Oklahoma Press, 1949.

The Home Book of the Picturesque: Or American Scenery, Art, and Literature. 1852. Introduction. Motley F. Deakin. Gainesville, Florida: Scholars' Facsimiles & Reprints, 1967.

Horizon: Writings of the Canadian Prairie. Ed. Ken Mitchell. Toronto: Oxford, 1977.

Jeffrey, Julie Roy. *Frontier Women: The Trans-Mississippi West, 1840–1880.* New York: Hill & Wang, 1979.

Johannsen, Albert. *The House of Beadle and Adams and Its Dime and Nickel Novels: The Story of a Vanishing Literature.* Foreword John T. McIntyre. 2 vols. Norman: University of Oklahoma Press, 1950.

Jones, Howard Mumford. *The Frontier in American Fiction.* Jerusalem: Magness Press, 1956.

————. *O Strange New World: American Culture: The Formative Years.* New York: Viking, 1952.

Josephy, Alvin M., Jr. *The Artist Was a Young Man: The Life Story of Peter Rindisbacher.* Fort Worth: Amon Carter Museum, 1970.

Karl Bodmer's America. Introduction. William H. Goetzmann. Annot. David C. Hunt and Marsha V. Gallagher. Biog. William J. Orr. Omaha and Lincoln: Joslyn Art Museum and University of Nebraska Press, 1984.

Kazin, Alfred. *On Native Grounds: An Interpretation of American Prose Literature.* 1942. New York: Harcourt Brace Jovanovich, 1970.

Keith, W. J. *Epic Fiction: The Art of Rudy Wiebe.* Edmonton: University of Alberta Press, 1981.

Kelly, William P. *Plotting America's Past: Fenimore Cooper and the Leatherstocking Tales.* Carbondale: Southern Illinois University Press, 1983.

Kline, Marcia B. *Beyond the Land Itself: Views of Nature in Canada and the United States.* Cambridge: Harvard University Press, 1970.

Kolodny, Annette. *The Land Before Her: Fantasy and Experience of the American Frontiers, 1630–1860.* Chapel Hill: University of North Carolina Press, 1984.

LaHood, Marvin J. *Conrad Richter's America.* The Hague: Mouton, 1975.

Latrobe, Charles Joseph. *The Rambler in North America.* 2 vols. New York: Harper, 1835.

Lauriston, Victor. *Arthur Stringer: Son of the North, Biography and Anthology.* Toronto: The Ryerson Press, 1941.

Lawrence, D. H. *Studies in Classic American Literature.* 1923. New York: Viking, 1973.

Lecker, Robert. *Robert Kroetsch.* Boston: Twayne, 1986.

Lee, Robert Edson. *From West to East: Studies in the Literature of the American West.* Urbana: University of Illinois Press, 1966.

Lessing, Gotthold Ephraim. *Laocoon: An Essay upon the Limits of Painting and Poetry.* Trans. Ellen Prothingham. New York: Noonday, 1968.

Lewis, R. W. B. *The American Adam: Innocence, Tragedy, and Tradition in the Nineteenth Century.* Chicago: University of Chicago Press, 1955.

Lewis, Meriwether and William Clark. *History of the Expedition Under the Command of Lewis and Clark.* Ed. Elliott Coues. 4 vols. 1893. New York: Dover, 1965.

Limerick, Patricia Nelson. *Desert Passages: Encounters with the American Deserts.* Albuquerque: University of New Mexico Press, 1985.

A Literary History of the American West. Ed. J. Golden Taylor et al. Fort Worth: Texas Christian University Press, 1987.

Lord, Barry. *The History of Painting in Canada: Toward a People's Art.* Toronto: NC Press, 1974.

Lutwack, Leonard. *The Role of Place in Literature.* Syracuse: Syracuse University Press, 1984.

Macoun, John. *Manitoba and the Great North-West.* Guelph, Ontario: World Publishing, 1882.

McCourt, Edward. *The Canadian West in Fiction.* Rev. ed. Toronto: Ryerson, 1970.

———. *Remember Butler: The Story of Sir William Francis Butler.* London: Routledge & Kegan Paul, 1967.

McLeod, Gordon Duncan. "A Descriptive Bibliography of the Prairie Novel, 1871–1970." Ph.D. diss. University of Manitoba 1974.

McMullen, Lorraine. *Sinclair Ross.* Boston: G. K. Hall, 1979.

Madden, David. *Wright Morris.* New York: Twayne, 1964.

Mandel, Eli. *Another Time.* Erin, Ont.: Press Porcépic, 1977.

Merritt, John L. *Baronets and Buffalo: The British Sportsman in the American West, 1833–1881.* Missoula: Mountain Press, 1985.

Marx, Leo. *The Machine in the Garden: Technology and the Pastoral Ideal in America.* New York: Oxford, 1964.

Meyer, Roy W. *The Middle Western Farm Novel in the Twentieth Century.* Lincoln: University of Nebraska Press, 1965.

Milton, John R. *The Novel of the American West.* Lincoln: University of Nebraska Press, 1980.

Mitchell, Ken. *Sinclair Ross: A Reader's Guide.* Moose Jaw, Sask.: Coteau, 1981.

Mitchell, Lee Clark. *Witnesses to a Vanishing America: The Nineteenth-Century Response.* Princeton: Princeton University Press, 1981.

Monk, Samuel H. *The Sublime: A Study of Critical Theories in XVIII-Century England.* New York: MLA, 1935.

Morley, Patricia. *Margaret Laurence.* Boston: Twayne, 1981.

Myres, Sandra L. *Westering Women and the Frontier Experience, 1800–1915.* Albuquerque: University of New Mexico Press, 1982.

Narratives of the Coronado Expedition, 1540–1542. Trans. and ed. George P. Hammond and Agapito Rey. Albuquerque: University of New Mexico Press, 1940.

Nash, Roderick. *Wilderness and the American Mind.* New Haven: Yale University Press, 1967.

The Native Muse: Theories of American Literature. Ed. Richard Ruland. 2 vols. New York: E. P. Dutton, 1976.

Neuman, Shirley and Robert Wilson. *Labyrinths of Voice: Conversations with Robert Kroetsch.* Edmonton: NeWest Press, 1982.

Nevius, Blake. *Cooper's Landscapes: An Essay on the Picturesque Vision.* Berkeley: University of California Press, 1976.

New, W. H. *Articulating West: Essays on Purpose and Form in Modern Canadian Literature.* Toronto: New Press, 1972.

Novak, Barbara. *Nature and Culture: American Landscape and Painting 1825–1875.* New York: Oxford, 1980.

Nye, Russell B. *Society and Culture in America, 1830–1860.* New York: Harper & Row, 1974.

Obrégon's History of Sixteenth-Century Exploration in Western America. Trans. and ed. George P. Hammond and Agapito Rey. Los Angeles: Wetzel, 1928.

O'Brien, Sharon. *Willa Cather: The Emerging Voice.* New York: Oxford, 1986.

Olson, Charles. *Call Me Ishmael.* New York: Grove, 1947.

Överland, Orm. *The Making and Meaning of an American Classic: James Fenimore Cooper's The Prairie.* Oslo: Universitestsforlaget, and New York: Humanities Press, 1973.

Owram, Doug. *Promise of Eden: The Canadian Expansionist Movement and the Idea of the West, 1856–1900.* Toronto: University of Toronto Press, 1980.

Painters in a New Land. Ed. Michael Bell. Toronto: McClelland and Stewart, 1973.

The Papers of the Palliser Expedition, 1857–1860. Ed. Irene M. Spry. Toronto: The Champlain Society, 1968.

Parrington, Vernon L. *Main Currents in American Thought: An Interpretation of American Literature from the Beginnings to 1920.* 3 vols. New York: Harcourt, Brace, 1927–30.

Peck, H. Daniel. *A World by Itself: The Pastoral Moment in Cooper's Fiction.* New Haven: Yale University Press, 1977.

Pizer, Donald. *Realism and Naturalism in Nineteenth-Century American Literature.* Preface Harry T. Moore. Carbondale: Southern Illinois University Press, 1966.

A Place to Stand On: Essays By and About Margaret Laurence. Ed. George Woodcock. Edmonton: NeWest Press, 1983.

Plains Woman: The Diary of Martha Farnsworth, 1882–1922. Ed. Marlene Springer and Haskell Springer. Bloomington: Indiana University Press, 1986.

Portales, Count Albert-Alexandre de. *On the Western Tour with Washington Irving.* Norman: University of Oklahoma Press, 1968.

Randall, John H., III. *The Landscape and the Looking Glass: Willa Cather's Search for Value.* Boston: Houghton Mifflin, 1960.

Rasmussen, Linda et al. *A Harvest Yet To Reap: A History of Prairie Women.* Toronto: The Women's Press, 1976.

Raymond, Catherine Elizabeth. "Down to Earth: Sense of Place in Midwestern Literature." Ph.D. diss. University of Pennsylvania, 1979.

Reigstad, Paul. *Rölvaag: His Life and Art.* Lincoln: University of Nebraska Press, 1972.

Rees, Ronald. *Land of Earth and Sky: Landscape Painting of Western Canada.* Saskatoon: Western Producer Prairie Books, 1985.

Ricou, Laurence. *Vertical Man/Horizontal World: Man and Landscape in Canadian Prairie Fiction.* Vancouver: University of British Columbia Press, 1973.

Riley, Glenda. *Women and Indians on the Frontier, 1825–1915.* Albuquerque: University of New Mexico Press, 1984.

———. *The Female Frontier: A Comparative View of Women on the Prairie and the Plains.* Lawrence: University Press of Kansas, 1988.

———. *Frontierswoman: The Iowa Experience.* Ames: Iowa State University Press, 1981.

Ringe, Donald A. *The Pictorial Mode: Space and Time in the Art of Bryant, Irving, and Cooper.* Lexington: University Press of Kentucky, 1971.

Robinson, Forest and Margaret Robinson. *Wallace Stegner.* Boston: Twayne, 1977.

Rosowski, Susan J. *The Voyage Perilous: Willa Cather's Romanticism.* Lincoln: University of Nebraska Press, 1986.

Rusk, Ralph Leslie. *The Literature of the Middle Western Frontier.* New York: Columbia University Press, 1925.

Sandoz, Mari. *Love Song to the Plains.* New York: Harper, 1961.

Schlissel, Lillian. *Women's Diaries of the Westward Journey.* Preface. Carl N. Degler. New York: Schocken, 1982.

Schubnell, Matthias. *N. Scott Momaday: The Cultural and Literary Background.* Norman: University of Oklahoma Press, 1985.

Sealts, Merton M. *Melville's Reading: A Check-List of Books Owned and Borrowed.* Madison: University of Wisconsin Press, 1966.

Sergeant, Elizabeth Shepley. *Willa Cather: A Memoir.* Lincoln: University of Nebraska Press, 1953.

Shephard, Paul. *Man in Landscape: A Historic View of the Esthetics of Nature.* New York: Alfred A. Knopf, 1967.

Silverman, Eliane Leslau. *The Last Best West: Women on the Alberta Frontier, 1880–1930.* Montreal: Eden, 1984.

Slotkin, Richard. *Regeneration Through Violence: The Mythology of the American Frontier.* Middleton, Conn.: Wesleyan University Press, 1973.

Smith, Henry Nash. *Virgin Land: The American West as Symbol and Myth.* Cambridge: Harvard University Press, 1950.

Spettigue, Douglas O. *FPG: The European Years.* Ottawa: Oberon, 1973.

Stegner, Wallace and Richard W. Etulain. *Conversations with Wallace Stegner on Western History and Literature.* Salt Lake City: University of Utah Press, 1983.

Stouck, David. *Willa Cather's Imagination.* Lincoln: University of Nebraska Press, 1975.

Stratton, Joanna L. *Pioneer Women: Voices From the Kansas Frontier.* Introduction Arthur M. Schlesinger, Jr. New York: Simon and Schuster, 1981.

Taft, Robert. *Artists and Illustrators of the Old West, 1850–1900.* 1953. Princeton: Princeton University Press, 1982.

Thomas, Clara. *The Manawaka World of Margaret Laurence.* Toronto: McClelland and Stewart, 1975.

———. *Margaret Laurence.* Toronto: McClelland and Stewart, 1969.

Thomas, Peter. *Robert Kroetsch.* Vancouver: Douglas & McIntyre, 1980.

Thompson, Eric Callum. "The Prairie Novel in Canada: A Study in Changing Form and Perception." Ph.D. diss. University of New Brunswick, 1974.

Trace: Prairie Writers on Writing. Ed. Birk Sproxton. Winnipeg: Turnstone, 1986.

Truettner, William H. *The Natural Man Observed: A Study of Catlin's Indian Gallery.* Washington, D.C.: Smithsonian Institution Press, 1979.

Tuan, Yi-Fu. *Topophilia: A Study of Environmental Perception, Attitudes, and Values.* Englewood Cliffs, NJ: Prentice-Hall, 1974.

———. *Space and Place: The Perspective of Experience.* Minneapolis: University of Minnesota Press, 1977.

Tunnard, Christopher. *A World with a View: An Inquiry into the Nature of Scenic Values.* New Haven: Yale University Press, 1978.

Turner, Frederick Jackson. *The Frontier in American History.* New York: Holt, 1921.

Unruh, John D. Jr. *The Plains Across: The Overland Emigrants and the Trans-Mississippi West, 1840–60.* Urbana: University of Illinois Press, 1979.

Van Kirk, Sylvia. *"Many Tender Ties": Women in Fur Trade Society in Western Canada, 1670–1870.* Winnipeg: Watson & Dwyer, 1980.

A Voice in the Land: Essays By and About Rudy Wiebe. Ed. W. J. Keith. Edmonton: NeWest, 1981.

Wade, Mason. *Francis Parkman: Heroic Historian.* New York: Viking, 1942.

Wallace, James D. *Early Cooper and His Audience.* New York: Columbia University Press, 1986.

The Western Interior of Canada: A Record of Geographical Discovery, 1612–1917. Ed. John Warkentin. Toronto: McClelland and Stewart, 1964.

Warwick, Susan J. "Telling Tales: Voice, Time and Image in the Fiction of Margaret Laurence and Willa Cather." Ph.D. diss. York University, 1983.

Webb, Walter Prescott. *The Great Plains.* 1931. Lincoln: University of Nebraska Press, 1981.

Williams, Stanley T. *The Life of Washington Irving.* 2 vols. New York: Oxford, 1935.

Women and Western American Literature. Ed. Helen Stauffer and Susan J. Rosowski. Troy, NY: Whitson, 1982.

Women, Women Writers, and the West. Ed. L. L. Lee and Merrill Lewis. Troy, NY: Whitson, 1980.

Wood, Susan Joan. "The Land in Canadian Prose, 1840–1945." Ph.D. diss. University of Toronto, 1975.

Woodress, James. *Willa Cather: Her Life and Art.* 1970. Lincoln: University of Nebraska Press, 1982.

———. *Willa Cather: A Literary Life.* Lincoln: University of Nebraska Press, 1987.

Writers of the Prairies. Ed. Donald G. Stephens. Vancouver: University of British Columbia Press, 1973.

Articles and Introductions

Allen, John L. "The Garden-Desert Continuum: Competing Views of the Great Plains in the Nineteenth Century." *Great Plains Quarterly,* 5 (1985), 207–20.

Baker, Joseph E. "Western Man Against Nature in *Giants in the Earth.*" *College English,* 4 (October 1942), 19–26.

Baum, Rosalie Murphy. "Martha Ostenso's *Wild Geese:* More Insight into the Naturalistic Sensibility." *Journal of Canadian Culture,* 1 (Fall 1984), 117–35.

Beard, James Franklin. "Cooper and his Artistic Contemporaries." *New York History,* 35 (1954), 480–95.

Bier, Jesse. "Lapsarians on *The Prairie:* Cooper's Novel." *Texas Studies in Literature and Language,* 4 (1962), 49–57.

Brown, E. K. "Willa Cather and the West." *University of Toronto Quarterly,* 5 (1935–36), 544–66.

Bowden, Martyn J. "The Perception of the Western Interior of the United States, 1800–1870: A Problem in Historical Geosophy." *Proceedings of the Association of American Geographers,* 1 (1969), 16–21.

Clark, William Bedford. "How the West Won: Irving's Comic Inversion of the Westering Myth in *A Tour on the Prairies.*" *American Literature,* 50 (1978), 334–47.

Comeau, Paul. "Sinclair Ross's Pioneer Fiction." *Canadian Literature,* No. 103 (Winter 1984), pp. 174–84.

Davidson, Cathy N. "Geography as Psychology in the Writings of Margaret Laurence." In *Regionalism and the Female Imagination: A Collection of Essays.* Ed. Emily Toth. New York: Human Sciences Press, 1985, pp. 129–38.

Denham, Paul. "Narrative Technique in Sinclair Ross's *As For Me and My House.*" *Studies in Canadian Literature,* 5 (1980), 116–24.

Dula, Martha. "Audience Response to *A Tour on the Prairies.*" *Western American Literature,* 8 (1973), 67–74.

Flanagan, John T. "The Authenticity of Cooper's *The Prairie.*" *Modern Language Quarterly,* 2 (1941), 99–104.

Francis, R. Douglas. "Changing Images of the West." *Journal of Canadian Studies,* 17, No. 3 (Fall 1982), pp. 5–19.

———. "From Wasteland to Utopia: Changing Images of the Canadian West in the Nineteenth Century." *Great Plains Quarterly,* 7 (Summer 1987), 178–94.

Fraser, Keith. "Futility at the Pump: The Short Stories of Sinclair Ross." *Queen's Quarterly,* 77 (1970), 72–80.

Gelfant, Blanche H. "The Forgotten Reaping-Hook: Sex in *My Ántonia.*" *American Literature,* 43 (1971), 60–82.

Godard, Barbara. "El Greco in Canada: Sinclair Ross's *As For Me and My House.*" *Mosaic,* 14, No. 2, (1981), 55–76.

Goetzmann, William H. "James Fenimore Cooper: *The Prairie.*" In *Landmarks of American Writing.* Ed. Henning Cohen. New York: Basic, 1969, pp. 66–78.

Grider, Susan. "Madness and Personification in *Giants in the Earth.*" In *Women, Women Writers and the West.* Ed. L. L. Lee and Merrill Lewis. Troy, NY: Whitston, 1980, pp. 111–17.

Hahn, Steve. "Vision and Reality in *Giants in the Earth.*" *South Dakota Review,* 17, No. 1 (Spring 1979), 85–100.

Harrison, Dick. "Popular Fiction of the Canadian Prairies: Autopsy on a Small Corpus." *Journal of Popular Culture,* 14 (1980), 326–32.

———. "Rölvaag, Grove, and Pioneering on the American and Canadian Plains." *Great Plains Quarterly,* 1 (1981), 252–62.

Hinz, Evelyn J. "Willa Cather's Technique and the Ideology of Populism." *Western American Literature,* 7 (1972), 47–61.

——— and John J. Teunissen. "Who's the Father of Mrs. Bentley's Child?: 'As For Me and My House' and the Conventions of Dramatic Monologue." *Canadian Literature,* No. 111 (Winter 1986), pp. 101–13.

Jacobson, Joanne. "Time and Vision in Wright Morris's Photographs of Nebraska." *Great Plains Quarterly,* 7 (1987), 3–21.

James, Stuart B. "Western American Space and the Human Imagination." *Western Humanities Review,* 24 (1970), 147–55.

Jeffrey, Julie Roy. " 'There Is Some Splendid Scenery': Women's Responses to the Great Plains Landscape." *Great Plains Quarterly,* 8 (1988), 69–78.

Jones, Howard Mumford. "The Image of the New World." In *Elizabethan Studies and Other*

Essays in Honour of George F. Reynolds. Boulder, Colorado: University of Colorado, 1945, pp. 62–84.

———. "Prose and Pictures: James Fenimore Cooper." *Tulane Studies in English,* 3 (1972), 140–47.

Kaye, Frances W. "Hamlin Garland and Frederick Philip Grove: Self-Conscious Chroniclers of the Pioneers." *Canadian Review of American Studies,* 10 (1979), 31–40.

Kime, Wayne R. "The Completeness of Washington Irving's *A Tour on the Prairies.*" *Western American Literature,* 8 (1973), 55–65.

———. "Poe's Use of Irving's *Astoria* in 'The Journal of Julius Rodman.' " *American Literature,* 40 (1968), 215–22.

Kroetsch, Robert. "Unhiding the Hidden: Recent Canadian Fiction." *Journal of Canadian Fiction,* 3, No. 3 (1974), 43–45.

Lamar, Howard R. Introduction. *Account of an Expedition from Pittsburgh to the Rocky Mountains.* By Edwin James. Barre, MA: Imprint Society, 1972, xv–xxxvi.

Lambert, Deborah. "The Defeat of a Hero: Autonomy and Sexuality in *My Ántonia.*" *American Literature,* 53 (1982), 666–90.

Lecker, Robert. "An Annotated Bibliography of Works By and About Robert Kroetsch." *Essays on Canadian Writing,* Nos. 7–8 (Fall 1977), 74–96.

Lenoski, Daniel S. "Martha Ostenso's *Wild Geese:* The Language of Silence." *North Dakota Quarterly,* 52, No. 3 (Summer 1984), 279–96.

Lewis, Merrill. "Lost and Found—In the Wilderness: The Desert Metaphor in Cooper's *The Prairie.*" *Western American Literature,* 5 (1970), 195–204.

Lowenthal, David. "The American Scene." *Geographical Review,* 58 (1968), 61–88.

Luebke, Frederick C. "Regionalism and the Great Plains: Problems of Concept and Method." *Western Historical Quarterly,* 15 (1984), 19–38.

MacLulich, T. D. "The Explorer as Sage: David Thompson's *Narrative.*" *Journal of Canadian Fiction,* No. 16 (1976), 99–107.

Madden, David. "The Great Plains in the Novels of Wright Morris." *Critique,* 4 (1961–62), 5–23.

McDermott, John Francis. Introduction. *A Tour on the Prairies.* By Washington Irving. Norman: University of Oklahoma Press, 1956, xv–xxxii.

MacLaren, I. S. "Aesthetic Mappings of the West by the Palliser and Hind Expeditions, 1857–59." *Studies in Canadian Literature,* 10 (1985), 24–52.

———. "Retaining Captaincy of the Soul: Response to Nature in the First Franklin Expedition." *Essays on Canadian Writing,* No. 28 (Spring 1984), 57–92.

———. "Samuel Hearne & the Landscape of Discovery." *Canadian Literature,* No. 103 (Winter 1984), 27–41.

McMullin, Stanley E. "Evolution versus Revolution: Grove's Perception of History." In *The Grove Symposium.* Ottawa: University of Ottawa Press, 1974, 77–88.

———. "Grove and the Promised Land." *Canadian Literature,* No. 49 (Summer 1971), 10–19.

Martin, Terence. "The Drama of Memory in *My Ántonia.*" *PMLA,* 84 (1969), 304–11.

Miller, James E., Jr. "*My Ántonia* and the American Dream." *Prairie Schooner,* 48 (1974), 112–23.

———. "*My Ántonia*: A Frontier Drama of Time." *American Quarterly,* 10 (1958), 476–84.

———. "The Nebraska Encounter: Willa Cather and Wright Morris." *Prairie Schooner,* 41 (1967), 165–67.

Milton, John. "Plains Landscapes and Changing Visions." *Great Plains Quarterly,* 2 (1982), 55–62.

Moorhead, Max L. Introduction. *Commerce of the Prairies.* By Josiah Gregg. Norman: University of Oklahoma Press, 1954, xvii–xxxviii.

Moseley, Ann. "The Land as Metaphor in Two Scandinavian Immigrant Novels." *MELUS,* 5, no. 2 (Summer 1978), 33–38.

Murphy, John J. "A Comprehensive View of Cather's *O Pioneers!.*" In *Critical Essays on Willa Cather.* Ed. John J. Murphy. Boston: G. K. Hall, 1984, 113–27.

Muszynska-Wallace, E. Sotoris. "The Sources of *The Prairie.*" *American Literature,* 21 (1949), 191–200.

Neinstein, Raymond L. "Wright Morris: The Metaphysics of Home." *Prairie Schooner,* 53 (Summer 1979), 121–54.

Nichol, John W. "Melville and the Midwest." *PMLA,* 66 (1951), 613–25.

O'Connor, John J. "Saskatchewan Sirens: The Prairie as Sea in Western Canadian Literature." *Journal of Canadian Fiction,* 28/29 (1980), 157–71.

Peterman, Michael. " 'The Good Game': The Charm of Willa Cather's *My Ántonia* and W. O. Mitchell's *Who Has Seen the Wind.*" *Mosaic,* 14, No. 2 (1981), 93–106.

Rainwater, Catherine. "Poe's Landscape Tales and the 'Picturesque' Tradition," *Southern Literary Journal,* 16 (1984), 30–43.

Redekop, Ernest H. "Picturesque and Pastoral: Two Views of Cooper's Landscapes." *Canadian Review of American Studies,* 8 (1977), 184–205.

Rees, Ronald. "Images of the Prairie: Landscape Painting and Perception in the Western Interior of Canada." *Canadian Geographer,* 20 (1976), 259–78.

Ricou, Laurence. "Empty as Nightmare: Man and Landscape in Recent Canadian Prairie Fiction." *Mosaic,* 6, No. 2 (1973), 143–60.

Ringe, Donald A. "Chiaroscuro as an Artistic Device in Cooper's Fiction." *PMLA,* 78 (1963), 349–57.

———. "James Fenimore Cooper and Thomas Cole: An Analogous Technique." *American Literature.* 30 (1958), 26–36.

———, "Man and Nature in Cooper's *The Prairie.*" *Nineteenth-Century Fiction,* 15 (1961), 313–23.

Rosowski, Susan J. "Willa Cather and the Fatality of Place: *O Pioneers!, My Ántonia,* and *A Lost Lady.*" In *Geography and Literature: A Meeting of the Disciplines.* Ed. William E. Mallory and Paul Simpson-Housley. Syracuse: Syracuse University Press, 1987, 81–94.

———. "Willa Cather's *A Lost Lady:* Art Versus the Closing Frontier," *Great Plains Quarterly,* 2 (1982), 239–48.

———. "Willa Cather—A Pioneer in Art: *O Pioneers!* and *My Ántonia.*" *Prairie Schooner,* 55, Nos. 1 and 2 (1981), 141–54.

———. "Willa Cather's Pioneer Women: A Feminist Interpretation." In *Where the West Begins: Essays on Middle Border and Siouxland Writing in Honor of Herbert Krause.* Ed. Arthur R. Huseboe and William Geyer. Sioux Falls, SD: Center for Western Studies, Augustana College, 1978, 135–42.

———. "Willa Cather's Women." *Studies in American Fiction,* 9 (1981), 261–75.

Ross, Morton. "The Canonization of *As For Me and My House:* A Case Study." In *Figures in a Ground: Canadian Essays on Modern Literature Collected in Honor of Sheila Watson.* Ed. Diane Bessai and David Jackel. Saskatoon: Western Producer Prairie Books, 1978, 189–205.

Rucker, Mary E. "Perspective Focus in *My Ántonia.*" *Arizona Quarterly,* 29 (1973), 303–16.

Rudd, Curtis D. "Beret and the Prairie in *Giants in the Earth.*" *Norwegian-American Studies,* 28 (1979), 217–44.

Ryder, Mary R. "Prosodic Variations in Willa Cather's Prairie Poems." *Western American Literature,* 20 (1985), 223–37.

Scherting, Jack. "Tracking the *Pequod* Along *The Oregon Trail.*" *Western American Literature,* 22 (1987), 3–15.

Schieck, William J. "Frontier Robin Hood: Wilderness, Civilization and the Half-Breed in Irving's *A Tour on the Prairie.*" *Southwestern American Literature,* 4 (1978), 14–21.

Schneider, Richard J. "Thoreau and Nineteenth-Century American Landscape Painting." *Emerson Society Quarterly,* 31, no. 2 (1985), 67–88.

Sellars, Richard West. "The Interrelationship of Literature, History, and Geography in Western Writing." *Western Historical Quarterly,* 4 (1973), 171–85.

Seim, Jeanette. "Horses & Houses: Further Readings in Kroetsch's *Badlands* and Sinclair Ross's *As For Me and My House.*" In *Essays on Robert Kroetsch, Open Letter,* 5th series, Nos. 8–9, 99–115.

Smith, Henry Nash. Introduction. *The Prairie: A Tale.* By James Fenimore Cooper. New York: Holt, 1950, v–xxii.

Stegner, Wallace. "Willa Cather: *My Ántonia.*" In *The American Novel: From James Fenimore Cooper to William Faulkner.* Ed. Wallace Stegner. New York: Basic Books, 1965, 144–53.

Stouck, David. "The Mirror and the Lamp in Sinclair Ross's *As For Me and My House.*" *Mosaic,* 7, No. 2 (1974), 142–50.

———. "Perspective as Structure and Theme in *My Ántonia.*" *Texas Studies in Literature and Language,* 12 (1970), 285–94.

Teunissen, John J. and Evelyn J. Hinz. "Poe's *Journal of Julius Rodman* as Parody." *Nineteenth-Century Fiction,* 27 (1972), 317–38.

Thacker, Robert. " 'Where is the Voice Coming From?': Toward a Western-Canadian Aesthetic." *Western American Literature,* 19 (May 1984), 41–47.

——— and Ann Davis. "Pictures and Prose: Romantic Sensibility and the Great Plains in Catlin, Kane, and Miller." *Great Plains Quarterly,* 6 (Winter 1986), 3–20.

Thomas, Clara. "Proud Lineage: Willa Cather and Margaret Laurence." *Canadian Review of American Studies,* 2 (1971), 1–12.

Todd, Edgeley W. "Washington Irving Discovers the Frontier." *Western Humanities Review,* 11 (1957), 29–39.

Vance, William L. " 'Man and Beast': The Meaning of Cooper's *The Prairie.*" *PMLA,* 89 (1974), 323–31.

Waldeland, Lynne. "*Plains Song:* Women's Voices in the Fiction of Wright Morris." *Critique,* 24 (Fall 1982), 7–19.

Walker, Don D. "The Western Humanism of Willa Cather." *Western American Literature,* 1 (1966), 75–90.

Watson, J. Wreford. "The Role of Illusion in North American Geography: A Note on the Geography of North American Settlement." *Canadian Geographer,* 13 (1969), 10–27.

Webb, Walter Prescott, "The American West: Perpetual Mirage." *Harper's,* (May, 1957), 25–31.

Wee, Morris Owen. "Specks on the Horizon: Individuals and the Land in Canadian Prairie Fiction." *South Dakota Review,* 19, No. 4 (Winter 1982), 18–32.

Williams, David. "The 'Scarlet' Rompers: Toward a New Perspective in *As For Me and My House.*" *Canadian Literature,* No. 103 (Winter 1984), 156–66.

Whitford, Kathryn. "Romantic Metamorphosis in Irving's Western Tour." *American Transcendental Quarterly,* No. 5 (First Quarter, 1970), 31–36.

Index